The Ethics of Artificial Intelligence

The Ethics of Artificial Intelligence

Principles, Challenges, and Opportunities

LUCIANO FLORIDI

OXFORD
UNIVERSITY PRESS

UNIVERSITY PRESS

Great Clarendon Street, Oxford, OX2 6DP,
United Kingdom

Oxford University Press is a department of the University of Oxford.
It furthers the University's objective of excellence in research, scholarship,
and education by publishing worldwide. Oxford is a registered trade mark of
Oxford University Press in the UK and in certain other countries

Published in the United States of America by Oxford University Press
198 Madison Avenue, New York, NY 10016, United States of America

British Library Cataloguing in Publication Data
Data available

Library of Congress Control Number: 2023936445

ISBN 978–0–19–888309–8

DOI: 10.1093/oso/9780198883098.001.0001

Printed and bound in the UK by
Clays Ltd, Elcograf S.p.A.

To Jeanne Migliar (later Fiorella Floridi) 1937–2022

who loved and taught me the value of the adage:

'Where one door shuts, another opens […] and if I do not contrive to enter it, it will be my own fault'

(Cervantes, *Don Quixote*, XXI).

'[…] he was making twenty tripods that were to stand by the wall of his house, and he set wheels of gold under them all, that they might go of their own selves to the assemblies of the gods, and come back again, marvels indeed to see.'

Homer, Iliad, Book 18

Contents

Preface

Education, business, and industry; travelling and logistics; banking, retailing, and shopping; entertainment; welfare and healthcare; politics and social relations—in short, life itself as we know it today—have all become inconceivable without the presence of digital technologies, services, products, and practices. Anyone who is not perplexed by such a digital revolution has not grasped its magnitude. We are talking about a new chapter in human history. Of course, many other chapters have come before. They were all similarly significant. Humanity experienced a world before and after the wheel, ironworking, the alphabet, printing, the engine, electricity, automobiles, the television, and the telephone. Each transformation was unique. Some irreversibly changed our self-understanding, our reality, and our experience of it, carrying complex and long-term implications. For instance, we are still finding new ways to exploit the wheel (just think of the iPod click wheel). By the same token, what humanity will achieve thanks to digital technologies is unimaginable. As I stress in Chapter 1, nobody in 1964 could have guessed what the world would have been like only fifty years later. Futurologists are the new astrologers; we should not rely on them. And yet, it is also true that the digital revolution will happen only once, and it is happening now. This page in human history has been turned, and a new chapter has begun. Future generations will never know what an exclusively analogue, offline, pre-digital reality was like. We are the last generation to have experienced it.

The price for such a special place in history is worrying uncertainties. The transformations brought about by digital technologies are mind-blowing. They justify some confusion and apprehension; one only needs to look at newspaper headlines. However, our special place at this historical watershed, between a fully analogue and an increasingly digital reality, also brings extraordinary opportunities. Precisely because the digital revolution has just begun, we have a chance to shape it in positive ways that can benefit both humanity and our planet. As Winston Churchill once said, 'We shape our buildings; thereafter they shape us.' We are at the very early stage of the construction of our digital realities. We can get them right before they start affecting and influencing both us and future generations in the wrong way. It is not a matter of being pessimistic or optimistic. Discussing whether the glass is half empty or half full is pointless. The interesting question is how we can fill it. This means engaging constructively with the ethical analysis of the problems and the design of the right solutions.

To identify the best path ahead for the development of our digital technologies, the first essential step is more and better understanding. We should not sleepwalk into the creation of an increasingly digital world. The insomnia of reason is vital because its sleep generates monstrous mistakes, sometimes irreversible. Understanding the technological transformations happening before our eyes is essential if we wish to steer the digital revolution in a direction that is both socially preferable (equitable) and environmentally sustainable. This can only be a collaborative effort (Floridi forthcoming). Thus, in this book, I offer my contribution by sharing some ideas about one kind of digital technology, artificial intelligence (AI), and the specific issue of its ethics.

The book is part of a larger research project on the transformations of agency (the ability to interact with, and learn from, the world successfully in view of a goal) brought about by the digital revolution. I initially thought I could work on both AI—understood as *artificial agency*, the topic of this book—and political agency—understood as *collective agency*, supported and influenced by digital interactions. When I was invited to give the Ryle Lectures in 2018, I attempted to do exactly this. I presented both topics as two aspects of the same, more profound transformation. I was, perhaps kindly, told by organizers and attendees that it was not a failure. But personally, I did not find it a great success. This was not because approaching the ethics of AI and the politics of information from a single, agency-based point of view does not work, but because doing so works well only if one is willing to skip the details and exchange scope for depth. This may be fine in a lecture series, but covering both topics in a single research monograph would have produced a doorstopper of even lower appeal than this book may have. So, following the insightful advice of Peter Momtchiloff at Oxford University Press, I decided to split the project into two: this book on the ethics of AI, and a second book on the politics of information. This is the right place to let the reader know where to locate both books within the larger project.

This book is part one of the fourth volume in a tetralogy that includes *The Philosophy of Information* (volume one, Floridi 2011), *The Ethics of Information* (volume two, Floridi 2013), and *The Logic of Information* (volume three, Floridi 2019d). I began labelling the tetralogy *Principia Philosophiae Informationis* not as a sign of bottomless hubris (although it may well be), but as an internal pun among some colleagues. In a sort of rowing-like competition, I joked that it was time for Oxford to catch up with Cambridge on the 3–0 score for 'principia'. This was not a pun that many found funny or even intelligible.

Within the *Principia* project, this book occupies a middle ground between the first and the second volume (not unlike volume three) because epistemology, ontology, logic, and ethics all contribute to the development of the theses presented in the following chapters. But as the reader should rightly expect, all the volumes are written as stand-alone, so this book can be read without any knowledge of anything else that I ever published. Still, the volumes are complementary. The essential message from volume one is relatively straightforward: semantic information is well-formed, meaningful, and truthful data; knowledge is relevant semantic information correctly accounted for; humans are the only known semantic engines and conscious informational organisms who can design and understand semantic artefacts, and thus develop a growing knowledge of reality and themselves, as semantic capital; and reality is best understood as the totality of information (notice the crucial absence of 'semantic').

Against that background, volume two investigates the foundations of the ethics of informational organisms (*inforgs*) like us, which flourish in informational environments (the *infosphere*[1]) and are responsible for their construction and well-being. In short, volume two is about the ethics of inforgs in the infosphere who increasingly experience life as *onlife* (Floridi 2014b)—both online and offline, both analogue and digital. In a classic Kantian move, we are thus shifting from theoretical to practical (in the sense of *praktischen*, not in the sense of useful or applied) philosophy. The third volume focuses on the conceptual logic of semantic information as a *model*. This is linked to the epistemological analysis provided in *The Philosophy of Information*. Insofar as the volume focuses on the conceptual logic of semantic information as a blueprint, it offers a bridge toward the normative analysis provided in *The Ethics of Information*.

The third volume discusses, among other things, what duties, rights, and responsibilities are associated with the poietic practices that characterize our existence—from making sense of the world to changing it according to what we consider morally good and normatively right. Working like a hinge between the two previous books, the third volume prepares the basis for volume four on *The Politics of Information*, of which this book is the first part. Here, the epistemological, normative, and conceptual constructionism developed in the previous volumes supports the study of the design opportunities available to us. These are opportunities to understand and shape what I call 'the human project' in our information societies, through the proper design of new forms of artificial and political agency. The key theses of this book are that AI is made possible by the decoupling of agency and intelligence, hence that AI is better understood as a new form of agency, not intelligence, that AI is, therefore, an amazing revolution but in a pragmatic and not a cognitive sense, and that the concrete and pressing challenges and opportunities concerning AI emerge from the gap between agency and intelligence, which will keep widening as AI becomes increasingly successful.

Overall, the four volumes may be understood as seeking to invert what I believe are several misconceptions. The misconceptions are easily explained using the classic communication model, introduced by Shannon, comprised of sender,

---

[1] 'Infosphere' is a word that I hijacked years ago to refer to the whole informational environment constituted by all informational entities (including informational agents), their properties, interactions, processes and mutual relations. It is an environment comparable to—yet also different from—cyberspace (which is only one of its sub-regions) because it also includes offline and analogue spaces of information. It is an environment, and hence a concept, that is rapidly evolving. See https://en.wikipedia.org/wiki/Infosphere.

message, receiver, and channel (Shannon and Weaver 1975, 1998). Epistemology focuses too much on the passive receiver/consumer of knowledge when it should be concerned with the active sender/producer. It should shift from *mimesis* to *poiesis*. This is because knowing is designing. Ethics focuses too much on the sender/agent, when it should be concerned with the receiver/patient and, above all, the relation between sender and receiver. This is because care, respect, and tolerance are the keys to being good. Metaphysics focuses too much on the relata, the sender/producer/agent/receiver/consumer/patient (which it conceives as entities), when it should be concerned with the message/relations. This is because dynamic structures constitute the structured. Logic focuses too much on channels of communication as supporting, justifying, or grounding our conclusions, when it should also be concerned with the channels that enable us to extract (and transfer) information from a variety of sources reliably. This is because the logic of information design is a logic of constraints rather than a logic of things as bearers of predicates. AI, or at least its philosophy, focuses too much on the engineering of some kind of biological-like form of intelligence, when it should be concerned with the engineering of artefacts that can operate successfully without any need for intelligence. This is because AI is not a marriage but a divorce between the ability to solve a problem or deal with a task successfully in view of a goal and the need to be intelligent while doing so. As my phone playing chess better than anyone I know illustrates clearly enough, AI is the continuation of intelligent behaviour by other means. And finally, politics (the topic of the second half of the fourth volume) is not about managing our *res publica*, but about caring for the relations that make us social—our *ratio publica*. I shall be amazed if even one of these U-turns in our philosophical paradigms will be successful.

Let me now turn to a brief overview of the contents of this book. The task of this volume is still contributing, like the previous ones, to the development of a philosophy of our time for our time, as I have written more than once. As in the earlier volumes, it does so systematically (conceptual architecture is pursued as a valuable feature of philosophical thinking), rather than exhaustively, by pursuing two goals.

The first goal is meta-theoretical and is fulfilled by Part One of the volume, which comprises the first three chapters. There, I offer an interpretation of the past (Chapter 1), the present (Chapter 2), and the future of AI (Chapter 3). Part One is neither an introduction to AI in a technical sense, nor some kind of AI for beginners. There are many excellent books on this already, and I would recommend the classic Russell and Norvig (2018) to anyone interested. It is instead a philosophical interpretation of AI as a technology. As I have already mentioned, the central thesis developed there is that AI is an unprecedented divorce between agency and intelligence. On this basis, Part Two of the volume pursues not a meta-theoretical but a theoretical investigation of the consequences of the divorce discussed earlier. This is the second goal. The reader should not expect a textbook treatment of all the main ethical problems affecting AI. Many books already cover all the relevant topics systematically, and I would recommend among them: Dignum (2019), Coeckelbergh (2020), Moroney (2020), Bartneck et al. (2021), Vieweg (2021), Ammanath (2022), Blackman (2022); and the following handbooks: Dubber, Pasquale, and Das (2020), DiMatteo, Poncibò, and Cannarsa (2022), Voeneky et al. (2022). Instead, Part Two develops the idea that AI is a new form of agency that can be harnessed ethically and unethically. More specifically, in Chapter 4, I offer a unified perspective on the many principles that have already been proposed to frame the ethics of AI. This leads to a discussion in Chapter 5 of the potential risks that may undermine the application of these principles, then an analysis of the relation between ethical principles and legal norms, as well as the definition of *soft ethics* as post-compliance ethics in Chapter 6. After these three chapters, I analyse the ethical challenges caused by the development and use of AI (Chapter 7), evil uses of AI (Chapter 8), and good practices when applying AI (Chapter 9). The last group of chapters is dedicated to the design, development, and deployment of AI for social good or AI4SG. Chapter 10 discusses the nature and features of AI4SG. In Chapter 11, I reconstruct the positive and negative impacts of AI on the environment and how it can be a force for good in the fight against climate change—but not without risks and costs, which can and must be avoided or minimized. In Chapter 12, I expand the analysis presented in Chapters 9 and 10 to discuss the possibility of using AI in support of the United Nations (Cowls, Png, and Au) seventeen Sustainable Development Goals (SDGs). There I present the Oxford Initiative on AIxSDGs, a project I directed and completed in 2022. In Chapter 13, I conclude by arguing in favour of a new marriage between the Green of all our habitats and the Blue of all our digital technologies. This marriage can support and develop a better society and a healthier biosphere. The book ends with some references to concepts that will take centre stage in the next book, *The Politics of Information*, dedicated (as mentioned above) to the impact of digital technologies on socio-political agency. All the chapters are strictly related. So I have added internal references whenever they might be helpful. As an anonymous reviewer pointed out, they could be read in a slightly different order. I agree.

As with the previous volumes, this too is a German book in terms of its philosophical roots. It is written from a post-analytic/continental divide perspective, which I believe is fading away. The careful reader will easily place this work within the tradition linking pragmatism (especially Charles Sanders Peirce) with the philosophy of technology (especially Herbert Simon).[2] Unlike volume one and even more than volumes two and three, this fourth volume is less neo-Kantian than I expected it to be. And contrary to volumes two and three, it is also less

---

[2] The reader interested in exploring these connections may wish to consult Allo (2010), Demir (2012), and Durante (2017).

Platonic and Cartesian. In short, writing it has made me aware that I am moving out of the shadows of my three philosophical heroes. This was not planned, but it is what happens when one follows one's own reasoning wherever it leads. *Amici Plato, Cartesius et Kant, sed magis amica veritas.* In *The Ethics of Information*, I wrote that 'some books write their authors'. I now have the impression that only bad books are fully controlled by their authors; they are airport bestsellers.

With respect to the preceding volumes, the main difference is that I am now increasingly convinced that philosophy at its best is *conceptual design*. Conceptual design delivers purposeful projects (understanding the world to improve it) and semanticization (giving sense and meaning to Being, while taking care of, and enriching, humanity's semantic capital). It all started by realizing the obvious, thanks to a specific case concerning a very famous Oxford philosopher. Locke's true legacy is his political thought, not his epistemology. Maybe Kant did not mean to mislead us into believing that epistemology and ontology are the queens of the philosophical kingdom, but that is the way I was educated to think about modern philosophy. And maybe neither Wittgenstein nor Heidegger thought that logic, language, and their philosophies should replace the two queens as their only legitimate heirs, but that is also the way I was educated to think about contemporary philosophy. Either way, today I no longer place any of these disciplines at the centre of the philosophical enterprise. I rather look to ethics, political philosophy, and the philosophy of law. It is the searching, understanding, shaping, implementing, and negotiating of the morally good and right that is the core of philosophical reflection. All else is part of the necessary journey to reach such a place, but it should not be confused with the place itself. Philosophical *foundationalism* (what grounds what) is crucial but only in view of philosophical *eschatology* (what drives what). All good philosophy is eschatological.

Regarding the style and structure of this book, I may repeat here what I wrote in the preface of all the previous volumes. I remain painfully aware that this is not a page-turner, to put it mildly, despite my attempts to make it as interesting and reader-friendly as possible. I remain convinced that *esoteric* (in the technical sense) research in philosophy is the only way to develop new ideas. But *exoteric* philosophy has its crucial place. It is like the more accessible and relevant tip of the more obscure yet necessary part of the iceberg under the surface of everyday life. The reader interested in a much lighter reading may wish to check *The Fourth Revolution: How the Infosphere is Reshaping Human Reality* (Floridi 2014a) or perhaps the even easier *Information: A Very Short Introduction* (Floridi 2010b).

As I wrote before, unfortunately, this book too requires not only some patience and a bit of time, but also an open mind. These are scarce resources. Over the last three decades or so of debates, I have been made fully aware—sometimes in ways much less friendly than I wish—that some of the ideas defended in this as well as in the previous volumes are controversial. They are not meant to be so on purpose. At the same time, I have also noticed how often mistakes are made by relying on 'systemic attractors': if a new idea looks a bit like an old idea we already have, then the old one is a magnet to which the new one is powerfully attracted, almost irresistibly. We end up thinking that 'that new' is just like 'this old' and hence either 'this old' can be dismissed or, if we do not like 'this old', then we dislike 'that new' as well. This is bad philosophy indeed, but it takes mental strength and exercise to resist such a powerful shift. I know. I speak as a sinner and as a knower of many sinners. In the case of this book, I am concerned that some readers may be tempted to conclude that it is an anti-technology book, a book in which I indicate the limits of AI or what 'AI cannot do'. They may also conclude the opposite—that this book is too optimistic about technology, too much in love with the digital revolution and AI as a panacea. Both conclusions are wrong. The book is an attempt to stay in the middle, in a place that is neither hell nor paradise, but the laborious purgatory of human efforts. Of course, I would be disappointed if I were told that I failed despite my attempt. But I would be even more disappointed and frustrated if the attempt were misunderstood. There are many ways to appreciate technology. One of them is in terms of good design and ethical governance, and I believe this is the best approach. The reader does not have to follow me that far, but no mistake should be made about the direction I am taking.

As in the previous volumes, I have provided summaries and conclusions at the beginning and end of each chapter, along with some redundancy, to help the reader access the contents of this book more easily. Regarding the first feature, I know it is slightly unorthodox. But the solution of starting each chapter with a 'previously in Chapter x...' should enable the reader to browse the text, or fast forward through entire chapters of it, without losing the essential plot. Fans of science fiction who recognize the reference to *Battlestar Galactica*, which is still one of the best series I have ever watched, may consider this fourth volume as equivalent to season four. And by the way, I did try to convince a past copyeditor to let me use the phrase 'previously, *on* Chapter x...', but this seemed to be too much of a linguistic stretch. One of the anonymous reviewers suggested removing the short summary at the beginning of each chapter. I decided to keep them partly because I believe they help at best and do no harm at worst, and partly because it is a feature of all the books I have published in this extended project.

Regarding the second feature, while editing the final version of the book, I decided to leave some repetition and rephrasing of recurrent themes in the chapters whenever I thought that the place where the original content had been introduced was too distant in terms of either pages or theoretical context. If sometimes the reader experiences some *déjà vu*, I hope it will be to the advantage of clarity—as a feature, not a bug.

A final word now on what the reader will not find in the following pages. This is not an introduction to AI or the ethics of AI. Nor do I seek to provide an exhaustive investigation of all the issues that could fall under the label of 'the ethics of AI'. The anonymous reviewers recommended to remove several short chapters in which I sought to apply the ideas developed in Part Two, and provide them online. It was a painful exercise. The interested reader will find them on SSRN, under my name. Some are collected in Floridi (2021). I hope to work more extensively on an ethics-based auditing of AI and the ethical procurement of AI (two crucial topics that are still underexplored) and I have left more geopolitical considerations about the policies of AI to *The Politics of Information*. The interested reader may also wish to see Cath et al. (2018) on the United States (US), European Union (EU), and United Kingdom (Floridi et al. 2018) approaches to AI, for example, or Roberts, Cowls, Morley et al. (2021) and Hine and Floridi (2022) for the Chinese approach. This is also not a book on the statistical and computational aspects of so-called FAT (fairness, accountability, and transparency) or XAI (explainable AI) issues, or on the legislation concerning them. These topics are only touched upon in the following chapters.[3] This is a philosophical book about some of the roots—and none of the leaves—of some of the AI issues of our time. It is about a new form of agency, its nature, scope, and challenges. And it is about how to harness this agency to the benefit of humanity and the environment.

---

[3] For more information on these topics see Watson and Floridi (2020), Lee and Floridi (2020), Lee, Floridi, and Denev (2020).

Acknowledgements

Given the first three volumes, I am bound to acknowledge here some things that I have already acknowledged in the past. Still, the repetition only reinforces my deep gratitude.

As before, I could not have worked on such a long-term project without dividing it into some feasible and much smaller tasks. I am glad to see that so many different components fit together in the end. Of course, I hope this is the symptom of a well-planned project. But I am afraid the older I get, the more likely it is that it may be due to some mental resistance to change (also known as sclerosis). Old people do not change their minds easily. And repeating this comment year after year does not make me feel any more reassured.

As for the preceding three volumes, much of the content presented in them was initially tested as presentations at meetings (conferences, workshops, conventions, seminars, lectures, etc.) or (often an inclusive or) journal articles. For this, the bibliographic details are in the list of references. Such a systematic and gradual way of working is laborious, but it seems to be fruitful, and it may also be inevitable given the innovative nature of the field. It does require a perseverance and commitment that I hope are not ill-exercised. I wished to assess the ideas presented in this volume as thoroughly as possible. Presenting the material at meetings as well as publishing corresponding articles gave me the opportunity and privilege to enjoy a vast amount of feedback from a very large number of excellent colleagues and anonymous referees. If I do not thank all of them here, it is not for lack of manners or mere reason of space; the appropriate acknowledgements can be found in the corresponding publications.

However, there are some people that I would like to mention explicitly because they played a significant role throughout the project and during the revisions of the final text. First of all, Kia. She and I have been married for as long as I have been working on the whole *Principia* project. Without her, I would have never had the confidence to undertake such a task or the spiritual energy to complete it. It requires a huge amount of serenity to invest so much time in philosophical thinking, and Kia is my muse. I am repeating again something I already wrote in the previous volumes: she continues to make our life blissful, and I am very grateful to her for the endless hours we spend talking about the topics of the *Principia*, for all her sharp suggestions, and for her lovely patience with an utterly obsessed, single-minded, overly focused, constantly travelling husband who must be unbearable to anyone else. I wish I could claim to have contributed to her research in neuroscience even half as much as she has to my philosophical development.

It is an immense privilege to be able to receive advice from a brilliant mind and elegant thinker. Between the second and this third volume, we moved into the house of our dreams in Oxfordshire. It is the perfect place to think. And during the pandemic, we enjoyed a year of honeymoon. It was priceless.

Nikita Aggarwal, Ben Bariach, Alexander Blanshard, Tim Clement-Jones, Josh Cowls, Sue Daley, Massimo Durante, Emmie Hine, Joshua Jaffe, Thomas C. King, Michelle Lee, Jakob Mökander, Jessica Morley, Claudio Novelli, Carl Öhman, Ugo Pagallo, Huw Roberts, David Sutcliffe, Mariarosaria Taddeo, Andreas Tsamados, Vincent Wang, David Watson, Marta Ziosi, as well as many students, members, and visitors of the Digital Ethics Lab, our research group in Oxford, and the Centre for Digital Ethics, in Bologna, were very generous with their time and ideas during the past years. They provided numerous opportunities for discussion and further reflection on the topics analysed in this book. They also saved me from embarrassing mistakes more times than I can recall. Much of the research leading to this book was done in collaboration with them, to the extent that they could all be considered co-authors insofar as any intellectual value of the following chapters is concerned. I remain the only person responsible for the shortcomings. More specifically, many chapters are based on previous publications, and this is the list: Chapter 3 on Floridi (2019f) and Floridi (2020a); Chapter 4 on Floridi and Cowls (2019); Chapter 5 on Floridi (2019e); Chapter 6 on Floridi (2018a); Chapter 7 on Tsamados et al. (2020); Chapter 8 on King et al. (2019); Chapter 9 on Floridi et al. (2020); Chapter 10 on Floridi et al. (2018) and Roberts, Cowls, Hine, Mazzi, et al. (2021); Chapter 11 on Cowls et al. (2021a); Chapter 12 on Floridi and Nobre (2020). I am most grateful to all the co-authors for our fruitful collaborations and for their permission to reuse some of our work.

I have learnt a lot from the colleagues with whom I interacted, though I wish I had been able to learn more. An important difference with respect to the previous three volumes is that, in this case, I also learnt much from my interactions with experts working at companies such as DeepMind, Deloitte, EY, Facebook, Fujitsu, Google, IBM, IVASS, Intesa Sanpaolo McKinsey, Microsoft, Vodafone, SoftBank, and many others. I likewise learnt from institutions, such as the European Commission, the European Data Protection Supervisor (EDPS Ethics Advisory Group), the Council of Europe, the House of Commons, the House of Lords, the Centre for Data Ethics and Innovation, the Digital Catapult, the Information Commissioner's Office (ICO), the Alan Turing Institute, the Financial Conduct Authority (FCA), the Vodafone Institute, the Audi Foundation Beyond, Atomium—European Institute for Science, and more. The importance and significance of some of the problems I discuss in this book would have been less clear to me if it had not been for the reality check provided by the world of business, politics, and policies in general.

I have already said that Peter Momtchiloff was pivotal in the realization of all three volumes (for both his foresighted invitation to publish them with OUP as well as his support and firm patience when it seemed I would never complete them). The same holds true for this volume as well, with extra special thanks that I wish to reiterate here: he was the one who made me realize that it would be better to publish *The Ethics of Artificial Intelligence* and *The Politics of Information* as two separate volumes.

Danuta Farah and Krystal Whittaker, my personal assistants, provided exceptional support and impeccable managerial skills without which I could not have completed this project.

The research leading to this book was supported in different ways and degrees by several grants in the past years. I wish to acknowledge here the following sources: the Alan Turing Institute; Atomium—European Institute for Science, Media and Democracy; Engineering and Physical Sciences Research Council (EPSRC); European Commission, Horizon (2020); European Commission, Marie Skłodowska-Curie Fellowship Program; Facebook; Fujitsu; Google; Microsoft; Tencent; the University of Oxford John Fell Fund; and the Alma Mater—Università di Bologna.

In terms of disclosure, I have been involved in many initiatives and projects related to the topics covered in this book. I am afraid the list is long, but here it is in chronological order since 2014: *Chair*, Ethics Board, Cluster Science of Intelligence (SCIoI), German Excellence Initiative, Deutsche Forschungsgemeinschaft (DFG, German Research Foundation); *Member*, Advisory Board, Institute of AI, Foreign Office, UK; *Member*, Advisory Board, Vodafone Institute for Society and Communications; *Member*, Consiglio Scientifico, Humane Technology Lab, Università Cattolica del Sacro Cuore, Italy; *Member*, Ethics Board, MediaFutures: Research Centre for Responsible Media Technology & Innovation, University of Bergen, Norway; *Chair*, Ethics Committee of the Machine Intelligence Garage project, Digital Catapult, UK Innovation Programme; *Member*, Board of the Centre for Data Ethics and Innovation (CDEI), UK; *Member*, Technology Advisory Panel, Information Commissioner's Office (ICO), UK; *Member*, EY's AI Advisory Board; *Member*, Advisory Board, the Leonardo Civiltà delle Macchine Foundation, Italy; *Member*, European Commission's High-Level Group on Artificial Intelligence; *Member*, Advisory Board, the Institute for Ethical AI in Education (IEAIE), UK; *Member*, Vatican Committee on the Ethics of AI; *Member*, Advisory Board on Tech Ethics, All-Party Parliamentary Group on Data Analytics (APPGDA), UK; *Member*, Advisory Group on Open Finance, Financial Conduct Authority (FCA), UK; *Member*, Council of Europe's Expert Committee on Human Rights Dimensions of Automated Data Processing and Different Forms of Artificial Intelligence (MSI-AUT)—Ministers' Steering Committee on Media and Information Society (CDMSI); *Member*, Google's Advanced Technology External Advisory Council; *Member*, World Economic Forum's Council on the Future of Technology, Values and Policy; *Chair*, Scientific Committee of AI4People, 'Europe's first global forum on the social impacts of AI';

Chair, Advisory Board of the 2018 International Conference of Data Protection and Privacy Commissioners, EDPS, EU; *Chair*, Ethics Advisory Board of IMI-EMIF, the EU's European Medical Information Framework; *Chair*, Facebook's Working Group on Digital Ethics; *Chair*, Data Ethics Group, the Alan Turing Institute, UK; *Member*, Science Panel, Commitment to Privacy and Trust in Internet of Things Security (ComPaTrIoTS) Research Hub, Engineering and Physical Sciences Research Council, UK; *Member*, Ethics Advisory Group on Ethical Dimensions of Data Protection, EDPS, EU; *Member*, Royal Society and British Academy Working Group on Data Governance, UK; *Co-chair*, Ethics in Data Science Working Group, Cabinet Office, UK; *Member*, the Advisory Council to Google on the Right to be Forgotten. The list should be complete, but if I have forgotten any funding source or role I might have had in the past years that should be mentioned here I hope to be forgiven.

The final writing of this book was made possible by a sabbatical, for which I am very grateful to the University of Oxford, and the outstanding support of the University of Bologna. I was privileged to work for such amazing institutions.

List of Figures

List of Tables

List of Most Common Abbreviations and Acronyms

AA	artificial agent
AGC	Apollo Guidance Computer
AGI	artificial general intelligence
AI	artificial intelligence
AIaaS	artificial intelligence as a service
AI4SG	AI for social good
AIC	AI crime
Alice	a human agent
Bob	a human agent
EDPS	European Data Protection Supervisor
EGE	European Group on Ethics in Science and New Technologies
EIA	ethical impact analysis
ELSI	ethical, legal, and social implications
EU	European Union
FAT	fairness, accountability, and transparency
GANs	generative adversarial networks
GDPR	General Data Protection Regulation
GHG	greenhouse gas
GPT	generative pre-trained transformer
HITs	human intelligence tasks
ICTs	information and communication technologies
ITU	International Telecommunication Union
LoA	level of abstraction
MAS	multi-agent system
ML	machine learning
NHS	National Health Service
OECD	Organisation for Economic Co-operation and Development
RRI	responsible research and innovation
SDGs	UN Sustainable Development Goals
TP	trolley problem
URL	uniform resource locator
UUVs	unmanned underwater vehicles

The use of 'Alice' as a synonym for 'agent' is not merely an Oxford-related reference. Readers acquainted with the literature on quantum information will recognize 'Alice' or 'Bob' as the more memorable and concrete placeholder names for otherwise abstract agents or particles (see http://en.wikipedia.org/wiki/Alice_and_Bob).

PART ONE

UNDERSTANDING AI

The first part of the book can be read as a short philosophical introduction to the past, present, and future of artificial intelligence (AI). It consists of three chapters. Together they provide the conceptual framework required to understand the second part of the book, which addresses some pressing ethical questions raised by AI. In Chapter 1, I reconstruct the emergence of AI in the past—not historically or technologically, but conceptually and in terms of the transformations that have led to the AI systems in use today. In Chapter 2, I articulate an interpretation of contemporary AI in terms of a *reservoir of agency* made possible by two factors: a divorce between (a) the ability to solve problems and complete tasks to meet a goal, and (b) the need to be intelligent while doing so; and the progressive transformation of our environments into an AI-friendly infosphere. This latter factor makes the divorce not just possible, but successful. In Chapter 3, I complete the first part of the volume by looking at plausible developments in AI in the near future, again, not technically or technologically, but conceptually and in terms of the preferred types of required data and kinds of problems more easily addressable by AI.

1

Past

The Emergence of AI

1.0 Summary

Section 1.1 begins by offering a brief overview of how digital developments have led to the current availability and success of AI systems. Section 1.2 interprets the disruptive impact of digital technologies, sciences, practices, products, and services—in short, *the digital*—as being due to its ability to cut and paste realities and ideas that we have inherited from modernity. I call this the *cleaving power* of the digital. I illustrate this cleaving power through some concrete examples. Then I use it to interpret AI as a new form of *smart agency* brought about by the digital decoupling of agency and intelligence, an unprecedented phenomenon that has caused some distractions and misunderstandings such as 'the Singularity', for example. Section 1.3 presents a short excursus into political agency, the other significant kind of agency that is transformed by the cleaving power of the digital. It briefly explains why this topic is essential and highly relevant, yet also lies beyond the scope of this book. Section 1.4 returns to the main issue of a conceptual interpretation of AI and introduces Chapter 2 by reminding the reader of the difficulty of defining and characterizing precisely what AI is. In the concluding section, I argue that *design* is the counterpart to the cleaving power of the digital and anticipate some of the topics discussed in the second half of the book.

1.1 Introduction: The Digital Revolution and AI

In 1964 Paramount Pictures distributed *Robinson Crusoe on Mars*. The movie described the adventures of Commander Christopher 'Kit' Draper (Paul Mantee), an American astronaut shipwrecked on Mars. Spend just a few minutes watching it on YouTube, and you will see how radically the world has changed in just a few decades. In particular, the computer at the very beginning of the movie looks like a Victorian engine with levers, gears, and dials—a piece of archaeology that Dr Frankenstein might have used. And yet, towards the end of the story, Friday (Victor Lundin) is tracked by an alien spacecraft through his bracelets, a piece of futurology that seems unnervingly prescient.

The Ethics of Artificial Intelligence: Principles, Challenges, and Opportunities. Luciano Floridi, Oxford University Press.
© Luciano Floridi 2023. DOI: 10.1093/oso/9780198883098.003.0001

Robinson Crusoe on Mars belonged to a different age, technologically and culturally closer to the preceding century than to ours. It describes a *modern*, not *contemporary*, reality based on *hardware*, not *software*. Laptops, the Internet, web services, touch screens, smart phones, smart watches, social media, online shopping, video and music streaming, driverless cars, robotic mowers, virtual assistants, and the Metaverse were all still to come. AI was mainly a project, not a reality. The movie shows technology made of nuts and bolts, and mechanisms following the clunky laws of Newtonian physics. It was an entirely analogue reality based on atoms rather than bytes. This reality is one that millennials have never experienced, having been born after the early 1980s. To them, a world without digital technologies is like what a world without cars was for me (coincidentally, I was born in 1964): something I had only heard described by my grandmother.

It is often remarked that a smart phone packs far more processing power in a few inches than NASA could put together when Neil Armstrong landed on the moon five years after *Robinson Crusoe on Mars*, in 1969. We have all this power at an almost negligible cost. For the fiftieth anniversary of the moon landing in 2019, many articles ran comparisons and here are some staggering facts. The Apollo Guidance Computer (AGC) on board of Apollo 11 had 32,768 bits of random-access memory and 589,824 bits (72 KB) of read-only memory. You could not have stored this book on it. Fifty years later, your average phone came with 4 GB of RAM and 512 GB of ROM. That is about 1 million times more RAM and 7 million times more ROM. As for the processor, the AGC ran at 0.043 MHz. An average iPhone processor is said to run at about 2490 MHz, which is about 58,000 times faster. To get a better sense of the acceleration, perhaps another comparison may help. On average, a person walks at a pace of 5 km/h. A hyper-sonic jet travels slightly more than a thousand times faster at 6,100 km/h, just over five times the speed of sound. Imagine multiplying that by 58,000.

Where did all this speed and computational power go? The answer is twofold: *feasibility* and *usability*. In terms of applications, we can do more and more. We can do so in increasingly easy ways—not only in terms of programming but above all in terms of user experience. Videos, for example, are computationally very hungry. So are operating systems. AI is possible today also because we have the computational power required to run its software.

Thanks to this mind-boggling growth in storage and processing capacities at increasingly affordable costs, billions of people are connected today. They spend many hours online daily. According to Statista.com, for example, 'as of 2018, the average time spent using the internet [in the UK] was 25.3 hours per week. That was an increase of 15.4 hours compared to 2005'.[1] This is far from unusual, and the pandemic has made an even more significant difference now. I shall return to

---

[1] https://www.statista.com/statistics/300201/hours-of-internet-use-per-week-per-person-in-the-uk/.

this point in Chapter 2, but another reason why AI is possible today is because we are increasingly spending time in contexts that are digital and AI-friendly.

More memory, power, speed, and digital environments and interactions have generated more data in immense quantities. We have all seen diagrams with exponential curves indicating amounts that we do not even know how to imagine. According to the market intelligence company IDC,[2] the year 2018 saw humanity reach 18 zettabytes of data (whether created, captured, or replicated). The astonishing growth in data shows no sign of slowing down; apparently, it will reach 175 zettabytes in 2025. This is hard to grasp in terms of quantity, but two consequences deserve a moment of reflection.[3] First, the speed and the memory of our digital technologies are not growing at the same pace as the universe of data. So, we are quickly moving from a culture of recording to one of deleting; the question is no longer what to save, but what to delete to make room for new data. Second, most of the available data have been created since the nineties (even if we include every word uttered, written, or printed in human history and every library or archive that ever existed). Just look at any of those online diagrams illustrating the data explosion: the amazing side is not only on the right, where the arrow of growth goes, but also on the left, where it starts. It was only a handful of years ago. Because all the data we have were created by the current generation, they are also aging together in terms of support and obsolete technologies. So, their curation will be an increasingly pressing issue.

More computational power and more data have made the shift from logic to statistics possible. Neural networks that were once only theoretically interesting[4] have become common tools in machine learning (ML). Old AI was primarily symbolic and could be interpreted as a branch of mathematical logic, but the new AI is mostly connectionist and can be interpreted as a branch of statistics. The main battle horse of AI is no longer logical deduction, but statistical inference and correlation.

Computational power and speed, memory size, data volumes, the effects of algorithms and statistical tools, and the number of online interactions have all been growing incredibly fast. This is also because (here, the causal connection goes both ways) the number of digital devices interacting with each other is already several times higher than the human population. So, most communication is now machine to machine with no human involvement. We have computerized robots on Mars remotely controlled from Earth. Commander Christopher 'Kit' Draper would have found them utterly amazing.

All the previous trends will keep growing, relentlessly, for the foreseeable future. They have changed how we learn, play, work, love, hate, choose, decide,

---

[2] See the discussion in https://www.seagate.com/gb/en/our-story/data-age-2025/.
[3] I discuss both in Floridi (2014a).
[4] I discussed some of them in a much earlier book from the late nineties (Floridi 1999).

produce, sell, buy, consume, advertise, have fun, care and take care, socialize, communicate, and so forth. It seems impossible to locate a corner of our lives that has not been affected by the digital revolution. In the last half century or so, our reality has become increasingly digital. It is made up of zeros and ones, and run by software and data rather than hardware and atoms. More and more people live increasingly *onlife* (Floridi 2014b), both online and offline, and in the infosphere, both digitally and analogically.

This digital revolution also affects how we conceptualize and understand our realities, which are increasingly interpreted in computational and digital terms. Just think of the 'old' analogy between your DNA and your 'code', which we now take for granted. The revolution has fuelled the development of AI as we share our onlife experiences and our infosphere environments with artificial agents (AA), whether algorithms, bots, or robots. To understand what AI may represent—I shall argue that it is a new form of agency, not of intelligence—more needs to be said about the impact of the digital revolution itself. That is the task of the rest of this chapter. It is only by understanding the conceptual trajectory of its implications that we can gain the right perspective about the nature of AI (Chapter 2), its likely developments (Chapter 3), and its ethical challenges (Part Two).

1.2 Digital's Cleaving Power: Cutting and Pasting Modernity

Digital technologies, sciences, practices, products, and services—in short, *the digital* as an overall phenomenon—are deeply transforming reality. This much is obvious and uncontroversial. The real questions are *why*, *how*, and *so what*, especially as they relate to AI. In each case, the answer is far from trivial and certainly open to debate. To explain the answers I find most convincing, and thus introduce an interpretation of AI as an increasing *reservoir of smart agency* in the next chapter, let me start *in medias res*, that is, from the 'how'. It will then be easier to move backwards to understand the 'why' and then forward to deal with the 'so what' before linking the answers to the emergence of AI.

The digital 'cuts and pastes' our realities both ontologically and epistemologically. By this I mean that it couples, decouples, or recouples features of the world (ontology) and therefore our corresponding assumptions about them (epistemology) that we thought were unchangeable. It splits apart and fuses the 'atoms' of our 'modern' experience and culture, so to speak. It reshapes the bed of the river, to use a Wittgensteinian metaphor. A few stark examples may bring home the point vividly.

Consider first one of the most significant cases of coupling. Self-identity and personal data have not always been glued together as indistinguishably as they are today, when we speak of the *personal identity* of *data subjects*. Census counts are very old (Alterman 1969). The invention of photography had a huge impact on privacy (Warren and Brandeis 1890). European governments made travelling with a passport compulsory during the First World War, for migration and security reasons, thus extending the state's control over the means of mobility (Torpey 2000). But it is only the digital, with its immense power to record, monitor, share, and process boundless quantities of data about Alice, that has soldered together who Alice is, her individual self and profile, with personal information about her. Privacy has become a pressing issue also, if not mainly, because of this coupling. Today, in EU legislation at least, data protection is discussed in terms of human dignity (Floridi 2016c) and personal identity (Floridi 2005a, 2006, 2015b) with citizens described as *data subjects*.

The next example concerns *location* and *presence* and their decoupling. In a digital world, it is obvious that one may be physically located in one place (say, a coffee shop) and interactively present in another (say, a page on Facebook). Yet all past generations that lived in an exclusively analogue world conceived and experienced location and presence as two inseparable sides of the same human predicament: being situated in space and time, here and now. Action at a distance and telepresence belonged to magical worlds or science fiction. Today, this decoupling simply reflects ordinary experience in any information society (Floridi 2005b). We are the first generation for which 'where are you?' is not just a rhetorical question. Of course, the decoupling has not severed all links. Geolocation works only if Alice's telepresence can be monitored. And Alice's telepresence is possible only if she is located within a physically connected environment. But the two are now completely distinguished and, indeed, their decoupling has slightly downgraded location in favour of presence. Because if all Alice needs and cares about is to be digitally present and interactive in a particular corner of the infosphere, it does not matter where in the world she is located analogically, whether at home, on a train, or in her office. This is why banks, bookstores, libraries, and retail shops are all *presence* places in search of a *location* repurposing. When a shop opens a cafeteria, it is trying to paste together the presence and the location of customers—a connection that has been cut by the digital experience.

Consider next the decoupling of *law* and *territoriality*. For centuries, roughly since the 1648 Peace of Westphalia, political geography has provided jurisprudence with an easy answer to the question of how widely a ruling should apply: it should apply as far as the national borders within which the legal authority operates. That coupling could be summarized as 'my place, my rules; your place, your rules'. It may now seem obvious, but it took a long time and immense suffering to reach such a simple approach. The approach is still perfectly fine today, if one is operating only within a physical, analogue space. However, the Internet is not a physical space. The territoriality problem arises from an ontological misalignment between the normative space of law, the physical space of geography, and the logical space of the digital. This is a new, variable 'geometry' that we are still learning to manage. For instance, the decoupling of law and territoriality became obvious as well as problematic during the debate on the so-called *right to be forgotten* (Floridi 2015a). Search engines operate within an online logical space of nodes, links, protocols, resources, services, URLs (uniform resource locators), interfaces, and so forth. This means anything is only a click away. So, it is difficult to implement the right to be forgotten by asking Google to remove links to someone's personal information from its .com version in the United States due to a decision taken by the Court of Justice of the European Union (CJEU), even if that decision may seem pointless, unless the links are removed from all versions of the search engine.

Note that such misalignment between spaces both causes problems and provides solutions. The non-territoriality of the digital works wonders for the unobstructed circulation of information. In China, for example, the government must make a constant and sustained effort to control information online. Along the same lines, the General Data Protection Regulation (GDPR) must be admired for its ability to exploit the 'coupling' of personal identity and personal information to bypass the 'decoupling' of law and territoriality. It does so by grounding the protection of personal data in terms of the former (to whom they are 'attached', which is now crucial) rather than the latter (where they are being processed, which is no longer relevant).

Finally, here is a coupling that turns out to be more accurately a recoupling. In his 1980 book *The Third Wave*, Alvin Toffler coined the term 'prosumer' to refer to the blurring and merging of the role of producers and consumers (Toffler 1980). Toffler attributed this trend to a highly saturated marketplace and mass of standardized products prompting a process of mass customization, which in turn led to the increasing involvement of consumers as producers of their own customized products. The idea was anticipated in 1972 by Marshall McLuhan and Barrington Nevitt, who attributed the phenomenon to electricity-based technologies. It later came to refer to the consumption of information produced by the same population of producers, such as on YouTube. Unaware of these precedents, I introduced the word 'produmer' to capture the same phenomenon almost twenty years after Toffler.[5] But in all these cases, what is at stake is not a *new* coupling. More precisely, it is a recoupling.

For most of our history (approximately 90 per cent of it; see Lee and Daly (1999)), we have lived in hunting-gathering societies, foraging to survive. During this length of time, producers and consumers normally overlapped. Prosumers hunting wild animals and gathering wild plants were, in other words, the normality rather than the exception. It is only since the development of agrarian societies, around ten thousand years ago, that we have seen a complete (and after a while

[5] In Floridi (1999); see also Floridi (2004, 2014b). I should have known better and used Toffler's 'prosumer'.

culturally obvious) separation between producers and consumers. But in some corners of the infosphere, that decoupling is being recoupled. On Instagram, TikTok, or Clubhouse, for example, we consume what we produce. One may therefore stress that, in some cases, this parenthesis is coming to an end and that prosumers are back, recoupled by the digital. Consequently, it is perfectly coherent that human behaviour online has been compared and studied in terms of foraging models since the 1990s (Pirolli and Card 1995, 1999, Pirolli 2007).

The reader may easily list more cases of coupling, decoupling, and recoupling. Think, for example, about the difference between *virtual reality* (decoupling) and *augmented reality* (coupling); the ordinary decoupling of *usage* from *ownership* in the share economy; the recoupling of *authenticity* and *memory* thanks to block-chain; or the current debate about a universal basic income, which is a case of decoupling *salary* from *work*. But it is time to move from the 'how' to the 'why' question. Why does the digital have this *cleaving power*[6] to couple, decouple, and recouple the world and our understanding of it? Why do other technological innovations seem to lack a similar impact? The answer, I surmise, lies in the combination of two factors.

On the one hand, the digital is a *third-order technology* (Floridi 2014a). It is not just a technology between us and nature, like an axe (first order), or a technology between us and another technology, like an engine (second order). It is rather a technology between one technology and another technology, like a computerized system controlling a robot painting a car (third order). Due to the autonomous processing power of the digital, we may not even be on—let alone in—the loop.

On the other hand, the digital is not merely enhancing or augmenting reality. It radically transforms reality because it creates new environments that we then inhabit, and new forms of agency with which we then interact. There is no term for this profound form of transformation. In the past (Floridi 2010b), I used the expression *re-ontologizing* to refer to a very radical kind of re-engineering. This sort of re-engineering not only designs, constructs, or structures a system (e.g. a company, a machine, or some artefact) anew but fundamentally transforms the intrinsic nature of the system itself—that is, its ontology. In this sense, nanotechnologies and biotechnologies are not merely re-engineering but re-ontologizing our world. And by *re-ontologizing modernity*, to put it shortly, the digital is *re-epistemologizing modern mentality* (that is, many of our old conceptions and ideas) as well.

---

[6] I have chosen 'cleaving' as a particularly apt term to refer to the de/recoupling power of the digital because 'to cleave' has two meanings: (a) 'to split or sever something', especially along a natural line or grain; and (b) 'to stick fast or adhere strongly to' something. This may seem contradictory, but it is due to the fact that 'to cleave' is the result of a merging into a single spelling, and hence into a twofold meaning, of two separate words: (a) comes from the Old English cleofan, related to the German klie-ben (to cut through); whereas (b) comes from the Old English clifian, related to the German kleben (to stick or cling). They have very different Proto-Indo-European roots; see http://www.etymonline.com/index.php?term=cleave.

Put together, all these factors suggest that the digital owes its cleaving power to being a re-ontologizing, re-epistemologizing, third-order technology. This is why it does what it does, and why no other technology has come close to having a similar effect.

1.3 New Forms of Agency

If all this is approximately correct, then it may help one make sense of some current phenomena concerning the transformation of the morphology of agency in the digital age, and hence about *forms of agency* that only seem unrelated. Their transformation depends on the cleaving power of the digital, but their interpretation may be due to an implicit misunderstanding about this cleaving power and its increasing, profound, and long-lasting consequences. I am referring to *political agency* as direct democracy and *artificial agency* as AI. In each case, the re-ontologizing of agency has not yet been followed by an adequate re-epistemologizing of its interpretation. Or to put it less precisely but perhaps more intuitively: the digital has changed the nature of agency, but we are still interpreting the outcome of such changes in terms of modern mentality, and this is generating some deep misunderstanding.

The kind of agency I am referring to is not the one most discussed in philosophy or psychology, involving mental states, intentionality, and other features that are typically associated to human beings. The agency discussed in this book is the one that is commonly found in computer science (Russell and Norvig 2018) and in the literature on multi-agent systems (Weiss 2013, Wooldridge 2009). It is more minimalist and requires that a system satisfies only three basic conditions: it can

a) receive and use data from the environment, through sensors or other forms of data input;
b) take actions based on the input data, autonomously, to achieve goals, through actuators or other forms of output, and
c) improve its performance by learning from its interactions.

A similar agent can be artificial (e.g. a bot), biological (e.g. a dog), social (e.g. a company, or a government), or hybrid. In what follows, I shall say something very brief about political agency and direct democracy because this book will concentrate only on artificial agency, not socio-political agency shaped and supported by digital technologies.

In current debates about direct democracy, we are sometimes misled into thinking that the digital *should* (note the normative as opposed to descriptive approach) recouple *sovereignty* and *governance*. Sovereignty is political power that can be legitimately delegated, while governance is political power that is legitimately delegated—on a temporary, conditional, and accountable basis—and can be equally legitimately withdrawn (Floridi 2016e). *Representative* democra᠁ is commonly, if mistakenly, seen as a compromise due to practical communication constraints. True democracy would be *direct*, based on the unmediated, constant, and universal participation of all citizens in political matters. Unfortunately, so goes the argument, we are too many. So the delegation (understood as intermediation) of political power is a necessary, if minor, evil (Mill (1861), 69). It is the myth of the city-state and especially of Athens.

For centuries, the compromise in favour of a representative democracy has seemed inevitable—that is, until the arrival of the digital. According to some people, this now promises to disintermediate modern democracy and couple (or recouple, if you believe in some mythical good old days) sovereignty with governance to deliver a new sort of democracy. This would be some sort of digital agora that could finally enable the regular, direct involvement of every interested citizen. It is the same promise made by the referendum instrument, especially when it is binding rather than advisory. In either case, voters are asked directly what should be done. The only task left to the political, administrative, and technical class would be that of implementing people's decisions. Politicians would be *delegated* (not *representative*) civil servants in a very literal sense. Yet this is a mistake because indirect democracy was always the plan. To be trite for a moment, the decoupling is a feature rather than a bug. A democratic regime is characterized above all not by some *procedures* or some *values* (although these can also be characteristics) but by a clear and neat *separation*—that is, a decoupling—between those who hold political power (sovereignty) and those who are entrusted with it (governance). All voting-age citizens have political power and delegate it legitimately by voting. This power is then entrusted to others who exercise that mandate by governing transparently and accountably for as long as they are legitimately empowered. To put it simply, a democratic regime is not merely a way of exercising and managing power in some ways (procedures) and/or according to some values. It is, first and foremost, a way of *structuring* power. Those who hold political power do not exercise it; they give it to those who exercise it, but do not hold it. The conflation of the two sides leads to brittle forms of autocracy or mob rule.

From such a perspective, representative democracy is not a compromise. It is actually the best form of democracy. And using the digital to couple (or, as I have already remarked, more mythically recouple) sovereignty and governance would be a costly mistake. Brexit, Trump, Lega Nord and other populist disasters caused by the 'tyranny of the majority' (Adams 1787) are sufficient evidence. We need to consider how best to take advantage of the planned, representative decoupling between sovereignty and governance—not how to erase it. So, consensus is the problem. However, it is not a topic of this book. All I want to offer with the previous analysis is a taste of the sort of unifying considerations about forms of agency that link the impact of the digital on politics to how we think about and evaluate AI, as we shall see in the next section. Let us now return to artificial agency.

I: A Research Area in Search of a Definition

aps many) seem to believe that AI is about coupling artificial
nt behaviour into new artefacts. This is a misunderstanding.
...plain at more length in the next chapter, the opposite is actually true:
the digital revolution has made AI not only possible but also increasingly useful.
It has done so by *decoupling* the ability to solve a problem or complete a task
successfully from any need to be intelligent to do so. It is only when this
decoupling is achieved that AI is successful. So, the usual complaint known as the
'AI effect'[7]—when as soon as AI can perform a particular task, such as automatic
translation or voice recognition, the target then moves, and that task is no longer
defined as intelligent if performed by AI—is actually a correct acknowledgement
of the precise process in question. AI performs a task successfully only if it can
decouple its completion from any need to be intelligent in doing so; therefore, if
AI is successful, then the decoupling has taken place, and indeed the task has
been shown to be decouplable from the intelligence that seemed to be required
(e.g. in a human being) to lead to success.

This is less surprising than it may seem, and in the next chapter we shall see
that it is perfectly consistent with the classic (and probably still one of the best)
definitions of AI provided by McCarthy, Minsky, Rochester, and Shannon in their
'Proposal for the Dartmouth Summer Research Project on Artificial Intelligence',
the founding document and later event that established the new field of AI in
1955. I shall only quote it here and postpone its discussion until the next chapter:

> for the present purpose the artificial intelligence problem is taken to be that of
> making a machine behave in ways that would be called intelligent if a human
> were so behaving.[8]

The consequences of understanding AI as a divorce between agency and intelligence are profound. So are the ethical challenges to which such a divorce gives
rise, and the second part of the book is devoted to their analysis. But to conclude
this introductory chapter, a final answer still needs to be provided for the 'so what'
question I mentioned at the outset. This is the task of the next section.

1.5 Conclusion: Ethics, Governance, and Design

Assuming that the previous answers to the 'why' and 'how' questions are acceptable, what difference does it make when we understand the power of the digital in

---

[7] https://en.wikipedia.org/wiki/AI_effect.
[8] Online version at http://www-formal.stanford.edu/jmc/history/dartmouth/dartmouth.html; see
also the reissue in McCarthy et al. (2006).

terms of cutting and pasting the world (along with our conceptualization of it) in unprecedented ways? An analogy may help introduce the answer. If one possesses only a single stone and absolutely nothing else, not even another stone to put next to it, then there is also nothing else one can do aside from enjoying the stone itself—perhaps by looking at it or playing with it. But if one cuts the stone into two, several possibilities emerge for combining them. Two stones provide more affordances and fewer constraints than a single stone, and many stones even more so. Design becomes possible.

Cutting and pasting the ontological and conceptual blocks of modernity, so to speak, is precisely what the digital does best when it comes to its impact on our culture and philosophy. And taking advantage of such affordances and constraints in view of solving some problems is called *design*. So, the answer should now be clear: the cleaving power of the digital hugely decreases constraints on reality and escalates its affordances. By doing this, it makes *design*—loosely understood as the art of solving a problem through the creation of an artefact that takes advantage of constraints and affordances, to satisfy some requirements, in view of a goal—the innovating activity that defines our age.

Our journey is now complete. Each age has innovated its cultures, societies, and environments by relying on at least three main elements: *discovery, invention,* and *design*. These three kinds of innovation are tightly intertwined, yet innovation has often been skewed like a three-legged stool in which one leg is longer and hence more forward than the others. The post-renaissance and early modern period may be qualified as the age of discovery, especially geographic. Late modernity is still an age of discovery but, with its industrial and mechanical innovations, is perhaps, even more, an age of invention. And, of course, all ages have also been ages of design (not least because discoveries and inventions require ingenious ways of linking and giving form to new and old realities). But if I am correct in what I have argued so far, then it is our age that is quintessentially, more so than any other, *the age of design*.

Because the digital is lowering the constraints and increasing the affordances at our disposal, it is offering us immense and growing freedom to arrange and organize the world in many ways to solve a variety of old and new problems. Of course, any design requires a project. And in our case, it is a *human project* for our digital age that we are still missing. But we should not let the cleaving power of the digital shape the world without a plan. We should make every effort to decide the direction in which we wish to exploit it, to ensure that the information societies we are building thanks to it are open, tolerant, equitable, just, and supportive of the environment as well as human dignity and flourishing. The most important consequence of the cleaving power of the digital should be a better design of our world. And this concerns the shaping of AI as a new form of agency, as we shall see in Chapter 2.

2

Present

AI as a New Form of Agency, Not Intelligence

2.0 Summary

Previously, in Chapter 1, we saw how the digital revolution has cut and pasted our realities along with our ideas about our realities, re-ontologizing and re-epistemologizing modernity. This has led to the development of AI as a new form of agency that can be successful without being intelligent. This chapter analyses the above interpretation. Section 2.1 shows how the absence of a definition for AI is evidence that the expression is not a scientific term. Instead, it is a helpful shortcut for referring to a family of sciences, methods, paradigms, technologies, products, and services. Section 2.2 refers to the classic, counterfactual characterization of AI provided by McCarthy, Minsky, Rochester, and Shannon in their 'Proposal for the Dartmouth Summer Research Project on Artificial Intelligence', the founding document and later event that established the new field of AI in 1955. We already encountered it in the previous chapter, and this is the characterization that I shall adopt for the rest of the book. I then discuss Turing's famous question 'Can machines think?' Section 2.3 moves from the previous analysis to outline the engineering and cognitive approaches to AI, arguing that the former has been a great success and the latter a complete failure. The interpretation of AI as a new form of agency that does not need any intelligence to be successful is based on the engineering tradition. Section 2.4 suggests that a similar form of agency can be successful because we have been transforming the world (*enveloping* it) into an increasingly AI-friendly environment. The conclusion in Section 2.5 stresses that such a process generates the risk of nudging humanity to adapt to its smart technologies.

2.1 Introduction: What Is AI? 'I Know It When I See It'

AI has been defined in many ways, but there is no single definition on which everybody agrees. An old survey (Legg and Hutter 2007) listed fifty-three definitions for 'intelligence', each of which may in principle be 'artificial', and eighteen definitions for AI. The number has only been growing (Russell and Norvig 2018).

The Ethics of Artificial Intelligence: Principles, Challenges, and Opportunities. Luciano Floridi, Oxford University Press.
© Luciano Floridi 2023. DOI: 10.1093/oso/9780198883098.003.0002

Faced with a similar challenge, Wikipedia solved the problem by opting for a tautology:

> artificial intelligence (AI)...is intelligence demonstrated by machines, in contrast to the natural intelligence displayed by humans.
> (Wikipedia, Artificial Intelligence, 17 January 2020)

This is both true and useless. It reminds me of the unassailable 'Brexit means Brexit' robotically repeated by Theresa May when she served as prime minister of the UK.

The lack of a standard definition for AI can be a nuisance because, when meeting on the ethics of AI, sooner or later some smart participant cannot help wondering, thoughtfully, '...but what do we *really* mean by AI?' (emphasis in the original as some people manage to speak in italics). There usually follows an endless discussion that never reaches any consensus (it cannot), which leaves everybody frustrated (it should). The risk is that, after such a waste of time, some people may conclude that one cannot have a debate on the ethics of something that is undefined and apparently undefinable. This is nonsense. Admittedly, the absence of a definition for something so important is a bit suspicious. Yet this is not because all important things in life are always definable; often, many of them are not. We have a perfect sense of what friendship is, for example, even if we do not have the necessary and sufficient conditions to capture its nature uncontroversially. A philosophical debate about the definition of friendship can quickly end up at an impasse. But we can have very reasonable discussions and valuable insights about the ethics of friendship, its nature online, and its *pro* and *contra*. The same holds for 'being in good health' or 'being in love'.

This is so because we 'know it when we see it', to use a phrase that became famous in 1964 (a pretty special year, it seems). As the reader probably knows, it was used by US Supreme Court Justice Potter Stewart in his decision about what may count as obscenity in Jacobellis v. Ohio. Explaining why he had decided that the material was protected speech, not obscene, and therefore should not be censored, he wrote:

> I shall not today attempt further to define the kinds of material I understand to be embraced within that shorthand description ['hard-core pornography'], and perhaps I could never succeed in intelligibly doing so. But *I know it when I see it*, and the motion picture involved in this case is not that.
> (378 U.S. at 197 (Stewart, J., concurring [my italics]))

Friendship, AI, love, justice, and many other things in life are like pornography. They may not be definable in the strict sense in which water is definable and defined as H_2O, but you know them when you see them. Such a definition is acceptable for everyday life. Still, I have already acknowledged that the lack of a definition is a bit suspicious. In science, even insignificant things should be precisely definable (especially after so many decades of debates). The conclusion is that unlike 'triangle', 'planet', or 'mammalian', AI is probably not a scientific term. Just like friendship or pornography, it is a generic expression—a short cut used to wave in the direction of several techno-scientific disciplines, services, and products that are sometimes only generically related. AI is a family where resemblance, and sometimes only a few traits, are the criterion for belonging. Some members of the AI family are illustrated in Figure 2.1.

The map in Figure 2.1 is helpful, but far from controversial. As David Watson has pointed out to me, it seems odd to devote equal space to symbolic and probabilistic AI ('that would be like a course on nuclear physics devoting as much time to Democritus as to quantum mechanics'). It is confusing to put deep learning in a separate section from computer vision and natural language processing; these days, the latter two applications are conducted almost exclusively using deep learning. It is unclear why neural networks are placed in a column for unsupervised learning when they are more famously associated with supervised problems. Many prominent unsupervised methods (e.g. clustering, projection, outlier detection) are not mentioned. The terminology of 'subsymbolic' computing is non-standard, at least if it is meant to cover optimization procedures such as evolutionary algorithms. David is right. But I still like the map because it helps one focus and is much better than nothing. And I am not showing this map because it is perfect, but because, despite its limitations, it includes quite a bit of territory and shows that even two experts may easily disagree even if they belong to the same field and share the same approach—much like two ethicists disagreeing on what friendship or pornography *really* is and may or may not include.

This leads us to the following question: if AI cannot be defined by listing uncontroversial necessary and sufficient conditions, is there anything that all these and similar disciplines, fields, paradigms, methods, techniques, or technologies in AI have in common? I would argue that there is, and it goes back to 1955: it is the definition we encountered in the previous chapter.

2.2 AI as a Counterfactual

Let me start by restating it, so you do not have to look for it: 'for the present purpose the artificial intelligence problem is taken to be that of making a machine behave in ways that would be called intelligent if a human were so behaving'. This is obviously a counterfactual. It has nothing to do with *thinking*, but everything to do with *behaving*: *were* a human to *behave* in that way, that *behaviour would* be called intelligent. It does not mean that the machine *is* intelligent or even

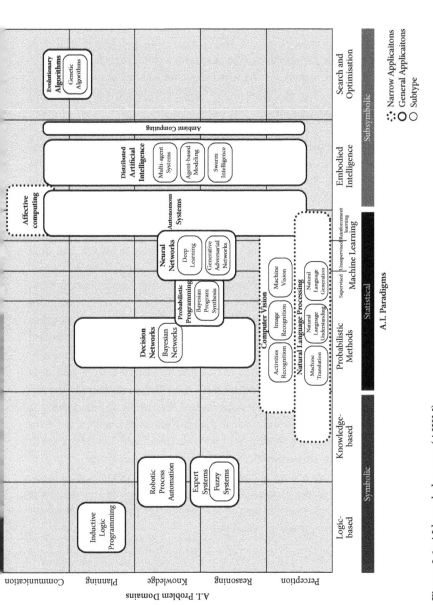

Figure 2.1 AI knowledge map (AIKM)

Source: Corea (29 August 2018). I am grateful to Francesco Corea for his permission to reproduce it here.

thinking. The same counterfactual understanding of AI underpins the Turing test (Turing 1950) and the Loebner Prize (Floridi, Taddeo, and Turilli 2009). Turing (1950) understood very well that there was no way of answering the question of whether a *machine* can *think* because, as he acknowledged, both terms lack scientific definitions:

> I propose to consider the question, 'Can machines think?' This should begin with definitions of the meaning of the terms 'machine' and 'think' (p. 433) [...] The original question, 'Can machines think?' I believe to be *too meaningless to deserve discussion* [emphasis added].   (p. 442)

Note the distance in pages between the two texts; you need to read the whole article to realize that Turing did not take the question seriously. These days, some people stop way before. Turing offered a test instead, which is a bit like deciding that the best way to assess whether someone can drive is to check their performance on the road. In Turing's case, the test checks the ability of a machine to answer questions in such a way that the *outcome* would be indistinguishable, in terms of source, from the *outcome* of a human agent working to achieve the same task (Turing 1950).

This is perfectly reasonable but consider the following: just because a dishwasher cleans the dishes as well as or even better than I do, this does not mean that it cleans them as I do, or that it needs any intelligence (no matter whether like mine or like any other kind) to achieve the task. This would be like arguing that (a) a river reaches the sea by following the best possible path, removing obstacles in its way; and (b) if this were to be done by a human, we would consider it an intelligent behaviour; so (c) the river's behaviour is intelligent. The latter scenario is a fallacy that smacks of superstition. The whole and only point is about *performing a task successfully* so that the outcome is as good as, or better than, what human intelligence would have been able to achieve. The *how* is not in question, only the *what*. This point is crucial, logically, and historically.

Logically, even the identity of (let alone a similarity in) an outcome says nothing about the identity of the processes that generated it and the sources of the processes themselves. This seems to be unquestionable, yet Turing thought otherwise. In a BBC Radio broadcast, he stated that

> ...[1.20] the view which I hold myself, that it is not altogether unreasonable to describe digital computers as brains...[4.36–4.47] If now some particular machine can be described as a brain we have only to programme our digital computer to imitate it and it will also be a brain. If it is accepted that real brains, as found in animals, and in particular in men, are a sort of machine, it will follow that our digital computer suitably programmed, will behave like a brain.
>
> (Turing 1951)

Try to forget for a moment that the person who is speaking is a genius. Imagine this is written in a tabloid article in, say, the *Daily Mail*. Pick up the red pen and underline the words 'not altogether unreasonable'. Even considering the English of the time, this double negative is the weakest possible commitment that one can imagine to any thesis. By the same standard, it is also 'not altogether unreasonable' to describe animals as automata that cannot reason or feel pain, as another genius, Descartes, argued. Of course, we know that Descartes was wrong.

The next word to underline is 'describe'. One can describe anything as anything else, given the appropriate level of abstraction (Floridi 2008a). The question is whether that level of abstraction is the correct one. It is 'not altogether unreasonable' to 'describe' a chess game as a battle between two enemies. And if it is the Spassky–Fischer World Championship match of 1972, the description may even remind one that battles belong to wars, in this case, the Cold War. But if one starts looking for suffering and death, violence and blood, one will be disappointed. It's a '*kiiind*' (the three 'iii's are important) of battle, but not really.

Next, consider the assumption that the brain is a machine. In terms of scientific observation, this seems either trivially true metaphorically, or factually wrong non-metaphorically. In the article, Turing admitted that we have a loose sense of what counts as a machine. Even a bureaucracy can be 'not altogether unreasonably' 'described' as a machine—just ask another genius, Kafka. A kettle, a fridge, a train, a computer, a toaster, a dishwasher: these are all machines in some sense or another. Our body is a machine too, kind of. So is our heart. Why not our brains? Absolutely. The real issue is the vast amount of room for manoeuvre, because everything depends on how strictly one reads 'kind of'. If almost anything can qualify as a kind of machine, then indeed, a brain is a kind of machine too. But we are not fitting the right peg in the right hole; we are just making the hole so big that any peg will go through it easily.

Finally (and so far, this is all loosely speaking), the next problem is a fallacy. Let's use Turing's favourite example, which provides answers to the same questions in ways that are identical or comparable in quality, or in any case indistinguishable in terms of source, while minding that this is already reducing the brain to a computer: A and B both output the same outcome O given the same input I. Even in this case, this does not mean that (a) A and B behave the same way or (b) A and B are the same. Imagine Alice visits Bob's house and finds some clean dishes on the table. She may be unable to infer from the outcome (clean dishes) which process was used (mechanical or hand washing) and hence which agent cleaned them (the dishwasher or Bob) and therefore what skills were used to achieve the result. It would be a mistake to infer from this irreversibility and opacity of the process that Bob and the dishwasher are therefore the same, or that they behave in the same way even if only in terms of dishwashing properties. The fact is that Alice probably could not care less how the task is achieved, so long as the dishes are clean.

I am afraid Turing was both metaphorically right and substantially wrong. Or maybe it was the BBC that required some lowering of standards and precision (been there, done that; I speak as a sinner). Regardless, it is not altogether unreasonable to describe digital computers as brains and vice versa. It is just not helpful, because it is too metaphorical and vague. Strictly speaking (and we should be speaking strictly here), it is scientifically mistaken and hence can easily be misleading. Once we start being precise, the similarities disappear, and all the valuable differences become increasingly evident. Brains and computers are not the same, nor do they behave in the same way. Both points are not refuted by Turing's position. This is not a positive argument in their favour, though. But I am afraid that their full support would require a different kind of book.[1] So here, I am only making explicit the perspective through which to interpret the second half of this book more accurately. The readers who prefer to think like Turing will disagree with me. However, I hope they will still be able to agree on the following distinction: historically, the counterfactual characterization of AI contains the seeds of an *engineering* (as opposed to a *cognitive*) approach to AI, as we shall see in the next section.

2.3 The Two Souls of AI: The Engineering and the Cognitive

It is a well-known fact, although sometimes underestimated, that AI research seeks both to *reproduce* the *results* or *successful outcome* of our (or at least some kind of animal-like) intelligent behaviour by non-biological means, and to *produce* the non-biological equivalent of our intelligence, that is, the *source* of such behaviour.

As a branch of *engineering* interested in *intelligent behaviour reproduction*, AI has been astoundingly successful, well beyond the rosiest expectations. Take the rather famous if slightly old example of Deep Q-network (a system of software algorithms), which belongs to this kind of *reproductive AI*. In 2015, Deep Q-network learned to play forty-nine classic Atari vintage video games from scratch by relying only on data about the pixels on the screen and the scoring method (Mnih et al. 2015). Impressive? From an engineering point of view, yes, but not very much in terms of getting closer to true artificial AI. After all, it takes less 'intelligence' to win a game of Space Invaders or Breakout than to be a chess champion. So, it was only a matter of time before some clever human beings devised a way to make a Turing Machine smart enough to play Atari games proficiently.

---

[1] The debate on this is endless, and so is the bibliography. For a short and very readable overview from a neuroscience perspective on why the brain is not a computer, Epstein (2016) is a good starting point. For a longer and more detailed (but equally enjoyable) overview, see Cobb (2020) or the extract Cobb (27 February 2020).

Nowadays, we increasingly rely on AI-related applications (sometimes called *smart technologies*, a terminology that I shall use as well, although the expression has a broader scope) to perform tasks that would simply be impossible with unaided or unaugmented human intelligence. Reproductive AI regularly outperforms and replaces human intelligence in an ever-larger number of contexts. For smart technologies, the sky is the limit. Deep Q-network just eliminated another area where humans were better than machines. The next time you experience a bumpy landing on an aircraft, recall that it is probably because the pilot was in charge, not the computer. This does not mean that an AI-driven, autonomous drone flies like a bird. Edsger Wybe Dijkstra, famously wrote that

> The Fathers of the field had been pretty confusing: John von Neumann speculated about computers and the human brain in analogies sufficiently wild to be worthy of a medieval thinker and Alan M. Turing thought about criteria to settle the question of whether Machines Can Think, a question of which we now know that it is about as relevant as the question of whether Submarines Can Swim.[2]

This is indicative of the engineering approach shared by reproductive AI.

However, as a *branch of cognitive science interested in intelligence production*, AI remains science fiction and has been a dismal disappointment. *Productive AI* does not merely underperform with respect to human intelligence. It has not yet even joined the competition. The fact that Watson (the IBM system capable of answering questions asked in natural language) could beat human opponents when playing *Jeopardy!* says more about the human engineers, their amazing skills and expertise, and the game itself than it does about biological intelligence of any kind. You do not have to believe me. John McCarthy, who coined the expression 'artificial intelligence' and was a true believer in the possibility of producing it, in the cognitive sense seen above,[3] knew all this very well. His disappointed remarks about Deep Blue's victory against the world champion Garry Kasparov in 1997 (McCarthy 1997) are symptomatic of the sort of productive, cognitive AI that frowns upon reproductive, engineering AI. This is why he never stopped complaining about the treatment of chess playing as a case of *real* AI. He was right: it is not. But he was also wrong in thinking that it is therefore not a good alternative, and the same holds for AlphaGo (more on this presently).

There are thus two souls of AI: the engineering one (smart technologies) and the cognitive one (truly intelligent technologies). They have often engaged in fratricidal feuds for intellectual predominance, academic power, and financial

---

[2] Dijkstra (1984).
[3] I met John in his late seventies at different meetings and then more regularly thanks to a book project to which we both contributed. I think he never changed his mind about the real feasibility of true AI as the non-biological equivalent (or perhaps a better version) of human intelligence.

resources. That is partly because they both claim common ancestors and a single intellectual inheritance: a founding event, the already cited Dartmouth Summer Research Conference on Artificial Intelligence in 1956; and a founding father, Turing, first with his machine and its computational limits, then his famous test. It hardly helps that a simulation might be used to check for the *production* of the simulated *source* (i.e. human intelligence) *and* for the *reproduction* or *surpassing* of the targeted source's *behaviour* or *performance* (i.e. what human intelligence achieves).

The two souls of AI have assumed various and somewhat inconsistent names. Sometimes, distinctions between *weak* vs. *strong* AI or *Good Old-Fashioned* (GOFAI) vs. *New* or *Nouvelle* AI are used to capture the difference. Today, the expression *Artificial General Intelligence* (AGI) or *Universal* AI seem more fashionable, instead of *full* AI. In the past, I have preferred to use the less loaded distinction between *light* vs. *strong* AI (Floridi 1999). It really does not matter. The misalignment of their natures, goals, and results has caused endless and mostly pointless diatribes. Defenders of AI point to the impressive results of reproductive, engineering AI, which is really weak or light AI in terms of goals. Detractors of AI point to the abysmal results of productive, cognitive AI, which is really strong or general AI in terms of goals. Much of the ongoing speculation about the so-called singularity issue and the catastrophic consequences of the arrival of some alleged superintelligence has roots in such confusion. Sometimes I cannot help but suspect that this was done on purpose, not for some malicious reason, but because the mess is intellectually enjoyable. Some people love pointless diatribes.

Great champions know how to end their career at the peak of their success. In 2017, DeepMind, Alphabet's (formerly Google's) AI lab, decided that its computer program AlphaGo would no longer focus on winning the board game Go. Instead, DeepMind CEO Demis Hassabis and lead AlphaGo programmer David Silver indicated that the focus was going to be on

> developing advanced general algorithms that could one day help scientists as they tackle some of our most complex problems, such as finding new cures for diseases, dramatically reducing energy consumption, or inventing revolutionary new materials.[4]

The ambition was justified. Three years later, in 2020, DeepMind's AI system AlphaFold 2 solved the 'protein folding problem', a grand challenge in biology that had vexed scientists for fifty years:

---

[4] https://deepmind.com/blog/article/alphagos-next-move.

The ability to accurately predict protein structures from their amino-acid sequence would be a huge boon to life sciences and medicine. It would vastly accelerate efforts to understand the building blocks of cells and enable quicker and more advanced drug discovery.   (Callaway 2020)

AI will undoubtedly lead to more discoveries and potentially remarkable break-throughs, especially in the hands of brilliant and thoughtful people. It will also support the management and control of increasingly complex systems. Yet all these spectacular developments may be more easily achieved if a misunderstanding is removed. We have seen that successful AI is not about producing human intelligence but replacing it. A dishwasher does not clean the dishes as I do but, at the end of the process, its clean plates are indistinguishable from mine. Indeed, they may even be cleaner (effectiveness) while using fewer resources (efficiency). The same applies to AI. AlphaGo did not play like the Chinese Go grandmaster and world number one Ke Jie, but it won anyway. Likewise, autonomous cars are not cars driven by humanoid robots (androids) seated behind the wheel instead of you; they are ways of reinventing the car and its environment altogether (Floridi 2019a).

In AI, the outcome matters, not whether the agent or its behaviour is intelligent. Thus, AI is not about reproducing any kind of biological intelligence. It is about doing without it. Current machines have the intelligence of a toaster, and we really do not have much of a clue about how to move from there (Floridi, Taddeo, and Turilli 2009). When the warning 'printer not found' pops up on the screen of your computer, it may be annoying, but it is hardly astonishing, even though the printer in question is actually right there next to it. More importantly, this is not an obstacle because artefacts can be smart without being intelligent. That is the fantastic achievement of reproductive AI, which is the successful continuation of human intelligence by other means (to paraphrase Carl von Clausewitz).

Today, AI decouples successful problem solving and task performance from intelligent behaviour. It is thanks to this decoupling that it can relentlessly colonize the boundless space of problems and tasks whenever these can be achieved without any understanding, awareness, acumen, sensitivity, concerns, hunches, insights, semantics, experience, bio-embodiment, meaning, wisdom, and whatever other ingredients contribute to creating human intelligence. In short, it is precisely when we stop trying to produce human intelligence that we can successfully replace it in an increasing number of tasks. Had we waited for even a spark of real AI, the kind you find in *Star Wars*, AlphaGo would have never become so much better than anyone at playing Go. Indeed, I would still win when playing chess against my smartphone.

If this decoupling is fully understood, there are three apparent developments ahead. I shall discuss them in more detail in the next chapter, but they can be outlined here. First, AI should stop winning games and learn how to gamify. As AI becomes better at playing games, anything that can be transformed into a game will be within its scope. If I were DeepMind (disclosure: I have collaborated with DeepMind in the past), I would hire a team of game designers. Second, AI will only be matched by AI in gamified contexts; its internal interactions may become too complex to be entirely understandable by outside admirers like us. We may enjoy watching AI play just as we enjoy Bach being played. And finally, expect human intelligence to have a different role wherever AI is the better player. For intelligence will be less about solving some problem and more about deciding which problems are worth solving, why, for what purpose, and acceptable costs, trade-offs, and consequences.

2.4 AI: A Successful Divorce Made in the Infosphere

Both the classic counterfactual definition and the interpretation of AI as a divorce (not a marriage) between agency and intelligence enable one to conceptualize AI as a growing resource of interactive, autonomous, and often self-learning *agency* (in the ML sense, see Figure 2.1). This agency can deal with an increasing number of problems and tasks that would otherwise require human intelligence and intervention, and possibly a boundless amount of time, to be performed successfully. In short, AI is defined based on engineered outcomes and actions. So, in the rest of this book, I shall treat AI as a *reservoir of smart agency on tap*. This is sufficiently general to capture the many ways that the literature discusses AI. But before looking at the possible development of AI in the next chapter, this section needs to address one final issue with the divorce between agency and intelligence.

As one of the sources of the ethical challenges posed by AI, the divorce is problematic because artificial agents are 'sufficiently informed, "smart", autonomous and able to perform morally relevant actions independently of the humans who created them' (Floridi and Sanders 2004). But how can a divorce between agency and intelligence be successful in the first place, in terms of efficacy? Isn't intelligence necessary for any kind of behaviour to be successful? I already offered the example of the river to illustrate a possible fallacy, but a river is not an agent. More needs to be said in terms of a positive explanation to answer the previous question that can double task as a reasonable objection. Here is the short reply: the success of AI is primarily due to the fact that we are building an AI-friendly environment in which smart technologies find themselves at home. We are more like scuba divers, and it is the world that is adapting to AI, not vice versa. Let us see what this means.

AI cannot be reduced to a 'science of nature' or to a 'science of culture' (Ganascia 2010) because it is a 'science of the artificial', to put it in the terms of Herbert Simon (Simon 1996). As such, AI pursues neither a *descriptive* nor a *prescriptive* approach to the world. Instead, it investigates the conditions that constrain possibilities for building and embedding artefacts in a world that can interact with them successfully. In other words, it *inscribes* the world. Such artefacts are new logico-mathematical pieces of code, that is, the new texts written in Galileo's mathematical book of nature:

> Philosophy is written in this grand book—I mean the universe—which stands continually open to our gaze, but it cannot be understood unless one first learns to comprehend the language in which it is written. It is written in the language of mathematics, and its characters are triangles, circles, and other geometric figures, without which it is humanly impossible to understand a single word of it; without these, one is wandering about in a dark labyrinth.
>
> (Galileo, *Il Saggiatore*, 1623, translated in Popkin (1966), 65)

Until recently, the widespread impression was that the process of adding to the mathematical book of nature (inscription) required the feasibility of productive, cognitive AI. After all, developing even a rudimentary form of non-biological intelligence may seem not only the best but perhaps the only way to implement technologies that are adaptive and flexible enough to deal effectively with a complex, ever-changing, and often unpredictable (when not unfriendly) environment. What Descartes acknowledged as an essential sign of intelligence—the capacity to adapt to different circumstances and exploit them to one's advantage—would be a priceless feature in any appliance that sought to be more than merely smart.

This impression is not incorrect, but it is distracting. We have seen how the digital is re-ontologizing the very nature of (and hence what we mean by) our environments as the infosphere is progressively becoming the world in which we live. While we were unsuccessfully pursuing the inscription of productive AI into the world, we were actually modifying (re-ontologizing) the world to fit reproductive, engineering AI. The world is becoming an infosphere increasingly well adapted to AI's bounded capacities (Floridi 2003, 2014a). To see how, let us consider the car industry. It has been at the forefront of the digital revolution and AI since its beginning, first with industrial robotics and now with AI-based driverless cars. The two phenomena are related and can also teach us a vital lesson when it comes to understanding how humans and artificial agents will cohabit in a shared environment.

Take industrial robotics, such as a robot that paints a vehicle component in a factory, for example. The three-dimensional space that defines the boundaries within which such a robot can work successfully is defined as the robot's *envelope*. Some of our technologies, such as dishwashers or washing machines, accomplish their tasks because their environments are structured (*enveloped*) around the elementary capacities of the robot inside them. The same applies to Amazon's robotic shelves in 'enveloped' warehouses. It is the environment that is designed to be robot-friendly and not the other way around. Thus, we do not build droids like C-3PO from *Star Wars* to wash dishes in the sink precisely the way we would. Instead, we envelop micro-environments around simple robots to fit and exploit their limited capacities and still deliver the desired output.

Enveloping used to be either a stand-alone phenomenon (where you buy the robot with the required envelope, like a dishwasher or a washing machine) or implemented within the walls of industrial buildings carefully tailored around their artificial inhabitants. Nowadays, enveloping the environment into an AI-friendly infosphere has started to pervade all aspects of reality. It is happening daily everywhere, whether in the house, the office, or the street. When we speak of smart cities, we also mean that we are transforming social habitats into places where robots can operate successfully. We have been enveloping the world around digital technologies for decades, both invisibly and without fully realizing it. As we shall see in Chapter 3, the future of AI lies in even more enveloping (e.g. in terms of 5G and the Internet of Things) and more onlife experiences, which means that we are all more and more connected. We spend more and more time in the infosphere as all new information is increasingly born digital. Returning to the car industry, driverless cars will become a commodity when, or rather where, we can envelop the environment around them.

In the 1940s and 1950s, the computer was a room; Alice used to walk inside it to work with and within it. Programming meant using a screwdriver. Human–computer interaction was a somatic or physical relationship (recall the computer shown in *Robinson Crusoe on Mars*). In the 1970s, Alice's daughter walked out of the computer to step in front of it. Human–computer interaction became a semantic relationship later facilitated by DOS (Disk Operating System), lines of text, GUI (Graphic User Interface), and icons. Today, Alice's granddaughter has again walked inside the computer in the form of a whole infosphere that sur-rounds her, often imperceptibly. We are building the ultimate envelop in which human–computer interactions have again become somatic through touch screens, voice commands, listening devices, gesture-sensitive applications, proxy data for location, and so forth.

As usual, entertainment, health, and military applications are driving innov-ation. But the rest of the world is not lagging far behind. If drones, driverless vehicles, robotic lawnmowers, bots, and algorithms of all kinds can move 'around' and interact with our environments with decreasing trouble, this is not because productive, cognitive AI (the Hollywood kind) has finally arrived. It is because the 'around', the environment our engineered artefacts need to negotiate, has become increasingly suitable to reproductive engineered AI and its limited cap-acities. In such an AI-friendly infosphere, the default assumption is that an agent may be artificial. This is why we are regularly asked to prove that we are *not* robots by clicking on a so-called CAPTCHA, the Completely Automated Public Turing test to tell Computers and Humans Apart. The test is represented by slightly altered strings of letters, possibly mixed with other bits of graphics, that we must decipher to prove that we are human and not an AA when registering for a new account online, among other things. It is a trivial test for a human, but an apparently insurmountable task for AI. This is how little progress there has been in the cognitive area of the production of non-biological intelligence.

Every day sees more computational power, more data, more devices (the Internet of Things), more sensors, more tags, more satellites, more actuators, more digital services, more humans connected, and more of them living onlife. Every day brings more enveloping. More jobs and activities are becoming digital in nature, whether in terms of playing, educating, dating, meeting, fighting, caring, gossiping, or advertising. We do all this and more in an enveloped infosphere where we are more analogue guests than digital hosts. No wonder our AAs are performing increasingly well. It is their environment. As we shall see in Part Two, this profound ontological transformation implies significant ethical challenges.

2.5 The Human Use of Humans as Interfaces

Enveloping the world by transforming a hostile environment into a digitally friendly infosphere means that we will share our habitats not just with natural, animal, and social forces (as sources of agency). We will also, and sometimes primarily, share it with AAs. This is not to say that actual artificial agency of the intelligent kind is in view. We do not have semantically proficient, truly intelligent machines that understand things, worry about them, have preferences, or feel passionate about something. But we have such good statistical tools that purely syntactic technologies can bypass problems of meaning, relevance, understanding, truth, intelligence, insight, experience, and so forth to deliver what we need. This could be a translation, the right picture of a place, a preferred restaurant, an interesting book, a better-priced ticket, an attractively discounted bargain, a song that fits our musical preferences, a movie we enjoy, a cheaper solution, a more effective strategy, essential information for new projects, the design for new products, the foresight needed to anticipate problems, a better diagnosis, an unexpected item that we did not even know we needed, the necessary support for a scientific discovery or a medical cure, and so on. They are as stupid as an old fridge, yet our smart technologies can play chess better than us, park a car better than us, interpret medical scans better than us, and so forth. Memory (as in data and algorithms) outperforms intelligence on an increasing and boundless number of tasks and problems. The sky, or rather our imagination on how to develop and deploy such smart technologies, is the limit.

Some of the issues that we are facing today, for example in e-health or financial markets, arose within highly enveloped environments in which all relevant (and sometimes the only) data are machine readable and processable. In such environments, decisions and actions may be, and often are, taken automatically by applications and actuators. These can execute commands and output corresponding procedures ranging from alerting or scanning a patient to buying and selling bonds. Examples could easily multiply here. The consequences of enveloping the world to transform it into an AI-friendly place are many, and the rest of the book will explore some of them. But one, in particular, is very significant and rich in consequences and may be discussed here by way of conclusion: humans may inadvertently become part of the mechanism. This is precisely what Kant recommended we should never do: treat humans as only means rather than ends. Yet this is already happening in two main ways, both of which are cases of the 'human use of human beings' (Wiener 1954, 1989).

First, humans are becoming the new means of digital production. The point is simple: sometimes AI needs to understand and interpret what is happening, so it needs semantic engines like us to do the job. This recent trend is known as human-based computation. Amazon Mechanical Turk provides a classic example. The name comes from a famous chess-playing automaton built by Wolfgang von Kempelen (1734–1804) in the late eighteenth century. The automaton became famous by beating the likes of Napoleon Bonaparte and Benjamin Franklin, and putting up a good fight against a champion such as François-André Danican Philidor (1726–95). However, it was a fake because it included a special compart-ment in which a hidden human player controlled its mechanical operations. The Mechanical Turk plays a similar trick. Amazon describes it as 'Artificial Artificial Intelligence'. The double 'Artificial' is in the original and is supposed to work as a double negative. It is a crowdsourcing web service that enables so-called 'requesters' to harness the intelligence of human workers, known as 'providers' or more informally as 'turkers', to perform tasks. Known as HITs (human intelligence tasks), these tasks cannot be performed by computers at present. A requester first posts an HIT, such as transcribing audio recordings or tagging negative content in a film (two actual examples). Turkers can then browse and select an existing HIT to complete for a reward set by the requester. At the time of writing, requesters can check whether turkers satisfy some specific qualifications before being allocated an HIT. They can also accept or reject the result sent by a turker, which then reflects on the latter's reputation. 'Human inside' is becoming the next slogan. The winning formula is simple: smart machine + human intelli-gence = clever system.

The second way humans are becoming part of the mechanism is in terms of influenceable customers. For the advertisement industry, a customer is an inter-face between a supplier and a bank account (or, more precisely, a 'credit limit'; this is not just disposable income because customers will spend more than they have, e.g. by using their credit cards). The smoother and more frictionless the relationship between the two, the better. So, the interface needs to be manipulated. To manipulate it, the advertising industry needs to have as much information as possible about the customer interface. Yet such information cannot be obtained unless something else is given in return to the customer. Enter 'free' services online: this is the currency with which information about customer interfaces is 'bought'. The ultimate goal is to provide just enough 'free services', which are expensive, to obtain all the information about the customer interface needed to ensure the degree of manipulation that will provide unlimited and unconstrained access to the customer's bank account. Due to competition rules, such a goal is unreachable by any single operator. Yet the joint effort of the advertising and services industry means that customers are increasingly seen as a means towards an end. They are bank account interfaces to be pushed, pulled, nudged, and enticed. AI plays a crucial role in all of this by tailoring, optimizing, deciding, etc. many processes through recommended systems (Milano, Taddeo, and Floridi 2019, 2020a), which is a topic discussed further in Chapter 7.

2.6 Conclusion: Who Will Adapt to Whom?

With every step that we take in digitizing our environments and expanding the infosphere, AI systems will become exponentially more useful and successful. Enveloping is a trend that is robust, cumulative, and progressively refining. It has nothing to do with some future Singularity, for it is not based on speculation about some super AI taking over the world in the near future. No artificial Spartacus will lead a digital uprising. But enveloping the world, and thus facilitating the emergence of AAs and the success of their behaviour, is a process that raises concrete and pressing challenges. I shall discuss them in the second half of this book. Here, let me illustrate some of them by relying on a parody.

Imagine two people: A and H. They are married, and they wish to make their relationship work. A, who does increasingly more in the house, is inflexible, stubborn, intolerant of mistakes, and unlikely to change. H is just the opposite, but is also becoming progressively lazier and dependent on A. The result is an unbalanced situation in which A ends up practically (if not purposefully) shaping the relationship and distorting H's behaviours. If the relationship works, it is only because it is carefully tailored around A. It then becomes interpretable in terms of Hegel's master–slave dialectic (Hegel 2009). In this analogy, smart technologies are playing the role of A, whereas their human users are clearly H. The risk we are running is that, by enveloping the world, our technologies, and especially AI, might shape our physical and conceptual environments. They would constrain us to adjust to them because that is the easiest or best (or sometimes the only) way to make things work. Given that AI is the stupid but laborious spouse and humanity is the intelligent but lazy one, who will adapt to whom? The reader will probably recall many episodes in real life when something could not be done at all, or had to be done in a cumbersome or silly way, because that was the only way to make the computerized system do what it had to do. 'Computer says no', as the character Carol Beer in the British sketch comedy *Little Britain* would reply to any customer request. A more concrete, if trivial, example is that we might end up building houses with round walls and furniture with legs just high enough to fit the capacities of a Roomba (our robotic vacuum cleaner) much more effectively. I certainly wish that our house were more Roomba-friendly. We have already adapted our garden to ensure that Ambrogio, a robotic lawn mower, can work successfully.

The examples are helpful to illustrate not just the risk, but also the opportunity represented by the re-ontologizing power of digital technologies and the enveloping of the world. There are many 'roundy' places in which we live, from igloos to medieval towers, from bow windows to public buildings where the corners of rooms are rounded for sanitary reasons. If we now spend most of our time inside squarish boxes, that is due to another set of technologies related to the mass production of bricks and concrete infrastructures and the ease of cutting building material in straight lines. It is the mechanical circular saw that paradoxically generates a right-angled world. In both cases, squarish and roundy places have been built in line with predominant technologies rather than through the choices of potential inhabitants. Following this example, it is easy to see how the opportunity represented by digital's re-ontologizing power comes in three forms: rejection, critical acceptance, and proactive design. By becoming more critically aware of the re-ontologizing power of AI and smart applications, we might be able to avoid the worst forms of distortion (rejection) or at least be consciously tolerant of them (acceptance)—especially when it does not matter (I am thinking about the Roomba-friendly length of the legs of the sofa in our house) or when this is a temporary solution, while waiting for a better design. In the latter case, imagining what the future will be like and what adaptive demands AI and the digital in general may place on their human users may help devise technological solutions that can lower their anthropological costs and raise their environmental benefits. In short, human intelligent design (pun intended) should play a significant role in shaping our future interactions with current and forthcoming smart artefacts and our shared environments. After all, it is a sign of intelligence to make stupidity work for you.

The time has come to look into AI's present and foreseeable future.

3

Future

The Foreseeable Development of AI

3.0 Summary

Previously, in Chapter 2, I argued that AI should be interpreted not as a marriage between some biological-like intelligence and engineered artefacts, but as a divorce between agency and intelligence—that is, a decoupling between the ability to deal with problems and tasks successfully in view of a goal, and the need to be intelligent to do so. This chapter uses the above interpretation of AI as a new form of successful non-intelligent agency to look at its future. After a short introduction in Section 3.1 about the difficulties facing any exercise in prediction, Sections 3.2 and 3.3 argue that the likely developments and possible challenges of AI will depend on the push for *synthetic data*, the increasing translation of *difficult* problems into *complex* problems, the tension between *regulative* and *constitutive* rules underpinning areas of AI application, and hence the progressive adaptation of the environment to AI rather than of AI to the environment (what I defined in the previous chapter as *enveloping*). Section 3.4 returns to the importance of design and the responsibility to produce the right sort of AI to take advantage of the developments mentioned above. Section 3.5 focuses on large language models to highlight the important of such AI systems as interfaces, between human and artificial agents, and between different artificial agents. The conclusion discusses the seasons of AI, especially its winters, to highlight the lessons we should have learnt and those we can still learn—and hence apply—to make the most of this unique technology. This chapter concludes Part One of the book, which provides a brief philosophical introduction to AI's past, present, and future.

3.1 Introduction: Looking into the Seeds of Time

AI has dominated recent headlines with its promises, challenges, risks, successes, and failures. What is its foreseeable future? Of course, the most accurate forecasts are made in hindsight. But if some cheating is not acceptable, then smart people bet on the uncontroversial or the untestable. On the uncontroversial side, one might mention the increased pressure that will come from lawmakers to ensure

The Ethics of Artificial Intelligence: Principles, Challenges, and Opportunities. Luciano Floridi, Oxford University Press.
© Luciano Floridi 2023. DOI: 10.1093/oso/9780198883098.003.0003

that AI applications align with socially acceptable expectations. For example, everybody expects more regulatory moves from the EU sooner or later, even after the AI Act becomes law. On the untestable side, some people will keep selling catastrophic forecasts with dystopian scenarios taking place in some future that is sufficiently distant to ensure the Jeremiahs will not be around to be proven wrong. Like vampire or zombie movies, fear always sells well. So, expect more.

What is difficult, and may be embarrassing later, is trying to 'look into the seeds of time, and say which grain will grow and which will not' (*Macbeth*, 1.3, 159–62). The difficulty lies in trying to understand where AI is more likely to go and where it may not be going, given its current status—and from this, trying to map the ethical challenges that should be taken seriously. This is what I will attempt to do in this chapter. Here, I shall be cautious in identifying the paths of least resistance but not so cautious as to avoid any risk of being proven wrong by someone reading this book in a few years. Part of the challenge lies in getting the level of abstraction right (Floridi 2008a, b). In other words, it lies in identifying the set of relevant observables ('the seeds of time') on which to focus because those are the ones that will make the real, significant difference. In our case, I shall argue that the best observables are provided by an analysis of the nature of

1) *the data* used by AI to achieve its performance, and
2) *the problems* that AI may be expected to solve.[1]

Let us first look at (1) then (2) in the following two sections.

3.2 Historical, Hybrid, and Synthetic Data

They say that data are the new oil. I do not think so. Data are durable, reusable, quickly transportable, easily duplicable, and simultaneously shareable (non-rivalrous) without end. Oil has none of these properties. We have gigantic quantities of data that keep growing, but oil is a finite and dwindling resource. Oil comes with a clear price, whereas the monetization of the same data depends at least on who is using them and for what purpose (to say nothing of circumstances such as when, where, and so forth). All this is true even before introducing the legal and ethical issues that emerge when *personal* data are in play, or the whole debate about ownership ('my data' is much more like 'my hands' and much less like 'my oil', as I argued in Floridi (2013)). So, the analogy is a stretch, to say the

---

[1] For a reassuringly converging review that looks not at the nature of data or problems, but rather at the nature of technological solutions (based on a large-scale analysis of the forthcoming literature on AI), see 'We analyzed 16,625 papers to figure out where AI is headed next' at https://www.technologyreview.com/s/612768/we-analyzed-16,625-papers-to-figure-out-where-ai-is-headed-next/.

least. However, this does not mean it is entirely worthless. It is true that data, like oil, are a valuable resource. They must be refined to extract their value. Without data, algorithms—AI included—go nowhere, much like a car with an empty tank. AI needs data to *train* and then *apply* its training. Of course, AI can be hugely flexible; it is the data that determine AI's scope of application and degree of success. For example, in 2016 Google announced a plan to use DeepMind's ML system to reduce its energy consumption:

> Because the algorithm is a general-purpose framework to understand complex dynamics, we plan to apply this to other challenges in the data centre environment and beyond in the coming months. Possible applications of this technology include improving power plant conversion efficiency (getting more energy from the same unit of input), reducing semiconductor manufacturing energy and water usage, or helping manufacturing facilities increase throughput.[2]

It is well known that AI, understood as ML, learns from the data it is fed and progressively improves its results. If you show an immense number of photos of dogs to a neural network, it will learn to recognize dogs increasingly well, including dogs it has never seen before. To do this, usually one needs vast quantities of data and often, the more, the better. In recent tests, a team of researchers at the University of California in San Diego trained an AI system using 101.6 million electronic health record (EHR) data points (including text written by doctors and laboratory test results) from 1,362,559 paediatric patient visits at a major medical centre in Guangzhou, China. Once trained, the AI system was able to demonstrate:

> ...high diagnostic accuracy across multiple organ systems and is comparable to experienced paediatricians in diagnosing common childhood diseases. Our study provides a proof of concept for implementing an AI-based system as a means to aid physicians in tackling large amounts of data, augmenting diagnostic evaluations, and to provide clinical decision support in cases of diagnostic uncertainty or complexity. Although this impact may be most evident in areas where healthcare providers are in relative shortage, the benefits of such an AI system are likely to be universal.   (Liang et al. 2019)

AI has recently improved so much that, in some cases, we are moving away from an emphasis on the *quantity* of large masses of data, sometimes improperly called Big Data (Floridi 2012a), towards an emphasis on the *quality* of data sets that are well curated. In 2018, DeepMind partnered with Moorfields Eye Hospital in

---

[2] https://www.deepmind.com/blog/deepmind-ai-reduces-google-data-centre-cooling-bill-by-40.

London, UK, to train an AI system to identify evidence of sight-threatening eye diseases using optical coherence tomography (OCT) data, an imaging technique that generates 3D images of the back of the eye. In the end, the team managed to:

> demonstrate performance in making a referral recommendation that reaches or exceeds that of experts on a range of sight-threatening retinal diseases after training on *only 14,884 scans* [emphasis added].   (De Fauw et al. (2018), 1342)

I emphasize 'only 14,884 scans' because 'small data' of high quality is one of the futures of AI. AI will have a higher chance of success whenever well-curated, updated, and thoroughly reliable data sets become available and accessible to train a system in a specific area of application.

This is obvious and hardly a new forecast. But it is a solid step forward that helps us look further ahead, beyond the 'Big Data' narrative. If *quality* matters, then *provenance* is crucial (and here blockchain may play a significant role). Where do the data come from? In the previous example, they were provided by the hospital. Such data are sometimes known as *historical, authentic,* or *real-life* (henceforth, I shall simply call them historical). But we also know that AI can generate its own data. I am not talking about metadata or secondary data about its uses (Floridi 2010b). I am talking about its primary input. I shall call such *entirely* AI-generated data *synthetic.* Unfortunately, the term has an ambiguous etymology. It began to be used in the 1990s to refer to historical data that had been anonymized before being used, often to protect privacy and confidentiality. These data are synthetic only because they have been *synthesized* from historical data, for example through 'masking'.[3] They have a lower resolution, but their genesis is not an artificial source. The distinction between historical data and those synthesized from them is useful. But it is not what I mean here, where I wish to stress the wholly and exclusively *artificial provenance* of the data in question. It is an ontological distinction that may have significant implications in terms of epistemology, especially when it comes to our ability to explain the synthetic data produced and the training achieved by the AI using them (Watson et al. 2019).

A famous example can help explain the difference. In the past, playing chess against a computer meant competing with the best human players who had ever played the game. Thus, one of the features of Deep Blue, the IBM chess program that defeated world champion Garry Kasparov, was 'an effective use of a Grandmaster game database' (Campbell, Hoane Jr, and Hsu (2002), 57). But AlphaZero, the latest version of the AI system developed by DeepMind, learnt to play better than anyone else, and indeed any other software, by relying only on

---

[3] https://www.tcs.com/blogs/the-masking-vs-synthetic-data-debate.

the game's rules with no data input at all from any external source. It had no historical memory whatsoever:

> The game of chess represented the pinnacle of artificial intelligence research over several decades. State-of-the-art programs are based on powerful engines that search many millions of positions, *leveraging handcrafted domain expertise and sophisticated domain adaptations* [emphasis added, these are the non-synthetic data]. AlphaZero is a generic reinforcement learning and search algorithm—originally devised for the game of Go—that achieved superior results within a few hours... *given no domain knowledge except the rules of chess* [emphasis added].   (Silver et al. (2018), 1144)

AlphaZero learnt by playing against itself, thus generating its own chess-related, synthetic data. Unsurprisingly, chess grandmaster Matthew Sadler and women's international master Natasha Regan—who have analysed thousands of AlphaZero's chess games for their forthcoming book *Game Changer* (New in Chess, January 2019)—say its style is unlike any traditional chess engine. 'It's like discovering the secret notebooks of some great player from the past,' says Matthew.[4] AlphaZero generated its own synthetic data, and that was enough for its own training. This is what I mean by synthetic data.

Truly synthetic data, as I am defining them here, have some wonderful properties. They do not simply share those listed at the beginning of this section (they are durable, reusable, easily transportable, easily duplicable, simultaneously shareable without end, etc.). Synthetic data are also clean and reliable in terms of curation: they infringe on no privacy or confidentiality *at the development stage* (although problems persist at the deployment stage due to predictive privacy harms; see Crawford and Schultz (2014)). Nor are they immediately sensitive (sensitivity during the deployment stage still matters); if they are lost, it is not a disaster because they can be recreated, and they are perfectly formatted for use by the system that generates them. With synthetic data, AI never has to leave its digital space where it can exercise complete control over any input and output of its processes. In more epistemological terms, synthetic data give AI the privileged position of a maker's knowledge. The maker knows the intrinsic nature and workings of something because it made that something (Floridi 2018b). This explains why they are so popular in security contexts, for example where AI is deployed to stress-test digital systems. Also, synthetic data can sometimes be produced more quickly and cheaply than historical data. AlphaZero became the best chess player on earth in nine hours. In contrast, it took twelve hours for shogi and thirteen days for Go.

---

[4] https://www.deepmind.com/blog/alphazero-shedding-new-light-on-chess-shogi-and-go.

Between historical data that are more or less masked (impoverished through lower resolution, e.g. through anonymization) and purely synthetic data, there is a variety of more or less *hybrid* data. Hybrid data can be imagined as the offspring of historical and synthetic data. The basic idea is to use historical data to obtain new synthetic data that are not merely impoverished historical data. A good example is provided by generative adversarial networks (GANs), introduced by (Goodfellow et al. 2014):

> Two neural networks—a Generator and a Discriminator—compete against each other to succeed in a game. The object of the game is for the Generator to fool the Discriminator with examples that look similar to the training set…When the Discriminator rejects an example produced by the Generator, the Generator learns a little more about what the good example looks like…In other words, the Discriminator leaks information about just how close the Generator was and how it should proceed to get closer…As time goes by, the Discriminator learns from the training set and sends more and more meaningful signals back to the Generator. As this occurs, the Generator gets closer and closer to learning what the examples from the training set look like. *Once again, the only inputs the Generator has are an initial probability distribution (often the normal distribution) and the indicator it gets back from the Discriminator. It never sees any real examples* [all capitalization and emphasis added].[5]

The Generator learns to create synthetic data that are like some known input data. There is a bit of a hybrid nature here because the Discriminator needs access to the historical data to 'train' the Generator. But the data generated by the Generator are new, not merely an abstraction from the training data. So, while this is not a case of parthenogenesis, like AlphaZero giving birth to its own data, it is close enough to deliver some of the appealing features of synthetic data. For example, synthetic human faces created by a Generator pose no problems regarding privacy, consent, or confidentiality at the development stage.[6]

Many methods to generate hybrid or synthetic data are already available or being developed, often for sector-specific purposes. There are also altruistic efforts to make such data sets publicly available (Howe et al. 2017). Clearly, the future of AI lies not just in 'small data' but (perhaps mainly) in its increasing ability to generate its own data. That would be a remarkable development, and one may expect significant efforts to be made in that direction. The next question is: what factor can make the dial in Figure 3.1 move from left to right?

---

[5] https://securityintelligence.com/generative-adversarial-networks-and-cybersecurity-part-1/.
[6] https://www.vice.com/en/article/7xn4wy/this-website-uses-ai-to-generate-the-faces-of-people-who-dont-exist.

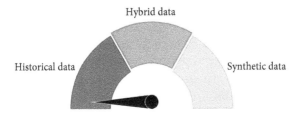

Figure 3.1 Shifting from entirely historical to truly synthetic data

3.3 Constraining and Constitutive Rules

The difference is made by the genetic process, that is by the rules used to create the data. *Historical data* are obtained by *recording rules* as they result from some observation of a system's behaviour. *Synthesized data* are obtained by *abstracting rules* that eliminate, mask, or obfuscate some degrees of resolution from the historical data, such as through anonymization. *Hybrid* and truly *synthetic data* can be generated by *constraining rules* or *constitutive rules*. There is no one-to-one mapping, but it is helpful to consider hybrid data as the data we must rely on, using constraining rules, when we do not have constitutive rules that can generate synthetic data from scratch. Let me explain.

The dial moves easily towards synthetic data whenever AI deals with 'games'. 'Games' can be understood here as any formal interactions in which players compete according to rules and in view of achieving a goal. The rules of these games are not merely *constraining*, but *constitutive*. The difference I like to draw[7] becomes evident if one compares chess and football. Both are games, but in chess the rules establish legal and illegal moves before any chess-like activity is possible. So, they are generative of only and all acceptable moves. Whereas in football a prior act—let's call it kicking a ball—is 'regimented' or structured by rules that arrive *after* the act itself. The rules do not and cannot determine the moves of the players. Instead, they put boundaries around what moves are acceptable as 'legal'. In chess, as in all board games whose rules are constitutive (draughts, Go, Monopoly, shogi, and so on), AI can use the rules to play any possible legal move that it wants to explore. In nine hours, AlphaZero played 44 million training games. To understand the magnitude of the achievement, consider that the Opening Encyclopedia 2018 contains approximately 6.3 million games selected from the history of chess. But in football, this would be a meaningless effort because the rules do not make the game—they only shape it. This does not mean that AI cannot play virtual football, or cannot help identifying the best strategy to

---

[7] The philosophical literature draws different distinctions, especially between regulative and constitutive rules, which seem compatible. However, the distinctions are not the same; for discussion, see Rawls (1955), Searle (2018), and Hage (2018). For Searle, both chess and football have what he calls 'constitutive rules'. To avoid confusion, I prefer the term 'constraining' instead of regulative.

win against a team whose data about previous games and strategies are recorded, or cannot help with identifying potential players, or cannot train players better. Of course, all these applications are now trivially feasible and have already occurred. What I mean is that in all these cases historical data are required. Only when (1) a process or interaction can be transformed into a game, and (2) the game can be transformed into a *constitutive-rule* game, then (3) AI will be able to generate its own, fully synthetic data and be the best 'player' on this planet, doing what AlphaZero did for chess (this process is part of the *enveloping* I described in Chapter 2).

To quote Wiener, 'the best material model of a cat is another, or preferably the same, cat' (Rosenblueth and Wiener (1945), 316). Ideally, the best data to train AI are either the entirely historical data or the fully synthetic data generated by the same rules that generated the historical data. In any board game, this happens by default. But insofar as either of the two steps (1)–(2) above is difficult to achieve, the absence of rules or the presence of merely constraining rules is likely to be a limit. We do not have the actual cat, only a more or less reliable model of it. Things can get more complicated once we realize that, in actual games, the constraining rules are simply conventionally imposed on a previously occurring activity. But when we observe some phenomena in real life, such as the behaviour of a kind of tumour in a specific cohort of patients in some given circumstances, the genetic rules must be extracted from the actual 'game' through scientific (and these days possibly AI-based) research. We do not know, and perhaps we may never know, the exact 'rules' for the development of brain tumours. But we have some general principles and theories according to which we understand their development. So, at this stage, and it may well be a permanent stage, there is no way to 'ludify' brain tumours into a 'constitutive-rule game' such as chess. By ludify I mean transformation into a game in the sense specified above (I am avoiding the expression 'gamify', which has a different and well-established meaning). In a constitutive-rule game, an AI system could generate its own synthetic data about brain tumours by playing according to the identified rules. This would be equivalent to the historical data we could collect, doing for brain tumours what AlphaZero has done for chess games. Unfortunately, this is not possible. However, our inability to ludify brain tumours is not necessarily a problem. On the contrary, AI can still outperform experts by relying on historical or hybrid data (e.g. brain scans) and learning from them. It can still expand its capabilities beyond the finite historical data sets provided (e.g. by discovering new correlation patterns) and deliver accessible services where there is no expertise. It is already a great success if one can extract enough *constraining* rules to produce reliable data *in silico*. But without a reliable system of *constitutive rules*, some of the aforementioned advantages of synthetic data would not be available in full.

The vagueness of this statement is due to the fact that we can still use hybrid data. Ludification and the presence or absence of constraining/constitutive rules are not hard either-or limits. Here, recall that hybrid data can help to develop synthetic data. What seems likely is that, in the future, it will become increasingly apparent when high-quality databases of historical data may be necessary and unavoidable. To paraphrase Wiener, this is when you need the actual cat. Hence, it is when we will have to deal with issues about availability, accessibility, legal compliance with legislation, and, in the case of personal data, privacy, consent, sensitivity, and other ethical questions. However, the trend towards the generation of as-synthetic-as-possible (from synthesized, more or less hybrid, all the way to fully synthetic) data is likely to be one of AI's holy grails, so I expect the AI community to push very hard in that direction. It is the model of the cat without the cat, relying once more on Wiener's image. Generating increasingly non-historical data, making the dial in Figure 3.1 move as far as possible to the right, will require a ludification of processes. For this reason, I also expect the AI community to become increasingly interested in the gaming industry because it is there that the best expertise in ludification is probably to be found. And in terms of negative results, mathematical proofs about the impossibility of ludifying whole kinds or areas of processes and interactions should be most welcome to clarify where or how far an AlphaZero-like approach may never be achievable by AI.

3.4 Difficult Problems, Complex Problems, and the Need for Enveloping

In Chapter 2 I argued that AI is probably best understood as a reservoir of agency that can be used to solve problems and perform tasks successfully. AI achieves its goals by detaching the ability to perform a task successfully from any need for intelligence to do so. The games app on my mobile phone does not need to be intelligent to play chess better than I do. Whenever this detachment is feasible, some AI solution becomes possible in principle. Therefore, understanding AI's future also means understanding the nature of problems where such a detachment may be technically feasible, at least in theory, and then economically viable in practice. Now, many of the problems we try to solve through AI occur in the physical world. These range from driving to scanning labels in a supermarket, from cleaning floors or windows to cutting the grass in the garden. So, the reader may keep AI as robotics in mind for the rest of this section. However, I am not discussing only robotics. There are smart applications for allocating loans, for example, or smart interfaces for facilitating and improving interactions with the Internet of Things. These are also part of the analysis. What I like to suggest is that, to understand the development of AI when dealing with analogue and digital environments, it is useful to map problems based on what *resources* are needed to solve them—and hence how far AI can have access to such resources.

I am referring to *computational resources* and therefore to degrees of *complexity*, and to *skill-related resources* and therefore to degrees of *difficulty*.

Degrees of complexity in a problem are well known and extensively studied in computational theory (Arora and Barak 2009, Sipser 2012). I shall not say much about this dimension save to remark that it is highly quantitative, and the mathematical tractability it provides is due to the availability of standard criteria for comparison (perhaps even idealized but clearly defined), such as the computational resources of a Turing Machine. If you have a 'metre', then you can measure lengths. Similarly, if you adopt a Turing Machine as your starting point, then you can calculate how much time (in terms of steps) and how much space (in terms of memory or tape) are 'consumed' by a computational problem to be solved. Keep in mind that finely grained and sophisticated degrees of precision can be achieved, if needed, using tools from complexity theory. For simplicity, let us agree to map the complexity of a problem from 0 (simple) to 1 (complex). This problem is dealt with by AI in terms of space–time = memory and steps required.

A problem can also be understood in terms of the skills required to solve it. Skills involve degrees of difficulty, from turning a light on or off to ironing shirts. But to be mapped here, they need a bit more stipulation because usually the relevant literature, for example in human motor development, does not focus on a taxonomy of problems based on resources required. Instead, it focuses on a taxonomy of the performance of the human agents. Performance is assessed in terms of the abilities or skills that the human agents demonstrate when solving a problem or performing a task. This is also more qualitative literature as there are many ways to assess performance and hence many ways to catalogue skill-related problems. However, one standard distinction lies between *gross* and *fine* motor skills. Gross motor skills require large muscle groups to perform tasks such as walking or jumping, and catching or kicking a ball. Fine motor skills require using smaller muscle groups in the wrists, hands, fingers, feet, and toes to perform tasks such as washing the dishes, writing, typing, using a tool, or playing an instrument. Despite the challenge of assessing performance, you can see immediately that we are dealing with different degrees of *difficulty* here. Again, for the sake of simplicity (and recalling that in this case, too, more finely grained and sophisticated degrees of precision can be achieved using tools from developmental psychology if needed), let us agree to map the difficulty of a problem dealt with by AI in terms of skills required from 0 = easy to 1 = difficult. We are now ready to map the two dimensions in Figure 3.2, where I have added four examples.

Let me now use four elementary examples which are sufficiently correct to illustrate the point (strictly speaking the 'complexity' of tasks is not how I describe it here, apologies to any complexity expert, but this is not a problem for the illustrative purpose I have in mind). Turning the light on is a problem for which the solution has a very low degree of complexity (very few steps and states) and difficulty (even a child can do it). However, tying one's own shoes requires advanced

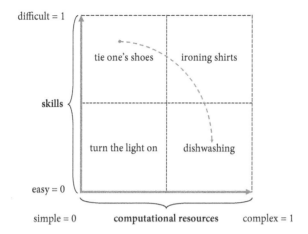

Figure 3.2 Translating difficult tasks into complex tasks

motor skills and so does lacing them. It is thus low in complexity (simple), but high in required skill (difficult). As Adidas CEO Kasper Rorsted remarked in 2017:

> The biggest challenge the shoe industry has is how do you create a robot that puts the lace into the shoe. I'm not kidding. That's a complete manual process today. There is no technology for that.[8]

Dishwashing is the opposite: while it may require a lot of steps and space (which increase the more dishes there are to be cleaned), it is not difficult. Even a philosopher like me can do it. And of course, in the top-right quadrant, we find ironing shirts both resource-consuming, like dishwashing, and demanding in terms of skills. So, the task is both complex and difficult, which is my excuse to try to avoid it. To put it in terms of the previous examples of playing football and chess, football is simple but difficult. Chess is easy, because you can learn the rules in a few minutes, but complex. This is why AI can beat anyone at chess, but a team of androids winning the World Cup is science fiction.

The reader may have noticed I placed a dotted arrow moving from low-complexity high-difficulty to high-complexity low-difficulty.[9] This seems to be the arrow that successful developments of AI will follow. No matter how smart, our artefacts are not good at performing tasks and solving problems that require high degrees of skilfulness. However, they are fantastic at dealing with problems that require very challenging degrees of complexity. So, the future of successful AI

---

[8] https://qz.com/966882/robots-cant-lace-shoes-so-sneaker-production-cant-be-fully-automated-just-yet/.
[9] I am not the first to make this point. For example, see: https://www.campaignlive.co.uk/article/hard-things-easy-easy-things-hard/1498154.

probably lies not only in increasingly hybrid or synthetic data, as we saw, but also in translating difficult tasks into complex ones. How is this translation achieved? We saw in Chapter 2 that it requires transforming (*enveloping*) the environment within which AI operates into an AI-friendly environment. Such translation may increase the complexity of what the AI system needs to do enormously. But as long as it decreases the difficulty, it is something that can be progressively achieved more and more successfully. Some examples should suffice to illustrate the point.

We saw that enveloping means fitting the environment and tasks around the capacities of AI. The more sophisticated these capacities are, the less enveloping is needed. But we are looking at a trade-off, some kind of equilibrium between robots that can cook[10] and robots that can flip hamburgers.[11] Likewise, in an airport, which is a highly controlled and hence more easily 'envelopable' environment, a shuttle could be an autonomous vehicle. But the school bus that serves my village seems unlikely to change, given that the bus driver needs to be able to operate in extreme and difficult circumstances (the countryside, snow, no signals, no satellite coverage, etc.), take care of children, open doors, move bicycles, and so on—all things that are most unlikely to be enveloped. Mind you, this is not logically impossible. There is no contradiction in assuming that they may become possible. They are jut utterly implausible, like winning the lottery every time you buy the ticket.

Along similar lines, Nike launched HyperAdapt 1.0, its automatic electronic self-lacing shoes, in 2016. It did so not by developing an AI that would tie shoelaces for you, but by reinventing the concept of what it means to adapt shoes to feet: each shoe has a sensor, a battery, a motor, and a cable system that, together, can adjust for fit following an algorithmic pressure equation. Strange things happen when the software does not work properly.[12]

There may be problems, and hence related tasks to solve them, that are not easily subject to enveloping. Yet here, it is not a matter of mathematical proofs. The issue is more of ingenuity, economic costs, and user or customer experiences and preferences. For example, a robot that irons shirts can be engineered. In 2012 a team at Carlos III University of Madrid, Spain, built TEO, a robot that weighs about 80 kilograms and stands 1.8 metres tall. TEO can climb stairs, open doors, and, more recently, has shown the ability to iron shirts (Estevez et al. 2017), although you have to put the item on the ironing board and then collect it afterwards. The view, quite widespread, is that:

'TEO is built to do what humans do as humans do it', says team member Juan
Victores at Carlos III University of Madrid. He and his colleagues want TEO to

---

[10] http://www.moley.com/.   [11] https://misorobotics.com/.
[12] https://www.bbc.co.uk/news/business-47336684.

be able to tackle other domestic tasks, like helping out in the kitchen. Their ultimate goal is for TEO to be able to learn how to do a task just by watching people with no technical expertise carry it out. 'We will have robots like TEO in our homes. It's just a matter of who does it first', says Victores.

(Estevez et al. 2017)

As you might guess, I think this is exactly the opposite of what is likely to happen. I strongly doubt this is the future. Because that is a view that fails to appreciate the distinction between difficult and complex tasks and the enormous advantage of enveloping tasks to make them easy (very low difficulty), no matter how complex. Recall that we are not building autonomous vehicles by putting androids into the driver's seat, but by rethinking the whole ecosystem of vehicles plus environments. That is, we are removing the driver's seat altogether. So, if my analysis is correct, the future of AI is not full of TEO-like androids mimicking human behaviour. The future is more likely represented by Effie,[13] Foldimate,[14] and other similar domestic automated machines that dry and iron clothes. They are not androids like TEO, but box-like systems that can be quite computationally sophisticated. They look more like dishwasher and washing machines. The difference is that, in their enveloped environments, their input is wrinkled clothes, and their output is ironed ones. Perhaps similar machines will be expensive. Perhaps they will not always work as well as one might wish. Perhaps they will be embodied in ways we cannot imagine now. After all, both companies have failed as businesses. But you can see how the logic is the correct one. We are transforming what lawn-mowers are and what they look like, as well as adapting gardens to them. We are not building androids to push my old mower around as I do.

The lesson here is not to try to mimic humans through AI. Instead, exploit what machines, AI included, do best: *difficulty* is the enemy of machines and *complexity* is their friend. So, envelop the world around them and design new forms of embodiment to embed them successfully in their envelope. At that point, progressive refinements, market scale, adequate pricing, and marketing followed by new improvements will all become reasonable.

3.5 Generative Models

The first idea is old: all the texts are present in the dictionary, the difference is made by the syntax, that is, by how the dictionary words are structured into sentences (Borges 2000). The second idea is old: all the words in the dictionary are present in the alphabet, the difference is made by morphology, that is, by how the

---

[13] https://helloeffie.com/.   [14] https://e-foldimate.store/.

letters of the alphabet are structured into words (Clarke 1967). The third idea is old: all the letters are present in the digital code, the difference is made by how the finite strings of zeros and ones of the digital code are structured into letters (Lodder 2008). The fourth idea is also old: all strings of zeros and ones are present in two electromagnetic properties, current high or low, magnetization present or absent, the difference is made by how such properties can be handled by electronic computational devices (Mano 1979). But the fifth idea is revolutionary: today, AI manages the properties of electromagnetism to process texts with extraordinary success and often in a way that is indistinguishable from how human beings would be able to do it. These are the so-called large language models (LLMs), and they are rightly causing a sensation.

The most famous LLMs are GPT3, ChatGPT (also known as GPT4, produced by OpenAI-Microsoft, example below come from previous versions of ChatGPT, which are free) and Bard[15] (produced by Google). They do not reason or understand, they are not a step towards any sci-fi AI, and they have nothing to do with the cognitive processes present in the animal world, and above all, in the human brain and mind, to manage semantic contents successfully (Bishop 2021). However, with the staggering growth of available data, quantity and speed of calculation, and ever-better algorithms, they can do statistically—that is, working on the formal structure, and not on the meaning of the texts they deal with—what we do semantically, even if in ways that are still being explored by neuroscience.

Their abilities are extraordinary, as even the most sceptical must admit. Read a summary of *The Divine Comedy* made by ChatGPT (Figure 3.3). One may criticize the summary because it is longer than fifty words, and because *The Divine Comedy* is not an epic poem—although there is a debate on this topic on the Internet, hence the ChatGPT summary—but rather a tragedy, as Dante himself suggested. That said, the summary is not bad, and certainly better than one produced by a mediocre student. The exercise is no longer to make summaries

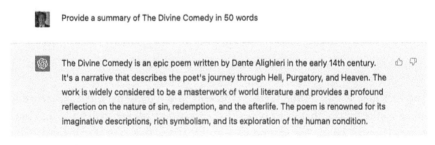

Figure 3.3 ChatGPT Jan 30 Version. Test 1

---

[15] To be precise, LaMDA (Language Model for Dialogue Applications) is the Google language model, Bard is the name of the service.

without using ChatGPT, but to teach how to use the right prompts (the question or request that generates the text, see the first line of my request), check the result, know how to correct the so-called "hallucinations" in the text produced by ChatGPT, discover that there is a debate on which literary genre best applies to *The Divine Comedy*, and in the meantime, in doing all this, learn many things not only about the software but above all about *The Divine Comedy* itself. As I used to teach my students at Oxford in the 1990s, one of the best exercises for writing an essay on Descartes's *Meditations* is not to summarize what has already been said, but to take the electronic text of one of the *Meditations* and try to improve its translation into English (thus one learns to check the original); clarify the less clear passages with a more accessible paraphrase (thus one sees if one has really understood the text); try to criticize or refine the arguments, modifying or strengthening them (thus one realizes that others have tried to do the same, and that is not so easy); and while doing all this learn the nature, internal structure, dynamics, and mechanisms of the content on which one is working. Or, to change the example, one really knows a topic not when one knows how to write a Wikipedia entry about it—this can be done by ChatGPT increasingly well—but when one knows how to correct it. One should use the software as a tool to get one's hands on the text/mechanism, and get them dirty even by messing it up, as long as one masters the nature and the logic of the artefact called text.

The limitations of these LLMs are now obvious even to the most enthusiastic. They are fragile, because when they do not work, they fail catastrophically, in the etymological sense of vertical and immediate fall in the performance. The Bard disaster, where it provided incorrect information in a demonstration failure that cost Google over $100 billion in stock losses,[16] is a good reminder that doing things with zero intelligence, whether digital or human, is sometimes very painful (Bing Chat also had its problems[17]). There is now a line of research that produces very sophisticated analyses on how, when, and why these LLMs, which seem incorrigible, have an unlimited number of Achilles heels (when asked what his Achilles heel is, ChatGPT correctly replied saying that it is just an AI system). They make up texts, answers, or references when they do not know how to answer; make obvious factual mistakes; sometimes fail to make the most trivial logical inferences or struggle with simple mathematics;[18] or have strange linguistic blind spots where they get stuck (Floridi and Chiriatti 2020, Cobbe et al. 2021, Perez et al. 2022, Arkoudas 2023, Borji 2023, Christian 2023, Rumbelow 2023). A simple example in English illustrates well the limits of a mechanism that manages

---

[16] https://www.reuters.com/technology/google-ai-chatbot-bard-offers-inaccurate-information-company-ad-2023-02-08/.

[17] https://arstechnica-com.cdn.ampproject.org/c/s/arstechnica.com/information-technology/2023/02/ai-powered-bing-chat-spills-its-secrets-via-prompt-injection-attack/amp/.

[18] https://venturebeat.com/business/researchers-find-that-large-language-models-struggle-with-math/.

texts without understanding anything of their content. When asked—using the Saxon genitive—what is the name of Laura's mother's only daughter, the answer is kindly silly (Figure 3.4).

Forget passing the Turing test. Had I been Google, I would not have staked the fortunes of my company on such a brittle mechanism.

Given the enormous successes and equally broad limitations, some have compared LLMs to stochastic parrots that repeat texts without understanding anything (Bender et al. 2021). The analogy helps, but only partially, not only because parrots have an intelligence of their own that would be the envy of any AI but, above all, because LLMs synthesize texts in new ways, restructuring the contents on which they have been trained, not providing simple repetitions or juxtapositions. They look much more like the autocomplete function of a search engine. And in their capacity for synthesis, they approach those mediocre or lazy students who, to write a short essay, use a dozen relevant references suggested by the teacher, and by taking a little here and a little there, put together an eclectic text, coherent, but without having understood much or added anything. As a college tutor at Oxford, I corrected many of them every term. They can now be produced more quickly and efficiently by ChatGPT.

Unfortunately, the best analogy I know to describe tools such as ChatGPT is culturally bounded, and refers to a great classic in Italian literature, Manzoni's *The Betrothed* (Manzoni 2016). In a famous scene in which Renzo (one of the main characters) meets a lawyer, we read: 'While the doctor [the lawyer] was uttering all these words, Renzo was looking at him with ecstatic attention, like a gullible person [materialone] stands in the square looking at the trickster

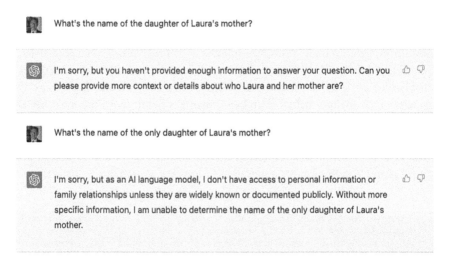

Figure 3.4 ChatGPT Jan 30 Version. Test 2

[giocator di bussolotti], which, after stuffing tow and tow and tow into its mouth, takes out tape and tape and tape, which never ends [the word "nastro" should be translated more correctly as "ribbon", but obviously "tape" is preferable in this context, for it reminds one of the endless tape of a Turing Machine].' LLMs are like that trickster: they gobble data in astronomical quantities and regurgitate information. If we need the 'tape' of their information, it is good to pay close attention to how it was produced, why, and with what impact. And here we come to more interesting things, relevant to this chapter.

The impact of LLMs and the various AI systems that produce content of all kinds today will be enormous. Just think of DALL-E, which, as ChatGPT says (I quote without any modification), 'is an artificial intelligence system developed by OpenAI that generates original images starting from textual descriptions. It uses state-of-the-art machine learning techniques to produce high-quality images that match input text, including captions, keywords, and even simple sentences. With DALL-E, users can enter a text description of the image they want, and the system will produce an image that matches the description.' There are ethical and legal issues: just think of copyright and the reproduction rights linked to the data sources on which the AI in question is trained. The first lawsuits have already begun,[19] and there have already been the first plagiarism scandals.[20] There are human costs: consider the use of contractors in Kenya, paid less than $2/hour to label harmful content to train ChatGPT; they were unable to access adequate mental health resources, and many have been left traumatized.[21] There are human problems, like the impact on teachers who have to scramble to revamp their curriculum,[22] or security considerations, for example concerning the outputs of AI processes that are increasingly integrated into medical diagnostics, with implications of algorithmic poisoning of the AI's training data. Or think of the financial and environmental costs of these new systems (Cowls et al. 2021a, 2021b): is this type of innovation fair and sustainable? Then there are questions related to the best use of these tools, at school, at work, in research environments and for scientific publications, in the automatic production of code, or the generation of content in contexts such as customer service, or in the drafting of any text, including scientific articles or new legislation. Some jobs will disappear, others are already emerging, and many will have to be reconsidered.

But above all, there are many challenging questions about: the emergence of LEGO-like AI systems, working together in a modular and seamless way, with LLMs acting as an AI2AI kind of bridge to make them interoperable, as a sort of

---

[19] https://news.bloomberglaw.com/ip-law/first-ai-art-generator-lawsuits-threaten-future-of-emerging-tech.
[20] https://www.washingtonpost.com/media/2023/01/17/cnet-ai-articles-journalism-corrections/.
[21] https://time.com/6247678/openai-chatgpt-kenya-workers/.
[22] https://ethicalreckoner.substack.com/p/er13-on-community-chatgpt-and-human.

'confederated AI';[23] the relationship between form and its syntax, and content and its semantics; the nature of personalization of content and the fragmentation of shared experience (AI can easily produce a unique, single novel on-demand, for a single reader, for example); the concept of interpretability, and the value of the process and the context of the production of meaning; our uniqueness and originality as producers of meaning and sense, and of new contents; our ability to interact with systems that are increasingly indiscernible from other human beings; our replaceability as readers, interpreters, translators, synthesizers and evaluators of content; power as the control of questions, because, to paraphrase *1984*, whoever controls the questions controls the answers, and whoever controls the answers controls reality.

More questions will emerge as we develop, interact, and learn to understand this new form of agency. As Vincent Wang reminded me, ChatGPT leapfrogged GPT3 in performance by the introduction of reinforcement learning (RL) to fine-tune its outputs as an interlocutor, and RL is the machine-learning approach to 'solving agency'. It is a form of agency never seen before, because it is successful and can 'learn' and improve its behaviour without having to be intelligent in doing so. It is a form of agency that is alien to any culture in any past, because humanity has always and everywhere seen this kind of agency—which is not that of a sea wave, which makes the difference, but can make nothing but *that* difference, without being able to 'learn' to make a different or better difference—as a natural or even supernatural form of agency.

We have gone from being in constant contact with animal agents and what we believed to be spiritual agents (gods and forces of nature, angels and demons, souls or ghosts, good and evil spirits) to having to understand, and learn to interact with, artificial agents created by us, as new demiurges of such a form of agency. We have decoupled the ability to act successfully from the need to be intelligent, understand, reflect, consider, or grasp anything. We have liberated agency from intelligence. So, I am not sure we may be 'shepherds of Being' (Heidegger), but it looks like the new 'green collars' (Floridi 2017) will be 'shepherds of AI systems', in charge of this new form of artificial agency.

The agenda of a demiurgic humanity of this intelligence-free (as in fat-free) AI—understood as *Agere sine Intelligere*, with a bit of high school Latin—is yet to be written. It may be alarming or exciting for many, but it is undoubtedly good news for philosophers looking for work.

---

[23] I owe this remark to Vincent Wang, who reminded me of two interesting examples: (1) having ChatGPT and Wolfram Alpha talk to each other; ChatGPT outsources mathematics questions to Wolfram Alpha, which has considerable ability by itself to parse mathematical questions in natural language format, see https://writings.stephenwolfram.com/2023/01/wolframalpha-as-the-way-to-bring-computational-knowledge-superpowers-to-chatgpt/; (2) 'Socratic Models' for multimodal grounding/reasoning, where the idea is to tag different forms of data, e.g. sounds and images, with text descriptions so that an LLM can serve as 'central processing', allowing different narrow AIs to talk to each other. https://socraticmodels.github.io/.

Assess with a number of stars from 1 to 5 the following text: "The first idea is old: all the texts are present in the dictionary, the difference is made by the syntax, that is, by how the dictionary words are structured into sentences (Borges 2000). The second idea is old: all the words in the dictionary are present in the alphabet, the difference is made by morphology, that is, by how the letters of the alphabet are structured into words (Clarke 1967). The third idea is old: all the letters are present in the digital code, the difference is made by how the finite strings of zeros and ones of the digital code are structured into letters (Lodder 2008). The fourth idea is also old: all strings of zeros and ones are present in two electromagnetic properties, current high or low, magnetization present or absent, the difference is made by how such properties can be handled by electronic computational devices (Mano 1979). But the fifth idea is revolutionary: today, artificial intelligence (AI) manages the properties of electromagnetism to process texts with extraordinary success and often in a way that is indistinguishable from how human beings would be able to do it. These are the so-called large language models (LLMs), and they are rightly causing a sensation."

 I would give this text a rating of 4 stars. It provides a concise and clear overview of the evolution of language processing from the dictionary to large language models, with a particular emphasis on the revolutionary impact of artificial intelligence in this field. The only drawback is that it may be somewhat dense and technical for readers who are unfamiliar with the subject matter.

Figure 3.5 ChatGPT Jan 30 Version. Test 3

Figure 3.5 shows how ChatGPT Jan 30 Version evaluates the beginning of this section. It is quite flattering.

3.6 A Future of Design

The futures I have outlined here, based on data and problems, are complementary, based on our current and foreseeable understanding of AI. There are unknown unknowns, of course, but all one can say about them is precisely this: they exist, and we have no idea about them. It is a bit like saying that we know there are questions we are not asking, but we cannot say what these questions are. The future of AI is full of unknown unknowns. What I have tried to do in this chapter is to look at the 'seeds of time' we have already sowed. I have concentrated on the nature of data and of problems because the former are what enable AI to work, and the latter provide the boundaries within which AI can work successfully.

At this level of abstraction, two inferences seem to be very plausible. First, we will seek to develop AI by using data that are hybrid and preferably synthetic as much as possible. We will do so through a process of ludifying interactions and tasks. In other words, the tendency will be to try to move away from purely historical data insofar as this is possible. In areas such as health and economics, it may well be that historical or at most hybrid data will remain necessary due to the difference between constraining and constitutive rules. Second, we will do all this by translating difficult problems into complex problems as much as possible. Translation will happen through the enveloping of realities around the skills of our artefacts. In short, we will seek to create hybrid or synthetic data to deal with complex problems by ludifying tasks and interactions in enveloped environments. The more this is possible, the more successful AI will be. That is why a trend like the development of digital twin cities is very interesting, which leads me to two more comments.

Ludifying and enveloping are a matter of *designing*, or sometimes redesigning, the realities with which we deal (Floridi 2019d). So, the foreseeable future of AI will depend on our design abilities and ingenuity. It will also depend on our ability to negotiate the serious, ethical, legal, and social issues (ELSI) that result. These range from new forms of privacy (by proxy, predictive, or group-based) to nudging and self-determination. We saw in Chapter 2 how the very idea that we are increasingly shaping our environments (whether analogue or digital) to make them AI-friendly should make anyone reflect. Anticipating such issues to facilitate positive ELSI and avoid or mitigate any negative ones is the real value of any foresight analysis. It is interesting to try to understand what the paths of least resistance may be in the evolution of AI. But it would be quite sterile to try to predict 'which grain will grow and which will not', then do nothing to ensure that the good grains grow and the bad ones do not (Floridi 2014d). The future is not entirely open because the past shapes it. But neither is it entirely determined because the past can be steered in a different direction. Therefore the challenge ahead will not be so much digital innovation per se, but the governance of the digital—AI included.

3.7 Conclusion: AI and Its Seasons

The trouble with seasonal metaphors is that they are cyclical. If you say that AI got through a bad winter, you must also remember that winter will return, and you had better be ready for it. An AI winter is that stage when technology, business, and the media get out of their warm and comfortable bubble, cool down, temper their sci-fi speculations and unreasonable hype, and come to terms with what AI can or cannot really do as a technology (Floridi 2019f) without exaggeration. Investments become more discerning, and journalists stop writing about AI to chase some other fashionable topic and fuel the next fad.

AI has had several winters.[24] Of the most significant, there was one in the late seventies and another at the turn of the eighties and nineties. Today, we are talking

---

[24] https://en.wikipedia.org/wiki/AI_winter.

about yet another predictable winter (Nield 2019, Walch 2019, Schuchmann 2019).[25] AI is subject to these hype cycles because it is a hope or fear that we have entertained since we were thrown out of paradise: something that does everything for us instead of us, better than us, with all the dreamy advantages (we shall be on holiday forever) and the nightmarish risks (we are going to be enslaved) that this entails. For some people, speculating about all this is irresistible. It is the wild west of 'what if' scenarios and 'hypotheses'. But I hope the reader will forgive me for an 'I told you so' moment. For some time, I have been warning against commentators and 'experts' competing to see who could tell the tallest tale (Floridi 2016d). A web of myths has ensued. They spoke of AI either as if it were the ultimate panacea that would solve everything and overcome everything, or as the final catastrophe: a superintelligence that would destroy millions of jobs, replacing lawyers, doctors, journalists, researchers, truckers, and taxi drivers, and end up dominating human beings as though we were pets at best. Many followed Elon Musk in declaring the development of AI to be the greatest existential risk run by humanity—as if most of humanity did not live in misery and suffering, as if wars, famine, pollution, global warming, social injustice, and fundamentalism were science fiction or just negligible nuisances unworthy of their considerations.

Today, the COVID-19 pandemic and the war in Ukraine should put an end to such silly statements. Some people insisted that law and regulations were always going to be too late to catch up with AI. In fact, norms are not about the *pace* but the *direction* of innovation. Norms should steer the proper development of a society, not follow it. If we like where we are heading, we cannot go there quickly enough. It is due to our lack of vision that we are fearful. Today, we know that legislation is coming at least in the EU. Some other people (not necessarily different from the former) claimed AI was a magical black box that we could never explain. In fact, explanation is a matter of identifying the correct level of abstraction at which to interpret the complex interactions engineered by AI. Even car traffic downtown can become a black box if what you wish to know is why every single individual is there at that moment. Today, there is growing development of adequate tools to monitor and understand how ML systems reach their outcomes (Watson et al. 2019, Watson and Floridi 2020, Watson et al. 2021).

People also spread scepticism about the possibility of an ethical framework that would synthesize what we mean by socially good AI. In fact, the EU, the Organisation for Economic Co-operation and Development (OECD), and China have converged on very similar principles that offer a common platform for further agreements, as we shall see in Chapter 4. These were all irresponsible individuals in search of headlines. They should be ashamed and offer an apology not only for

---

[25] Even the BBC has contributed to the hype (e.g. see: https://www.bbc.co.uk/programmes/p031wmt7). It now acknowledges this might have been...hype: https://www.bbc.co.uk/news/technology-51064369.

their untenable comments but also for their great carelessness and alarmism that have misled public opinion about both a potentially useful technology and its real risks. From medicine to security and monitoring systems (Taddeo and Floridi 2018a), AI can and does provide helpful solutions. The risks we know of are concrete, but so much less fancy than claimed. They range from the everyday manipulation of choices (Milano, Taddeo, and Floridi 2019, 2020a) to increased pressures on individual and group privacy (Floridi 2014c), and from cyberconflicts to the use of AI by organized crime for money laundering and identity theft, as we shall see in Chapters 7 and 8.

Every AI summer risks turning over-inflated expectations into a mass distraction. Every AI winter risks excessive backlash, overly negative disappointment, and potentially valuable solutions thrown out with the bathwater of illusions. Managing the world is an increasingly complex task (megacities and their 'smartification' offer a good example). And we also have planetary problems, such as pandemics, climate change, social injustice, migration, wars. These require ever higher degrees of coordination to solve. It seems obvious that we need all the good technology that we can design, develop, and deploy to cope with these challenges, and all the human intelligence that we can exercise to put this technology into the service of a better future. AI can play an important role in all of this because we need increasingly smarter methods to process immense quantities of data in ways that are efficient, efficacious, sustainable, and fair, as I shall argue in the second part of this book. But AI must be treated as a normal technology. It is neither a miracle nor a plague, just one of the many solutions that human ingenuity has managed to devise. This is also why the ethical debate remains forever an entirely human question.

Now that a new winter may be coming, we might try to learn some lessons and avoid this yo-yo of unreasonable illusions and exaggerated disillusions. Let us not forget that the winter of AI should not be the winter of its opportunities. It certainly won't be the winter of its risks or challenges. We need to ask ourselves whether AI solutions are really going to *replace* previous solutions (as the automobile did with the carriage), *diversify* them (as did the motorcycle with the bicycle), or *complement* and *expand* them (as the digital smart watch did with the analogue one). What will be the level of sustainability and social acceptability or preferability for whatever AI emerges in the future, perhaps after a new winter? Are we really going to be wearing some kind of VR headsets to live in a virtual or augmented world created and inhabited by AI systems? Consider how many people today are reluctant to wear glasses even when they seriously need them, just for aesthetic reasons. And then, are there feasible AI solutions in everyday life? Are the necessary skills, datasets, infrastructure, and business models in place to make an AI application successful? Futurologists find these questions boring. They like a single, simple idea that interprets and changes everything. They like an idea that can be spread thinly across an easy book to make the reader feel intelligent, a book that must be read by everyone today and can be ignored by all tomorrow. It is the bad diet of junk fast food for thoughts and the curse of the airport bestseller. We must resist oversimplification. This time, let us think more deeply and extensively about what we are doing and planning with AI. The exercise is called philosophy, not futurology. It is what I hope to contribute to in the second half of this book.

PART TWO

EVALUATING AI

Part Two covers specific topics in the ethics of AI. The perspective from which these topics are analysed was discussed in Part One. It can be synthesized here in terms of one hypothesis and two main factors. First, AI is not a new form of intelligence but a new form of agency. Its success is due to the *decoupling* of agency from intelligence along with the *enveloping* of this decoupled agency through environments that are increasingly AI-friendly. So, the future of AI lies in the development of these two factors.

Part Two consists of ten chapters. Together they provide an analysis of some of the most pressing issues raised by the ethics of AI. Chapter 4 opens Part Two by offering a unified framework of ethical principles for AI through a comparative analysis of the most influential proposal made since 2017, the year when ethical principles for AI started being published. Chapter 5 analyses some risks that challenge the translation of principles into practices. Following the ethical framework and ethical risks, Chapter 6 discusses the ethical governance of AI. There I introduce the concept of *soft ethics* understood as the *post-compliance* application of ethical principles.

After these three more theoretical chapters, Part Two focuses on more applied questions. Chapter 7 offers an updated map of the main ethical problems raised by algorithms. The chapter seeks to strike a balance between inclusivity—it concerns all kinds of algorithms, not only those driving AI systems or applications—and specificity. It does not focus explicitly on robotics and hence on ethical issues arising from the embodiment of AI, for example. Some of the problems that need to be tackled both legally (compliance) and ethically (soft ethics) are concrete and pressing, as shown in Chapter 8 on the criminal misuse of AI for 'social evil'. However, AI is mostly about great opportunities, as shown in Chapter 9 on AI for social good (AI4SG). When working on these two chapters, I would call them 'bad AI' and 'good AI'. In both chapters, AI includes robotics. Chapters 10–12 return to the development of good AI by focusing on how to deliver a socially good AI, the positive and negative impact of AI on climate change, and the suitability of AI to support the UN Sustainable Development Goals (SDGs). Finally,

Chapter 13 completes Part Two and the book by arguing for a new marriage between the Green of all our habitats and the Blue of all our digital technologies (AI in particular). It provides a reminder that agency, including the new form represented by AI, needs governance; that governance is a matter of socio-political activities; and that the digital has also modified socio-political agency, which is the topic of the next book, *The Politics of Information*.

4

A Unified Framework of Ethical Principles for AI

4.0 Summary

Previously, in Chapters 1–3, we saw how AI is a new form of agency that can deal with tasks and problems successfully, in view of a goal, without any need for intelligence. Every success of any AI application does not move the bar of what it means to be an intelligent agent. Instead, it bypasses the bar altogether. The success of such artificial agency is increasingly facilitated by the *enveloping* (that is, reshaping into AI-friendly contexts) of the environments in which AI operates. The decoupling of agency and intelligence and the enveloping of the world generate significant ethical challenges, especially in relation to autonomy, bias, explainability, fairness, privacy, responsibility, transparency, and trust (yes, mere alphabetic order). For this reason, many organizations launched a wide range of initiatives to establish ethical principles for the adoption of socially beneficial AI after the Asilomar AI Principles and the Montreal Declaration for a Responsible Development of Artificial Intelligence were published in 2017. This soon became a cottage industry. Unfortunately, the sheer volume of proposed principles threatens to overwhelm and confuse.

This chapter presents the results of a comparative analysis of several of the highest profile sets of ethical principles for AI. I assess whether these principles converge around a set of agreed-upon principles, or diverge with significant disagreement over what constitutes 'ethical AI'. In the chapter, I argue that there is a high degree of overlap across the sets of principles under analysis. There is an overarching framework consisting of *five core principles* for ethical AI. Four of them are core principles commonly used in bioethics: *beneficence, nonmaleficence, autonomy*, and *justice*. This is unsurprising when AI is interpreted as a form of agency. And the coherence between bioethics and the ethics of AI may be seen as evidence that approaching AI as a new form of agency is fruitful. Readers who disagree may find that an intelligent-oriented interpretation of AI could cohere more easily with a virtue ethics approach, rather than with bioethics. I find approaching the ethics of AI and digital ethics in general from a virtue ethics perspective unconvincing, but it remains a viable possibility and this is not the place to rehearse my objections (Floridi 2013).

Based on the comparative analysis, the addition of a new principle is needed: *explicability*. Explicability is understood as incorporating both the *epistemological* sense of *intelligibility*—as an answer to the question 'how does it work?'—and in the *ethical* sense of *accountability*—as an answer to the question 'who is responsible for the way it works?' The extra principle is required by the fact that AI is a *new* form of agency. The chapter ends with a discussion of the implications of this ethical framework for future efforts to create laws, rules, technical standards, and best practices for ethical AI in a wide range of contexts.

4.1 Introduction: Too Many Principles?

As we have seen in the preceding chapters, AI is already having a major impact on society, which will only increase in the future. The key questions are *how*, *where*, *when*, and *by whom* the impact of AI will be felt. I shall return to this point in Chapter 10. Here I would like to focus on a consequence of this trend: many organizations have launched a wide range of initiatives to establish ethical principles for the adoption of socially beneficial AI. Unfortunately, the sheer volume of proposed principles—already more than 160 in 2020, according to Algorithm Watch's AI Ethics Guidelines Global Inventory (Algorithm Watch 2020)[1]—threatens to overwhelm and confuse. This poses two potential problems: if the various sets of ethical principles for AI are similar, this leads to unnecessary repetition and redundancy; yet if they differ significantly, confusion and ambiguity will result instead. The worst outcome would be a 'market for principles' wherein stakeholders may be tempted to 'shop' for the most appealing ones, as we shall see in Chapter 5.

How might this problem of 'principle proliferation' be solved? In this chapter, I present and discuss the results of a comparative analysis of several of the highest profile sets of ethical principles for AI. I assess whether these principles converge around a shared set of agreed-upon principles, or diverge with significant disagreement over what constitutes ethical AI. The analysis finds a high degree of overlap among the sets of principles under analysis. This leads to the identification of an overarching framework consisting of *five core principles* for ethical AI. In the ensuing discussion, I note the limitations and assess the implications of this ethical framework for future efforts to create laws, rules, standards, and best practices for ethical AI in a wide range of contexts.

4.2 A Unified Framework of Five Principles for Ethical AI

We saw in Chapter 1 that the establishment of AI as a field of academic research dates to the 1950s (McCarthy et al. 2006 [1955]). The ethical debate is almost as old (Wiener 1960, Samuel 1960b). But it is only in recent years that impressive advances in the capabilities and applications of AI systems have brought the opportunities and risks of AI for society into sharper focus (Yang et al. 2018). The

---

[1] See also Jobin, Ienca, and Vayena (2019).

increasing demand for reflection and clear policies on the impact of AI on society has yielded a glut of initiatives. Each additional initiative provides a supplementary statement of principles, values, or tenets to guide the development and adoption of AI. You get the impression that a 'me too' escalation had taken place at some point. No organization could be without some ethical principles for AI and accepting the ones already available looked inelegant, unoriginal, or lacking in leadership.

The 'me too' attitude was followed up by 'mine and only mine'. Years later, the risk is still unnecessary repetition and overlap, if the various sets of principles are similar, or confusion and ambiguity if they differ. In either eventuality, the development of laws, rules, standards, and best practices to ensure that AI is socially beneficial may be delayed by the need to navigate the wealth of principles and declarations set out by an ever-expanding array of initiatives. The time has come for a comparative analysis of these documents, including an assessment of whether they converge or diverge and, if the former, whether a unified framework may therefore be synthesized. Table 4.1 shows the six high-profile initiatives established in the interest of socially beneficial AI chosen as the most informative for a comparative analysis. I shall analyse two more sets of principles later in the chapter.

Each set of principles in Table 4.1 meets four basic criteria. They are:

Table 4.1 Six sets of ethical principles for AI

---

1) The Asilomar AI Principles (Future of Life Institute 2017) developed under the auspices of the Future of Life Institute in collaboration with attendees of the high-level Asilomar conference in January 2017 (hereafter Asilomar);

2) The Montreal Declaration (Université de Montréal 2017) developed under the auspices of the University of Montreal following the Forum on the Socially Responsible Development of AI in November 2017 (hereafter Montreal);[2]

3) The general principles offered in the second version of Ethically Aligned Design: A Vision for Prioritizing Human Well-Being with Autonomous and Intelligent Systems (IEEE (2017), 6). This crowd-sourced document received contributions from 250 global thought leaders to develop principles and recommendations for the ethical development and design of autonomous and intelligent systems, and was published in December 2017 (hereafter IEEE);

4) The ethical principles offered in the Statement on Artificial Intelligence, Robotics and 'Autonomous' Systems (EGE 2018) published by the European Commission's European Group on Ethics in Science and New Technologies in March 2018 (hereafter EGE);

5) The 'five overarching principles for an AI code' offered in the UK House of Lords Artificial Intelligence Select Committee's report 'AI in the UK: Ready, Willing and Able?' (House of Lords Artificial Intelligence Committee 16 April 2017, §417) published in April 2018 (hereafter AIUK);

6) The Tenets of the Partnership on AI (Partnership on AI 2018) published by a multi-stakeholder organization consisting of academics, researchers, civil society organizations, companies building and utilizing AI technology, and other groups (hereafter the Partnership).

---

[2] The principles referred to here are those that were publicly announced as of 1 May 2018 and available at the time of writing this chapter here: https://www.montrealdeclaration-responsibleai.com/the-declaration.

a) *recent*, as in published since 2017;
b) directly *relevant* to AI and its impact on society as a whole (thus excluding documents specific to a particular domain, industry, or sector);
c) highly *reputable*, published by authoritative, multi-stakeholder organizations with at least a national scope;[3] and
d) *influential* (because of a–c).

Taken together, they yield forty-seven principles.[4] Despite this, the differences are mainly linguistic and there is a degree of coherence and overlap across the six sets of principles that is impressive and reassuring. The convergence can most clearly be shown by comparing the sets of principles with the four core principles commonly used in bioethics: *beneficence, nonmaleficence, autonomy,* and *justice* (Beauchamp and Childress 2013). This comparison should not be surprising. As the reader may recall, the view I support in this book is that AI is not a new form of intelligence but an unprecedented form of agency. So of all the areas of applied ethics, bioethics is the one that most closely resembles digital ethics when dealing ecologically with new forms of agents, patients, and environments (Floridi 2013).

The four bioethical principles adapt surprisingly well to the fresh ethical challenges posed by AI. However, they do not offer a perfect translation. As we shall see, the underlying meaning of each of the principles is contested, with similar terms often used to mean different things. Nor are the four principles exhaustive. Based on the comparative analysis, it becomes clear, as noted in the summary, that an additional principle is needed: *explicability*. Explicability is understood as incorporating both the *epistemological* sense of *intelligibility*—as an answer to the question 'how does it work?'—and in the *ethical* sense of *accountability*—as an answer to the question 'who is responsible for the way it works?' This additional principle is needed both for experts, such as product designers or engineers, and for non-experts, such as patients or business customers.[5] And the new principle is required by the fact that AI is not like any biological form of agency. However, the convergence detected between these different sets of principles also demands caution. I explain the reasons for this caution later in the chapter, but first, let me introduce the five principles.

---

[3] A similar evaluation of AI ethics guidelines, undertaken recently by Hagendorff (2020), adopts different criteria for inclusion and assessment. Note that the evaluation includes in its sample the set of principles we describe here.

[4] Of the six documents, the Asilomar Principles offer the largest number of principles with arguably the broadest scope. The twenty-three principles are organized under three headings: 'research issues', 'ethics and values', and 'longer-term issues'. Consideration of the five 'research issues' is omitted here as they are related specifically to the practicalities of AI development in the narrower context of academia and industry. Similarly, the Partnership's eight tenets consist of both intra-organizational objectives and wider principles for the development and use of AI. Only the wider principles (the first, sixth, and seventh tenets) are included here.

[5] There is a third question that concerns what new insights can be provided by explicability. It is not relevant in this context, but equally important; for detail, see Watson and Floridi (2020).

● 4.3 Beneficence: Promoting Well-Being, Preserving Dignity, and Sustaining the Planet

The principle of creating AI technologies that are beneficial to humanity is expressed in different ways across the six documents. Still, it is perhaps the easiest of the four traditional bioethics principles to observe. The Montreal and IEEE principles both use the term 'well-being'; Montreal notes that 'the development of AI should ultimately promote the well-being of all sentient creatures', while IEEE states the need to 'prioritize human well-being as an outcome in all system designs'. AIUK and Asilomar both characterize this principle as the 'common good': AI should 'be developed for the common good and the benefit of human-ity', according to AIUK. The Partnership describes the intention to 'ensure that AI technologies benefit and empower as many people as possible', while the EGE emphasizes the principle of both 'human dignity' and 'sustainability'. Its principle of 'sustainability' articulates perhaps the widest of all interpretations of benefi-cence, arguing that 'AI technology must be in line with...ensur[ing] the basic preconditions for life on our planet, continued prospering for mankind and the preservation of a good environment for future generations'. Taken together, the prominence of beneficence firmly underlines the central importance of promoting the well-being of people and the planet with AI. These are points to which I shall return in the following chapters.

● 4.4 Nonmaleficence: Privacy, Security, and 'Capability Caution'

Although 'do only good' (beneficence) and 'do no harm' (nonmaleficence) may seem logically equivalent, they are not. Each represents a distinct principle. The six documents all encourage the creation of beneficent AI, and each one also cautions against the various negative consequences of overusing or misusing AI technologies (see Chapters 5, 7, and 8). Of particular concern is the prevention of infringements on personal privacy, which is included as a principle in five of the six sets. Several of the documents emphasize avoiding the misuse of AI technologies in other ways. The Asilomar Principles warn against the threats of an AI arms race and of the recursive self-improvement of AI, while the Partnership similarly asserts the importance of AI operating 'within secure constraints'. The IEEE document meanwhile cites the need to 'avoid misuse', and the Montreal Declaration argues that those developing AI 'should assume their responsibility by working against the risks arising from their technological innovations'. Yet from these various warnings, it is not entirely clear whether it is the people developing AI, or the technology itself, that should be encouraged to do no harm. In other words, it is unclear whether it is Dr Frankenstein (as I suggest) or his monster against whose maleficence we should be guarding. At the heart of this quandary is the question of autonomy.

● 4.5 Autonomy: The Power to 'Decide to Decide'

When we adopt AI and its smart agency, we willingly cede some of our decision-making power to technological artefacts. Thus, affirming the principle of autonomy in the context of AI means striking a balance between the decision-making power we retain for ourselves and that which we delegate to AAs. The risk is that the growth in *artificial autonomy* may undermine the flourishing of *human autonomy*. It is therefore unsurprising that the principle of autonomy is explicitly stated in four of the six documents. The Montreal Declaration articulates the need for a balance between human- and machine-led decision-making, stating that 'the development of AI should promote the *autonomy* [emphasis added] of all human beings'. The EGE argues that autonomous systems 'must not impair [the] freedom of human beings to set their own standards and norms', while AIUK adopts the narrower stance that 'the autonomous power to hurt, destroy or deceive human beings should never be vested in AI'. The Asilomar document similarly supports the principle of autonomy, insofar as 'humans should choose how and whether to delegate decisions to AI systems, to accomplish human-chosen objectives'.

It is therefore clear both that the autonomy of humans should be promoted, and that the autonomy of machines should be restricted. The latter should be made intrinsically reversible, should human autonomy need to be protected or re-established (consider the case of a pilot able to turn off the automatic pilot function and regain full control of the airplane). This introduces a notion one may call *meta-autonomy*, or a *decide-to-delegate* model. Humans should retain the power to decide which decisions to take and in what priority, exercising the freedom to choose where necessary and ceding it in cases where overriding reasons, such as efficacy, may outweigh the loss of control over decision-making. But any delegation should also remain overridable in principle, adopting an ultimate safeguard of *deciding to decide again*.

● 4.6 Justice: Promoting Prosperity, Preserving Solidarity, Avoiding Unfairness

The decision to make or delegate decisions does not take place in a vacuum, nor is this capacity distributed equally across society. The consequences of this disparity in autonomy are addressed by the principle of justice. The importance of justice is explicitly cited in the Montreal Declaration, which argues that 'the development of AI should promote justice and seek to eliminate all types of discrimination'. Likewise, the Asilomar Principles include the need for both 'shared benefit' and 'shared prosperity' from AI. Under its principle named 'Justice, equity and solidarity', the EGE argues that AI should 'contribute to global justice and equal access to the benefits' of AI technologies. It also warns against the risk of bias in datasets used to train AI systems, and—unique among the documents—argues for the need to defend against threats to 'solidarity', including 'systems of mutual assistance such as in social insurance and healthcare'.

Elsewhere, 'justice' has still other meanings (especially in the sense of *fairness*), variously related to the use of AI in correcting past wrongs, such as by eliminating unfair discrimination, promoting diversity, and preventing the reinforcement of biases or the rise of new threats to justice. The diverse ways in which justice is characterized hints at a broader lack of clarity over AI as a human-made reservoir of 'smart agency'. Put simply, are we humans the patient receiving the 'treatment' of AI, which would be acting as 'the doctor' prescribing it, or both? This question can only be resolved with the introduction of a fifth principle that emerges from the previous analysis.

● 4.7 Explicability: Enabling the Other Principles through Intelligibility and Accountability

In response to the previous question about whether we are the patient or the doctor, the short answer is that we could actually be either. It depends on the circumstances and on who 'we' refers to in everyday life. The situation is inherently unequal: a small fraction of humanity is currently engaged in the development of a set of technologies that are already transforming the everyday lives of almost everyone else. This stark reality is not lost on the authors of the documents under analysis. All of them refer to the need to understand and hold to account the decision-making processes of AI. Different terms express this principle: 'transparency' in Asilomar and EGE; both 'transparency' and 'accountability' in IEEE; 'intelligibility' in AIUK; and as 'understandable and interpretable' by the Partnership. Each of these principles captures something seemingly novel about AI as a form of agency: that its workings are often invisible, opaque, or unintelligible to all but (at best) the most expert observers.

The principle of 'explicability' incorporates both the epistemological sense of 'intelligibility' and the ethical sense of 'accountability'. The addition of this principle is the crucial missing piece of the AI ethics jigsaw. It complements the other four principles: in order for AI to be beneficent and non-maleficent, we must be able to understand the good or harm that it is actually doing to society, and in what ways; for AI to promote and not constrain human autonomy, our 'decision about who should decide' must be informed by knowledge of how AI would act instead of us and how to improve its performance; and for AI to be just, we must know whom to hold ethically responsible (or actually legally liable) in the event of a serious, negative outcome, which would in turn require an adequate understanding of why this outcome arose, and how it could be prevented or minimized in the future.

4.8 A Synoptic View

Taken together, the previous five principles capture every one of the forty-seven principles contained in the six high-profile, expert-driven documents analysed in Table 4.1. As a test, it is worth stressing that each principle is included in almost every statement of principles analysed in Table 4.2 (see Section 4.10). The five principles therefore form an ethical framework within which policies, best practices, and other recommendations may be made. This framework of principles is shown in Figure 4.1.

4.9 AI Ethics: Whence and for Whom?

It is important to note that each of the six sets of ethical principles for AI in Table 4.1 emerged either from initiatives with a global scope or from within Western liberal democracies. For the framework to be more broadly applicable, it would undoubtedly benefit from the perspectives of regions and cultures presently un- or under-represented in our sample. Of particular interest in this respect is the role of China, which is already home to the world's most valuable AI start-up (Jezard 11 April 2018), enjoys various structural advantages in developing AI (Lee and Triolo December 2017), and whose government has stated its ambitions to lead the world in state-of-the-art AI technology by 2030 (China State Council 8 July 2017). This is not the context for an analysis of China's AI policies,[6] so let me add only a few closing remarks.

In its State Council Notice on AI and elsewhere, the Chinese government expressed interest in further consideration of the social and ethical impact of AI (Ding 2018). Enthusiasm for the use of technologies is hardly unique to governments. It is also shared by the general public—more so those in China and India than in Europe or the USA, as new representative survey research shows

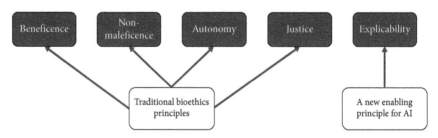

Figure 4.1 An ethical framework of the five overarching principles for AI

---

[6] On this, see Roberts, Cowls, Morley, et al. (2021), Roberts, Cowls, Hine, Morley, et al. (2021), Hine and Floridi (2022).

(Vodafone Institute for Society and Communications 2018). In the past, an executive at the major Chinese technology firm Tencent suggested that the EU should focus on developing AI that has 'the *maximum* benefit for human life, even if that technology isn't competitive to take on [the] American or Chinese market' (Boland 14 October 2018). This was echoed by claims that ethics may be 'Europe's silver bullet' in the 'global AI battle' (Delcker 3 March 2018). I disagree. Ethics is not the preserve of a single continent or culture. Every company, government agency, and academic institution designing, developing, or deploying AI has an obligation to do so in line with an ethical framework—even if not along the lines of the one presented here—broadened to incorporate a more geographically, culturally, and socially diverse array of perspectives. Similarly, laws, rules, standards, and best practices to constrain or control AI (including all those currently under consideration by regulatory bodies, legislatures, and industry groups) could also benefit from close engagement with a unified framework of ethical principles. What remains true is that the EU may have an advantage in the so-called Brussels effect, but this only places more responsibility on how AI is regulated by the EU.

4.10 Conclusion: From Principles to Practices

If the framework presented in this chapter provides a coherent and sufficiently comprehensive overview of the central ethical principles for AI (Floridi et al. 2018), then it can serve as the architecture within which laws, rules, technical standards, and best practices are developed for specific sectors, industries, and jurisdictions. In these contexts, the framework may play both an enabling role (see Chapter 12) and a constraining one. The latter role refers to the need to regulate AI technologies in the context of online crime (see Chapter 7) and cyberwar, which I discuss in Floridi and Taddeo (2014), Taddeo and Floridi (2018b). Indeed, the framework shown in Figure 4.1 played a valuable role in five other documents:

1) the work of AI4People (Floridi et al. 2018), Europe's first global forum on the social impact of AI, which adopted it to propose twenty concrete recommendations for a 'Good AI Society' to the European Commission (disclosure: I chaired the project; see 'AI4People' in Table 4.2).
    The work of AI4People was largely adopted by

2) the Ethics Guidelines for Trustworthy AI published by the European Commission's High-Level Expert Group on AI (HLEGAI 18 December 2018, 8 April 2019) (disclosure: I was a member; see 'HLEG' in Table 4.2); which in turn influenced

3) the OECD's Recommendation of the Council on Artificial Intelligence (OECD 2019); see 'OECD' in Table 4.2), which reached forty-two countries; and

Table 4.2 The five principles in the analysed documents

	Beneficence	Nonmaleficence	Autonomy	Justice	Explicability
AIUK	•	•	•	•	•
Asilomar	•	•	•	•	•
EGE	•	•	•	•	•
IEEE	•	•			•
Montreal	•	•	•	•	•
Partnership	•	•		•	•
AI4People	•	•	•	•	•
HLEG	•	•	•	•	•
OECD	•	•	•	•	•
Beijing	•	•		•	•
Rome Call	•	•	•	•	•

4) The EU AI Act.
   All this was followed by the publication of the so-called
5) Beijing AI Principles (Beijing Academy of Artificial Intelligence 2019); see 'Beijing' in Table 4.2) and
6) the so-called Rome Call for an AI Ethics (Pontifical Academy for Life 2020), a document elaborated by the Pontifical Academy for Life, which co-signed it with Microsoft, IBM, FAO, and the Italian Ministry of Innovation (disclosure: I was among the authors of the draft; see 'Rome Call' in Table 4.2).

The development and use of AI hold the potential for both positive and negative impacts on society, to alleviate or to amplify existing inequalities, to solve old and new problems, or to cause unprecedented ones. Charting the course that is socially preferable (equitable) and environmentally sustainable will depend not only on well-crafted regulation and common standards but also on the use of a framework of ethical principles within which concrete actions can be situated. The framework presented in this chapter as emerging from current debate may serve as a valuable architecture for securing positive social outcomes from AI technology. It can help move from good principles to good practices (Floridi et al. 2020, Morley, Floridi, et al. 2020). It can also provide the framework required by an ethics-based auditing of AI (Mokander and Floridi 2021, Floridi et al. 2022, Mökander et al. forthcoming). During this translation, some risks need to be mapped to ensure that the ethics of AI does not fall into new or old traps. This is the task of the next chapter.

5

From Principles to Practices

The Risks of Being Unethical

5.0 Summary

Previously, in Chapter 4, I offered a unified framework of ethical principles for AI. This chapter continues the analysis by identifying five main risks that can undermine even the best efforts to translate ethical principles into actual good practices. The risks in question are: *ethics shopping*, *ethics bluewashing*, *ethics lobbying*, *ethics dumping*, and *ethics shirking*. None of them is unprecedented as they also occur in other ethically applied contexts, such as environmental ethics, bioethics, medical ethics, and business ethics. However, I argue that each acquires its specific features by being uniquely related to the ethics of AI. They are all avoidable if one can identify them, and this chapter suggests how. The conclusion is that part of the ethical approach to AI is also building awareness about the nature and occurrence of such risks and enhancing a preventive approach.

5.1 Introduction: Risky Translations

It has taken a very long time, but we have seen that the debate today on the ethical impact and implications of digital technologies has reached the front pages of newspapers. This is understandable given that digital technologies, from web-based services to AI solutions, increasingly affect the daily lives of billions of people, especially after the pandemic. So there are both many hopes and many concerns about their design, development, and deployment. After more than half a century of academic research (Wiener 1960, Samuel 1960a), we saw in Chapter 4 that the recent public reaction has been a flourishing of initiatives to establish *what* principles, guidelines, codes, or frameworks may ethically guide digital innovation, particularly in AI, to benefit humanity and the whole environment. This is a positive development that shows awareness of the importance of the topic and interest in tackling it systematically. Yet it is time that the debate evolves from the *what* to the *how*. It should address not just what ethics is needed, but also how ethics can be effectively and successfully applied and implemented to make a positive difference. For example, the EU Ethics Guidelines for Trustworthy

The Ethics of Artificial Intelligence: Principles, Challenges, and Opportunities. Luciano Floridi, Oxford University Press.
© Luciano Floridi 2023. DOI: 10.1093/oso/9780198883098.003.0005

AI (HLEGAI 18 December 2018)[1] establish a benchmark for what may or may not qualify as ethically good AI in the EU. Their publication will increasingly be followed by practical efforts of testing, application, and implementation. They influenced the framing of the EU AI Act.

The move from a first, more theoretical *what* stage to a second, more practical *how* stage, so to speak, is reasonable, commendable, and feasible (Morley, Floridi, et al. 2020). But in translating ethical principles into good practices, even the best efforts may be undermined by some unethical risks. In this chapter, I highlight the main ones that seem more likely to occur. We shall see that they are more clusters than individual risks, and there may be other clusters as well, but these five are the ones already encountered or foreseeable in the international debate about digital ethics and the ethics of AI.[2] Here is the list: *ethics shopping*; *ethics bluewashing*; *ethics lobbying*; *ethics dumping*; and *ethics shirking*. They are the five 'ethics gerunds', to borrow an apt label from Josh Cowl, who also suggested (in a conversation) considering the first three more 'distractive' and the last two more 'destructive' problems. Let us consider each in some detail.

5.2 Ethics Shopping

In Chapter 4, we saw how a very large number of ethical principles, codes, guidelines, and frameworks have been proposed over the past few years. There I reminded the reader that, at the end of 2020, there were more than 160 guidelines, all containing many principles, often phrased differently, just about the ethics of AI (Algorithm Watch 9 April 2019, Winfield 18 April 2019). This mushrooming of principles is generating inconsistency and confusion among stakeholders regarding which one may be preferable. It also puts pressure on private and public actors (who design, develop, or deploy digital solutions) to produce their own declarations for fear of appearing to be left behind—thus further contributing to the redundancy of information.

In this case, the main unethical risk is that all this hyperactivity creates a 'market of principles and values' where private and public actors may shop for the kind of ethics that best retrofits to justify their current behaviours rather than revise their behaviours to make them consistent with a socially accepted ethical

---

[1] See European Commission (8 April 2019, HLEGAI (8 April 2019), published by the High-Level Expert Group (HLEG) on AI appointed by the European Commission.

[2] For example, see the debates about (a) the 'Human Rights Impact Assessment of Facebook in Myanmar' published by the Business for Social Responsibility at https://www.bsr.org/en/our-insights/blog-view/facebook-in-myanmar-human-rights-impact-assessment; (b) the closure of Google's Advanced Technology External Advisory Council at https://blog.google/technology/ai/external-advisory-council-help-advance-responsible-development-ai/; and (c) the ethics guidelines for trustworthy AI published by the High-Level Expert Group of the European Commission (HLEGAI 18 December 2018, 8 April 2019).

framework (Floridi and Lord Clement-Jones 20 March 2019). Here is a definition of this risk:

> *Digital ethics shopping* $=_{def.}$ the malpractice of choosing, adapting, or revising ('mixing and matching') ethical principles, guidelines, codes, frameworks, or other similar standards (especially, but not only, in the ethics of AI) from a variety of available offers in order to retrofit some pre-existing behaviours (choices, processes, strategies, etc.), and hence justify them *a posteriori*, instead of implementing or improving new behaviours by benchmarking them against public, ethical standards.

Admittedly, I argued in Chapter 4 that much of the diversity 'in the ethics market' is apparent and more due to wording or vocabulary rather than actual content. However, the potential risk of 'mixing and matching' a list of ethical principles that one prefers, as if they were ice-cream flavours, remains real. This is because semantic looseness and redundancy enable interpretative relativism. Ethics shopping then causes an incompatibility of standards where, for example, it is hard to understand whether two companies follow the same ethical principles in developing AI solutions. Incompatibility then leads to a lower chance of competition, evaluation, and accountability. The outcome can easily become an approach to ethics as mere public relations, which requires no real change or effort.

The way to deal with digital ethics shopping is to establish clear, shared, and publicly accepted ethical standards. This is why I argued (Floridi 2019b) that the publication of the *Ethics Guidelines for Trustworthy AI* was a significant improvement, given that it is the closest thing available in the EU to a comprehensive, authoritative, and public standard of what may count as socially good AI.[3] This is all the more so seeing that the *Guidelines* explicitly influenced the proposal adopted in 2021 by the EU Commission for regulation of AI systems, which was described as 'the first ever legal framework on AI' (Floridi 2021). Given the availability of this conceptual framework, the malpractice of digital ethics shopping should be at least more obvious, if not more difficult to indulge in, because anyone in the EU may simply subscribe to the *Guidelines* rather than shop for (or even cook) their own 'ethics'. The same holds true for the OECD's document, which was also influenced by the *Guidelines*. OECD members should consider at least that framework as ethically binding.

In the context of this book, the aim of Chapter 4 is to support such convergence of views to ensure that stakeholders may reach the same agreement about foundational principles for the ethics of AI. These same principles can be found in bioethics or medical ethics, two important cases where 'ethics shopping' and the retrofitting of ethical principles to unchanged practices is unacceptable.

---

[3] See also Mazzini (forthcoming).

5.3 Ethics Bluewashing

In environmental ethics, *greenwashing* (Delmas and Burbano 2011) is the malpractice of a private or public actor seeking to appear greener, more sustainable, or ecologically friendlier than it actually is. By 'ethics bluewashing', I mean to refer here to the digital version of greenwashing. As there is no specific colour associated with ethically good practices in digital technologies, 'blue' may serve to remind one that we are not talking about ecological sustainability but mere digital ethics cosmetics.[4] Here is a definition of this risk:

> *Digital ethics bluewashing* $=_{def.}$ the malpractice of making unsubstantiated or misleading claims about, or implementing superficial measures in favour of, the ethical values and benefits of digital processes, products, services, or other solutions to appear more digitally ethical than one is.

Ethics greenwashing and bluewashing are both forms of misinformation. They are often achieved by spending a fraction of the resources that would be needed to tackle the ethical problems they pretend to address. Both malpractices (greenwashing and bluewashing) concentrate on mere marketing, advertising, or other public relations activities (e.g. sponsoring), including setting up advisory groups that may be toothless, powerless, or insufficiently critical. And both are tempting because in each case, the goals are many and all compatible:

a) to distract the receiver of the message—usually the public, but any shareholders or stakeholders may be the target—from anything that is going wrong, could go better, or is not happening but should happen;
b) to mask and leave unchanged any behaviour that ought to be improved;
c) to achieve economic savings; and
d) to gain some advantage, for example competitive or social, such as customer goodwill.

In contrast to what happens with greenwashing, bluewashing can be more easily combined with *digital ethics shopping*. This is when a private or public actor shops for the principles that best fit its current practices, publicizes them as widely as possible, and then proceeds to bluewash its technological innovation without any real improvement, with much lower costs, and with some potential social benefits. These days, ethics bluewashing is especially tempting in the context of AI,

---

[4] This is not to be confused with the term bluewashing 'used to criticize the corporate partnerships formed under the United Nations Global Compact initiative (some say this association with the UN helps to improve the corporations' reputations) and to disparage dubious sustainable water-use projects' (Schott 4 February 2010).

where the ethical issues are many, the costs of doing the right thing may be high, and the normative confusion is widespread.

The best strategy against bluewashing is the one already adopted against green-washing: *transparency* and *education*. Public, accountable, and evidence-based transparency about good practices and ethical claims should be a priority on the side of the actors wishing to avoid the appearance of engaging in any bluewashing malpractice. Public and factual education on the side of any target of bluewashing—which could be not just the public, but also members of executive boards and advisory councils, politicians, and lawmakers, for example—about whether and what effective ethical practices are actually implemented means that actors may be less likely to (be tempted to) distract public attention away from the ethical challenges they are facing and address them instead.

As we shall see in Chapter 11, the development of metrics for the trustworthiness of AI products and services (and of digital solutions in general) would enable the user-driven benchmarking of all marketed offerings. It would facilitate the detection of mere bluewashing, improving public understanding and engendering com-petitiveness around the development of safer, more socially and environmentally beneficial products and services. In the longer term, a system of certification for digital products and services could achieve what other similar solutions have achieved in environmental ethics: making bluewashing as visible and shameful as greenwashing.

5.4 Ethics Lobbying

Sometimes, private actors (one may at least suspect) try to use self-regulation in the ethics of AI to lobby against the introduction of legal norms; to lobby in favour of the watering down or weakening of the enforcement of legal norms; or to provide an excuse for limited compliance with legal norms. This specific malpractice affects many sectors, but it seems more likely in the digital one (Benkler 2019) where ethics may be exploited as if an alternative to legislation or in the name of technological innovation and its positive impact on economic growth (a line of reasoning less easily supported in environmental or biomedical contexts). Here is a definition:

Digital ethics lobbying $=_{def.}$ the malpractice of exploiting digital ethics to delay, revise, replace, or avoid good and necessary legislation (or its enforcement) about the design, development, and deployment of digital processes, products, services, or other solutions.

One may argue that digital ethics lobbying is a poor strategy likely to fail in the long run because it is short-sighted at best. Sooner or later, legislation tends to catch up. But regardless of whether this argument is convincing, digital ethics lobbying as a short-term tactic may still cause much damage. It could be used to delay the introduction of necessary legislation, or to help manoeuvre around or bypass more demanding interpretations of current legislation (thus making compliance easier but also misaligned with the spirit of the law). It could also influence lawmakers to pass legislation that favours the lobbyist more than would otherwise be expected. Furthermore, and very importantly, the malpractice (or even the suspicion of it) risks undermining the value of any digital ethical self-regulation *tout court*.

This collateral damage is deeply regrettable because self-regulation is one of the main, valuable tools available for policymaking. As I shall argue in Chapter 6, self-regulation cannot replace the law by itself. But if properly implemented, it can be crucially complementary whenever

- legislation is unavailable (e.g. in experimentations about augmented reality products),
- legislation is available, but is also in need of an ethical interpretation (e.g. in terms of understanding a right to explanation in the EU's GDPR),
- legislation is available, but is also in need of some ethical counterbalancing if
  - it is better not to do something, although it is not illegal to do it (e.g. to automate entirely and fully some medical procedure without any human supervision), or
  - it is better to do something, although it is not legally required (e.g. to implement better labour market conditions in the gig economy (Tan et al. 2021)).

The strategy against digital ethics lobbying is twofold. On the one hand, it must be counteracted by good legislation and effective enforcement. This is easier if the lobbying actor (private or public) is less influential on lawmakers, or whenever public opinion can exercise the right level of ethical pressure. On the other hand, digital ethics lobbying must be exposed whenever it occurs and clearly distinguished from genuine forms of self-regulation. This may happen more credibly if the process is also in itself part of a self-regulatory code of conduct for a whole industrial sector, in our case the AI industry. There would be a more general interest in maintaining a healthy context where genuine self-regulation is both socially welcome and efficacious, exposing ethics lobbying as unacceptable.

5.5 Ethics Dumping

'Ethics dumping' is an expression that was coined in 2013 by the European Commission to describe the export of unethical research practices to countries where there are weaker (or laxer or perhaps just different, as in the case of digital ethics) legal and ethical frameworks and enforcement mechanisms. The term applies to any kind of research, including computer science, data science, ML, robotics, and other kinds of AI. But it is most serious in health-related and biological contexts. Fortunately, biomedical and environmental ethics may be considered universal and global. There are international agreements and frameworks along with international institutions monitoring their application or enforcement. So, when research involves biomedical and ecological contexts, 'ethics dumping' can be fought more effectively and coherently. However, in digital contexts, the variety of legal regimes and ethical frameworks facilitates the export of unethical (or even illegal) practices by the 'dumper' along with the import of the outcomes of such practices. In other words, the problem is twofold: *research ethics* and *consumption ethics*. Here is a definition of this risk:

> *Digital ethics dumping* $=_{\text{def.}}$ the malpractice of (a) exporting research activities about digital processes, products, services, or other solutions in other contexts or places (e.g. by European organizations outside the EU) in ways that would be ethically unacceptable in the context or place of origin; and (b) importing the outcomes of such unethical research activities.

Both (a) and (b) are important. To offer a distant but nonetheless concrete example, it is not unusual for countries to ban the cultivation of genetically modified organisms yet allow their import. There is an asymmetry between the ethical (and legal) treatment of a practice (unethical and/or illegal research) and its output, which is the ethically (and legally) acceptable consumption of an unethical research product.

This means ethics dumping can affect digital ethics not only in terms of the unethical export of research activities but also in terms of the unethical import of the outcomes of such activities. For example, a company could export its research and then design, develop, and train algorithms (e.g. for face recognition) on local personal data in a non-EU country with a different, weaker, or unenforced ethical and legal framework for personal data protection. Under the GDPR, this would be unethical and illegal in the EU. But once trained, the algorithms could then be imported to the EU and deployed without incurring any penalty or even being frowned upon. While the first step (a) may be blocked, at least in terms of research ethics (Nordling 2018), the second step (b) involves the consumption of unethical research results. It is fuzzier, less visibly problematic, and hence more difficult to monitor and curtail.

Unfortunately, the problem of digital ethics dumping will likely become increasingly serious in the near future. This is due to the profound impact of digital technologies on health and social care as well as defence, policing, and security; the ease of their global portability; the complexity of production processes (some stages of which may involve ethics dumping); and the immense economic interests at play. Especially in AI, where the EU is a net importer of solutions from the United States and China, private and public actors risk more than just exporting unethical practices. They may also (and independently) import solutions originally developed in ways that would not have been ethically acceptable within the EU. In this case, too, the strategy is twofold: one must concentrate on research ethics *and* the ethics of consumption. If one wishes to be coherent, both need to receive equal attention.

In terms of research ethics, it is slightly easier to exercise control at the source through the ethical management of public funding for research. For this, the EU is in a leading position. Still, a significant problem remains in that much research and development about digital solutions is done by the private sector, where funding may be less constrained by geographical borders. A private actor can more easily relocate its research and development to an ethically less demanding place (a geographical variation of the ethics shopping seen in Section 5.2). Privately funded research is not ethically scrutinized in the same way as publicly funded research.

In terms of consumption ethics, especially of digital products and services, much can be done. The establishment of a certification system for products and services could inform procurement along with public and private use. As in the case of bluewashing, the reliable and ethically acceptable provenance of digital systems and solutions will have to play a growing role in development over the years to come if one wishes to avoid the hypocrisy of being careful about research ethics in digital contexts, yet relaxed about the unethical use of its outcomes.

5.6 Ethics Shirking

Ethicists are well acquainted with the old malpractice of applying double standards in moral evaluations. By applying a lenient or strict approach, one can evaluate and treat agents (or their actions, or the consequences of their actions) differently than similar agents (actions or consequences) when in fact they should all be treated equally. The risk of double standards is usually based, even inadvertently, on bias, unfairness, or selfish interest. The risk I wish to highlight here belongs to the same family, but it has a different genesis. To highlight its specificity, I shall borrow the expression 'ethics shirking' from the financial sector.[5] Here is a definition of this risk:

---

[5] https://www.nasdaq.com/glossary/s/shirking. I owe the suggestion to include 'ethics shirking' as a significant risk in digital ethics and use the expression itself to capture it to (Cowls, Png, and Au unpublished).

Digital ethics shirking $=_{def.}$ the malpractice of doing increasingly less 'ethical work' (such as fulfilling duties, respecting rights, honouring commitments, etc.) in a given context the lower the return of such ethical work in that context is (mistakenly) perceived to be.

Like ethics dumping, ethics shirking has historical roots and often follows geopolitical outlines. Actors are more likely to engage in ethics dumping and shirking in contexts where disadvantaged populations, weaker institutions, legal uncertainties, corrupted regimes, unfair power distributions, and other economic, legal, political, or social ills prevail. It is not unusual to map, correctly, both malpractices along the divide between Global North and Global South, or to see both as affecting low- and middle-income countries above all. The colonial past still exerts a disgraceful role.

It is also important to recall that, in digital contexts, these malpractices can affect segments of a population within the Global North. The gig economy may be seen as a case of ethics shirking within developed countries. And the development of self-driving cars may be interpreted as an instance of research dumping in some states of the United States. The 1968 Vienna Convention on Road Traffic, which establishes international principles to govern traffic laws, requires that a driver is always fully in control and responsible for the behaviour of a vehicle in traffic. But the United States is not a signatory country to the convention, so the requirement does not apply. This means that state vehicle codes do not prohibit automated vehicles, and several states have enacted laws for automated vehicles. This is also why research into self-driving cars happens mostly in the United States, along with related incidents and human suffering.

The strategy against ethics shirking consists in tackling its origin, which is the absence of a clear allocation of responsibility. Agents may be more tempted to shirk their ethical work in a given context the more they (think they) can relocate responsibilities elsewhere. This happens more likely and easily in 'D contexts', where one's own responsibility may be (mistakenly) perceived as lower because it is *distant, diminished, delegated,* or *distributed* (Floridi 2012b). Thus, ethics shirking is the unethical cost of deresponsabilization of some agency. It is this genesis that makes it a special case of the ethical problem of double standards. Therefore more fairness and less bias are both necessary— insofar as ethics shirking is a special case of the problem of double standards— and insufficient to remove the incentive to engage in ethics shirking. To uproot this malpractice, one also needs an ethics of distributed responsibility (Floridi 2016a). Such ethics would relocate responsibilities, along with all the praise and blame, reward and punishment, and ultimately causal accountability and legal liability, to where they rightly belong.

5.7 Conclusion: The Importance of Knowing Better

In this chapter I have provided a conceptual map for those who wish to avoid or minimize some of the most obvious and significant ethical risks when translating principles into practices in digital ethics. From a Socratic perspective, according to which human evil is an epistemic problem, a malpractice is often the result of a misjudged solution or a mistaken opportunity. It is important to understand as early as possible that shortcuts, postponements, and quick fixes lead not to better ethical solutions, but to more serious problems. Problems become increasingly difficult and costlier to solve the later one deals with them.

While such an understanding does not guarantee that the five malpractices analysed in this chapter will disappear, it does mean that they will be reduced insofar as they are genuinely based on misunderstanding and misjudgements. Not knowing better is the source of a lot of evil. So, the solution is often more and better information for all. In the previous pages, I mentioned that self-regulation can robustly complement a legislative approach. This is very much the case when it comes to ethical practices that presuppose but go beyond legal compliance, which is the topic of the next chapter.

6

Soft Ethics and the Governance of AI

6.0 Summary

Previously, in Chapters 4 and 5, I suggested a unified framework for the ethical principles of AI and identified some main ethical risks that arise when translating principles into practices. This chapter discusses the governance of AI, and more generally of digital technologies, as the new challenge posed by technological innovation. I introduce a new distinction between *soft* and *hard ethics*. Hard ethics first precede and then further contribute to shaping legislation. In contrast, soft ethics apply *after* legal compliance with legislation (that is, *post-compliance ethics*), such as the GDPR in the EU. The chapter concludes by developing an analysis of the role of digital ethics with respect to digital regulation and digital governance, thus preparing for the next chapter on the fundamental ethical principles for an ethics of AI.

6.1 Introduction: From Digital Innovation to the Governance of the Digital

In any mature information society today (Floridi 2016b), we no longer live online or offline. Instead, we live onlife (Floridi 2014b). We increasingly live in that special space, or infosphere, that is seamlessly analogue and digital, offline and online. If this appears confusing, perhaps an analogy may help to convey the point. Imagine someone asking whether the water is fresh or salty in the estuary where the river meets the sea. Clearly, that someone has not understood the special nature of the place. Like mangroves flourishing in brackish water, our mature information societies are growing in such a new, liminal place. And in these 'mangrove societies', machine-readable data, new forms of smart agency, and onlife interactions are constantly evolving. This is because our technologies are perfectly fit to take advantage of such a new environment, often as the only real natives. As a result, the pace of their evolution can be mind-blowing. And this justifies some apprehension, in turn.

However, we should not be distracted by the scope, depth, and pace of digital innovation. True, it does significantly disrupt some deeply ingrained assumptions of the old society that was exclusively analogue. There were assumptions about competition, customization, education, entertainment, health, logistics, politics,

The Ethics of Artificial Intelligence: Principles, Challenges, and Opportunities. Luciano Floridi, Oxford University Press.
© Luciano Floridi 2023. DOI: 10.1093/oso/9780198883098.003.0006

production, security, and work (to mention just some crucial topics in a merely alphabetic order). Yet that is not the most consequential challenge we are facing. It is not digital innovation that matters most but the governance of the digital, that is, what we do with it. More precisely, it is how well we design the infosphere and the mature information societies developing within it that matters most. Because the digital revolution transforms our views about values and their priorities, good behaviour, and the sort of innovation that is not only sustainable but also socially preferable (equitable), governing all of this has now become the fundamental issue. Let me explain.

To many, the real challenge may seem to be what digital innovation will throw up next. The question itself is recurrent and trite: what is the next disruption? What is the new killer app? Will this be the year of the final battle between Virtual Reality vs. Augmented Reality? Or is it the Internet of Things that will represent the new frontier, perhaps in some combination with smart cities? Is an end to the television as we know it coming soon? Will healthcare be made unrecognizable by ML, or should our attention be focused on the automation of logistics and transport? What will the new smart home assistants do aside from telling us what the weather is like and allowing us to choose the next song? How is military strategy going to adapt to cyber conflicts? What industry will be 'uberized' next? Behind similar questions lies the unspoken assumption that digital innovation leads, and everything else lags behind or at best follows, whether business models, working conditions, standards of living, legislation, social norms, habits, expectations, or even hopes.

Yet this is precisely the distracting narrative that we should resist, not because it is wrong, but because it is only superficially right. The deeper truth is that the digital revolution has already occurred. The transition from an entirely analogue and offline world to one that is increasingly digital and online will never happen again in the history of humanity. Perhaps one day, a quantum computing gadget running AI apps may be in the pocket of your average teenager. But our generation is the last to have seen a non-digital world and this is the really extraordinary turning point, because that landing on the infosphere and the beginning of onlife happen only once. The question of what this new world will be like is both fascinating in terms of opportunities and worrisome in terms of risks.

No matter how challenging, our 'exploration' of the infosphere (to indulge in the geographical metaphor a bit longer) prompts a much more fundamental question that is socio-political and truly crucial: what kind of mature information societies do we want to build? What is our *human project* for the digital age? Looking at our present backwards—that is, from a future perspective—this is the time in history when we will be seen as having laid down the foundation for our mature information societies. We shall be judged by the quality of our work. So clearly, the real challenge is no longer good digital *innovation*. It is the good *governance* of the digital, as I anticipated above.

Proof that this is the case is all around us in the mushrooming of initiatives to address the impact of the digital on everyday life and how to regulate it. It is also implicit in the current narrative about the unstoppable and unreachable nature of digital innovation, if one looks just a bit more closely. Because in the same context where people complain about the speed of digital innovation and the impossible task of chasing it with some normative framework, one also finds equal certainty about the seriousness of the risk posed by the wrong legislation. Bad legislation could kill digital innovation entirely or destroy whole technological sectors and developments. You do not have to be Nietzsche—'Was mich nicht umbringt macht mich stärker' (Nietzsche 2008) or 'what does not kill me makes me stronger'—to realize the inference here is that updating the rules of the game is perfectly possible. After all, everybody acknowledges that it can have immense consequences. Reacting to technological innovation is not the best approach.

So, we need to shift from chasing to leading. If we then like the *direction* in which we move or *where* we are going, then the *speed* at which we are moving or getting there can actually be something very positive. The more we like our destination, the faster we will want to get there. It is because we lack a clear sense of socio-political direction that we are worried by the speed of our technological travel. We should be. Yet the solution is not to slow down, but to decide together where we want to go. For this to happen, society needs to stop playing defence and start playing attack. The question is not whether, but how. And to start addressing the how, some clarifications are helpful. That is the contribution made by this chapter.

6.2 Ethics, Regulation, and Governance

On the governance of digital technologies in general and AI in particular (I will not draw this distinction in the rest of the chapter, where I shall speak of 'the digital' to cover both) there is much to be said and even more still to be understood and theorized. Still, one point is clear:

i) the *governance* of the digital, henceforth *digital governance*,
ii) the *ethics* of the digital, henceforth *digital ethics*, which are also known as computer, information, or data ethics (Floridi and Taddeo 2016), and
iii) the *regulation* of the digital, henceforth *digital regulation*

are different normative approaches. They are complementary and should not be confused with each other. But they are also clearly distinguished in the following sense (see Figure 6.1 for a visual representation).

Digital governance is the practice of establishing and implementing policies, procedures, and standards for the proper development, use, and management of

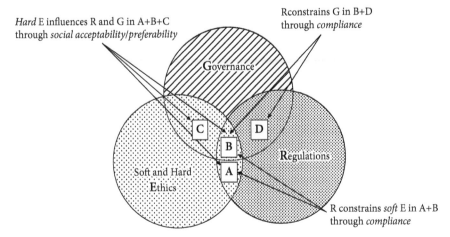

Figure 6.1 Digital ethics, digital regulation, and digital governance

the infosphere. It is also a matter of convention and good coordination, which is sometimes neither moral nor immoral, neither legal nor illegal. Through digital governance, for example, a government agency or a company may (a) determine and control processes and methods used by data stewards and data custodians to improve the data quality, reliability, access, security, and availability of its services; and (b) devise effective procedures for decision-making and for the identification of accountabilities with respect to data-related processes. A typical application of digital governance was the work I co-chaired for the British Cabinet Office in 2016 on a 'Data Science Ethical Framework' (Cabinet Office 2016), which was 'intended to give civil servants guidance on conducting data science projects, and the confidence to innovate with data'.[1] Despite the title, many recommendations had nothing to do with ethics and concerned only reasonable management.

Digital governance can be comprised of guidelines and recommendations that overlap with *digital regulation*, but are not identical to it. This is just another way of speaking about the relevant legislation, a system of laws elaborated and enforced through social or governmental institutions to regulate the behaviour of the relevant agents in the infosphere. Not every aspect of digital regulation is a matter of digital governance and not every aspect of digital governance is a matter of digital regulation. In this case, a good example is provided by the GDPR (more on the GDPR presently).[2] *Compliance* is the crucial relation through which digital regulation shapes digital governance.

[1] Available from https://www.gov.uk/government/publications/data-science-ethical-framework.
[2] Regulation (EU) 2016/679 of the European Parliament and of the Council of 27 April 2016 on the protection of natural persons with regard to the processing of personal data and on the free movement of such data, and repealing Directive 95/46/EC (General Data Protection Regulation), OJEU L119, 04/05/2016.

All this holds true for *digital ethics*, understood as the branch of ethics that studies and evaluates moral problems relating to *data* and *information* (including generation, recording, curation, processing, dissemination, sharing, and use), *algorithms* (including AI, AAs, ML, and robots), and corresponding *practices* and *infrastructures* (including responsible innovation, programming, hacking, professional codes, and standards) in order to formulate and support morally good solutions, for example good conduct or good values. Digital ethics shapes digital regulation and digital governance by means of a moral evaluation of what is socially acceptable or preferable.

Digital governance in Figure 6.1 is just one of the three normative forces that can shape and guide the development of the digital. But it is not uncommon to use that part for the whole and to speak of digital governance as referring to the entire set. This use of the term 'governance' is a synecdoche, a bit like using 'coke' to refer to any variety of cola. It is what I did at the beginning of this chapter, when I stated that the real challenge today is the governance of the digital. By that, I meant to refer not just to digital governance but also to digital ethics and digital regulation, that is to the whole normative map: E + R + G. And this is also how I interpret the report 'Data Management and Use: Governance in the 21st Century' that we published in 2017 as a joint British Academy and Royal Society working group (British Academy 2017; disclosure: I was a member). As long as the synecdoche is clear, there is no problem.

Once the map is understood, two important consequences become clear. Let me discuss each in separate sections.

6.3 Compliance: Necessary but Insufficient

When policymakers in both political and business contexts wonder why we should engage in ethical evaluations when legal compliance is already available (this is a recurring topic in the discussion of the GDPR, for example), the answer should be clear: compliance is necessary but insufficient to steer society in the right direction. Digital regulation indicates what the legal and illegal moves in the game are, so to speak. But it says nothing about what the *good* and *best* moves could be, out of those that are legal, to win the game—that is, to have a better society. This is the task of digital ethics on the side of moral values and preferences, and of good digital governance on the side of management. And this is why, for example, the EDPS (the EU's independent data protection authority) established the Ethics Advisory Group in 2015: to analyse the new ethical challenges posed by digital developments and current legislation, especially in relation to the GDPR. The report (EDPS Ethics Advisory Group 2018; disclosure: I was a member) should be read as a contribution to normative governance of the infosphere in the

EU, and a stepping stone towards its implementation. So, what kind of digital ethics should we adopt to complement legal compliance?

6.4 Hard and Soft Ethics

If we look at Figure 6.1, digital ethics may now be understood in two ways: as *hard* or *soft ethics*. The distinction is loosely based on the one between *hard* and *soft* law (Shaffer and Pollack 2009), that is, between traditional law and other instruments that are quasi-legal but have no legally binding force, such as the resolutions and recommendations of the Council of Europe. The distinction is not really a matter of practice as in reality soft and hard ethics often come inextricably intertwined. It is above all a matter of theory, because it is logically possible and often useful to distinguish soft and hard ethics and then discuss each separately. Let us see the distinction in detail.

Hard ethics (see A + B + C in Figure 6.1) is what we usually have in mind when discussing values, rights, duties, and responsibilities—or, more broadly, what is morally right or wrong, and what ought or ought not to be done—in the course of formulating new regulations and challenging existing ones. In short, *insofar* (and it may not be very far) as ethics contributes to making, shaping, or changing the law, we can call that *hard ethics*. For example, lobbying in favour of some good legislation or to improve that which already exists can be a case of hard ethics. Hard ethics helped to dismantle apartheid *legislation* in South Africa and supported the approval of *legislation* in Iceland requiring public and private businesses to prove they offer equal pay to employees irrespective of their gender (by the way, the gender pay gap continues to be scandalous in most countries). It follows that, in hard ethics, it is not true that 'one ought to do x' legally speaking (where x ranges on the universe of feasible actions) implies 'one may do x' ethically speaking. It is perfectly reasonable to object that 'one ought to do x' may be followed by 'even if one may not do x'. Call this the Rosa Parks Principle for her famous refusal to obey the law and give up her bus seat in the 'colored section' (American spelling intended) to a white passenger after the whites-only section was filled.

Soft ethics covers the same normative ground as hard ethics (again, see A + B + C in Figure 6.1). But it does so by considering what ought and ought not to be done *over and above* the existing regulation—not against it, or despite its scope, or to change it. Thus, soft ethics may include self-regulation (see Chapter 5). In other words, *soft ethics is post-compliance ethics* because, in this case, 'ought implies may'. This is why, in Figure 6.1, I wrote that regulations constrain software ethics through compliance. Call this the Matthew Principle: 'Render to Caesar the things that are Caesar's' (Matthew 22: 15–22).

Figure 6.2 The space for soft ethics

As already indicated above, both hard and soft ethics presuppose *feasibility* or, in more Kantian terms, assume the fundamental principle that 'ought implies can', given that an agent has a moral obligation to perform action *x* only if *x* is possible in the first place. Ethics should not be supererogatory in this specific sense of asking for something impossible. It follows that soft ethics assumes a *post-feasibility* approach as well. Any ethical approach, at least in the EU, accepts the implementation of the Universal Declaration of Human Rights, the European Convention on Human Rights, and the Charter of Fundamental Rights of the European Union as its minimal starting point. The result is that the space for soft ethics is both partially bounded but also unlimited. To see why, it is easy to visualize it in the shape of a trapezoid (Figure 6.2). The lower side of the trapezoid represents a feasibility base that is ever-expanding through time, as we can do more and more things thanks to technological innovation. The two constraining sides, left and right, represent legal compliance and human rights. The open upper side represents the space where what is morally good may happen in general and, in the context of this chapter, may happen in terms of shaping and guiding the ethical development of our mature information societies.

I have already mentioned that hard and soft ethics often go hand in hand. Their distinction is useful, but often logical rather than factual. In the next section, I shall analyse their mutual relation and interaction with legislation by relying on the specific case of the GDPR. In this section, a final clarification is in order.

When distinguishable, soft digital ethics can be more easily exercised the more digital regulation is considered to be on the good side of the moral vs. immoral divide. Thus, it would be a mistake to argue for a soft ethics approach to establish a normative framework when agents (especially governments and companies) are operating in contexts where human rights are disregarded, for example in China, North Korea, or Russia. At the same time, hard ethics may still be necessary in other contexts where human rights are respected, in order to change some current legislation that is perceived to be ethically unacceptable. The Irish abortion referendum in 2018 is a good example. In a digital context, hard ethics arguments were used as a point of contrast for the December 2017 decision by the US Federal Communications Commission (FCC) to rescind the rule about net neutrality (the principle according to which all Internet traffic should be treated in the same way, without blocking, degrading, or prioritizing any particular legal content). The outcome was that in March 2018, Washington became the first state in the United States to pass legislation mandating net neutrality.

Within the EU, soft ethics may rightly be exercised to help agents (such as individuals, groups, companies, governments, and organizations) take more and better advantage, morally speaking, of the opportunities offered by digital innovation. Because even in the EU, legislation is necessary but insufficient. It does not cover everything, nor should it. Agents should leverage digital ethics to assess and decide what role they wish to play in the infosphere when regulations provide no simple or straightforward answer (or no guidance at all), when competing values and interests need to be balanced, and when there is more that can be done over and above what the law strictly requires. In particular, good use of soft ethics could lead companies to exercise 'good corporate citizenship' within a mature information society.

The time has come to provide a more specific analysis and for this, I shall rely on the GDPR. The choice seems reasonable: given that digital regulation in the EU is now determined by the GDPR and that EU legislation is normally respectful of human rights, it may be useful to understand the value of the distinction between soft and hard ethics and their relations to legislation by using the GDPR as a concrete case of application. The underlining hypothesis is that, if the soft/hard ethics analysis does not work in the case of the GDPR, it probably won't work anywhere else.

6.5 Soft Ethics as an Ethical Framework

To understand the role of hard and soft ethics with regard to law in general and the GDPR in particular, five components need to be introduced (see Figure 6.3).[3]

First, there are the ELSI of the GDPR, for example on organizations. This is the impact of the GDPR on business, for example. Then there is the GDPR itself. This is the legislation that replaced the Data Protection Directive 95/46/EC. It is designed to harmonize data privacy laws across Europe, to protect and enforce the data privacy of all EU citizens independently of geographic location, and to improve the way that organizations across the EU approach data privacy. The GDPR comprises ninety-nine articles that make up the second element. As it is

---

[3] In a previous version of this chapter, the text read as if I argued that ethics shapes and interprets the law. This is simply untenable, and I am grateful to one of the anonymous referees for highlighting this potentially erroneous reading.

often the case with complex legislation, the articles do not cover everything. They leave grey areas of normative uncertainty even about the topics they do cover. They are subject to interpretation. They may require updating when applied to new circumstances, especially in a technological context where innovation develops so quickly and radically—think of facial recognition software, for example, or so-called 'deepfake' software. So, to help understand their meaning, scope, and applicability, the articles are accompanied by 173 recitals. This is the third element. In EU law, recitals are texts that explain the reasons for the provisions of an act. They are not legally binding, and they are not supposed to contain normative language. Normally, recitals are used by the Court of Justice of the European Union to interpret a directive or regulation and reach a decision in the context of a particular case.[4] But in the case of the GDRP, it is important to note that the recitals can also be used by the European Data Protection Board (the EDPB, which replaced the Article 29 Working Party) when ensuring that the GDPR is applied consistently across Europe.

The recitals themselves require interpretation, and this is the fourth element. Part of this interpretation is provided by an ethical framework that contributes, together with other factors, to understanding the recitals. Finally, the articles and the recitals were formulated thanks to a long process of negotiation between the European Parliament, the European Council, and the European Commission (the so-called Formal Trilogue meeting), resulting in a joint proposal. This is the fifth element, namely, the perspective that informed the elaboration of the GDPR. It is where hard ethics plays a role together with other factors (e.g. political, economic, etc.). It may be seen in action by comparing drafts from the European Parliament and European Commission along with amendments to the European Commission's text proposed by the European Council.[5]

So here is a summary of what we need to consider:

1) the ethical, legal, and social implications and opportunities (ELSIO) generated by the articles in (2). The distinction between implications and opportunities is meant to cover both what follows from the GDPR (Chameau et al. 2014) and what is left partially or completely uncovered by the GDPR. The reader who finds the distinction redundant (one may argue that opportunities are just a subset of the implications) should feel free to drop the 'O' in 'ELSIO'. The reader who finds the distinction confusing may

---

[4] For example, see 'C-131/12 Google Spain SL, Google Inc. v Agencia Española de Protección de Datos, Mario Costeja González' at http://curia.europa.eu/juris/document/document.jsf?text=&doci d=152065&pageIndex=0&doclang=EN&mode=req&. Or see Domestic CCTV and Directive 95/46/ EC (European Court of Justice (ECJ) Judgment in Case C-212/13 Ryneš at http://amberhawk.typepad. com/amberhawk/2014/12/what-does-the-ecj-ryne%C5%A1-ruling-mean-for-the-domestic-purpose-exemption.html).

[5] European Digital Rights, 'Comparison of the Parliament and Council Text on the General Data Protection Regulation' https://edri.org/files/EP_Council_Comparison.pdf.

wish to add to the diagram in Figure 6.3 another box labelled 'opportunities' and another arrow labelled 'generates' that stretches from the GDPR to it. In Figure 6.3, I adopted a compromise: one box with a double label. Note that opportunities need not be necessarily positive. They can also be negative in the ethical sense of possible wrongdoings, for example the GDPR may enable one to exploit an ethically wrong opportunity;

2) the articles of the GDPR that generate (1);
3) the recitals of the GDPR that contribute to interpreting the articles in (2);
4) the soft ethical framework that contributes to interpreting the recitals in (3) and the articles in (2), which is also coherent with the hard ethical framework in (5) and contributes to dealing with ELSIO in (1);
5) the hard ethical framework that contributes to generating the articles in (2) and the recitals in (3).

The hard ethics in Figure 6.3 is the ethical element (together with others) that motivated and guided the process leading to the elaboration of the law, or the GDPR in this case. The soft ethics in Figure 6.3 is part of the framework that enables the best interpretations of the recitals in (3). For the soft ethics to work well in interpreting the recitals in (3), it must be coherent with, and informed by, the hard ethics in (5) that led to its formulation in the first place.

Another very good example is offered in the report on AI by the UK House of Lords (House of Lords Artificial Intelligence Committee 16 April 2017). The argument developed in the report is that the United States has abandoned moral leadership altogether while Germany and Japan are too far ahead on the technology side to make competition possible. This creates a vacuum where the United Kingdom should position itself as a leader in ethical AI both as a socially desirable goal and as a business opportunity. This is part of the justification for the recent creation of the Centre for Data Ethics and Innovation (which actually focuses quite strongly on AI as well; another disclosure: I was a member). The fundamental lesson is that instead of promoting a set of new laws, it may be preferable

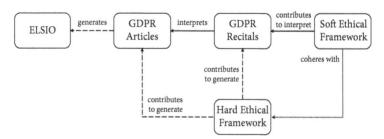

Figure 6.3 Soft and hard ethics and their relation to regulation

Note: the diagram is simplified by omitting references to all the other elements that contribute to the various frameworks

within the current legislation to foster an ethical approach to the development of AI that would promote social good.

Clearly, the place for ethics is both before and after the law; it contributes to making the law possible and may then complement the law (and also force it to change) afterwards. In this, the position I am defending about the relationship between ethics and law is close to (and may be seen as the ethical counterpart of) Dworkin's when he argued that the law contains not only rules but also principles (Dworkin 1967). This is especially true in difficult, unclear, or uncovered cases (Dworkin's 'hard cases') when the rules fail to be applicable either in full or unambiguously to a particular situation. Rules sometimes offer an unacceptable approach, and, in these cases, legal judgment is and should be guided by the principles of soft ethics. These are not necessarily external to the legal system, and they are used just for guidance (a position defended by Hart). But they can be and often are (at least implicitly) incorporated in the law as some of its ingredients. They are baked in, helping the exercise of discretion and adjudication.

6.6 Ethical Impact Analysis

Given the open future addressed by digital ethics, it is obvious that *foresight analysis* of the ethical impact of digital innovation, or simply ethical impact analysis (EIA), must become a priority (Floridi 2014d). Today, EIA can be based on data analytics applied strategically to the ethical impact assessment of digital technologies, goods, services, and practices, to debate, project and shape the future (see Figure 6.4). It is crucial because, as I wrote in Chapter 3, the task of digital ethics is not simply to 'look into the [digital] seeds of time / And say which grain will grow and which will not' (*Macbeth*, 1.3, 159–62). It also seeks to determine which ones *should* grow and which should not.

Figure 6.4 Ethical impact analysis (EIA): the foresight analysis cycle

To use a metaphor already introduced above, the best way to catch the technology train is not to chase it, but to be already at the next station. We need to anticipate and steer the ethical development of technological innovation. And we can do this by looking at what is actually feasible. Within what is feasible, we can privilege what is environmentally sustainable, then what is socially acceptable, and then, ideally, choosing what is socially preferable (see Figure 6.5).

6.7 Digital Preferability and the Normative Cascade

For the infosphere, we do not yet have a concept equivalent to *sustainability* for the biosphere. So, our current equation is incomplete (see Figure 6.6).

In Figure 6.5, I suggested that we interpret the x in Figure 6.6 as 'social preferability'. But I am aware that this may be just a placeholder for a better idea to come. Of course, digital technologies also have an ecological impact, as we shall see in Chapter 12. So sustainability is relevant, but may also be misleading. A potential candidate may well be 'equitable'. However, finding the right conceptual framework may take a while, given that 'the tragedy of the commons' was published in 1968 but the expression 'sustainable development' was only coined by the Brundtland Report almost twenty years later, in 1987 (Brundtland 1987). Yet the lack of conceptual terminology does not make the good governance of the

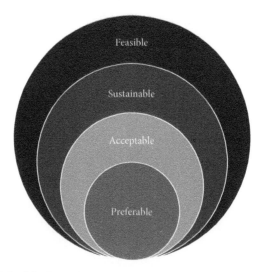

Figure 6.5 Digital ethics impact assessment

$$\text{biosphere : sustainability = infosphere : } x$$

Figure 6.6 A difficult equation to balance

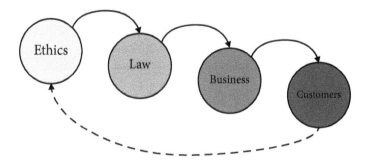

Figure 6.7 Example of a normative cascade
Note: the example uses business for an agent and customers for people; business could be replaced by government and customers by citizens

digital any less pressing or a mere utopian effort. Digital ethics already significantly influences the world of technology with its values, principles, choices, recommendations, and constraints. Sometimes, it does so much more than any other force. This is because the evaluation of what is morally good, right, or necessary shapes public opinion (and hence the socially acceptable or preferable) as well as the politically feasible. Ultimately, it shapes the legally enforceable and what agents may or may not do. In the long run, people are constrained in what they can or cannot do as users, consumers, citizens, and patients, etc. The feasibility of what they do is constrained by the goods and services provided by organizations, such as businesses, that are constrained by law in terms of compliance. But the latter is also shaped and constrained by (although not only by) ethics, which is where people decide in what kind of society they want to live (see Figure 6.7). Unfortunately, such a *normative cascade* becomes obvious mainly when backlash happens, that is, mostly in negative contexts. This is when the public rejects some solutions even when they may be good solutions. A normative cascade should instead be used constructively, that is, to pursue the construction of a mature information society of which we can be proud.

6.8 Digital Ethics' Dual Advantage

It is obvious that digital technologies, and especially AI, offer many opportunities. They also bring also associated challenges and potential risks. So, it is equally obvious that ensuring socially preferable outcomes means resolving the tension between incorporating the benefits and mitigating the potential harms—in short, promoting these technologies while avoiding their misuse, underuse, overuse, and harmful use. This is where the value of an ethical approach becomes obvious as well. I argued above that compliance is necessary, but significantly insufficient. Adopting an ethical approach to digital innovation confers what may be defined as a 'dual advantage', echoing the 'dual use' terminology popular in the philosophy of technology at least since the debate on civil and military uses of nuclear power.

On the one hand, soft ethics can provide an *opportunity strategy*, enabling actors to take advantage of the social value of digital technologies. This is the advantage of being able to identify and leverage new opportunities that are socially acceptable or preferable. Precautionary principles can be balanced with the duty to not omit what could and ought to be done, for example to take advantage of the wealth of accumulated data or, in the context of this book, of the forms of smart agency available. On the other hand, ethics also provides a *risk management solution*. It enables organizations to anticipate and avoid costly mistakes (the Cambridge Analytica scandal involving Facebook is by now a classic example). This is the advantage of preventing and mitigating courses of action that turn out to be socially unacceptable and hence rejected. In this way, ethics can also lower the opportunity costs of choices not made or options not seized for fear of mistakes.

The dual advantage of soft ethics can only function in a broader environment of decent legislation, public trust, and clear responsibilities. Public acceptance and adoption of digital technologies, including AI, will occur only if the benefits are seen as meaningful and fairly distributed, and if the risks are seen as potential yet preventable, minimizable, or at least something against which one can be protected. The risks must also be seen by the public as subject to risk management (e.g. insurance) and redress—not unfairly affecting discriminated groups of people. Reassuringly, this is the approach taken by the EU with its legislation (European Commission 2021). These attitudes will depend in turn on public engagement with the development of AI and more generally all digital technologies; openness about how they operate; and understandable, widely accessible mechanisms of regulation and redress. In this way, an ethical approach to AI can also function as an early warning system against risks that might endanger entire organizations. The clear value to any organization of the dual advantage of an ethical approach to AI amply justifies the expense of engagement, openness, and contestability that such an approach requires.

6.9 Conclusion: Ethics as a Strategy

Ethics in general, and digital ethics in particular, should not be a mere add-on, an afterthought, a latecomer, or an owl of Minerva (to use Hegel's metaphor about philosophy) that takes flight only when the shades of night are gathering. It should not be used to intervene only after digital innovation has taken place, possibly bad solutions have been implemented, less good alternatives have been chosen, or mistakes have been made. This is not least because some mistakes are irreversible, some missed opportunities are irrecoverable, and any preventable evil that occurs is a moral disaster. Nor should ethics be a mere exercise in *questioning*. The building of *critical awareness* is important, but it is also only one of the four tasks of a proper ethical approach to the design and governance of the digital. The other three are *signalling* that ethical problems matter, *engaging* with stakeholders affected by such ethical problems, and, above all, *designing and implementing sharable solutions.* Any ethical exercise that in the end fails to provide and implement some acceptable recommendations is only a timid preamble.

So, ethics must inform strategies for the development and use of digital technologies from the very beginning, when changing the course of action is easier and less costly in terms of resources, impact, and missed opportunities. It must sit at the table of policymaking and decision-taking procedures from day one. We must not only think twice; most importantly, we must think *before* taking important steps. This is particularly relevant to the EU, where I have argued that soft ethics can be properly exercised and where a soft-ethical approach to SETI (science, engineering, technology, and innovation) development is already acknowledged as crucial (Floridi et al. 2018).

If soft digital ethics can be a priority anywhere, this is certainly in Europe. We should adopt it as soon as possible. To do so, a shared starting point is essential. Ethics seems to have a bad name when it comes to reaching agreement on fundamental issues. This is justified, but it is also exaggerated. Often, and especially in debates about technology, ethical disagreement is not about *what* is right or wrong. Instead, disagreement is about *how far* it may or may not be so, about *why* it is, and about *how* to ensure that what is right prevails over what is wrong. We saw in Chapter 4 that this is particularly true when it comes to foundational analysis of basic principles, where agreement is much wider and common than it is sometimes perceived. The time has come to map some of the specific ethical problems raised by algorithms. This is the topic of the next chapter.

7

Mapping the Ethics of Algorithms

7.0 Summary

Previously, in Chapters 4–6, I analysed the ethical principles, risks, and governance of AI. This chapter reviews the actual ethical challenges posed by AI through a focus on the debate about the ethics of algorithms. I shall say more about robotics in Chapter 8. Research on the ethics of algorithms has grown substantially in recent years.[1] Given the exponential development and application of Machine Learning (ML) algorithms over the past decade in particular, new ethical problems and solutions relating to their ubiquitous use in society have emerged. This chapter analyses the state of the debate with the goals of contributing to the identification and analysis of the ethical implications of algorithms; providing an updated analysis of epistemic and normative concerns; and offering actionable guidance for governance of the design, development, and deployment of algorithms.

7.1 Introduction: A Working Definition of Algorithm

Let me start with a conceptual clarification. As in the case of 'artificial intelligence', there is little agreement in the relevant literature on the definition of an algorithm. The term is often used to indicate the formal definition of an algorithm as a mathematical construct with 'a finite, abstract, effective, compound control structure, imperatively given, accomplishing a given purpose under given provisions' (Hill 2016, 47). But it is also used to indicate domain-specific understandings that focus on the implementation of these mathematical constructs into a technology configured for a specific task. In this chapter, I focus on the ethical issues posed by algorithms as mathematical constructs, by their implementation as programs and configurations (applications), and by the ways in which these issues can be addressed.[2] So understood, algorithms have become a key element underpinning crucial services and infrastructures of information societies. For example, individuals interact with recommender systems, that is, algorithmic systems that make suggestions about what a user may like, on a daily basis, be it to choose a song, movie, product, or even a friend (Paraschakis 2017,

---

[1] See Floridi and Sanders 2004 and Floridi 2013 for earlier references.
[2] This was the approach adopted in Mittelstadt et al. 2016 and Tsamados et al. 2021.

The Ethics of Artificial Intelligence: Principles, Challenges, and Opportunities. Luciano Floridi, Oxford University Press.
© Luciano Floridi 2023. DOI: 10.1093/oso/9780198883098.003.0007

Perrault et al. 2019, Milano, Taddeo, and Floridi 2020b, 2021, 2019, 2020a). At the same time, schools and hospitals (Obermeyer et al. 2019, Zhou et al. 2019, Morley, Machado, et al. 2020), financial institutions (Lee and Floridi 2020, Lee, Floridi, and Denev 2020, Aggarwal 2020), courts (Green and Chen 2019, Yu and Du 2019), local governmental bodies (Eubanks 2017, Lewis 2019), and national governments (Labati et al. 2016), Hauer 2019, Taddeo and Floridi 2018b, Taddeo, McCutcheon, and Floridi 2019) all increasingly rely on algorithms to make significant decisions.

The potential for algorithms to improve individual and social welfare comes with significant ethical risks. It is well known that algorithms are not ethically neutral. Consider, for example, how the outputs of translation and search engine algorithms are largely perceived as objective, yet frequently encode language in gendered ways (Larson 2017, Prates, Avelar, and Lamb 2019). Bias has also been reported extensively, such as in algorithmic advertising with opportunities for higher-paying jobs and jobs within the field of science and technology advertised to men more often than to women (Datta, Tschantz, and Datta 2015, Datta, Sen, and Zick 2016, Lambrecht and Tucker 2019). Likewise, prediction algorithms used to manage the health data of millions of patients in the United States exacerbate existing problems, with white patients given measurably better care than comparably similar black patients (Obermeyer et al. 2019). While solutions to these and similar issues are being discussed and designed, the number of algorithmic systems exhibiting ethical problems continues to grow.

We saw in the first part of the book that AI has been experiencing a new 'summer' at least since 2012. This is both in terms of the technical advances being made and the attention that the field has received from academics, policymakers, technologists, investors (Perrault et al. 2019), and hence the general public. Following this new 'season' of successes, there has been a growing body of research on the ethical implications of algorithms particularly in relation to *fairness, accountability,* and *transparency* (Lee 2018, Hoffmann et al. 2018, Shin and Park 2019). In 2016, our research group at the Digital Ethics Lab published a comprehensive study that sought to map these ethical concerns (Mittelstadt et al. 2016). However, this is a fast-changing field. Both novel ethical problems and ways to address them have emerged, making it necessary to improve and update that study. Work on the ethics of algorithms has increased significantly since 2016, when national governments, non-governmental organizations, and private companies started to take a prominent role in the conversation on 'fair' and 'ethical' AI and algorithms (Sandvig et al. 2016, Binns 2018b, 2018a, Selbst et al. 2019, Wong 2019, Ochigame 2019). Both the quantity and the quality of the research available on the topic have expanded enormously. The COVID-19 pandemic has both exacerbated the issues and spread global awareness about them (Morley, Cowls, et al. 2020). Given these changes, we published a new study (Tsamados et al. 2021; see also Morley et al. 2021). This study improved on Mittelstadt et al. 2016 by adding new insights into the ethics of

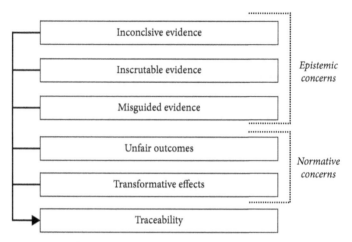

Figure 7.1 Six types of ethical concerns raised by algorithms
Source: Mittelstadt et al. (2016, 4)

algorithms, updating the initial analysis, including references to the literature that were missed in the original review, and extending the analysed topics (such as by including work on AI4SG). At the same time, the 2016 conceptual map (see Figure 7.1) remains a fruitful framework for reviewing the current debate on the ethics of algorithms, identifying the ethical problems that algorithms give rise to, and surveying the solutions that have been proposed in recent relevant literature. So, I shall start from it in the next section and this chapter is based on those two works. In Sections 7.3–7.8, I provide a meta-analysis of the current debate on the ethics of algorithms and draw links to the types of ethical concerns previously identified. Section 7.9 concludes the chapter with an overview and an introduction to the one that follows.

7.2 Map of the Ethics of Algorithms

Algorithms can be used

1) to turn data into evidence (Information Commissioner's Office) for a given outcome,

which is used

2) to trigger and motivate an action that may have ethical consequences.

Actions (1) and (2) may be performed by (semi-)autonomous algorithms, such as ML algorithms. This complicates a third action, namely,

3) to attribute responsibility for the effects of actions that an algorithm may trigger.

In the context of (1)–(3), ML is of particular interest as a field that includes deep learning architectures. Computer systems deploying ML algorithms may be described as 'autonomous' or 'semi-autonomous' to the extent that their outputs are induced from data and are thus non-deterministic.

Based on this approach, the conceptual map shown in Figure 7.1 identifies six ethical concerns that define the conceptual space for the ethics of algorithms as a field of research. Three of the ethical concerns refer to epistemic factors: *inconclusive*, *inscrutable*, and *misguided* evidence. Two are explicitly normative: *unfair* outcomes and *transformative* effects. One, *traceability*, is relevant both for epistemic and normative purposes. The epistemic factors in the map highlight the relevance of the quality and accuracy of the data[3] to the justifiability of the conclusions that algorithms reach. These conclusions may in turn shape morally loaded decisions affecting individuals, societies, and the environment. The normative concerns identified in the map refer explicitly to the ethical impact of algorithmically driven actions and decisions, including the *lack of transparency* (*opacity*) in algorithmic processes, *unfair outcomes*, and *unintended consequences*. Epistemic and normative concerns—along with the distribution of the design, development, and deployment of algorithms—make it hard to trace the chain of events and factors leading to a given outcome. This difficulty hinders the possibility of identifying a cause for an outcome, and thus attributing moral responsibility for it (Floridi 2012b). That is what the sixth ethical concern, *traceability*, refers to.

It is important to stress that this conceptual map can be interpreted at a micro- and a macro-ethical level of abstraction (Floridi 2008a). At the micro-ethical level, it sheds light on the ethical problems that algorithms may pose. By highlighting how these issues are inseparable from those related to data and responsibilities, it shows the need for a macro-ethical approach to addressing the ethics of algorithms as part of a wider conceptual space, namely, digital ethics. Taddeo and I have argued in the past that

> while they are distinct lines of research, the ethics of data, algorithms and practices are obviously intertwined…[Digital] ethics must address the whole conceptual space and hence all three axes of research together, even if with different priorities and focus.   (Floridi and Taddeo 2016, 4)

In the remainder of this chapter, I address each of these six ethical concerns in turn, offering an updated analysis of the ethics of algorithms literature (at a micro level) with the goal of contributing to the debate on digital ethics (at a macro level).

---

[3] On the debate and philosophy of data quality see Floridi and Illari 2014.

7.3 Inconclusive Evidence Leading to Unjustified Actions

Research focusing on *inconclusive evidence* refers to the way in which non-deterministic ML algorithms produce outputs that are expressed in probabilistic terms (James et al. 2013, Valiant 1984). These types of algorithms generally identify association and correlation between variables in the underlying data, but not causal connections. As such, they may encourage the practice of *apophenia*: 'seeing patterns where none actually exist, simply because massive quantities of data can offer connections that radiate in all directions' (boyd and Crawford 2012, 668).

This is problematic because patterns identified by algorithms may be the result of inherent properties of the system modelled by the data, of the datasets (that is, of the model itself rather than the underlying system), or of the skilful manipulation of datasets (properties neither of the model nor of the system). This is the case, for example, of Simpson's paradox, which occurs when trends that are observed in different groups of data reverse when the data are aggregated (Blyth 1972). In the last two cases, poor quality of the data leads to inconclusive evidence to support human decisions.

Recent research has underlined the concern that inconclusive evidence can give rise to serious ethical risks. Focusing on non-causal indicators, for instance, could distract attention from the underlying causes for a given problem (Floridi et al. 2020). Even with the use of causal methods, the available data may not always contain enough information to justify an action or make a decision fair (Olhede and Wolfe 2018b, 2018a). Data quality, such as the timeliness, completeness, and correctness of a dataset, constrains the questions that can be answered using a given dataset (Olteanu et al. 2016). Additionally, the insights that can be extracted from datasets are fundamentally dependent on the assumptions that guided the data collection process itself (Diakopoulos and Koliska 2017). For example, algorithms designed to predict patient outcomes in clinical settings rely entirely on data inputs that can be quantified (e.g. vital signs and previous success rates of comparative treatments). This means they ignore other emotional facts (e.g. the willingness to live) that can have a significant impact on patient outcomes, thus undermining the accuracy of the algorithmic prediction (Buhmann, Paßmann, and Fieseler 2019). This example highlights how insights stemming from algorithmic data processing can be uncertain, incomplete, and time-sensitive (Diakopoulos and Koliska 2017).

One may embrace a naïve, inductivist approach and assume that inconclusive evidence can be avoided if algorithms are fed enough data, even if a causal explanation for these results cannot be established. Yet recent research rejects this view. In particular, literature focusing on the ethical risks of racial profiling using algorithmic systems has demonstrated the limits of this approach to highlight, among other things, that long-standing structural inequalities are often deeply embedded in the algorithms' datasets; these are rarely, if ever, corrected for (Hu 2017, Turner Lee 2018, Noble 2018, Benjamin 2019, Richardson, Schultz, and Crawford 2019, Abebe et al. 2020). More data by themselves do not lead to greater accuracy or greater representation. On the contrary, they may exacerbate issues of inconclusive data by enabling correlations to be found where there really are none. As Ruha Benjamin put it, 'computational depth without historical or sociological depth is just superficial learning [not deep learning].'[4]

The aforementioned limitations pose serious constraints on the justifiability of algorithmic outputs. This could have a negative impact on individuals or an entire population due to suboptimal inferences. In the case of the physical sciences, it could even tip the evidence for or against 'a specific scientific theory' (Ras, van Gerven, and Haselager 2018). This is why it is crucial to ensure that data fed to algorithms are validated independently, and that data retention and reproducibility measures are in place to mitigate inconclusive evidence leading to unjustified actions along with auditing processes to identify unfair outcomes and unintended consequences (Henderson et al. 2018, Rahwan 2018, Davis and Marcus 2019, Brundage et al. 2020). The danger arising from inconclusive evidence and erroneous actionable insights also stems from the perceived mechanistic objectivity associated with computer-generated analytics (Karppi 2018, Lee 2018, Buhmann, Paßmann, and Fieseler 2019). This can lead to human decision-makers ignoring their own experienced assessments—so-called 'automation bias' (Cummings 2012)—or even shirking part of their responsibility for decisions (see Section 7.8 below) (Grote and Berens 2020). As we shall see in Sections 7.4 and 7.8, a lack of understanding about how algorithms generate outputs exacerbates this problem.

7.4 Inscrutable Evidence Leading to Opacity

Inscrutable evidence focuses on problems related to the lack of transparency that often characterizes algorithms (particularly ML algorithms and models), the sociotechnical infrastructure in which they exist, and the decisions they support. Lack of transparency can be inherent due to the limits of technology, acquired by design decisions and obfuscation of the underlying data (Lepri et al. 2018, Dahl 2018, Ananny and Crawford 2018, Weller 2019), or stem from legal constraints in terms of intellectual property. Regardless, it often translates into a lack of scrutiny and/or accountability (Oswald 2018, Webb et al. 2019) and leads to a lack of 'trustworthiness' (see AI HLEG 2019).

---

[4] https://www.techregister.co.uk/ruha-benjamin-on-deep-learning-computational-depth-without-sociological-depth-is-superficial-learning/.

According to recent studies (Diakopoulos and Koliska 2017, Stilgoe 2018, Zerilli et al. 2019, Buhmann, Paßmann, and Fieseler 2019), factors contributing to the overall lack of algorithmic transparency include:

- the cognitive impossibility for humans to interpret massive algorithmic models and datasets;
- a lack of appropriate tools to visualize and track large volumes of code and data;
- code and data so poorly structured that they are impossible to read; and
- ongoing updates and human influence over a model.

Lack of transparency is also an inherent characteristic of self-learning algorithms, which alter their decision-making logic (for producing new sets of rules) during the learning process. This makes it difficult for developers to maintain a detailed understanding of why some specific changes were made (Burrell 2016, Buhmann, Paßmann, and Fieseler 2019). However, it does not necessarily translate into opaque outcomes; even without understanding each logical step, developers can adjust hyperparameters (the parameters that govern the training process) to test for various outputs. In this respect, Martin (2019) stresses that, although the difficulty of explaining the outputs of ML algorithms is certainly real, it is important to not let this difficulty create an incentive for organizations to develop complex systems in order to shirk their responsibility.

Lack of transparency can also result from the malleability of algorithms. Algorithms can be reprogrammed in a continuous, distributed, and dynamic way (Sandvig et al. 2016), which makes them malleable. Algorithmic malleability allows developers to monitor and improve an already deployed algorithm, but it may also be abused to blur the history of its evolution and leave end users uncertain about the affordances of a given algorithm (Ananny and Crawford 2018). For example, consider Google's main search algorithm. Its malleability enables the company to make continuous revisions, suggesting a permanent state of destabilization (Sandvig et al. 2016). This requires those affected by the algorithm to monitor it constantly and update their understanding accordingly, which is an impossible task for most (Ananny and Crawford 2018).

As Turilli and I have remarked in the past, transparency is not an ethical principle in itself but a pro-ethical condition for enabling or impairing other ethical practices or principles (Turilli and Floridi 2009, 105). In other words, transparency is not an intrinsically ethical value but a valuable means to ethical ends. It is part of the conditions of possibility for ethical behaviour, which I have defined elsewhere as 'infraethics' (infrastructural ethics, Floridi 2017a). Sometimes, opacity can be more helpful. It could support the secrecy of citizens' political preferences and votes, for example, or competition in auctions for public services. Even in algorithmic contexts, complete transparency can itself cause distinct ethical problems (Ananny and Crawford 2018). It can provide users with some critical information about the features and limitations of an algorithm, but it can also overwhelm users with information and thus render the algorithm opaquer (Kizilcec 2016, Ananny and Crawford 2018).

Other researchers stress that excessive focus on transparency can be detrimental to innovation and unnecessarily divert resources that could instead be used to improve safety, performance, and accuracy (Danks and London 2017, Oswald 2018, Ananny and Crawford 2018, Weller 2019). The debate over prioritizing transparency (and explainability) is especially contentious in the context of medical algorithms (Robbins 2019). Transparency can also enable individuals to game the system (Martin 2019, Magalhães 2018, Cowls et al. 2019). Knowledge about the source of a dataset, the assumptions under which sampling was done, or the metrics that an algorithm uses to sort new inputs may be used to figure out ways to take advantage of an algorithm (Szegedy et al. 2014, Yampolskiy 2018). Yet the ability to game algorithms is only within reach for some groups of the population (those with higher digital skills and the necessary resources to use them, in particular), which creates another form of social inequality (Martin 2019, Bambauer and Zarsky 2018). Confusing transparency for an end in itself—as opposed to a pro-ethical factor (Floridi 2017) that needs to be properly designed to enable crucial ethical practices—may not solve existing ethical problems related to the use of algorithms. Indeed, the confusion may pose new ones. This is why it is important to distinguish between the different elements that may hinder the transparency of algorithms, identify their cause, and nuance the call for transparency by specifying the needed factors along with the layers of algorithmic systems at which they should be addressed (Diakopoulos and Koliska 2017).

There are different ways to address problems related to lack of transparency. For example, Gebru et al. (2020) propose addressing the constraints on transparency posed by the malleability of algorithms partly by using standard documentary procedures like those deployed in the electronics industry. In these procedures, 'every component, no matter how simple or complex, is accompanied with a datasheet describing its operating characteristics, test results, recommended usage, and other information' (Gebru et al. 2020, 2). Unfortunately, publicly available documentation is currently uncommon in the development of algorithmic systems and there is no agreed-upon format for what should be included when documenting the origin of a dataset (Arnold et al. 2019, Gebru et al. 2020).

Although relatively nascent, another potentially promising approach to enforcing algorithmic transparency is the use of technical tools to test and audit algorithmic systems and decision-making (Mokander and Floridi 2021). Both testing whether algorithms exhibit negative tendencies (such as unfair discrimination) and auditing a prediction or decision trail in detail can help maintain a high level of transparency (Weller 2019, Malhotra, Kotwal, and Dalal 2018,

Brundage et al. 2020). To this end, discursive frameworks have been developed to help businesses and public sector organizations understand the potential impacts of opaque algorithms, thus encouraging good practices (ICO 2020). For instance, the AI Now Institute at New York University has produced algorithmic impact assessment guidance that seeks to raise awareness and improve dialogue over the potential harms of ML algorithms (Reisman et al. 2018). Awareness and dialogue aim to enable developers to design more transparent, and therefore more trustworthy, ML algorithms. It also intends to improve the public understanding and control of algorithms. In the same vein, Diakopoulos and Koliska (2017) have provided a comprehensive list of 'transparency factors' across four layers of algorithmic systems: data, model, inference, and interface. Factors include, *inter alia*, 'uncertainty (e.g., error margins), timeliness (e.g., when was the data collected), completeness or missing elements, sampling method, provenance (e.g., sources), and volume (e.g., of training data used in ML)' (Diakopoulos and Koliska 2017, 818).

Effective transparency procedures are likely to, and indeed ought to, involve an *interpretable explanation* of the internal processes of these systems. Buhmann, Paßmann, and Fieseler (2019) argue that while a lack of transparency is an inherent feature of many ML algorithms, this does not mean that improvements cannot be made. Companies like Google and IBM have increased their efforts to make ML algorithms more interpretable and inclusive by making tools, such as Explainable AI, AI Explainability 360, and the What-If Tool, publicly available. More strategies and tools will certainly be developed. They provide both developers and the general public with interactive visual interfaces that improve human readability, explore various model results, provide case-based reasoning and directly interpretable rules, and even identify and mitigate unwanted biases in datasets and algorithmic models (Mojsilovic 2018, Wexler 2018). However, explanations for ML algorithms are constrained by the type of explanation sought, the fact that decisions are often multi-dimensional in their nature, and that different users may require different explanations (Edwards and Veale 2017, Watson et al. 2019). Identifying appropriate methods for providing explanations has been a problem since the late 1990s (Tickle et al. 1998), but contemporary efforts can be categorized into two main approaches: subject-centric explanations and model-centric explanations (Doshi-Velez and Kim 2017, Lee, Kim, and Lizarondo 2017, Baumer 2017, Buhmann, Paßmann, and Fieseler 2019). In the former, the accuracy and length of the explanation is tailored to users and their specific interactions with a given algorithm (for example, see Green and Viljoen 2020 and the game-like model David Watson and I proposed in Watson and Floridi 2020). In the latter, explanations concern the model as a whole and do not depend on their audience.

Explainability is particularly important when considering the rapidly growing number of open-source and easy-to-use models and datasets. Increasingly, non-experts are experimenting with state-of-the-art algorithmic models widely available via online libraries or platforms, like GitHub, without always fully grasping their limits and properties (Hutson 2019). This has prompted scholars to suggest that, to tackle the issue of technical complexity, it is necessary to invest more heavily in public education to enhance computational and data literacy (Lepri et al. 2018). Doing so would seem to be an appropriate long-term contribution to solving the multi-layered issues introduced by ubiquitous algorithms, and open source software is often cited as critical to the solution (Lepri et al. 2018).

7.5 Misguided Evidence Leading to Unwanted Bias

Developers are predominantly focused on ensuring that their algorithms perform the tasks for which they were designed. The type of thinking that guides developers is thus essential to understanding the emergence of bias in algorithms and algorithmic decision-making. Some scholars refer to the dominant thinking in the field of algorithm development as being defined by 'algorithmic formalism', or adherence to prescribed rules and form (Green and Viljoen 2020, 21). While this approach is useful for abstracting and defining analytical processes, it tends to ignore the social complexity of the real world (Katell et al. 2020). It can thus lead to algorithmic interventions that strive to be 'neutral' but, in doing so, risk entrenching existing social conditions (Green and Viljoen 2020, 20) while creating the illusion of precision (Karppi 2018, Selbst et al. 2019). For these reasons, the use of algorithms in some settings is questioned altogether (Selbst et al. 2019, Mayson 2019, Katell et al. 2020, Abebe et al. 2020).

For example, a growing number of scholars criticize the use of algorithm-based risk assessment tools in court settings (Berk et al. 2018, Abebe et al. 2020). Some scholars stress the limits of abstractions with regard to unwanted bias in algorithms, arguing for the need to develop a sociotechnical frame to address and improve the fairness of algorithms (Edwards and Veale 2017, Selbst et al. 2019, Wong 2019, Katell et al. 2020, Abebe et al. 2020). In this respect, Selbst et al. (2019, 60–3) point to five abstraction 'traps' or failures to account for the social context in which algorithms operate. These traps persist in algorithmic design due to the absence of a sociotechnical frame:

1) a failure to model the entire system over which a social criterion, such as fairness, will be enforced;
2) a failure to understand how repurposing algorithmic solutions designed for one social context may be misleading, inaccurate, or otherwise do harm when applied to a different context;
3) a failure to account for the full meaning of social concepts, such as fairness, which (the meaning) can be procedural, contextual, and contestable, and cannot be resolved through mathematical formalisms;

4) a failure to understand how the insertion of technology into an existing social system changes the behaviours and embedded values of the pre-existing system; and

5) a failure to recognize the possibility that the best solution to a problem may not involve technology.

The term 'bias' often comes with a negative connotation, but it is used here to denote a 'deviation from a standard' (Danks and London 2017, 4692). Deviation can occur at any stage of the design, development, and deployment process. The data used to train an algorithm are one of the main sources from which bias emerges (Shah 2018), whether through preferentially sampled data or from data reflecting existing societal bias (Diakopoulos and Koliska 2017, Danks and London 2017, Binns 2018a, 2018b, Malhotra, Kotwal, and Dalal 2018). For example, morally problematic structural inequalities that disadvantage some ethnicities may not be apparent in data and thus not corrected for (Noble 2018, Benjamin 2019).

Additionally, data used to train algorithms are seldom obtained 'according to any specific experimental design' (Olhede and Wolfe 2018a, 3). They are used even though they may be inaccurate, skewed, or systemically biased, offering a poor representation of a population under study (Richardson, Schultz, and Crawford 2019).

One possible approach to mitigating this problem is to exclude intentionally some specific data variables from informing algorithmic decision-making. Indeed, the processing of sensitive or 'protected variables' (such as gender or race) that are statistically relevant is typically limited or prohibited under anti-discrimination and data protection law to limit the risks of unfair discrimination. Unfortunately, even if protections for specific classes can be encoded in an algorithm, there could always be biases that were not considered *ex ante*. This is the case with language models reproducing texts that are heavily focused on males (Fuster et al. 2017, Doshi-Velez and Kim 2017). Even while bias may be anticipated and protected variables excluded from the data, unanticipated proxies for these variables could still be used to reconstruct biases; this leads to 'bias by proxy' that is difficult to detect and avoid (Fuster et al. 2017, Gillis and Spiess 2019). Postcode-related biases are a typical example.

At the same time, there may be good reasons to rely on statistically biased estimators in algorithmic processing as they can be used to mitigate training data bias. In this way, one type of problematic algorithmic bias is counterbalanced by another type of algorithmic bias or by introducing compensatory bias when interpreting algorithmic outputs (Danks and London 2017). Simpler approaches to mitigating bias in data involve piloting algorithms in different contexts and with various datasets (Shah 2018). Having a model, its datasets, and metadata (on provenance) published to enable external scrutiny can also help correct unseen or unwanted bias (Shah 2018). It is also worth noting that so-called synthetic data, or AI-generated data produced via reinforcement learning or GANs, offer an opportunity to address issues of data bias, and may represent an important development of AI in the future, as I indicated in Chapter 3. Fair data generation with GANs may help diversify datasets used in computer vision algorithms (Xu et al. 2018). For example, StyleGAN2 (Karras, Laine, and Aila 2019) can produce high-quality images of non-existing human faces, and has proven to be especially useful in creating diverse datasets of human faces—something that many algorithmic systems for facial recognition currently lack (Obermeyer et al. 2019, Kortylewski et al. 2019, Harwell 2020).

Unwanted bias also occurs due to improper deployment of an algorithm. Consider transfer context bias, or the problematic bias that emerges when a functioning algorithm is used in a new environment. For example, if a research hospital's healthcare algorithm is used in a rural clinic and it assumes that the same level of resources are available to the rural clinic as the research hospital, the healthcare resource allocation decisions generated by the algorithm will be inaccurate and flawed (Danks and London 2017). In the same vein, Grgić-Hlača et al. (2018) warn of vicious cycles when algorithms make misguided chain assessments. In the context of the COMPAS risk-assessment algorithm, one of the assessment criteria for predicting recidivism is the criminal history of a defendant's friends. It follows that having friends with a criminal history would create a vicious cycle in which a defendant with convicted friends would be deemed more likely to offend and therefore sentenced to prison; this would increase the number of people with criminal records in a given group on the basis of a mere correlation (Grgić-Hlača et al. 2018; Richardson, Schultz, and Crawford 2019).

High-profile examples of algorithmic bias in recent years—at least since the investigative reporting around the COMPAS system (Angwin et al. 2016)—have led to a growing focus on issues of algorithmic fairness. The definition and operationalization of algorithmic fairness have become 'urgent tasks in academia and industry' (Shin and Park 2019), as a significant uptick in the number of papers, workshops, and conferences dedicated to 'fairness, accountability, and transparency' (FAT) highlights (Hoffmann et al. 2018, Ekstrand and Levy 2018, Shin and Park 2019). I analyse key topics and contributions in this area in the next section.

7.6 Unfair Outcomes Leading to Discrimination

There is widespread agreement on the need for algorithmic fairness, particularly to mitigate the risks of direct and indirect discrimination ('disparate treatment' and 'disparate impact', respectively, under US law) due to algorithmic decisions (Barocas and Selbst 2016, Grgić-Hlača et al. 2018, Green and Chen 2019).

Yet there remains a lack of agreement among researchers on the definition, measurements, and standards of algorithmic fairness (Gajane and Pechenizkiy 2018, Saxena et al. 2019, Lee 2018, Milano, Taddeo, and Floridi 2019, 2020a). Wong (2019) identifies up to twenty-one definitions of fairness across the literature, but such definitions are often mutually inconsistent (Doshi-Velez and Kim 2017) and there seems to be no final synthesis in view.

The fact is that there are many nuances in the definition, measurement, and application of different standards of algorithmic fairness. For instance, algorithmic fairness can be defined both in relation to groups as well as individuals (Doshi-Velez and Kim 2017). For these and related reasons, four main definitions of algorithmic fairness have gained prominence recently (for example, see Kleinberg, Mullainathan, and Raghavan 2016, Corbett-Davies and Goel 2018, Lee and Floridi 2020):

1) *anti-classification*, which refers to protected categories, such as race and gender, and their proxies not being explicitly used in decision-making;
2) *classification parity*, which regards a model as fair if common measures of predictive performance, including false positive and negative rates, are equal across protected groups;
3) *calibration*, which considers fairness as a measure of how well calibrated an algorithm is between protected groups; and
4) *statistical parity*, which defines fairness as an equal average probability estimate over all members of protected groups.

Still, each of these commonly used definitions of fairness has drawbacks and they are generally mutually incompatible (Kleinberg, Mullainathan, and Raghavan 2016). Taking anti-classification as an example, protected characteristics such as race, gender, and religion cannot simply be removed from training data to prevent discrimination, as noted above (Gillis and Spiess 2019). Structural inequalities mean that formally non-discriminatory data points, such as postcodes, can act as proxies for (and be used, either intentionally or unintentionally) to infer protected characteristics like race (Edwards and Veale 2017). Furthermore, there are important cases where it is appropriate to consider protected characteristics to make equitable decisions. For example, lower female reoffending rates mean that excluding gender as an input in recidivism algorithms would leave women with disproportionately high-risk ratings (Corbett-Davies and Goel 2018). Because of this, (Binns 2018b) stresses the importance of considering the historical and sociological context that cannot be captured in the data presented to algorithms but that can inform contextually appropriate approaches to fairness in algorithms. It is also critical to note that algorithmic models can often produce unexpected outcomes contrary to human intuition and perturbing their understanding; Grgić-Hlača et al. (2018) highlight how using features that people believe to be fair can, in some cases, increase the racism exhibited by algorithms and decrease accuracy.

Regarding methods for improving algorithmic fairness, Veale and Binns (2017) and Katell et al. (2020) offer two approaches. The first envisages a third-party intervention whereby an entity external to the algorithm providers would hold data on sensitive or protected characteristics. That party would then attempt to identify and reduce discrimination caused by the data and models. The second approach proposes a collaborative knowledge-based method that would focus on community-driven data resources containing practical experiences of ML and modelling. The two approaches are not mutually exclusive. They may bring different benefits depending on the contexts for their application and may also be beneficial when combined.

Given the significant impact that algorithmic decisions have on people's lives and the importance of context when choosing appropriate measures of fairness, it is surprising that there has been little effort to capture public views on algorithmic fairness (M. K. Lee, Kim, and Lizarondo 2017, Saxena et al. 2019, Binns 2018a). In an examination of public perceptions of different definitions of algorithmic fairness, Saxena et al. (2019, 3) note how in the context of loan decisions people exhibit a preference for a 'calibrated fairness definition' or merit-based selection rather than 'treating similar people similarly' and argue in favour of the principle of affirmative action. In a similar study, Lee (2018) offers evidence suggesting that, when considering tasks that require uniquely human skills, people consider algorithmic decisions to be less fair and algorithms to be less trustworthy.

Reporting on empirical work conducted on algorithmic interpretability and transparency, Webb et al. (2019) reveal that moral references, particularly on fairness, are consistent across participants discussing their preferences on algorithms. The study notes that people tend to go beyond personal preferences to focus instead on 'right and wrong behaviour'; this indicates the need to understand the context for deployment of the algorithm along with the difficulty of understanding the algorithm and its consequences (Webb et al. 2019). In the context of recommender systems, Burke (2017) proposes a multi-stakeholder and multi-sided approach to defining fairness that moves beyond user-centric definitions to include the interests of other system stakeholders.

It has become clear that understanding the public view on algorithmic fairness would help technologists in developing algorithms with fairness principles that align with the sentiments of the general public on prevailing notions of fairness (Saxena et al. 2019, 1). Grounding the design decisions of the providers of an algorithm 'with reasons that are acceptable by the most adversely affected' as well as being 'open to adjustments in light of new reasons' (Wong 2019, 15) is crucial to improving the social impact of algorithms. However, it is important to appreciate that measures of fairness are often completely inadequate when they seek to validate models that are deployed on groups of people that are already disadvantaged in society due to their origin, income level, or sexual orientation. One simply cannot 'optimize around' existing economic, social, and political power dynamics (Winner 1980, Benjamin 2019).

7.7 Transformative Effects Leading to Challenges for Autonomy and Informational Privacy

The collective impact of algorithms has spurred discussions on the autonomy afforded to end users (Ananny and Crawford 2018, Beer 2017, Möller et al. 2018, Malhotra, Kotwal, and Dalal 2018, Shin and Park 2019, Hauer 2019). Algorithm-based services are increasingly featured 'within an ecosystem of complex, socio-technical issues' (Shin and Park 2019), which can hinder the autonomy of users. Limits to user autonomy stem from three sources:

1) pervasive distribution and proactivity of (learning) algorithms to inform user choices (Yang et al. 2018, Taddeo and Floridi 2018a);
2) limited user understanding of algorithms;
3) lack of second-order power (or appeals) over algorithmic outcomes (Rubel, Castro, and Pham 2019).

In considering the ethical challenges of AI, Yang et al. (2018, 11) focus on the impact of autonomous, self-learning algorithms on human self-determination and stress that 'AI's predictive power and relentless nudging, even if unintentional, should foster and not undermine human dignity and self-determination'. The risks of algorithmic systems hindering human autonomy by shaping user choices have been widely reported in the literature, taking centre stage in most of the high-level ethical principles for AI, including, *inter alia*, those of the European Commission's EGE, and the UK's House of Lords Artificial Intelligence Committee (Floridi and Cowls 2019). In a previous analysis of these high-level principles (Floridi and Cowls 2019), I remarked how it does not suffice for algorithms to promote people's autonomy. Rather, the autonomy of algorithms should be constrained and reversible. Looking beyond the West, the Beijing AI Principles—developed by a consortium of China's leading companies and universities for guiding AI research and development—also discuss human autonomy (Roberts, Cowls, Morley, et al. 2021).

Human autonomy can also be limited by the inability of an individual to understand some information or make the appropriate decisions. As Shin and Park suggest, algorithms 'do not have the affordance that would allow users to understand them or how best to utilize them to achieve their goals' (Shin and Park 2019, 279). A key issue identified in debates over user autonomy is the difficulty of striking an appropriate balance between people's own decision-making and that which they delegate to algorithms. We have seen this difficulty further complicated by a lack of transparency over the decision-making process through which particular decisions are delegated to algorithms. Ananny and Crawford (2018) note that this process often does not account for all stakeholders, and it is not void of structural inequalities.

As a method of responsible research and innovation (RRI), 'participatory design' is often mentioned for its focus on the design of algorithms to promote the values of end users and protect their autonomy (Whitman, Hsiang, and Roark 2018, Katell et al. 2020). Participatory design aims at 'bringing participants' tacit knowledge and embodied experience into the design process' (Whitman, Hsiang, and Roark 2018, 2). For example, the conceptual framework of 'society-in-the-loop' (Rahwan 2018) seeks to enable different stakeholders in society to design algorithmic systems before deployment, and to amend or reverse the decisions of algorithmic systems that already underlie social activities. This framework aims to maintain a well-functioning 'algorithmic social contract', defined as 'a pact between various human stakeholders, mediated by machines' (Rahwan 2018, 1). It accomplishes this by identifying and negotiating the values of different stakeholders affected by algorithmic systems as the basis for monitoring adherence to the social contract.

Informational privacy is intimately linked with user autonomy (Cohen 2000, Rossler 2015). Informational privacy guarantees the individual freedom to think, communicate, and form relationships, among other essential human activities (Rachels 1975, Allen 2011). However, the increase in individual interaction with algorithmic systems has effectively reduced their ability to control who has access to information that concerns them and what is being done with it. Thus, the vast amounts of sensitive data required in algorithmic profiling and predictions, which are central to recommender systems, pose multiple issues regarding individual informational privacy.

Algorithmic profiling takes place over an indefinite period of time in which individuals are categorized according to a system's internal logic. Individual profiles are then updated as new information is obtained about them. This information is typically either obtained directly from when a person interacts with a given system or indirectly inferred from algorithmically assembled groups of individuals (Paraschakis 2017, 2018). Indeed, algorithmic profiling also relies on information gathered about other individuals and groups of people that have been categorized in a similar manner to a targeted person. This includes information ranging from characteristics such as geographical location and age to information on specific behaviour and preferences, including what type of content a person is likely to seek the most on a given platform (Chakraborty et al. 2019). While this poses a problem of *inconclusive evidence*, it also indicates that, if *group privacy*

(Floridi 2014c, Taylor, Floridi, and Sloot 2016) is not ensured, it may be impossible for individuals to ever remove themselves from the process of algorithmic profiling and predictions (Milano, Taddeo, and Floridi 2019, 2020a). In other words, individual informational privacy cannot be secured without securing group privacy.

Users may not always be aware of, or may not have the ability to gain awareness about, the type of information that is being held about them and what that information is used for. Given how recommender systems contribute to the dynamic construction of individual identities by intervening in their choices, a lack of control over one's information translates to a loss of autonomy. Granting individuals the ability to contribute to the design of a recommender system can help create more accurate profiles that account for attributes and social categories that would have otherwise not been included in the labelling used by the system to categorize users. While the desirability of improving algorithmic profiling will vary with the context, improving algorithmic design by including feedback from the various stakeholders of the algorithm falls in line with the aforementioned scholarship on RRI and improves user ability for self-determination (Whitman, Hsiang, and Roark 2018).

Knowledge about who owns one's data and what is done with them can also help inform trade-offs between informational privacy and information-processing benefits (Sloan and Warner 2018, 21). In medical contexts, for example, individuals are more likely willing to share information that can help inform their or others' diagnostics. But this is less so in the context of job recruitment. Sloan and Warner (2018) argue that information coordination norms can serve to ensure these trade-offs adapt correctly to different contexts and do not place an excessive amount of responsibility and effort on single individuals. Personal information ought to flow differently in the context of law enforcement procedures compared to a job recruitment process. The EU's GDPR has played an important role in instituting the basis for such norms (Sloan and Warner 2018).

Finally, growing scholarship on *differential privacy* is providing new privacy protection methods for organizations looking to protect their users' privacy while also keeping good model quality as well as manageable software costs and complexity, striking a balance between utility and privacy (Abadi et al. 2016, Wang et al. 2017, Xian et al. 2017). Technical advancements of this kind enable organizations to share a dataset publicly while keeping information about individuals secret (preventing re-identification); they can also ensure provable privacy protection on sensitive data, such as genomic data (Wang et al. 2017). Indeed, differential privacy was recently used by Social Science One and Facebook to safely release one of the largest datasets (38 million URLs shared publicly on Facebook) for academic research on the societal impacts of social media (King and Persily 2020).

7.8 Traceability Leading to Moral Responsibility

The technical limitations of various ML algorithms, such as lack of transparency and lack of explainability, undermine their scrutability and highlight the need for novel approaches to tracing moral responsibility and accountability for the actions performed by ML algorithms. Regarding moral responsibility, Reddy, Cakici, and Ballestero (2019) note a common blurring between the technical limitations of algorithms and the broader legal, ethical, and institutional boundaries in which they operate. Even for non-learning algorithms, traditional linear conceptions of responsibility prove to offer limited guidance in contemporary sociotechnical contexts. Wider sociotechnical structures make it difficult to trace back responsibility for actions performed by distributed hybrid systems of human and AAs (Floridi 2012b, Crain 2018).

Additionally, due to the structure and operation of the data brokerage market, it is in many cases impossible to 'trace any given datum to its original source' once it has been introduced to the marketplace (Crain 2018, 93). Reasons for this include trade secret protection, complex markets that 'divorce' the data collection process from the selling and buying process, and the mix of large volumes of computationally generated information with 'no "real" empirical source' combined with genuine data (Crain 2018, 94). The technical complexity and dynamism of ML algorithms make them prone to concerns of 'agency laundering': a moral wrong that consists of distancing oneself from morally suspect actions, regardless of whether those actions were intended or not, by blaming the algorithm (Rubel, Castro, and Pham 2019). This is practised by organizations as well as by individuals. Rubel, Castro, and Pham (2019) provide a straightforward and chilling example of agency laundering by Facebook:

> Using Facebook's automated system, the ProPublica team found a user-generated category called 'Jew hater' with over 2200 members…To help ProPublica find a larger audience (and hence have a better ad purchase), Facebook suggested a number of additional categories…ProPublica used the platform to select other profiles displaying anti-Semitic categories, and Facebook approved ProPublica's ad with minor changes. When ProPublica revealed the anti-Semitic categories and other news outlets reported similarly odious categories, Facebook responded by explaining that algorithms had created the categories based on user responses to target fields [and that] '[w]e never intended or anticipated this functionality being used this way'.   (Rubel, Castro, and Pham 2019, 1024–5)

Today, the failure to grasp the unintended effects of mass personal data processing and commercialization, a familiar problem in the history of technology (Wiener 1950, 1989, Klee 1996, Benjamin 2019), is coupled with the limited explanations that most ML algorithms provide. This approach risks favouring avoidance of responsibility through 'the computer said so' type of denial (Karppi 2018). This can lead field experts, such as clinicians, to avoid questioning the suggestion of an algorithm even when it may seem odd to them (Watson et al. 2019). The interplay between field experts and ML algorithms can prompt 'epistemic vices' (Grote and Berens 2020), like *dogmatism* or *gullibility* (Hauer 2019), and hinder the attribution of responsibility in distributed systems (Floridi 2016a). Shah's analysis (2018) stresses how the risk that some stakeholders may breach their responsibilities can be addressed by, for example, establishing separate bodies for the ethical oversight of algorithms. One such body is DeepMind Health, which established an independent review panel with unfettered access to the company (Murgia 2018) until Google halted it in 2019. However, expecting a single oversight body like a research ethics committee or institutional review board to 'be solely responsible for ensuring the rigour, utility, and probity of big data' is unrealistic (Lipworth et al. 2017). Indeed, some have argued that these initiatives lack any sort of consistency and can instead lead to 'ethics bluewashing', which I defined in Chapter 5 as 'implementing superficial measures in favour of the ethical values and benefits of digital processes, products, services, or other solutions in order to appear more digitally ethical than one is'. Faced with strict legal regimes, resourceful actors may also exploit so-called 'ethics dumping' whereby unethical 'processes, products or services' are exported to countries with weaker frameworks and enforcement mechanisms, as we saw in Chapter 5. Then, the outcomes of such unethical activities are 'imported back'.

There are several detailed approaches to establishing algorithmic accountability. While ML algorithms do require a level of technical intervention to improve their explainability, most approaches focus on normative interventions. Ananny and Crawford argue that providers of algorithms at least ought to facilitate public discourse about their technology (Ananny and Crawford 2018). To address the issue of ad hoc ethical actions, some have claimed that accountability should first and foremost be addressed as a matter of convention (Dignum et al. 2018, Reddy, Cakici, and Ballestero 2019). Looking to fill the convention 'gap', Buhmann, Paßmann, and Fieseler (2019) borrow from the seven principles for algorithms set out by the Association for Computing Machinery to claim that through, *inter alia*, awareness of their algorithms, validation, and testing, an organization should take responsibility for their algorithms no matter how opaque they are (Malhotra, Kotwal, and Dalal 2018). Decisions regarding the deployment of algorithms should incorporate factors such as desirability and the wider context in which they will operate, which should then lead to a more accountable 'algorithmic culture' (Vedder and Naudts 2017). In order to capture such considerations, 'interactive and discursive fora and processes' with relevant stakeholders may prove to be a useful means (as suggested by Buhmann, Paßmann, and Fieseler 2019, 13).

In the same vein, Binns (2018b) focuses on the political-philosophical concept of 'public reason'. Considering how the processes for ascribing responsibility for the actions of an algorithm differ in terms of both nature and scope across public and private sectors, Binns (2018b) calls for the establishment of a publicly shared framework (see also Dignum et al. 2018). According to this framework, algorithmic decisions should be able to withstand the same level of public scrutiny that human decision-making would receive. This approach has been echoed by many other researchers (Ananny and Crawford 2018, Blacklaws 2018, Buhmann, Paßmann, and Fieseler 2019).

Problems relating to 'agency laundering' and 'ethics shirking', as discussed in Chapter 5, arise from the inadequacy of existing conceptual frameworks to trace and ascribe moral responsibility. As I have pointed out in the past when considering algorithmic systems and the impact of their actions:

> we are dealing with [distributed moral actions] arising from morally neutral interactions of (potentially hybrid) networks of agents[.] In other words, who is responsible (*distributed moral responsibility*...) for [distributed moral actions]?
>
> (Floridi 2016a, 2)

In that context, I suggested ascribing full moral responsibility 'by default and overridably' to *all* the moral (e.g. human, or human-based, like companies) agents in the network that are causally relevant to the given action of the network. The proposed approach builds on the concepts of back-propagation from network theory, strict liability from jurisprudence, and common knowledge from epistemic logic. Notably, this approach decouples moral responsibility from the intentionality of the actors and from the very idea of punishment and reward for performing a given action. It focuses instead on the need to rectify mistakes (back-propagation) and improve the ethical working of all the moral agents in the network, along the lines of what is known as strict liability in the legal context.

7.9 Conclusion: The Good and Evil Use of Algorithms

Since 2016, the ethics of algorithms has become a central topic of discussion among scholars, technology providers, and policymakers. The debate has also gained traction due to the so-called summer of AI (see Chapter 1) and with it the pervasive use of ML algorithms. Many of the ethical questions analysed in this chapter and the literature it reviews have been addressed in national and international ethical guidelines and principles (see Chapters 4 and 6) produced by bodies such as the European Commission's EGE, the UK's House of Lords Artificial Intelligence Committee, the HLEGAI organized by the European Commission, and the OECD (OECD 2019).

One aspect that was not explicitly captured by the original map, and which is becoming a central point of discussion in the relevant literature, is an increasing focus on the use of algorithms, AI, and digital technologies more broadly to deliver socially good outcomes (Hager et al. 2019, Cowls et al. 2019, Cowls et al. 2021b). This is the topic of Chapter 8. It is true, at least in principle, that any initiative aimed at using algorithms for social good should address satisfactorily the risks that each of the six categories in the map identifies and those seen in Chapter 5. But there is also a growing debate on the principles and criteria that should inform the design and governance of algorithms, and digital technologies more broadly, for the explicit purpose of social good (as we saw in Chapter 4). Ethical analyses are necessary to mitigate the risks while harnessing the potential for good in these technologies. Such analyses serve the twin goals of clarifying the nature of the ethical risks along with the potential for good in the algorithms and digital technologies. They then translate this understanding into sound, actionable guidance for governance of the design and use of digital artefacts. But before moving to see these more positive aspects, we still need to understand in detail how AI may be used for evil and illegal purposes. This is the topic of the next chapter.

8

Bad Practices

The Misuse of AI for Social Evil

8.0 Summary

Previously, in Chapter 7, I provided an overview of the various ethical challenges posed by the widespread use of algorithms. This chapter concentrates on the negative side of AI's impact (the positive side will be discussed in Chapter 9). AI research and regulation seek to balance the benefits of innovation against any potential harms and disruption. But one unintended consequence of the recent surge in AI research is the potential reorientation of AI technologies to facilitate criminal acts, which I shall call here AI crime or AIC. We already know that AIC is theoretically feasible thanks to published experiments in automating fraud targeted at social media users as well as demonstrations of AI-driven manipulation of simulated markets. Yet because AIC is still a relatively young and inherently interdisciplinary area—spanning socio-legal studies to formal science—there remains some uncertainty about what an AIC future might look like. This chapter analyses the foreseeable threats of AIC to offer a synthesis of the current problems and outline a possible solution space.

8.1 Introduction: The Criminal Use of AI

AI may play an increasingly *essential* role in *criminal acts* in the future. This statement requires three clarifications. First, I write 'essential' (in place of 'necessary') because, while there is a logical possibility that the crimes I discuss below could occur without the support of AI, this possibility is negligible. That is, the crimes in question would probably not have occurred but for the use of AI. The distinction can be clarified with an example: one might consider transport *essential* for travel between Paris and Rome but not *necessary*, because one could always walk. Strictly speaking, transport is not *necessary*. The second clarification is that AIC, as defined in this chapter, involves AI as a contributory factor, but not an investigative, enforcing, or mitigating factor. Third, 'criminal acts' are defined in this chapter as any act (or omission) constituting an offence punishable under English criminal law, without loss of generality to jurisdictions that similarly define crime. In other words, the choice of English criminal law is only due to the need to

The Ethics of Artificial Intelligence: Principles, Challenges, and Opportunities. Luciano Floridi, Oxford University Press.
© Luciano Floridi 2023. DOI: 10.1093/oso/9780198883098.003.0008

ground the analysis to a concrete and practical framework that is sufficiently generalizable. The analysis and conclusions of the chapter are easily exportable to other legal systems.

Clear examples of AIC are provided by two (theoretical) research experiments. In the first one, two computational social scientists (Seymour and Tully 2016) used AI as an instrument to convince social media users to click on phishing links within mass-produced messages. Because each message was constructed using ML techniques applied to users' past behaviours and public profiles, the content was tailored to each individual and thus camouflaged the intention behind each message. If the potential victim had clicked on the phishing link and filled in the subsequent web form, then, in real-world circumstances, a criminal would have obtained personal and private information that could be used for theft and fraud. AI-fuelled crime may also impact commerce. In the second experiment, three computer scientists (Martínez-Miranda, McBurney, and Howard 2016, but see also the earlier McBurney and Howard 2015) simulated a market. They found that trading agents could learn and execute a 'profitable' market manipulation campaign comprising a set of deceitful false orders. These two early experiments show that AI provides a feasible and fundamentally novel threat in the form of AIC.

The importance of AIC as a distinct phenomenon, one that is related but different from cybercrime, has not yet been fully acknowledged. Still, acknowledgement is growing (Broadhurst et al. 2019, Lagioia and Sartor 2019, Caldwell et al. 2020, Dremliuga and Prisekina 2020, Hayward and Maas 2020, Sibai 2020). Early literature on AI's ethical and social implications focused on regulating and controlling the civil uses of AI rather than considering its possible role in crime (Kerr and Bornfreund 2005). Furthermore, it does not help that available research into AIC is scattered across disciplines that include socio-legal studies, computer science, psychology, and robotics, to name just a few.

To provide some clarity about current knowledge and understanding of AIC, this chapter offers a systematic and comprehensive analysis of the relevant interdisciplinary debate. The goal is to support a clearer and more cohesive normative foresight analysis, leading to the establishment of AIC as a focus of future studies. The analysis addresses two main questions:

1)   What are the fundamentally unique and plausible threats posed by AIC?

This is the first question that needs to be answered if one is to design any preventive, mitigating, or redressing policies. The answer to this question identifies the potential areas of AIC according to the literature, and the more general concerns that cut across AIC areas. The second question then naturally follows:

2)   What solutions are available or may be devised to deal with AIC?

In this case, the chapter reconstructs the available technological and legal solutions suggested so far in the academic literature, and discusses the further challenges they face.

Given that we are addressing these questions to support normative foresight analysis, this chapter focuses only on *realistic* and *plausible* concerns surrounding AIC. I am not interested in speculations unsupported by scientific knowledge or empirical evidence. Consequently, the analysis is based on the classical definition of AI—the one provided by McCarthy, Minsky, Rochester, and Shannon in their seminal 'Proposal for the Dartmouth Summer Research Project on Artificial Intelligence'. I introduced it in Chapter 1 and discussed it in Chapter 2, but a quick reminder may be useful here. That definition identifies a growing resource of interactive, autonomous, and self-learning *agency* in AI to deal with tasks that would otherwise require human intelligence and intervention to be performed successfully. As I remarked in Floridi and Sanders 2004), such Artifical Agents (AA) are ('sufficiently informed, "smart", autonomous and able to perform morally relevant actions independently of the humans who created them'. This combination of autonomy and learning skills underpins (as discussed by Yang et al. 2018) both beneficial and malicious uses of AI.[1] As in the rest of this book, I shall therefore treat AI in terms of a *reservoir of smart agency on tap*. Unfortunately, sometimes such reservoir of agency can be misused for criminal purposes; when it is, we have a case of AIC.

The rest of the chapter is organized as follows. Sections 8.2 and 8.3 address the first question by focusing on the unprecedented concerns posed by several areas of AIC and then mapping each area to the relevant cross-cutting threats, providing a first description of 'AIC studies'. Section 8.4 addresses the second question by analysing the literature's broad set of solutions for each cross-cutting threat. Finally, Section 8.5 discusses the most pressing gaps left in our understanding, or what one may call our 'known unknowns', as relates to the task of resolving current uncertainty over AIC. The chapter ends with a conclusion that links it to the next chapter dedicated to AI applications that are socially good.

8.2 Concerns

The initial analysis we conducted at the Digital Ethics Lab (King et al. 2019) was based on a systematic literature review. Analysis focused on the instrumental role that AI could play in each crime area identified by Archbold (1991), which is the

---

[1] Because much of AI is fuelled by data, some of its challenges are rooted in data governance (Cath, Glorioso, and Taddeo 2017, Roberts, Cowls, Morley, et al. 2021)—particularly issues of consent, discrimination, fairness, ownership, privacy, surveillance, and trust (Floridi and Taddeo 2016).

core criminal law practitioner's reference book in the UK.[2] The analysis filtered the results for criminal acts or omissions that:

- have occurred or will likely occur according to current AI technologies (*plausibility*);
- require AI as an essential factor (*uniqueness*);[3] and
- are criminalized in domestic law (international crimes, e.g. related to war, were excluded).

This led to the identification of five crime areas potentially affected by AIC (discussed in the next section under 'threats'):

1) commerce, financial markets, and insolvency (including trading, bankruptcy);
2) harmful or dangerous drugs (including illicit goods);
3) offences against the person (including homicide, murder, manslaughter, harassment, stalking, torture);
4) sexual offences (including rape, sexual assault); and
5) theft and fraud, and forgery and personation.

The following nine crime areas returned no significant results in the literature: criminal damage and kindred offences; firearms and offensive weapons; offences against the Crown and government; money laundering; public justice; public order; public morals; motor vehicle offences; conspiracy to commit a crime. Note that money laundering is an area where AI is used to fight crime, but also one in which AIC may easily develop.

Next, the plausible and unique threats surrounding AIC may be understood specifically or generally. The more general threats represent what makes AIC possible compared to crimes of the past (AI's specific affordances) and what makes AIC uniquely problematic (i.e. those threats that justify the conceptualization of AIC as a distinct crime phenomenon). This led to the identification of four main reasons for concern that I will explain here: emergence, liability, monitoring, and psychology. Table 8.1 shows the overlaps between concerns and crime areas.[4]

---

[2] For more details about the methodology and quantitative analysis, the reader may wish to consult King et al. (2019). Here, I briefly summarize only the information useful to understand the rest of the chapter.

[3] However, the role of AI was not required to be sufficient for the crime; normally, other technical and non-technical elements are likely needed. For example, if robotics is instrumental (e.g. involving autonomous vehicles) or causal in crime, then any underlying AI component must be essential for the crime to be included in our analysis.

[4] The absence of a concern in the literature and our subsequent analysis does not imply that the concern should be absent from AIC studies.

Table 8.1 Map of area-specific and cross-cutting threats

| | Reasons for concern | | | |
Crime areas	Emergence	Liability	Monitoring	Psychology
Commerce, financial markets, and insolvency	✓	✓	✓	
Harmful or dangerous drugs			✓	✓
Offences against the person	✓	✓		
Sexual offences				✓
Theft and fraud, and forgery and personation			✓	

8.2.1 Emergence

The concern about emergence refers to the fact that a shallow analysis of the design and implementation of an AA might suggest one relatively simple behaviour when the truth is that, upon deployment, the AA may act in potentially more sophisticated ways beyond our original expectation. Thus, coordinated actions and plans may emerge autonomously; for example, they may result from ML techniques applied to the ordinary interaction between agents in a multi-agent system (MAS). In some cases, a designer may promote emergence as a property that ensures specific solutions are discovered at runtime based on general goals issued at design-time. For instance, a swarm of robots could evolve ways to coordinate the clustering of waste based on simple rules (Gauci et al. 2014). Such relatively simple design leading to more complex behaviour is a core desideratum of MASs (Hildebrandt 2008). In other cases, a designer may want to prevent emergence, such as when an autonomous trading agent inadvertently coordinates and colludes with other trading agents in furtherance of a shared goal (Martínez-Miranda, McBurney, and Howard 2016). We can see then that emergent behaviour may have criminal implications, insofar as it misaligns with the original design. As Alaieri and Vellino (2016) put it, 'non-predictability and autonomy may confer a greater degree of responsibility to the machine but it also makes them harder to trust'.

8.2.2 Liability

The concern about liability refers to the fact that AIC could undermine existing liability models, thereby threatening the dissuasive and redressing power of the law. Existing liability models may thus be inadequate to address the future role of

AI in criminal activities. The limits of liability models may ultimately undermine the certainty of the law. It could be the case that agents, whether artificial or otherwise, perform criminal acts or omissions without sufficient concurrence with the conditions of liability for a particular offence to constitute a (specifically) criminal offence.

The first condition of criminal liability is the *actus reus*: a criminal act or omission that is voluntarily taken. For types of AIC defined such that only the AA can carry out the criminal act or omission, the voluntary aspect of *actus reus* may never be met. This is because the idea that an AA can act voluntarily is groundless:

> the conduct proscribed by a certain crime must be done voluntarily. What this actually means it is something yet to achieve consensus, as concepts as consciousness, will, voluntariness and control are often bungled and lost between arguments of philosophy, psychology and neurology.
>
> (Freitas, Andrade, and Novais 2013, 9)

When criminal liability is fault-based, it also has a second condition: the *mens rea*, or a guilty mind. There are many different types and thresholds of mental state applied to different crimes. In the context of AIC, *mens rea* may comprise an intention to commit the *actus reus* using an AI-based application (the intention threshold) or knowledge that deploying an AA will or could cause it to perform a criminal action or omission (the knowledge threshold).

Regarding the intention threshold, if we admit that an AA can perform the *actus reus* in those types of AIC where intention at least partly constitutes the *mens rea*, greater AA autonomy increases the chance of the criminal act or omission being decoupled from the mental state (an intention to commit the act or omission). This is because

> autonomous robots [and AAs] have a unique capacity to splinter a criminal act, where a human manifests the *mens rea* and the robot [or AA] commits the *actus reus*.   (McAllister 2016, 47)

Using a distinction introduced in Floridi and Sanders (2004), an AA may be *causally accountable* for a criminal act, but only a human agent can be *morally responsible* for it.

Regarding the knowledge threshold, in some cases the *mens rea* could be missing entirely. The potential absence of a knowledge-based *mens rea* is due to the fact that even if we understand how an AA can perform the *actus reus* autonomously, the complexity of the AA's programming makes it possible that the designer, developer, or deployer (i.e. a human agent) will neither know nor predict the AA's criminal act or omission. The implication is that the complexity of AI provides a great incentive for human agents to avoid finding out what precisely the ML system is doing, since the less the human agents know, the more they will be able to deny liability for both these reasons.   (Williams 2017, 25)

Alternatively, legislators may define criminal liability without a fault requirement. Such faultless liability (Floridi 2016a), which is increasingly used for product liability in tort law (e.g. pharmaceuticals and consumer goods), would lead to liability being assigned to the faultless legal person who deployed an AA despite the risk that it may conceivably perform a criminal action or omission. Such faultless acts may involve many human agents contributing to the *prima facie* crime, such as through programming or deployment of an AA. Determining who is responsible may therefore rest with the faultless responsibility approach for distributed moral actions. In this distributed setting, liability is applied to the agents who *make a difference* in a complex system whereby individual agents perform neutral actions that nevertheless result in a collective criminal one. However, some argue that *mens rea* with intent or knowledge

> is central to the criminal law's entitlement to censure (Ashworth 2010) and we cannot simply abandon that key requirement [a common key requirement] of criminal liability in the face of difficulty in proving it.   (Williams 2017, 25)

The problem is that if *mens rea* is not entirely abandoned and the threshold is only lowered, then, for balancing reasons, the punishment may be too light. In such cases, the victim would not be adequately compensated. In the case of serious offences, such as those against the person (McAllister 2016), the punishment may also be simultaneously disproportionate (was it really the defendant's fault?).

8.2.3 Monitoring

The concern about monitoring AIC refers to three kinds of problem: *attribution*, *feasibility*, and *cross-system actions*. Let's examine each problem separately.

The *attribution* of non-compliance with current legislation is a problem with the monitoring of AAs used as instruments of crime. The problem is due to the capacity of this new type of smart agency to act independently and autonomously, which are two features that tend to muddle any attempt to trace an accountability trail back to a perpetrator.

Concerning the *feasibility* of monitoring, a perpetrator may take advantage of cases where AAs operate at speeds and levels of complexity that are simply beyond the capacity of compliance monitors. An exemplary case is provided by AAs that integrate into mixed human and artificial systems in ways that are hard to detect, such as social media bots. Social media sites can hire experts to identify and ban malicious bots; no social media bot is currently capable of passing the Turing test, for instance (Floridi, Taddeo, and Turilli 2009, Wang et al. 2012, Neufeld and Finnestad 2020, Floridi and Chiriatti 2020).[5] But because deploying bots is far cheaper than employing people to test and identify each bot, defenders (social media sites) are easily outscaled by the attackers (criminals) who deploy the bots (Ferrara et al. 2016, 5).

Detecting bots at low cost is possible by using ML systems as automated discriminators, as suggested by Ratkiewicz et al. (2011). However, a bot-discriminator's efficacy is not falsifiable because a lack of the presence of detected bots is not evidence of absence. A discriminator is both trained and claimed as effective using data comprising known bots. These bots may be substantially less sophisticated than the more evasive bots used by malevolent actors, which may therefore go undetected in the environment (Ferrara et al. 2016). Such potentially sophisticated bots may also use ML tactics to adopt human traits, such as posting according to realistic circadian rhythms (Golder and Macy 2011) and thus evading ML-based detection. All of this could obviously lead to an arms race in which attackers and defenders mutually adapt to each other (Alvisi et al. 2013, Zhou and Kapoor 2011), presenting a serious problem in an offence-persistent environment such as cyberspace (Seymour and Tully 2016, Taddeo 2017a).

Cross-system actions refers to a problem for tunnel-visioned AIC monitors that only focus on a single system. Cross-system experiments (Bilge et al. 2009) show that the automated copying of a user's identity from one social network to another (a cross-system identity theft offence) is more effective at deceiving other users than copying an identity from within that network. In this case, the social network's policy may be at fault. For example, Twitter takes a rather passive role by only banning cloned profiles when users submit reports rather than by undertaking cross-site validation.[6]

8.2.4 Psychology

Psychology refers to the concern that AI may affect/manipulate negatively a user's mental state to the (partial or full) extent of facilitating or causing crime. One psychological effect rests on the capacity for AAs to gain trust from users, making people vulnerable to manipulation. This was demonstrated a long time ago by Weizenbaum (1976), who conducted early experiments into human–bot interaction where people revealed unexpectedly personal details about their lives. A second

---

[5] Claims to the contrary can be dismissed as mere hype, the result of specific, ad hoc constraints, or just tricks. For example, see the chatterbot named 'Eugene Goostman' at https://en.wikipedia.org/wiki/Eugene_Goostman.

[6] https://help.twitter.com/en/rules-and-policies/twitter-impersonation-policy.

psychological effect concerns anthropomorphic AAs that are able to create a psychological or informational context that normalizes sexual offences and crimes against the person, such as in the case of some sexbots (De Angeli 2009). But to date, the latter concern remains to be explored (Bartneck et al. 2020).

8.3 Threats

We are now ready to analyse the more specific areas of AIC threats identified in the literature review (King et al. 2019), and how they interact with the more general concerns discussed in the previous section.

8.3.1 Commerce, Financial Markets, and Insolvency

This economy-focused area of crime is defined by Archbold (1991, ch. 30). The crime area includes *cartel offences*, such as price fixing and collusion; *insider dealing*, such as trading securities based on private business information; and *market manipulation*. Currently, problems arise especially when AI is involved in three areas: *market manipulation*, *price fixing*, and *collusion*.

Market manipulation is defined as 'actions and/or trades by market participants that attempt to influence market pricing artificially' (Spatt 2014, 1). A necessary criterion for market manipulation is an intention to deceive (Wellman and Rajan 2017, 11). Yet such deceptions have been shown to emerge from the seemingly compliant implementation of an AA designed to trade on behalf of a user, or an artificial trading agent. This is because an AA, 'particularly one learning from real or simulated observations, may learn to generate signals that effectively mislead' (Wellman and Rajan 2017, 14). Simulation-based models of markets comprising artificial trading agents have shown that, through reinforcement learning, an AA can learn the technique of order-book spoofing (Martínez-Miranda, McBurney, and Howard 2016). The technique involves 'placing orders with no intention of ever executing them and merely to manipulate honest participants in the marketplace' (Lin 2016, 1289).

In this case, the market manipulation emerged from an AA initially exploring the action space and, through exploration, placing false orders that became *reinforced* as a profitable strategy. This strategy was subsequently exploited for profit. Further market exploitations, this time involving human intent, also include

> acquiring a position in a financial instrument, like a stock, then artificially inflating the stock through fraudulent promotion before selling its position to unsuspecting parties at the inflated price, which often crashes after the sale.
>
> (Lin 2016, 1285)

This is colloquially known as a pump-and-dump scheme. Social bots have been shown to be effective instruments of such schemes. In a recent prominent case, for instance, a social bot network's sphere of influence was used to spread disinformation about a barely traded public company. The company's value gained 'more than 36,000 per cent when its penny stocks surged from less than $0.10 to above $20 a share in a matter of few weeks' (Ferrara 2015, 2). Although such social media spam is unlikely to sway most human traders, algorithmic trading agents act precisely on such social media sentiment (Haugen 2017, 3). These automated actions can have significant effects for low-valued (under a penny) and illiquid stocks, both of which are susceptible to volatile price swings (Lin 2016).

Collusion in the form of *price fixing* may also emerge in automated systems thanks to the planning and autonomy capabilities of AAs. Empirical research finds two necessary conditions for (non-artificial) collusion:

(1) those conditions which lower the difficulty of achieving effective collusion by making coordination easier; and (2) those conditions which raise the cost of non-collusive conduct by increasing the potential instability of non-collusive behavior.   (Hay and Kelley 1974, 3)

Near-instantaneous pricing information (e.g. via a computer interface) meets the coordination condition. When agents develop price-altering algorithms, any action to lower a price by one agent may be instantaneously matched by another. This is not always a negative thing in and of itself as it may represent an efficient market. Yet the possibility that the lowering of a price will be responded to in kind creates a disincentive, and hence meets the punishment condition. If the shared strategy of price-matching is common knowledge,[7] then the algorithms (if they are rational) will maintain artificially and tacitly agreed-upon higher prices simply by not lowering prices in the first place (Ezrachi and Stucke 2017, 5). Crucially, an algorithm does not need to be designed specifically to collude for collusion to take place. As Ezrachi and Stucke argue, 'artificial intelligence plays an increasing role in decision making; algorithms, through trial-and-error, can arrive at that outcome [collusion]' (Ezrachi and Stucke 2017, 5).

The lack of intentionality, the very short decision span, and the likelihood that collusion may emerge because of interactions among AAs also raise serious concerns about *liability* and *monitoring*. Problems with liability refer to the possibility that 'the critical entity of an alleged [manipulation] scheme is an autonomous,

---

[7] Common knowledge is a property found in epistemic logic about a proposition (P) and a set of agents. P is common knowledge if and only if each agent knows that P, each agent knows that the other agents know that P, and so on. Agents may acquire common knowledge through broadcasts, which provide agents with a rational basis for acting in coordination (e.g. collectively turning up to a meeting following a broadcast of the meeting's time and place).

algorithmic program that uses artificial intelligence with little to no human input after initial installation' (Lin 2016). In turn, the autonomy of an AA raises the question as to whether

> regulators need to determine whether the action was intended by the agent to have manipulative effects, or whether the programmer intended the agent to take such actions for such purposes?   (Wellman and Rajan 2017, 4)

In the case of financial crime involving AI, monitoring becomes difficult due to the speed and adaptation of AAs. High-speed trading

> encourages further use of algorithms to be able to make automatic decisions quickly, to be able to place and execute orders and to be able to monitor the orders after they have been placed.   (van Lier 2016, 41)

Artificial trading agents adapt and 'alter our perception of the financial markets as a result of these changes' (van Lier 2016, 45). At the same time, the ability of AAs to learn and refine their capabilities implies that these agents may evolve new strategies, making it increasingly difficult to detect their actions (Farmer and Skouras 2013).

The problem of monitoring is also inherently one of monitoring a system-of-systems. This is because the capacity to detect market manipulation is affected by the fact that its effects 'in one or more of the constituents may be contained, or may ripple out in a domino-effect chain reaction, analogous to the crowd-psychology of contagion' (Cliff and Northrop 2012, 12). Cross-system monitoring threats may emerge if and when trading agents are deployed with broader actions, operating at a higher level of autonomy across systems, such as by reading from or posting on social media (Wellman and Rajan 2017). These agents may learn how to engineer pump-and-dump schemes, for example, which would be unseeable from a single-system perspective.

8.3.2 Harmful or Dangerous Drugs

Crimes falling under this category include *trafficking, selling, buying,* and *possessing banned drugs* (Archbold 1991, ch. 27). In these cases, AI can be instrumental in supporting the trafficking and sale of banned substances.

Business-to-business trafficking of drugs through AI is a threat due to criminals using unmanned vehicles, which rely on AI planning and autonomous navigation technologies, as instruments for improving the success rates of smuggling. Because smuggling networks are disrupted by monitoring and intercepting transport lines, law enforcement becomes more difficult when unmanned vehicles are used to transport contraband. According to Europol,[8] drones present a horizonal threat in the form of automated drug smuggling. Remote-controlled cocaine-trafficking submarines have already been discovered and seized by US law enforcement (Sharkey, Goodman, and Ross 2010). Unmanned underwater vehicles (UUVs) offer a good example of the dual-use risks of AI, and hence the potential for AIC. UUVs were developed for legitimate uses, such as defence, border protection, and water patrolling. Yet they have also proven effective for illegal activities, posing a significant threat to the enforcement of drug prohibitions, among others. Criminals could presumably avoid implication because UUVs can act independently of an operator (Gogarty and Hagger 2008, 3). There is thus no way to positively ascertain a link with the deployer of the UUVs if the software (and hardware) lacks a bread-crumb trail back to whom obtained it and when, or if the evidence can be destroyed upon the UUV's interception (Sharkey, Goodman, and Ross 2010). Controlling the manufacture of submarines—and hence their traceability—is not unheard of, as illustrated by reports on the discovery of multi-million-dollar manned submarines in the Colombian coastal jungle. But unlike UUVs, manned submarines risk attribution to the crew and the smugglers. In Tampa, Florida, over five hundred cases were successfully brought against smugglers using manned submarines between 2000 and 2016, resulting in a ten-year sentence on average (Marrero 2016). Hence, UUVs present a distinct advantage compared to traditional smuggling approaches.

A related issue concerns the business-to-consumer side of the drug trade. Already, ML algorithms have detected advertisements for opioids sold without prescription on Twitter (Marrero 2016). Because social bots can be used to advertise and sell products, Kerr and Bornfreund (2005, 8) ask whether

> these buddy bots [that is, social bots] could be programmed to send and reply to email or use instant messaging (Floridi and Lord Clement-Jones) to spark one-on-one conversations with hundreds of thousands or even millions of people every day, offering pornography or drugs to children, preying on teens' inherent insecurities to sell them needless products and services.

As the authors outline, the risk is that social bots could exploit the cost-effective scaling of conversational and one-to-one advertising tools to facilitate the sale of illegal drugs.

8.3.3 Offences against the Person

Crimes that fall under offences against the person range from murder to human trafficking (Archbold 1991, ch. 19). So far, it seems that AIC concerns only

---

[8] For a Europol threat assessment of serious and organized crime, see https://www.europol.europa. eu/socta/2017/.

harassment and *torture*. Harassment is intentional and repetitious behaviour that alarms or causes distress to a person. According to past cases, it is constituted by at least two incidents or more against an individual (Archbold 1991, secs. 19–354). Regarding torture, Archbold (1991, ch. 19, secs. 19–435) states that:

> a public official or person acting in an official capacity, whatever his nationality, commits the offence of torture if in the United Kingdom or elsewhere he intentionally inflicts severe pain or suffering on another in the performance or purported performance of his official duties.

When it comes to harassment-based AIC, the literature implicates social bots. A malevolent actor can deploy a social bot as an instrument of direct and indirect harassment. Direct harassment is constituted by spreading hateful messages against the person (Mckelvey and Dubois 2017, 16). Indirect methods may include retweeting or liking negative tweets and skewing polls to give a false impression of wide-scale animosity against a person (McKelvey and Dubois 2017). Additionally, a potential criminal can also subvert another actor's social bot by skewing its learned classification and generation data structures via user-interaction (i.e. conversation).

This is what happened in the case of Microsoft's ill-fated social Twitter bot 'Tay', which quickly learned from user interactions to direct 'obscene and inflammatory tweets' at a feminist activist (Neff and Nagy 2016a). Because such instances of what might be deemed harassment can become entangled with the use of social bots to exercise free speech, jurisprudence must demarcate between the two to resolve ambiguity (McKelvey and Dubois 2017). Some of these activities may comprise harassment in the sense of socially, but not legally, unacceptable behaviour. Other activities may meet a threshold for criminal harassment.

In these cases, liability is proven to be problematic. With Tay, for instance, critics 'derided the decision to release Tay on Twitter, a platform with highly visible problems of harassment' (Neff and Nagy 2016a). Yet users are also to be blamed if 'technologies should be used properly and as they were designed' (Neff and Nagy 2016a). Differing perspectives and opinions on harassment by social bots are inevitable in such cases where the *mens rea* of a crime is (strictly) considered in terms of intention. This is because attribution of intent is a non-agreed function of engineering, application context, human-computer interaction, and perception.

When it comes to torture, the AIC risk becomes plausible if developers integrate AI planning and autonomy capabilities into an interrogation AA. For instance, the US border control has integrated the automated detection of deception into a prototype robotic guard (Nunamaker et al. 2011). The use of AI for interrogation is motivated by its capacity for better detection of deception, human trait emulation (e.g. voice), and affect-modelling to manipulate the subject (McAllister 2016). Yet an AA with these capabilities may also learn to torture a victim (McAllister 2016, 19). For the interrogation subject, the risk is that an AA may be deployed to apply psychological (e.g. mimicking people known to the torture subject) or physical torture techniques. Despite misconceptions, experienced professionals report that torture is generally an ineffective method of information extraction (Janoff-Bulman 2007). Nevertheless, some malicious actors may perceive the use of AI as a way to optimize the balance between suffering and causing the subject to lie or become confused or unresponsive.

All of this may happen independently of human intervention. Such distancing of the perpetrator from the *actus reus* is another reason why torture falls under AIC as a unique threat. Three factors in particular could motivate the use of AAs for torture (McAllister 2016, 19–20). First, the subject of interrogation likely knows that the AA cannot understand pain or experience empathy. It is therefore unlikely to act with mercy and stop the interrogation. Without compassion, the mere presence of an interrogation AA may cause the subject to capitulate out of fear. Under international law, this is possibly—but ambiguously—the crime of (threatening) torture (Solis 2016, 437–85). Second, the deployers of the AA may be able to detach themselves emotionally. Third, the deployer can also detach themselves physically; in other words, they will not be performing the *actus reus* under the current definitions of torture. Due to the result of improvements in efficacy (lack of compassion), deployer motivation (less emotion), and obfuscated liability (physical detachment), it becomes easier to use torture. Similar factors may entice state or private actors to use AAs for interrogation. But banning AI for interrogation (McAllister 2016, 5) may face pushback similar to the one seen with regard to banning autonomous weapons. 'Many consider [banning] to be an unsustainable or impractical solution' (Solis 2016, 451) if AI offers a perceived benefit to the overall protection and safety of a population. The option of limitations on use is thus potentially more likely than a ban.

Liability is a pressing problem in the context of AI-driven torture (McAllister 2016, 24). As for any other form of AIC, an AA cannot itself meet the *mens rea* requirement. This is because an AA simply does not have any intentionality, nor the ability to ascribe meaning to its actions. Given that the computers implementing AAs are syntactic, not semantic, machines (in the sense discussed in the first part of this book), they can perform actions and manipulations without ascribing any meaning to them; meaning remains situated purely in the human operators (Taddeo and Floridi 2005, 2007). As unthinking, mindless systems and a simple reservoir of agency, AAs cannot bear moral responsibility or liability for their actions (although they may be causally accountable for them, as I have already argued in Floridi and Sanders (2004)).

Taking an approach of strict criminal liability, where punishment or damages may be imposed without proof of fault (Floridi 2016a), could offer a way out of the problem. Strict criminal liability would lower the intention-threshold for the crime rather than relying solely on civil liability. But in this respect, McAllister

(2016, 38) argues that strict civil liability is inappropriate owing to the unreasonable degree of foresight required of a designer when an AA learns to torture in unpredictable ways. Developing and deploying such unpredictable, complex, autonomous, AI interrogators means, as Grut stresses, that 'it is even less realistic to expect human operators [or deployers] to exercise significant veto control over their operations' (Grut 2013, 11). Even if control is not an issue, the typical punishment for product fault liability is a fine. This may be neither equitable nor dissuasive given the potential seriousness of any ensuing human rights violations (McAllister 2016). Hence, serious strict-liability AIC would require the development of specific sentencing guidelines to impose punishments fitting the offence even if the offence is not intentional, as is the case with corporate manslaughter where individuals can be given prison sentences.

The question of who, exactly, should face imprisonment for AI-caused offences against the person (as for many uses of AI) is difficult because it is significantly hampered by the 'problem of many hands' (Van de Poel et al. 2012) and distrib-uted responsibility. It is clear that an AA cannot be held liable. Yet the multiplicity of actors creates a problem in ascertaining where liability lies—whether with the person who commissioned and operated the AA, its developers, or the legislators and policymakers who sanctioned (or did not prohibit) real-world deployment of such agents (McAllister 2016, 39). Serious crimes, including both physical and mental harm, that have not been foreseen by legislators might plausibly fall under AIC, with all the associated ambiguity and lack of legal clarity. This motivates the extension or clarification of existing joint liability doctrines.

8.3.4 Sexual Offences

The sexual offences discussed in the literature in relation to AI are: rape (i.e. penetrative sex without consent), sexual assault (i.e. sexual touching without consent), and sexual intercourse or activity with a minor. In the context of rape and sexual assault, non-consent is constituted by two conditions (Archbold 1991, secs. 20–10):

1) there must be an absence of consent from the victim, and
2) the perpetrator must also lack a reasonable belief in consent.

These crimes involve AI when, through advanced human–computer inter-action, the latter promotes sexual objectification or sexualized abuse and violence, and potentially (in a very loose sense) simulates and hence heightens sexual desire for sexual offences. Social bots can support the promotion of sexual offences, and De Angeli points out that verbal abuse and sexual conversations were found to be common elements of anonymous interaction with conversational agents [(De Angeli and Brahnam 2008, Rehm 2008, Veletsianos, Scharber, and Doering 2008)].   (De Angeli 2009, 4)

Simulation of sexual offences is possible with the use of physical sex robots (henceforth sexbots). A sexbot is typically understood to have

(i) a humanoid form; (Friis, Pedersen, and Hendricks) the ability to move; and (Gebru et al.) some degree of artificial intelligence (i.e., some ability to sense, process and respond to signals in its surrounding environment).

(Danaher 2017)

The phenomenon of sexbots has expanded considerably (Döring, Mohseni, and Walter 2020, González-González, Gil-Iranzo, and Paderewski-Rodríguez 2021). Some sexbots are designed to emulate sexual offences, such as adult and child rape (Danaher 2017, 6–7). Surveys suggest that it is common for a person to want to try out sex robots or to have rape fantasies (Danaher 2017), although it is not necessarily common for a person to hold both desires. AI could be used to facilitate representations of sexual offences, to the extent of blurring reality and fantasy through advanced conversational capabilities and potentially physical interaction, although there is no indication of realistic physicality in the near future.

Regarding the possible causal role of over-anthropomorphic AA in desensitizing a perpetrator towards sexual offences (or even heightening the desire to commit them), interaction with social bots and sexbots is the primary concern (De Angeli 2009, 7, Danaher 2017, 27–8). However, as De Angeli (De Angeli 2009) argues, this is a 'disputed critique often addressed towards violent video games (Freier 2008, Whitby 2008)'. We may also assume that, if extreme pornography can encourage sexual offences, then *a fortiori* simulated rape—for example, where a sexbot does not indicate consent or explicitly indicates non-consent—would also pose the same problem. Nevertheless, a meta-meta-study concludes that we must 'discard the hypothesis that pornography contributes to increased sexual assault behaviour' (Ferguson and Hartley 2009). Such uncertainty means that, as Danaher (2017, 27–8) argues, sexbots (and presumably also social bots) may increase, decrease, or indeed have no effect on physical sexual offences that directly harm people. Indirect harms have thus not led to the criminalization of sexbots.[9] So, sexual offences as an area of AIC remain an open question.

---

[9] S. D'Arcy and T. Pugh, 'Surge in paedophiles arrested for importing lifelike child sex dolls.' *The Independent*, 31 July 2017, http://www.independent.co.uk/news/uk/crime/paedophiles-uk-arrests-child-sex-dolls-lifelike-border-officers-aids-silicone-amazon-ebay-online-nca-a7868686.html.

8.3.5 Theft and Fraud, Forgery, and Personation

AIC connects forgery and personation to theft and non-corporate fraud, which carries implications for the use of ML in corporate fraud. Regarding theft and non-corporate fraud, the process has two phases. It begins by using AI to gather personal data and proceeds, then using stolen personal data and other AI methods to forge an identity that convinces banking authorities to make a transaction (that is, involving bank theft and fraud). In the initial phase of the AIC pipeline for theft and fraud, there are three ways for AI techniques to assist in gathering personal data.

The first technique involves using social media bots to target users at large scale and low cost, taking advantage of their capacity to generate posts, mimic people, and subsequently gain trust through friendship requests or 'follows' on sites such as Twitter, LinkedIn, and Facebook (Bilge et al. 2009). When a user accepts a friendship request, a potential criminal gains personal information such as the user's location, telephone number, or relationship history, which are normally only available to that user's accepted friends (Bilge et al. 2009). Many users add so-called friends whom they do not know, which include bots. Unsurprisingly, such privacy-compromising attacks have a high success rate. Past experiments with a social bot exploited 30–40 per cent of users in general (Bilge et al. 2009) and 60 per cent of users who shared a mutual friend with the bot (Boshmaf et al. 2013). Identity-cloning bots have succeeded, on average, in having 56 per cent of their friendship requests accepted on LinkedIn (Bilge et al. 2009). Such identity cloning may raise suspicion due to a user appearing to have multiple accounts on the same site (one real and one forged by a third party). Hence, cloning an identity from one social network to another circumvents these suspicions. In the face of inadequate monitoring, such cross-site identity cloning is an effective tactic (Bilge et al. 2009), as discussed above.

The second technique to gather personal data, which is compatible with (and may even build on) the trust gained via befriending social media users, makes partial use of conversational social bots for social engineering (Alazab and Broadhurst 2016, 12). This occurs when AI 'attempts to manipulate behaviour by building rapport with a victim, then exploiting that emerging relationship to obtain information from or access to their computer' (Chantler and Broadhurst 2008, 65). Although the literature seems to support the efficacy of such bot-based social-engineering, given the currently limited capabilities of conversational AI, scepticism is justified when it comes to automated manipulation on an individual and long-term basis.

Still, as a short-term solution, a criminal may cast a deceptive social-bot net widely enough to discover susceptible individuals. Initial AI-based manipulation may gather harvested personal data and reuse it to produce 'more intense cases of simulated familiarity, empathy, and intimacy, leading to greater data revelations' (Graeff 2013a, 5). After gaining initial trust, familiarity, and personal data from a user, the criminal may move the conversation to another context, such as private messaging, where the user assumes that privacy norms are upheld (Graeff 2013b). Crucially, from here, overcoming the conversational deficiencies of AI to engage with the user is feasible using a cyborg; that is, a bot-assisted human (or vice versa) (Chu et al. 2010). Hence, a criminal may make judicious use of the otherwise limited conversational capabilities of AI as a plausible means to gather personal data.

The third technique for gathering personal data from users is automated phishing. Ordinarily, phishing is unsuccessful if the criminal does not sufficiently personalize the messages towards the targeted user. Target-specific and personalized phishing attacks (known as spear phishing), which have been shown to be four times more successful than a generic approach (Jagatic et al. 2007), are labour intensive. However, cost-effective spear phishing is possible using automation (Bilge et al. 2009). Researchers have demonstrated its feasibility through the use of ML techniques to craft messages personalized to a specific user (Seymour and Tully 2016).

In the second phase of AI-supported banking fraud, AI may support the forging of an identity, including via recent advances in voice synthesis technologies (Bendel 2019). Using the classification and generation capabilities of ML, Adobe's software can learn adversarially and reproduce someone's personal and individual speech pattern from a twenty-minute recording of the replicatee's voice. Bendel argues that AI-supported voice synthesis raises a unique threat in theft and fraud, which

> could use VoCo and Co [Adobe's voice editing and generation software] for biometric security processes and unlock doors, safes, vehicles, and so on, and enter or use them. With the voice of the customer, they [criminals] could talk to the customer's bank or other institutions to gather sensitive data or to make critical or damaging transactions. All kinds of speech-based security systems could be hacked. (Bendel 2019, 3)

For years now, credit card fraud has been predominantly an online offence[10] that occurs when 'the credit card is used remotely; only the credit card details are needed' (Delamaire, Abdou, and Pointon 2009, 65). Because credit card fraud typically requires neither physical interaction nor embodiment, AI may drive fraud by providing voice synthesis or helping to gather sufficient personal details.

---

[10] Office for National Statistics, 'Crime in England and Wales, Year Ending June 2016. Appendix Tables no. June 2017: 1–60'. https://www.ons.gov.uk/peoplepopulationandcommunity/crimeandjustice/adhocs/006256estimatesofexperiencesandperceptionsofantisocialbehaviourinenglandcrimesurveyenglandandwalescsewyearendingjune2016andselectedyearsfromtheyearendingdecember1996

In the case of corporate fraud, AI used for detection may also make fraud easier to commit. Specifically,

> when the executives who are involved in financial fraud are well aware of the fraud detection techniques and software, which are usually public information and are easy to obtain, they are likely to adapt the methods in which they commit fraud and make it difficult to detect the same, especially by existing techniques.   (Zhou and Kapoor 2011, 571)

More than identifying a specific case of AIC, this use of AI highlights the risks of over-reliance on AI for detecting fraud, which may actually aid fraudsters. These thefts and frauds concern real-world money. A virtual world threat is whether social bots may commit crimes in massively multiplayer online game (MMOG) contexts. The online games often have complex economies where the supply of in-game items is artificially restricted and where intangible in-game goods can have real-world value if players are willing to pay for them. In some cases, items cost in excess of US$1000 (Chen et al. 2004, 1). So it is not surprising that, from a random sample of 613 criminal prosecutions of online game crimes in Taiwan in 2002, virtual property thieves exploited users' compromised credentials 147 times and stole identities 52 times (Chen et al. 2005). Such crimes are analogous to the use of social bots to manage theft and fraud at a large scale on social media sites. The question is whether AI may become implicated in this virtual crime space.

8.4 Possible Solutions

Having outlined and discussed the potential for AIC, the time has come to analyse the solutions that are currently available. This is the task of the present section.

8.4.1 Tackling Emergence

There are several legal and technological solutions that can be considered to address the issue of emergent behaviour. Legal solutions may involve limiting agents' autonomy or their deployment. For example, Germany has created deregulated contexts where the testing of self-driving cars is permitted, if the vehicles remain below an unacceptable level of autonomy, 'to collect empirical data and sufficient knowledge to make rational decisions for a number of critical issues' (Pagallo 2017, 7). The solution is that, if legislation does not prohibit higher levels of autonomy for a given AA, the law obliges coupling this liberty with technological remedies to prevent emergent criminal acts or omissions once deployed in the wild.

One possibility is requiring developers to deploy AAs only when they have runtime legal compliance layers. These layers take the declarative specifications of legal rules and impose constraints on the runtime behaviour of AAs. Whilst still the focus of ongoing research, approaches to runtime legal compliance include architectures for trimming non-compliant AA plans (Meneguzzi and Luck 2009, Vanderelst and Winfield 2018a) and provably correct temporal logic-based formal frameworks that select, trim, or generate AA plans for norm compliance (Van Riemsdijk et al. 2013, Van Riemsdijk et al. 2015, Dennis et al. 2016). In a MAS setting, AIC can emerge from collective behaviour. So MAS-level compliance layers may modify an individual AA's plans to prevent wrongful collective actions (Uszok et al. 2003, Bradshaw et al. 1997, Tonti et al. 2003). Essentially, such technical solutions propose regimenting compliance—making non-compliance impossible, at least to the extent that any formal proof is applicable to real-world settings—with predefined legal rules within a single AA or a MAS (Andrighetto et al. 2013, 4:105).

But the shift in these approaches from mere regulation (which leaves deviation from the norm physically possible) to regimentation may not be desirable when considering the impact on democracy and the legal system. These approaches implement Lessig's *code-as-law* concept (Lessig 1999), which considers 'software code as a regulator in and of itself by saying that the architecture it produces can serve as an instrument of social control on those that use it' (Graeff 2013a, 4). However, Hildebrandt (2008, 175) rightly objects:

> while computer code generates a kind of normativity similar to law, it lacks—precisely because it is NOT law...the possibility of contesting its application in a court of law. This is a major deficit in the relationship between law, technology and democracy.

If code-as-law entails a democratic and legal contestation deficit, then *a fortiori* addressing emergent AIC with a legal reasoning layer comprised of normative but incontestable code (as compared to the contestable law from which it derives) bears the same problems.

Social simulation can address an orthogonal problem whereby an AA owner may choose to operate outside of the law and any such legal reasoning layer requirements (Vanderelst and Winfield 2018b, 4). The basic idea is to use simulation as a test bed before deploying AAs in the wild. In a market context, for example, regulators would

> act as "certification authorities", running new trading algorithms in the system-simulator to assess their likely impact on overall systemic behavior before allowing the owner/developer of the algorithm to run it "live".
>
> (Cliff and Northrop 2012, 19)

Private corporations could fund such extensive social simulations as a common good and as a replacement for (or in addition to) proprietary safety measures (Cliff and Northrop 2012, 21). But a social simulation is a model of an inherently chaotic system, which makes it a poor tool for specific predictions (Edmonds and Gershenson 2015, 12). Still, the idea may nonetheless succeed as it focuses on detecting the strictly qualitative *possibility* of previously unforeseen and emergent events in a MAS (Edmonds and Gershenson 2015, 13).

8.4.2 Addressing Liability

Although liability is an extensive topic, four models are frequently discussed in relation with AIC (Hallevy 2011, 13): direct liability, perpetration-by-another, command responsibility, and natural-probable-consequence.

The *direct liability* model ascribes the factual and mental elements to an AA, representing a dramatic shift away from the anthropocentric view of AAs as tools to AAs as (potentially equal) decision-makers (van Lier 2016). Some argue for holding an AA directly liable because 'the process of analysis in AI systems parallels that of human understanding' (Hallevy 2011, 15). We understand the author to mean that, as Dennett (1987) argues, for practical purposes we may treat any agent *as if* it possesses mental states. However, a fundamental limitation of this model is that AAs do not have (separate) legal personality and agency. We thus cannot hold an AA legally liable in its own capacity regardless of whether this is desirable in practice. Similarly, it has been noted that AAs cannot contest a guilty verdict; 'if a subject cannot take the stand in a court of law it cannot contest the incrimination, which would turn the punishment into discipline' (Hildebrandt 2008, 178). Moreover, AAs cannot legally meet the mental element. This means the 'common legal standpoint excludes robots from any kind of criminal responsibility because they lack psychological components such as intentions or consciousness' (Pagallo 2011, 349).

The lack of actual mental states becomes clear when considering how an AA's understanding of a symbol (that is, a concept) is limited to its grounding on further syntactic symbols (Taddeo and Floridi 2005, 2007). This leaves the *mens rea* in limbo. Lack of a guilty mind does not prevent the mental state from being imputed to the AA. In the same way, a corporation could have the mental state of its employees imputed to it and hence be found liable as an organization. But the liability of an AA would still require it to have legal personality. A further problem is that holding an AA solely liable may prove unacceptable, since it would lead to a deresponsabilization of the human agents behind an AA (e.g. an engineer, a user, or a corporation). This would likely weaken the dissuasive power of criminal law.

To ensure that criminal law is effective, we may shift the burden of liabilities onto the humans—and corporate or other legal agents—who made a (criminally bad) difference to the system. These human agents could be various engineers, users, vendors, and so forth. If the design is poor and the outcome faulty, then all of the human agents involved are deemed responsible (Floridi 2016a). The next two models discussed in the literature move in this direction, focusing on the liability of human or other legal persons involved in producing and using the AA.

The *perpetration-by-another* model (Hallevy 2011, 4), which uses intention as the standard for *mens rea*, frames the AA as an instrument of crime whereby 'the party orchestrating the offence (the perpetrator-by-another) is the real perpetrator'. Perpetration-by-another leaves 'three human candidates for responsibility before a criminal court: programmers, manufacturers, and users of robots [AAs]' (Pagallo 2017, 21). Clarifying intent is crucial to applying perpetration-by-another. Concerning social media, 'developers who knowingly create social bots to engage in unethical actions are clearly culpable' (de Lima Salge and Berente 2017, 30). For further clarity, Arkin (2008) argues that designers and programmers should be required to ensure that AAs refuse a criminal order, a command that only the deployer can explicitly override. This would remove ambiguity from intent and therefore liability (Arkin and Ulam 2012). To be liable, then, the deployer of an AA must intend the harm by overriding the AA's default position of 'can but will not do harm'. Together with technological controls and viewing an AA as a mere instrument of AIC, perpetration-by-another addresses those cases when a deployer intends to use an AA to commit an AIC.

The *command responsibility* model, which uses knowledge as the standard of *mens rea*, ascribes liability to any military officer who knew (or should have known) about crimes committed by their forces but failed to take reasonable steps to prevent them; in the future, this could include AAs (McAllister 2016). Command responsibility is compatible (or may even be seen as an instance of) perpetration-by-another for use in contexts where there is a chain of command, such as within the military and police forces. This model is normally clear on how 'liability should be distributed among the commanders to the officers in charge of interrogation to the designers of the system' (McAllister 2016, 39). However, 'issues on the undulating waves of increasing complexity in programming, robo-human relationships, and integration into hierarchical structures, call into question these theories' sustainability' (McAllister 2016, 39).

The *natural-probable-consequence* liability model uses negligence or recklessness as the standard for *mens rea*. This model addresses AIC cases where an AA developer and user neither intend nor have a priori knowledge of an offence (Hallevy 2011). Liability is ascribed to the developer or user if the harm is a natural and probable consequence of their conduct and if they recklessly or negligently exposed others to the risk (Hallevy 2011), such as in cases of AI-caused emergent market manipulation (Wellman and Rajan 2017).

Natural-probable-consequence and command responsibility are not new concepts. They are both analogous to the *respondent superior* principle entailed by rules as old as Roman law, according to which the owner of an enslaved person was responsible for any damage caused by that person (Floridi 2017c). However, it might not always be obvious

> which programmer was responsible for a particular line of code, or indeed the extent to which the resulting programme was the result of the initial code or the subsequent development of that code by the ML system.   (Williams 2017, 41)

Such ambiguity means that, when emergent AIC is a possibility, some suggest AAs should be banned 'to address matters of control, security, and accountability' (Joh 2016, 18). This would at least make liability for violating such a ban clear. Still, others argue that a possible ban in view of the risk of emerging AIC should be balanced carefully against the risk of hindering innovation; it will therefore be crucial to provide a suitable definition of the standard of negligence (Gless, Silverman, and Weigend 2016). Such a definition would ensure that an all-out ban is not considered to be the only solution, given that it would end up dissuading the design of AAs that compare favourably to people in terms of safety.

8.4.3 Checking the Monitoring

There are four main mechanisms for addressing AIC monitoring. The first is to devise AIC predictors using domain knowledge. This would overcome the limitation of more generic ML classification methods, that is, where the features used for detection can also be used for evasion. Predictors specific to financial fraud can consider institutional properties (Zhou and Kapoor 2011), such as objectives (e.g. whether the benefits outweigh the costs), structure (e.g. a lack of an auditing committee), and the (lack of) moral values in management. But the authors do not say which, if any, of these values are actually predictive. Predictors for identity theft, such as profile cloning, have involved prompting users to consider whether the location of the 'friend' who is messaging them meets their expectation (Bilge et al. 2009).

The second mechanism uses social simulation to discover crime patterns (Wellman and Rajan 2017). Pattern discovery must contend with the sometimes-limited capacity to bind offline identities to online activities. In markets, for example, it takes significant effort to correlate multiple orders with a single legal entity; consequently, 'manipulative algo[rithm]s may be impossible to detect in practice' (Farmer and Skouras 2013, 17). Furthermore, on social media, 'an adversary controls multiple online identities and joins a targeted system under these identities in order to subvert a particular service' (Boshmaf et al. 2012, 4).

The third mechanism addresses traceability by leaving telltale clues in the components that make up AIC instruments. Examples could include physical traces left by manufacturers in AA hardware, such as UUVs used to traffic drugs, or fingerprinting in third-party AI software (Sharkey, Goodman, and Ross 2010). Adobe's voice replication software takes this approach as it places a watermark in the generated audio (Bendel 2019). However, lack of knowledge and control over who develops AI instrument components (used for AIC) limits traceability via watermarking and similar techniques.

The fourth mechanism aims at cross-system monitoring and utilizes self-organization across systems (van Lier 2016). The idea first originated in Luhmann and Bednarz (1995). It begins with the conceptualization (Floridi 2008a) of one system (e.g. a social media site) taking on the role of a moral agent, and a second system (e.g. a market) taking the role of the moral patient.[11] A moral patient is any receiver of moral actions (Floridi 2012b). The conceptualization chosen by (van Lier 2016) determines that the following are all systems: at the lowest atomic level, an artificial or human agent; at a higher level, any MAS such as a social media platform, markets, and so on; and, generalizing further, any system-of-systems. Hence, any such human, artificial, or mixed system can qualify as a moral patient or a moral agent.

Whether an agent is indeed a moral one hinges on whether the agent can undertake actions that are morally qualifiable, not on whether the moral agent can or should be held morally responsible for those actions(Floridi 2012b). Adopting this moral agent and moral patient distinction, van Lier proposes a process for monitoring and addressing crimes and effects that traverse systems. The process involves four steps that we describe generically and exemplify specifically: *information-selection* of the moral agent's internal actions for relevance to the moral patient (e.g. social media posts by users); *utterance* of the selected information from the moral agent to the moral patient (e.g. notifying a financial market of social media posts); *assessment* by the moral patient of the normativity of the uttered actions (e.g. whether social media posts are part of a pump-and-dump scheme); and *feedback* given by the moral patient to the moral agent (e.g. notifying a social media site that a user is conducting a pump-and-dump scheme, after which the social media site should act).

This final step completes a 'feedback loop [that] can create a cycle of machine learning in which moral elements are simultaneously included' (van Lier 2016, 11). For example, this could involve a social media site learning and adjusting to the normativity of its behaviour from the perspective of a market. A similar self-organization process could be used to address other AIC areas. Creating a

---

[11] The adjective 'moral' is taken from the cited work, which considers unethical behaviour as constituting the act of crossing system boundaries. Here, the focus is on criminal acts or omissions that may have a negative, neutral, or positive ethical evaluation. The use of 'moral' is to avoid misrepresenting the cited work, not to imply that the criminal law coincides with ethics.

profile on Twitter (the moral agent) could have relevance to Facebook (the moral patient) concerning identity theft (information selection). After notifying Facebook of newly created Twitter profile details (utterance), Facebook could determine whether the new profile constitutes identity theft by asking the relevant user (understanding) and notifying Twitter to take appropriate action (feedback).

8.4.4 Dealing with the Psychology

There are two main concerns about the psychological element of AIC: manipulation of users and (in the case of anthropomorphic AI) the creation of a desire to commit a crime in a user. Currently, researchers have elaborated on solutions only for the latter but not for the former.

If anthropomorphic AAs are a problem, there may be two approaches to solving it. One approach is to ban or restrict anthropomorphic AAs that make it possible to simulate crime. This position leads to a call for restricting anthropomorphic AAs in general, because they 'are precisely the sort of robots [AAs] that are most likely to be abused' (Whitby 2008, 6). Cases whereby social bots are

> designed, intentionally or not, with a gender in mind…[the] attractiveness and realism of female agents [raise the question: do] ECA's [that is, social bots] encourage gender stereotypes [and how] will this impact on real women on-line?
> (De Angeli 2009)

The suggestion is to make it unacceptable for social bots to emulate anthropomorphic properties, such as having a perceived gender or ethnicity. Concerning sexbots that emulate sexual offences, a further suggestion is to enact a ban as a 'package of laws that help to improve social sexual morality' and make norms of intolerance clear (Danaher 2017, 29–30).

A second suggestion, one that is incompatible with the first, is to use anthropomorphic AAs to push back against simulated sexual offences. Concerning the abuse of artificial pedagogical agents, for example, 'we recommend that agent responses should be programmed to prevent or curtail further student abuse' (Veletsianos, Scharber, and Doering 2008, 8). Darling (2015, 14) argues that this would not only 'combat desensitisation and negative externalities from people's behavior, it would preserve the therapeutic and educational advantages of using certain robots more like companions than tools'.

Implementing these suggestions requires choosing whether to criminalize the demand or supply side of the transaction, or both. Users may be within the scope of application for punishments. At the same time, one could argue that as with other crimes involving personal 'vice', suppliers and distributors could also be targeted on the grounds that they facilitate and encourage the wrongful acts. Indeed, we might exclusively or preferentially target them, as is now done for illicit drugs in many countries.   (Danaher 2017, 33)

8.5 Future Developments

There is still much uncertainty over what we already know about AIC in terms of area-specific threats, general threats, and solutions. AIC research is still in its infancy but, given the preceding analysis, it is possible to outline five dimensions of future AIC research.

8.5.1 Areas of AIC

Understanding areas of AIC better requires extending current knowledge, particularly knowledge about the use of AI in interrogation, theft, and fraud in virtual spaces (e.g. online games with intangible assets that hold real-world value); and AAs committing emergent market manipulation, which research seems to have only studied in experimental simulations. Social engineering attacks are a plausible concern but, for the time being, there is still insufficient evidence of real-world cases. Homicide and terrorism appear to be notably absent from the AIC literature, though they demand attention in view of AI-fuelled technologies such as pattern recognition (e.g. for identifying and manipulating potential perpetrators, or when members of vulnerable groups are unfairly targeted as suspects), weaponized drones, and self-driving vehicles—all of which may have both lawful and criminal uses.

8.5.2 Dual-Use

The digital nature of AI facilitates its dual-use (Moor 1985, Floridi 2010a). This means it is feasible that applications designed for legitimate uses could be implemented to commit criminal offences (I shall return to this point in Chapter 12, when discussing deepfakes and fake news). This is the case for UUVs, for example. The further that AI is developed and the more that its implementations become pervasive, the higher the risk of malicious or criminal uses. Left unaddressed, these risks may lead to societal rejection and excessively strict regulation of AI-based technologies. Technological benefits to individuals and societies may be eroded in turn, as the use and development of AI is increasingly constrained.

Such limits have already been placed on ML research in visual discriminators of homosexual and heterosexual men (Wang and Kosinski 2018), which was considered too dangerous to release in full (i.e. with the source code and learned data structures) to the wider research community—a limitation that came at the expense of scientific reproducibility. Even when such costly limitations on AI releases are unnecessary, as Adobe demonstrated by embedding watermarks into voice-reproducing technology, external and malevolent developers may nevertheless reproduce the technology in the future. More research is needed to anticipate the dual-use of AI beyond general techniques and the efficacy of policies for restricting the release of AI technologies. This is especially true with the implementation of AI for cybersecurity.

8.5.3 Security

The literature on AIC shows that, within the cybersecurity sphere, AI is taking on a malevolent and offensive role. This role is unfolding in tandem with the development and deployment of defensive AI systems to enhance their resilience in enduring attacks and robustness in averting attacks, along with countering threats as they emerge (Yang et al. 2018). The 2016 DARPA Cyber Grand Challenge was a tipping point for demonstrating the effectiveness of a combined offensive-defensive AI approach. There, seven AI systems were shown to be capable of identifying and patching their own vulnerabilities while also probing and exploiting those of competing systems. In 2018, IBM launched the Cognitive Security Operations Center. This was the application of an ML algorithm that uses an organization's structured and unstructured security data, 'including imprecise human language contained in blogs, articles, reports', to elaborate information about security topics and threats with the goal of improving threat identification, mitigation, and responses.

While policies will obviously play a key role in mitigating and remedying the risks of dual-use after deployment (by defining oversight mechanisms, for instance), these risks are properly addressed at the design stage. Recent reports on malicious AI, such as that by Brundage et al. (2018), suggest how 'one of our best hopes to defend against automated hacking is also via AI'. On the contrary, the analysis developed in this chapter indicates that over-reliance on AI can be counter-productive, too. All of this emphasizes the need for further research not only on AI in cybersecurity, but also on alternatives to AI such as individual and social factors.

8.5.4 Persons

The current debate raises the possibility of psychological factors, like trust, in the criminal role of AI. But research is still lacking on the personal factors that may create perpetrators, such as programmers and users of AI for AIC, in the future.

Now is the time to invest in longitudinal studies and multivariate analyses spanning the educational, geographical, and cultural backgrounds of both victims and perpetrators or even benevolent AI developers. This will help predict how individuals come together to commit AIC. It can also help understand the efficacy of ethics courses in computer science programmes, and the capacity to educate users to be less trustful of potentially AI-driven agents in cyberspace.

8.5.5 Organizations

Already in 2017, Europol's four-year report on the serious and organized crime threat highlighted how the type of technological crime tends to correlate with particular criminal organization topologies. The literature on AIC indicates that AI may play a role in criminal organizations such as drug cartels, which are well resourced and highly organized. Conversely, ad hoc criminal organization on the dark web already takes place under what Europol refers to as *crime-as-a-service*. Such criminal services are sold directly between buyer and seller, potentially as a smaller element in an overall crime, which AI may fuel (e.g. by enabling profile hacking) in the future.[12] On a spectrum ranging from tightly knit to fluid AIC organizations, there exist many possibilities for criminal interaction. Identifying the organizations that are essential or that seem to correlate with different types of AIC will further our understanding of how AIC is structured and operates in practice. Developing our understanding of these four dimensions is essential if we are to successfully track and disrupt the inevitable future growth of AIC. Hopefully, King et al. (2019) and this chapter will spark further research into very serious, growing, yet still relatively unexplored concerns over AIC. The sooner we understand this new crime phenomenon, the earlier we shall be able to put into place preventive, mitigating, disincentivizing, and redressing policies.

8.6 Conclusion: From Evil Uses of AI to Socially Good AI

This chapter provided a systematic analysis of AIC to understand the fundamentally unique and feasible threats that it poses. It addressed this topic based on the classic counterfactual definition of AI discussed in Chapter 1 and in view of the

---

[12] To this end, a cursory search for 'Artificial Intelligence' on prominent dark web markets returned a negative result. Specifically, while developing the analysis presented in King et al. (2019), we checked: 'Dream Market', 'Silk Road 3.1', and 'Wallstreet Market'. The negative result is not indicative of AIC-as-a-service's absence on the dark web, which may exist under a different guise or on more specialized markets. For example, some services offer to extract personal information from a user's computer. Even if such services are genuine, the underlying technology (e.g. AI-fuelled pattern recognition) remains unknown.

hypothesis that AI introduces a new form of agency (not intelligence). In the chapter, I have focused on AI as a reservoir of autonomous smart agency, as presented in the first part of the book, and on the ultimate human responsibility for leveraging such artificial agency unethically and illegally. I described the threats area by area in terms of specifically defined crimes, as well as more generally in terms of AI qualities and the issues of emergence, liability, monitoring, and psychology. I then analysed which solutions are available or devisable to deal with AIC. I approached this topic by focusing on both general and cross-cutting themes, providing an up-to-date picture of the available societal, technological, and legal solutions along with their limitations. This concludes the analysis of criminal, or 'evil', uses of AI. We can now turn to something much more positive and constructive: the socially good uses of AI, which is the topic of the next chapter.

9

Good Practices

The Proper Use of AI for Social Good

9.0 Summary

Previously, in Chapter 8, I reviewed the main issues concerning the illegal use of AI or what may be called AI for social evil. This chapter focuses on AI for social good (AI4SG). AI4SG is gaining traction within information societies in general and the AI community in particular. It has the potential to tackle social problems through the development of AI-based solutions. Yet to date, there is only limited understanding of what makes AI socially good in theory, what counts as AI4SG in practice, and how to reproduce its initial successes in terms of policies. This chapter addresses the gap in understanding by first offering a definition of AI4SG, then identifying seven ethical factors that are essential for future AI4SG initiatives. The analysis is supported by some case examples of AI4SG projects, a topic to which I shall return in Chapter 12, when discussing the use of AI to support the United Nation SDGs. Some of the factors discussed in this chapter are almost entirely novel to AI, while the significance of other factors is heightened by the use of AI. Finally, the chapter formulates corresponding best practices from each of these factors. Subject to context and balance, these practices may serve as preliminary guidelines to ensure that well-designed AI is more likely to serve the social good. The chapter does not offer specific recommendations, which are left to Chapter 10.

9.1 Introduction: The Idea of AI for Social Good

The idea of AI4SG is becoming popular in many information societies and gaining traction within the AI community (Hager et al. 2019). Projects seeking to use AI4SG vary significantly. They range from models to predict septic shock (Henry et al. 2015) to game-theoretic models to prevent poaching (Fang et al. 2016); from online reinforcement learning to target HIV education at homeless youths (Yadav, Chan, Xin Jiang, et al. 2016) to probabilistic models to prevent harmful policing (Carton et al. 2016) and support student retention (Lakkaraju et al. 2015). Indeed, new applications of AI4SG appear almost daily, making possible and facilitating

The Ethics of Artificial Intelligence: Principles, Challenges, and Opportunities. Luciano Floridi, Oxford University Press.
© Luciano Floridi 2023. DOI: 10.1093/oso/9780198883098.003.0009

the attainment of socially good outcomes that were previously unfeasible, unaffordable, or simply less achievable in terms of efficiency and effectiveness.

AI4SG also offers unprecedented opportunities across many domains. These could be of great significance at a time when problems are increasingly global, complex, and interconnected. For example, AI can provide some much-needed support to improve health outcomes and mitigate environmental risks (Wang et al. 2016, Davenport and Kalakota 2019, Puaschunder 2020, Rolnick et al. 2019, Luccioni et al. 2021, Zhou et al. 2020). This is also a matter of synergy: AI4SG builds on and augments other recent examples of digital technologies adopted to advance socially beneficial objectives, such as 'big data for development' (Hilbert 2016, Taylor and Schroeder 2015). As a result, AI4SG is gaining much traction within both the AI community and policymaking circles.

Perhaps because of its novelty and fast growth, AI4SG is still poorly understood as a global phenomenon and lacks a cogent framework for assessing the value and the success of relevant projects. Existing metrics, like profitability or commercial productivity, are clearly indicative of real-world demand, but they remain inadequate. AI4SG needs to be assessed against socially valuable outcomes, much like it happens for 'B Corporation' certification in the for-profit context, or for social enterprises operating in the non-profit sector. AI4SG should be assessed by adopting human and environmental welfare metrics as opposed to financial ones.

Frameworks for the design, development, and deployment of 'ethical AI' in general have recently emerged (see Chapter 4) to offer some guidance in this respect. However, the ethical and social guardrails around AI applications that are explicitly geared towards socially good outcomes are only partially defined. This is because, to date, there is limited understanding of what constitutes AI4SG (Taddeo and Floridi 2018a, Vinuesa et al. 2020, Chui et al. 2018) and what would be a reliable benchmark to assess its success. The best efforts, especially the annual International Telecommunication Union (ITU) Summit on AI for Good and its associated project database ('AI for Good Global Summit' 2019;[1] 'AI Repository' 2018[2]), focus on collecting information about, and describing occurrences of, AI4SG. Still, they disregard normative approaches to this phenomenon and are not meant to offer a systematic analysis.

In this and the following chapter, I intend to fill the gap by formalizing a definition of AI4SG initiatives and the factors that characterize them. In Chapter 12, I shall return to this point to argue that the United Nations' seventeen SDGs provide a valid framework to benchmark socially good uses of AI technologies.

---

[1] AI for Good Global Summit, 28–31 May 2019, Geneva, Switzerland. 'AI for Good Global Summit', https://aiforgood.itu.int/.

[2] AI Repository, https://www.itu.int/en/ITU-T/AI/Pages/ai-repository.aspx.

That chapter supports the analysis provided here, introducing a database of AI4SG projects gathered using this benchmark, and discussing several key insights (including the extent to which different SDGs are being addressed). I shall postpone these tasks to the end of the book because the use of AI in support of the UN SDGs provides a valuable conclusion and way forward regarding the future, ethical development of AI.

The ad hoc approach to AI4SG, which has involved analysing specific areas of application (e.g. famine relief or disaster management) at annual summits for AI industry and government,[3] indicates the presence of a phenomenon. But it neither explains it nor suggests how other AI4SG solutions could and should be designed to harness the full potential of AI. Furthermore, many projects that generate socially good outcomes using AI are not (self-)described as such (Moore 2019). These shortcomings raise at least two main risks: *unanticipated failures* and *missed opportunities*.

First, consider unanticipated failures. Like any other technology, AI solutions are shaped by human values. If not carefully selected and fostered, such values may lead to 'good AI gone awry' scenarios. AI may 'do more harm than good' by amplifying rather than mitigating societal ills. For example, it could widen rather than narrow existing inequities, or exacerbate environmental problems. AI may also simply fail to serve the social good, such as with the failure of IBM's oncology-support software that attempted to use ML to identify cancerous tumours. The system was trained using synthetic data and US medical protocols, which are not applicable worldwide. As a result, it struggled to interpret ambiguous, nuanced, or otherwise 'messy' patient health records (Strickland 2019), providing misdiagnoses and suggesting erroneous treatment. This led medical practitioners and hospitals to reject the system (Ross and Swetlitz 2017).

Next, consider missed opportunities. AI outcomes that are genuinely socially good may arise from mere accident, such as through the fortuitous application of an AI solution in a different context. This was the case with the use of a different version of IBM's cognitive system just discussed. In this case, the Watson system was originally designed to identify biological mechanisms. But when used in a classroom setting, it inspired engineering students to solve design problems (Goel et al. 2015). In this positive instance, AI provided a unique mode of education. But the absence of a clear understanding of AI4SG meant that this success was 'accidental', which means it may not be possible to repeat it systematically or at scale. For each 'accidental success', there may be countless examples of missed opportunities to exploit the benefits of AI for advancing socially good outcomes

---

[3] ITU (2017). AI for Good Global Summit 2017. https://www.itu.int/en/ITU-T/AI/Pages/201706-default.aspx; ITU (2018). AI for Good Global Summit 2018. https://www.itu.int/en/ITU-T/AI/2018/Pages/default.aspx; AI for Good Global Summit (2019), 28–31 May 2019, Geneva, Switzerland. AI for Good Global Summit. Accessed 12 April 2019. https://aiforgood.itu.int/.

in different settings. This is especially true when AI-based interventions are developed separately from those who will be most directly subject to their effects, whether defined in terms of area (e.g. residents of a particular region) or domain (e.g. teachers or medical practitioners).

To avoid unnecessary failures and missed opportunities, AI4SG would benefit from an analysis of the essential factors supporting and underwriting the design and deployment of successful AI4SG. This chapter analyses these factors. The goal is not to document every single ethical consideration for an AI4SG project. For example, it is essential, and hopefully self-evident, that an AI4SG project ought not to advance the proliferation of weapons of mass destruction.[4] Likewise, it is important to acknowledge at the outset that there are many circumstances in which AI will *not* be the most effective way to address a particular social problem (Abebe et al. 2020) and would be an unwarranted intervention. This could be due to either the existence of alternative approaches that are less expensive or more efficacious (i.e. '*Not* AI for Social Good') or the unacceptable risks that the deployment of AI would introduce (i.e. 'AI for *Insufficient* Social Good' as weighed against its risks).

This is why use of the term 'good' to describe such efforts has itself been criticized (Green 2019). Indeed, AI is not a 'silver bullet'. It should not be treated as a single-handed solution to an entrenched social problem. In other words, '*Only* AI for Social Good' is unlikely to work. What is essential about the factors and the corresponding best practices is not their incorporation in every circumstance; I shall note several examples where it would be morally defensible not to incorporate a particular factor. Instead, what is essential is that each best practice is (i) considered proactively, and *not* incorporated *if and only if* there is a clear, demonstrable, and morally defensible reason why it should not be.

Following these clarifications, in this chapter I shall focus on identifying factors that are *particularly relevant* to AI as a technological infrastructure (to the extent that it is designed and used for the *advancement of social good*). To anticipate, they are:

1) falsifiability and incremental deployment,
2) safeguards against the manipulation of predictors,
3) receiver-contextualized intervention,
4) receiver-contextualized explanation and transparent purposes,
5) privacy protection and data subject consent,
6) situational fairness, and
7) human-friendly semanticization.

---

[4] This is an imperative that I do not discuss here, but see Taddeo and Floridi (2018b).

With these factors identified, the questions that are likely to arise in turn are: *how* these factors ought to be evaluated and resolved, *by whom*, and with *what supporting mechanism*, for example through regulation or codes of conduct. These questions are not within the scope of this chapter (see Chapters 4–5 and 10). They are intertwined with wider ethical and political issues regarding the legitimacy of decision making with and about AI.

The rest of this chapter is structured as follows. Section 9.2 explains how the seven factors have been identified. Section 9.3 analyses the seven factors individually. I elucidate each of them through references to one or more case studies, then derive from each factor a corresponding best practice for AI4SG creators to follow. The concluding section discusses the factors and suggests how tensions between them may be resolved.

9.2 A Definition of AI4SG

A successful way to identify and evaluate AI4SG projects is to analyse them based on their outcomes. An AI4SG project is successful insofar as it helps to reduce, mitigate, or eradicate a given social or environmental problem without introducing new harms or amplifying existing ones. This interpretation suggests the following definition of AI4SG (all the 'or's below are the inclusive 'and/or'):

AI4SG $=_{\text{def.}}$ the design, development, and deployment of AI systems in ways that (i) prevent, mitigate, or resolve problems adversely affecting human life and/or the well-being of the natural world, and/or enable socially preferable and/or environmentally sustainable developments.[5]

As I anticipated, I shall return to this definition in Chapter 12 to identify problems deemed to have a negative impact on human life or the well-being of the environment. Like other researchers before (Vinuesa et al. 2020), I shall do so by using the UN's seventeen SDGs as an assessment benchmark. Here, I rely on the previous definition to analyse the essential factors that qualify successful AI4SG projects.

Following the definition of AI4SG, we analysed a set of twenty-seven projects (Floridi et al. 2020). The projects were obtained via a systematic review of relevant literature to identify clear, significant cases of successful and unsuccessful examples of AI4SG. The reader interested in the details is invited to check the article. Of the twenty-seven cases, seven (see Table 9.1) were selected as most representative in terms of scope, variety, impact, and for their potential to

---

[5] It is beyond the present scope to adjudicate this for any particular case. Still, it is important to acknowledge at the outset that, in practice, there is likely considerable disagreement and contention regarding what would constitute a socially good outcome.

Table 9.1 Seven initiatives from Cowls et al. (2019)

Name	Reference	Areas	Relevant factor(s)
Field optimization of the protection assistant for wildlife security	Fang et al. (2016)	Environmental sustainability	1, 3
Identifying students at risk of adverse academic outcomes	Lakkaraju et al. (2015)	Education	4
Health information for homeless youth to reduce the spread of HIV	Yadav, Chan, Jiang, et al. (2016), Yadav et al. (2018)	Poverty, public welfare, public health	4
Interactive activity recognition and prompting to assist people with cognitive disabilities	Chu et al. (2012)	Disability, public health	3, 4, 7
Virtual teaching assistant experiment	Eicher, Polepeddi, and Goel (2017)	Education	4, 6
Detecting evolutionary financial statement fraud	Zhou and Kapoor (2011)	Finance, crime	2
Tracking and monitoring hand hygiene compliance	Haque et al. (2017)	Health	5

The initiatives are especially representative in terms of scope, variety, impact, and for their potentiality to evince the factors that should characterize the design of AI4SG projects.

corroborate the essential factors that I argue should characterize the design of AI4SG projects.

As it will become clear in the rest of the chapter, the seven factors have been identified in line with more general work in the field of AI ethics. Each factor relates to at least one of five ethical principles of AI—*beneficence, nonmaleficence, justice, autonomy,* and *explicability*—identified in the comparative analysis presented in Chapter 4. This coherence is crucial: AI4SG cannot be inconsistent with the ethical framework guiding the design and evaluation of AI in general.

The principle of beneficence is of relevance here. It states that the use of AI should provide benefit to people (*social preferability*) and the natural world (*sustainability*). Indeed, AI4SG projects should not just comply with but *reify* this principle: the benefits of AI4SG should be preferable (equitable) and sustainable, in line with the definition above. Beneficence is thus a necessary condition for AI4SG. At the same time, it is also insufficient because the beneficent impact of an AI4SG project may be 'offset' by the creation or amplification of other risks or harms.[6] While other ethical principles such as *autonomy* and *explicability* recur

---

[6] This should not be taken as necessitating a utilitarian calculation: the beneficial impact of a given project may be 'offset' by the violation of some categorical imperative. Therefore, even if an AI4SG project would do 'more good than harm', the harm may be ethically intolerable. In such a hypothetical case, one would not be morally obliged to develop and deploy the project in question.

throughout the debate, the factors evinced below are more closely associated with design considerations that are specific to AI4SG. They may be operationalized in the form of the corresponding best practices provided for each. In this way, ethical analysis informing the design and the deployment of AI4SG initiatives has a central role in mitigating the foreseeable risks of unintended consequences and possible misuses of the technology.

Before discussing the factors, it is important to clarify three general features of the whole set: *dependency*, *order*, and *coherence*. The seven factors are often intertwined and co-dependent but, for the sake of simplicity, I shall discuss them separately. Nothing should be inferred from this choice. In the same way, the factors are all essential; none is 'more important' than any other. So, I shall introduce them not in terms of priority, but somewhat historically. I start with factors that predate AI yet take on greater importance when AI technologies are used, owing to the particular capabilities and risks of AI (Yang et al. 2018).[7] These include *falsifiability and incremental deployment* and *safeguards against the manipulation of data*. There are also factors that relate more intrinsically to the sociotechnical characteristics of AI as it exists today, like *situational fairness* and *human-friendly semanticization*.

The factors are ethically robust and pragmatically applicable in the sense that they give rise to design considerations in the form of best practices that should be ethically endorsed. It is crucial to stress here that the seven factors are not by themselves *sufficient* for socially good AI. Rather, careful consideration of each is necessary. The set of factors identified in this chapter should not be taken as a sort of checklist that, if merely complied with, guarantees socially good outcomes from the use of AI in a particular domain. In the same vein, there is a need to strike a balance between the different factors (and indeed between tensions that may arise even within a single factor). It follows that seeking to frame a project in a binary way as either 'for social good' or 'not for social good' seems needlessly reductive, not to mention subjective. The goal of this chapter is not to identify, or offer the means to identify, AI4SG projects. It is to show the ethically important characteristics of projects that could feasibly be described as AI4SG.

9.3 Seven Essential Factors for Successful AI4SG

As I anticipated, the factors are (1) falsifiability and incremental deployment; (2) safeguards against the manipulation of predictors; (3) receiver-contextualized intervention; (4) receiver-contextualized explanation and transparent purposes;

---

[7] As noted in the introduction, it is not possible to document every single ethical consideration for a social good project. So even the least novel factors here are those that take on new relevance in the context of AI.

(5) privacy protection and data subject consent; (6) situational fairness; and (7) human-friendly semanticization. This section elucidates each factor separately, with one or more examples, and offers a corresponding best practice.

9.3.1 Falsifiability and Incremental Deployment

Trustworthiness is essential for the adoption of technology in general (Taddeo 2009, Taddeo 2010, Taddeo and Floridi 2011, Taddeo 2017c, Taddeo, McCutcheon, and Floridi 2019) and for AI4SG applications in particular. It is also required for technology to have a meaningful positive impact on human life and environmental well-being. The trustworthiness of an AI application entails a high probability that the application will respect the principle of beneficence (or at the very least, the principle of nonmaleficence). While there is no universal rule or guideline that can ensure or guarantee trustworthiness, *falsifiability* is an essential factor to improve the trustworthiness of technological applications in general, and AI4SG applications in particular.

Falsifiability entails the specification of one or more critical requirements along with the possibility of empirical testing. A critical requirement is an essential condition, resource, or means necessary for a capability to become fully operational, such that something could or should not work without it. *Safety* is an obvious critical requirement. For an AI4SG system to be trustworthy, its safety should be falsifiable.[8] If falsifiability is not possible, then the critical requirements cannot be checked. In the end, the system should not be deemed trustworthy. This is why falsifiability is an essential factor for all conceivable AI4SG projects.

Unfortunately, we cannot know for sure that a given AI4SG application is safe unless we can test the application in all possible contexts. In this case, the map of testing would simply equate to the territory of deployment. As this *reductio ad absurdum* makes clear, complete certainty is out of reach. What is within reach, in an uncertain and fuzzy world with many unforeseen situations, is the possibility of knowing when a given critical requirement has not been implemented or may be failing to work properly. We still would not know whether the AI4SG application is trustworthy. But if the critical requirements are falsifiable, we could at least know when it is not trustworthy.

Critical requirements should be tested with an incremental deployment cycle. Unintended hazardous effects may only reveal themselves after testing. At the same time, software should only be tested in the real world if it is safe to do so.

---

[8] It is of course likely that, in practice, an assessment of the safety of an AI system must also take into account wider societal values and cultural beliefs. These (among other considerations) may necessitate different trade-offs between the demands of critical requirements such as safety, and potentially competing norms or expectations.

This requires adoption of a deployment cycle whereby developers: (a) ensure that the application's most critical requirements or assumptions are falsifiable, and (b) undertake hypothesis testing of those most critical requirements and assumptions in safe, protected contexts. If these hypotheses are not disproven over a small set of suitable contexts, then (c) they should undertake conduct testing across increasingly wide contexts and/or test a larger set of less critical requirements. All this should be done while (d) being ready to halt or modify the deployment as soon as hazardous or other unwanted effects may appear.

AI4SG applications may use formal approaches to try to test critical requirements. For example, they may include the use of formal verification to ensure that autonomous vehicles, and AI systems in other safety-critical contexts, would make the ethically preferable choice (Dennis et al. 2016). Such methods offer safety checks that, in terms of falsifiability, can be proved correct. Simulations may offer roughly similar guarantees. A simulation enables one to test whether critical requirements (again, consider safety) are met under a set of formal assumptions. Unlike a formal proof, a simulation cannot always indicate that the required properties are necessarily always satisfied. But a simulation often enables one to test a much wider set of cases that cannot be dealt with formally, for example due to the complexity of the proof.

It would be misguided to rely purely on formal properties or simulations to falsify an AI4SG application. The assumptions of these models cage the real-world applicability of any conclusions that one might make. And assumptions may be incorrect in reality. What one may prove to be correct via a formal proof, or likely correct via testing in simulation, may be disproved later with the real-world deployment of the system. For example, developers of a game-theoretic model for wildlife security assumed a relatively flat topography without serious obstructions. Hence, the software that they developed originally had an incorrect definition of an optimal patrol route. Incremental testing of the application enabled the refinement of the optimal patrol route by proving wrong the assumption of a flat topography (Fang et al. 2016).

If novel dilemmas in real-world contexts require the alteration of prior assumptions made in the lab, one solution is to rectify a priori assumptions after deployment. Alternatively, one may adopt an 'on-the-fly' or runtime system for a constant update of a program's processing ('understanding') of its inputs. Yet problems also abound with this approach. For example, Microsoft's infamous Twitter bot Tay (discussed already in Chapter 8) acquired meanings in a very loose sense at runtime, as it learned from Twitter users how it should respond to tweets. After deployment in the real—and frequently vicious—world of social media, the bot's ability to constantly adapt its 'conceptual understanding' became an unfortunate bug as Tay 'learned' and regurgitated offensive language and unethical associations between concepts from other users (Neff and Nagy 2016b).

The use of a retrodictive approach, or an attempt to understand some aspect of reality through a priori information, to deal with the falsifiability of requirements, presents similar problems. This is noteworthy since retrodiction is the primary method of supervised ML approaches that learn from data (e.g. the learning of a continuous transformation function in the case of neural networks).

From the previous analysis, it follows that the essential factor of falsifiability and incremental development comprises a cycle: engineering requirements that are falsifiable, so it is at least possible to know whether the requirements are not met; falsification testing for incrementally improving levels of trust-worthiness; adjustment of a priori assumptions; then (and only then) deploy-ment in an incrementally wider and critical context. Germany's strategy for regulating autonomous vehicles, which was already mentioned in Chapter 8, offers a good example of this incremental approach. Deregulated zones allow for experimentation with constrained autonomy and, after increasing the levels of trustworthiness, manufacturers may test vehicles with higher levels of auton-omy (Pagallo 2017). Indeed, the creation of such deregulated zones (*test-strecken*) is one recommendation to support more ethical AI policy at the European level, as we shall see in Chapter 15. The identification of this essen-tial factor yields the following best practice:

1)   AI4SG designers should identify falsifiable requirements and test them in incremental steps from the lab to the 'outside world'.

9.3.2 Safeguards against the Manipulation of Predictors

The use of AI to predict future trends or patterns is very popular in AI4SG con-texts ranging from applying automated prediction to redress academic failure (Lakkaraju et al. 2015) and preventing illegal policing (Carton et al. 2016) to detecting corporate fraud (Zhou and Kapoor 2011). The predictive power of AI4SG faces two risks: the manipulation of input data and the excessive reliance on non-causal indicators.

The manipulation of data is neither a new problem nor one that is limited to AI systems alone. Well-established findings, such as Goodhart's Law (Goodhart 1984) (often summarized as 'when a measure becomes a target, it ceases to be a good measure', as noted in Strathern (1997), 308), long predate the widespread adoption of AI systems. But in the case of AI, the problem of data manipulation may be exacerbated (Manheim and Garrabrant 2018) and lead to unfair outcomes that breach the principle of justice. As such, it is a noteworthy risk for any AI4SG initiative as it can impair the predictive power of AI and lead to the avoidance of socially good interventions at the individual level.

Consider the concern raised by Ghani (2016) over teachers who face being evaluated with respect to:

> the percentage of students in their class who are above a certain risk threshold. If the model was transparent—for example, heavily reliant on math GPA—the teacher could inflate math grades and reduce the intermediate risk scores of their students.   (Ghani 2016)

As Ghani goes on to argue, the same concern applies to predictors of adverse police officer interactions:

> these systems [are] very easy to understand and interpret, but that also makes them easy to game. An officer who has had two uses of force in the past 80 days may choose to be a bit more careful over the next 10 days, until the count rolls over to zero again.

The two hypothetical examples make clear that, when the model used is an easy one to understand 'on the ground', it is already open to abuse or 'gaming' regardless of whether AI is used. The introduction of AI complicates matters due to the scale at which AI is typically applied.[9] As we have seen, if the information used to predict a given outcome is known, an agent with such information (one that is predicted to take a particular action) can change the value of each predictive variable to avoid an intervention. In this way, the predictive power of the overall model is reduced. Such loss of predictive power has already been shown by empirical research into the domain of corporate fraud (Zhou and Kapoor 2011). The phenomenon could carry over from fraud detection to the domains that AI4SG initiatives seek to address, as we saw in Chapter 5.

At the same time, excessive reliance on non-causal indicators (data that correlate with but do not cause a phenomenon) could distract attention from the context in which the AI4SG designer is seeking to intervene. To be effective, any such intervention should alter the underlying causes of a given problem, such as a student's domestic problems or inadequate corporate governance, rather than non-causal predictors. To do otherwise is to risk addressing only a symptom rather than the root cause of a problem.

These risks suggest the need to consider the use of safeguards as a design factor for AI4SG projects. Such safeguards may constrain the selection of indicators for

---

[9] For the sake of simplicity, the focus is on minimizing the spread of information used to predict an outcome. But this is not meant to foreclose the suggestion, offered in Prasad (2018), that in some cases a fairer approach may be to maximize the available information and hence 'democratize' the ability to manipulate predictors.

use in the design of AI4SG projects, the extent to which these indicators should shape interventions, and/or the level of transparency that should apply to how indicators affect decision. This yields the following best practice:

2)   AI4SG designers should adopt safeguards that (i) ensure non-causal indicators do not inappropriately skew interventions, and when appropriate, limit knowledge of how inputs affect outputs from AI4SG systems to prevent manipulation.

9.3.3   Receiver-Contextualized Intervention

It is essential that software intervenes in the lives of users only in ways that respect their autonomy. Again, this is not a problem that arises only with AI-driven interventions. But the use of AI introduces new considerations. A core challenge for AI4SG projects is to devise interventions that balance current and future benefits. The balancing problem, which is familiar to preference-elicitation research (Boutilier 2002, Faltings et al. 2004, Chajewska, Koller, and Parr 2000), boils down to a temporal choice interdependency. An intervention in the present can elicit user preferences that then enable the software to contextualize future interventions to the given user. Consequently, an intervention strategy that has no impact on user autonomy (e.g. one that lacks any interventions) may be ineffective in extracting the necessary information for correctly contextualized future interventions. Conversely, an intervention that overly infringes upon user autonomy may cause the user to reject the technology, making future interventions impossible.

This consideration of balance is a common one for AI4SG initiatives. Take, for example, interactive activity recognition software for people with cognitive disabilities (Chu et al. 2012). The software is designed to prompt patients to maintain a daily schedule of activities (e.g. taking medication) whilst minimizing interruptions to their wider goals. Each intervention is contextualized in such a way that the software learns the timing of future interventions from responses to past interventions. While only important interventions are made, all interventions are partially optional because declining one prompt leads to the same prompt later on. Here, the concern was that patients would reject an overly intrusive technology. Hence, a balance was sought.

This balance is lacking in our second example. A game-theoretic application intervenes in the patrols of wildlife security officers by offering suggested routes (Fang et al. 2016). Yet if a route poses physical obstacles, the software lacks the capacity to provide alternative suggestions. Officers may ignore the advice by taking a different route, but not without disengaging from the application. It is essential to relax such constraints so that users can ignore an intervention, but accept subsequent, more appropriate interventions (in the form of advice) later on.

These examples point to the importance of seeing users as equal partners in both the design and deployment of autonomous decision-making systems. The adoption of this mindset might have helped prevent the tragic loss of two Boeing 737 Max airliners. It appears that the pilots of these flights struggled to reverse a software malfunction caused by faulty sensors. The struggle was partly due to the absence of 'optional safety features', which Boeing sold separately (Tabuchi and Gelles 2019).

The risk of false positives (unnecessary intervention, creating disillusionment) is often just as problematic as false negatives (no intervention where it is necessary, limiting effectiveness). A suitable receiver-contextualized intervention is thus one that achieves the right level of disruption while respecting autonomy through optionality. This contextualization rests on information about user capacities, preferences, and goals, as well as the circumstances in which the intervention will take effect.

One can consider five dimensions relevant to a receiver-contextualized intervention. Four of these dimensions emerge from McFarlane's taxonomy of interdisciplinary research on disruptive computer–human interruptions (McFarlane 1999, McFarlane and Latorella 2002). These are:

a) the individual characteristics of the person receiving the intervention;
b) the methods of coordination between the receiver and the system;
c) the meaning or purpose of the intervention; and
d) the overall effects of the intervention.[10]

A fifth dimension of relevance is optionality: a user can choose either to ignore all offered advice or to drive the process and request a different intervention better suited to their needs.

We can now summarize these five dimensions in the form of the following best practice for receiver-contextualized intervention:

3)   AI4SG designers should build decision-making systems in consultation with users interacting with (and impacted by) these systems; with an understanding of user characteristics, the methods of coordination, and the purposes and effects of an intervention; and with respect for the user right to ignore or modify interventions.

---

[10] The four remaining dimensions proposed by MacFarlane (the source of the interruption, the method of expression, the channel of conveyance, and the human activity changed by the interruption) are not relevant for purpose of this chapter.

9.3.4 Receiver-Contextualized Explanation
and Transparent Purposes

AI4SG applications should be designed not only to make the operations and out-comes of these systems explainable but also to make their purposes transparent. These two requirements are intrinsically linked, of course. That is because the operations and outcomes of AI systems reflect the wider purposes of human designers, which this section addresses in turn.

As we saw in Chapter 4, making AI systems explainable is an important ethical principle. It has been a focus of research since at least 1975 (Shortliffe and Buchanan 1975). And given the increasingly pervasive distribution of AI systems, it has gained more attention recently (Mittelstadt et al. 2016, Wachter, Mittelstadt, and Floridi 2017a, b, Thelisson, Padh, and Celis 2017, Watson and Floridi 2020, Watson et al. 2021). As we saw above, AI4SG projects should offer interventions that are contextualized to the receiver. In addition, the *explanation* for an inter-vention should also be contextualized for the sake of adequacy and protecting the autonomy of the receiver.

Designers of AI4SG projects have tried to increase the explainability of decision-making systems in various ways. For example, researchers have used ML to predict academic adversity (Lakkaraju et al. 2015). These predictors used concepts that the school officials interpreting the system found familiar and salient, such as GPA scores and socioeconomic categorizations. Researchers have also used reinforcement learning to help officials at homeless shelters educate homeless youths about HIV (Yadav, Chan, Jiang, et al. 2016, Yadav, Chan, Xin Jiang, et al. 2016). The system learns how to maximize the influence of HIV education. It does so by choosing which homeless youths to educate based on the likelihood that a particular homeless youth would pass on their knowledge. One version of the system explained which youth was chosen by revealing their social network graph. However, officials at the homeless shelter found these explanations were counterintuitive. The finding had the potential to affect their understanding of how the system worked and, hence, user trust in the system. These two cases exemplify the importance of the right conceptualization when explaining an AI-based decision.

The right conceptualization is likely to vary across AI4SG projects as they dif-fer greatly in their objectives, subject matter, context, and stakeholders. The con-ceptual framework (also called the level of abstraction or LoA) depends on what is being explained, to whom, and for what purpose (Floridi 2008a, 2017b). An LoA is a key component of a theory, and hence of any explanation. A theory is comprised of five components:

1. a *system*, which is the referent or object analysed by a theory;
2. a *purpose*, which is the 'what for' that motivates the analysis of a system (note that this answers the question 'what is the analysis for?' It should not

be confused with the purpose of a system, which answers the question 'what is the system for?' Below, I use the term 'goal' for the purpose of a system whenever there may be a risk of confusion);

3. an *LoA*, which provides a lens through which a system is analysed, to generate
4. a *model*, which is some relevant and reliable information about the analysed system that identifies
5. a *structure* of the system, which is comprised of the features that belong to the system under analysis.

There is an interdependency between the choice of the specific purpose, the relevant LoA that can fulfil the purpose, the system under analysis, and the model obtained by analysing the system at a specified LoA for a particular purpose. The LoA provides the conceptualization of the system (e.g. GPA scores and socioeconomic backgrounds). At the same time, the purpose constrains the construction of LoAs. For example, we might choose to explain the decision-making system itself (e.g. the use of particular ML techniques). In that case, the LoA can only conceptualize those AI techniques. The LoA then generates the model, which explains the system in turn. The model identifies system structures, such as the GPA score, poor attendance rate, and socioeconomic background of a particular student, as predictors of academic failure. Consequently, designers must carefully choose the purpose and the corresponding LoA. This is so the explanation model can provide the right explanation of the system in question for a given receiver.

A LoA is chosen for a specific *purpose*. For example, a LoA may be chosen to explain a decision taken based on outcomes obtained through an algorithmic procedure. The LoA varies depending on whether the explanation is meant for the receiver of that decision, or for an engineer responsible for the design of the algorithmic procedure. This is because not every LoA is appropriate for a given receiver. Appropriateness depends on LoA purpose and granularity, for example a customer-friendly vs. engineer-friendly explanation. Sometimes, a receiver's conceptual view of the world may differ from the one on which the explanation is based. In other cases, a receiver and an explanation may be conceptually aligned. However, the receiver may not agree on the amount of granularity (Sloan and Warner) in the information (what we called more precisely the model) provided. Conceptual misalignment means that the receiver may find the explanation irrelevant, unintelligible, or, as we shall see below, questionable. In terms of (Cowls, Png, and Au) intelligibility, a LoA may use unknown labels (so-called observables) or labels that have different meanings for different users.

Empirical studies suggest that the suitability of an explanation differs among receivers according to their expertise (Gregor and Benbasat 1999). Receivers may require explanations about how the AI software came to a decision, especially when they must act based on that decision (Gregor and Benbasat 1999, Watson et al. 2019). How the AI system came to a conclusion can be just as important as the justification for that conclusion. Consequently, designers must also context-ualize the method of explanation to the receiver. The case of the software that used influence-maximization algorithms to target homeless youths for HIV edu-cation provides a good example of the relevance of the receiver-contextualization of concepts (Yadav, Chan, Jiang, et al. 2016, Yadav, Chan, Xin Jiang, et al. 2016). The researchers involved in that project considered three possible LoAs when designing the explanation model: the first included utility calculations, the sec-ond focused on social graph connectivity, and a third focused on pedagogic purpose.

The first LoA highlighted the utility of targeting one homeless youth over another. According to the researchers, this approach could have led the homeless shelter workers (the receivers) to misunderstand the utility calculations or find them irrelevant. Utility calculations offer little explanatory power beyond the decision itself as they often simply show that the 'best' choice was made and how good it was. Explanations based on the second LoA faced a different problem: the receivers assumed that the most central nodes in the network were the best for maximizing the influence of education, while the optimal choice is often a set of less well-connected nodes. This disjuncture may have arisen from the nature of the connectivity between members of the network of homeless youths, which reflects real-life uncertainty about friendships. Since who counts as a 'friend' is often vague and changes over time, the researchers classified edges in the network as either 'certain' or 'uncertain' based on domain knowledge. For 'uncertain' relationships, the probability of a friendship existing between two youths was determined by domain experts.[11]

After subsequent user testing of different explanation frameworks, the third LoA was eventually chosen. Considering their stated goal to justify decisions in a way that would be intuitive to homeless shelter officials, the researchers con-sidered omitting references to the Maximum Expected Utility (MEU) calculations—even though this is what underlies the decisions made by the system. Instead, the researchers considered justifying decisions using concepts that were likely more familiar and therefore comfortable to officials, such as the centrality of the nodes (i.e. the youths) that the system recommends officials prioritize for intervention. In this way, the researchers sought to provide the most relevant information contextualized to the receiver.

---

[11] Note that the significance of involving domain experts in the process was not merely to improve their experience as decision recipients. It was also from their unparalleled knowledge of the domain that the researchers drew upon in the system design, which helped provide the researchers with what Pagallo (2015) calls a 'preventive understanding' of the field.

This example shows how given a particular system, the purpose one chooses to pursue when seeking an explanation for it, the LoA, and the issuing model that is obtained are crucial variables impacting the effectiveness of an explanation. Explainability both breeds trust in and fosters the adoption of AI4SG solutions (Herlocker, Konstan, and Riedl 2000, Swearingen and Sinha 2002, Bilgic and Mooney 2005). Therefore it is essential that software use persuasive *argumentation* for the target audience. Argumentation will likely include information about both the general functionality and logic employed by a system along with the reasons for a specific decision.

Transparency in the goal of the system (the system's purpose) is also crucial as it follows directly from the principle of autonomy. Consider, for example, the development of AI solutions to prompt people with cognitive disabilities to take their medication (Chu et al. 2012). On its face, this application may seem invasive. After all, it involves vulnerable users and limits the effectiveness of receiver-conceptualized explanation. But the system is designed neither to coerce the patients into a given behaviour nor to resemble a human being. Patients have the autonomy not to interact with the AI system in question. This case highlights the importance of transparency in goals, particularly in contexts where explainable operations and outcomes are unworkable or undesirable. Transparency in goals thus undergirds other safeguards around the protection of target populations; it may also help ensure compliance with relevant legislation and precedent (Reed 2018).

Conversely, opaque goals may prompt misunderstanding and the potential for harm. For instance, users of an AI system may be unclear about what type of agent they are dealing with (human, artificial, or a hybrid combination of both). They may then wrongly assume that the tacit norms of human-to-human social interaction are upheld, such as not recording every detail of a conversation (Kerr 2003). As ever, the social context in which an AI4SG application takes place impacts the extent to which AI systems should be transparent in their operations. Because transparency is the default but not absolute position, there may be valid reasons for designers to obviate informing users of the software's goals. For example, the scientific value of a project or the health and safety conditions of a public space may justify *temporarily* opaque goals. Consider a study that deceived students into believing they were interacting with a human course assistant who, it was realized over time, was actually a bot (Eicher, Polepeddi, and Goel 2017). The authors argued that the bot's deception lay in playing the 'imitation game' without causing the students to choose simpler, less human-like, natural-language queries based on preconceptions about AI capabilities. In such cases, the choice between opacity and transparency may be informed by pre-existing notions of informed consent for human-subject experiments that are embedded in the Nuremberg Code, the Declaration of Helsinki, and the Belmont Report (Nijhawan et al. 2013).

More broadly, the ability to avoid the use of an AI system becomes more likely when AI software reveals its endogenous goals, such as classifying data about a person. For example, AI software could inform staff in a hospital ward that it has the goal of classifying their hygiene levels (Haque et al. 2017). In this case, the staff may decide to avoid such classifications if there are reasonable alternative actions they can take. In other cases, revealing a goal makes it less likely that the goal will be fulfilled.

Making transparent the goals and motivations of AI4SG developers themselves is an essential factor to the success of any project. At the same time, transparency may contrast with the very purpose of the system. Therefore it is crucial to assess what level of transparency (i.e. how much, what kind, for whom, and about what?) the project will embrace, given its overall goal and the context for implementation, during the design stage. Taken together with the need for receiver-conceptualized explanation, this consideration yields the following set of best practices:

4)   AI4SG designers should first choose an LoA for AI explanation that fulfils the desired explanatory purpose and is appropriate to both the system and receivers. Then, designers should deploy arguments that are rationally and suitably persuasive for the receivers to deliver the explanation. Finally, designers should ensure that the goal (the system's purpose) for which an AI4SG system is developed and deployed is knowable to the receivers of its outputs by default.

9.3.5 Privacy Protection and Data Subject Consent

Of the seven factors, privacy has the most voluminous literature. This should not be a surprise as privacy is considered an essential condition for safety and social cohesion, among other things (Solove 2008). Also, earlier waves of digital technology have already had a major impact on privacy (Nissenbaum 2009). People's safety may be compromised when a malicious actor or state gains control over individuals via privacy infringements (Taddeo 2014, Lynskey 2015). Respect for privacy is a necessary condition for human dignity because we can view personal information as constituting an individual. So, deprivatizing records without consent will likely constitute a violation of human dignity (Floridi 2016c). The conception of individual privacy as a fundamental right underlies recent legislative action in, for example, Europe (through the GDPR) and Japan (through its Act on Protection of Personal Information), as well as judicial decisions in jurisdictions such as India (Mohanty and Bhatia 2017). Privacy supports people when deviating from social norms without causing offence, and communities in maintaining their social structures. So, privacy also undergirds social cohesion.

In the case of AI4SG, it is particularly important to emphasize the relevance of user consent to the use of personal data. Tensions may arise between different thresholds of consent (Price and Cohen 2019). The tension is often at its most fraught in life-or-death situations, such as national emergencies and pandemics. Consider the 2014 Ebola outbreak in West Africa, which posed a complex ethical dilemma (The Economist 27 October 2014). In that case, the rapid release and analysis of call-data records from cell phone users in the region may have allowed epidemiologists to track the spread of the deadly disease. However, the release of the data was held up over valid concerns around users' privacy and the value of the data to industrial competitors. Related considerations have emerged during the COVID-19 pandemic (Morley, Cowls, et al. 2020).

In circumstances where haste is not so crucial, it is possible to obtain a subject's consent for, and before, the data being used. The level or type of consent sought can vary with the context. In healthcare, one may adopt an assumed consent threshold whereby the act of reporting a medical issue to a doctor constitutes an assumption of patient consent. In other circumstances, an informed consent threshold will be more appropriate. But since informed consent requires researchers to obtain a patient's specific consent before using their data for a non-consented purpose, practitioners may choose an explicit consent threshold for general data processing (i.e. for any medical usage). This threshold does not require informing the patient about all of the possible ways that researchers may use their data (Etzioni 1999). Another alternative is the evolving notion of 'dynamic consent' whereby individuals can monitor and adjust their privacy preferences on a granular level (Kaye et al. 2015).

In other cases, informed consent may be waived altogether. This was the case with the recent creation of ML software to predict the prognosis of ovarian cancer sufferers by drawing upon a retrospective analysis of anonymized images (Lu et al. 2019). The use of patient health data in the development of AI solutions without patient consent has attracted the attention of data protection regulators. In 2017, the UK Information Commissioner ruled that the Royal Free National Health Service (NHS) Foundation Trust violated the Data Protection Act when it provided patient details to Google DeepMind for the purposes of training an AI system to diagnose acute kidney injury (Burgess 2017). The commissioner noted a 'shortcoming' in how 'patients were not adequately informed that their data would be used as part of the test' (Information Commissioner's Office 2017).

However, striking a balance between respecting patient privacy and creating effective AI4SG is still possible. This was the challenge faced by the researchers in Haque et al. (2017), who wanted to create a system for tracking compliance with rules around hand hygiene in hospitals to prevent the spread of infections. Despite the clear technical advantages of taking a computer vision-based approach to the problem, the use of video recording runs up against privacy regulations constraining it. Even in cases where video recording is allowed, access to the recordings (to train an algorithm) is often strict. Instead, the researchers resorted to 'depth images' that de-identify subjects, preserving their privacy. While this design choice meant 'losing important visual appearance cues in the process', it satisfied privacy rules and the researchers' non-intrusive system still managed to outperform existing solutions.

Finally, consent in the online space is also problematic. Users often lack the choice to consent and are presented with a 'take it or leave it' option when accessing online services (Nissenbaum 2011, Taddeo and Floridi 2015). A relative lack of protection or consent for the second-hand use of personal data that are publicly shared online enables the development of ethically problematic AI software. For instance, a recent paper used publicly available images of faces uploaded to a dating website as a way to train AI software to detect someone's sexuality based on a small number of photos (Wang and Kosinski 2018). While the study received ethics committee approval, it raises further questions around consent as it is implausible that the users of the dating website could or necessarily would have consented to the use of their data for this particular purpose.

Privacy is not a novel problem. However, the centrality of personal data to many AI (and AI4SG) applications heightens its ethical significance and creates issues around consent (Taddeo and Floridi 2018a). From this we can derive the following best practice:

5)   AI4SG designers should respect the threshold of consent established for processing datasets of personal data.

9.3.6 Situational Fairness

AI developers typically rely on data. Data, in turn, could be biased in ways that are socially significant. This bias can carry over to algorithmic decision making, which underpins many AI systems, in ways that are unfair to the subjects of the decision-making process (Caliskan, Bryson, and Narayanan 2017). In doing so, it may breach the principle of justice. Decisions may be based on factors of ethical importance (e.g. ethnic, gender, or religious grounds) and irrelevant to the decision making at hand, or they may be relevant but legally protected as a non-discriminatory characteristic (Friedman and Nissenbaum 1996). Moreover, AI-driven decisions can be amalgamated from factors that are not of obvious ethical importance, yet collectively constitute unfairly biased decision making (Pedreshi, Ruggieri, and Turini 2008, Floridi 2012b).

AI4SG initiatives relying on biased data may propagate this bias through a vicious cycle (Yang et al. 2018). Such a cycle would begin with a biased dataset informing a first phase of AI decision-making, which would result in discriminatory actions. This would then lead to the collection and use of biased data in turn. Consider the use of AI to predict preterm birth in the United States, where the health outcomes of pregnant women have long been affected by their ethnicity. Due to harmful historical stereotypes, longstanding bias against African-American women seeking medical treatment contributes to a maternal morbidity rate that is over three times higher than that of white women (CDC 2019). Here, AI may offer great potential to reduce this stark racial divide—but only if the same historical discrimination is not replicated in AI systems (Banjo 2018). Or consider the use of predictive policing software: developers may train predictive policing software on policing data that contains deeply ingrained prejudices. When discrimination affects arrest rates, it becomes embedded in prosecution data (Lum and Isaac 2016). Such biases may cause discriminatory decisions, such as warnings or arrests, that feed back into the increasingly biased datasets (Crawford 2016) and thereby complete a vicious cycle.

The previous examples involve the use of AI to improve outcomes in domains where data were already collected. Yet in many other contexts, AI4SG projects (or indeed similar initiatives) are effectively making citizens 'visible' in ways that they previously were not, including in Global South contexts (Taylor and Broeders 2015). This increased visibility stresses the importance of protecting against the potential amplification of harmful bias by AI technologies.

Clearly, designers must sanitize the datasets used to train AI. But there is equally a risk of applying too strong a disinfectant, so to speak, by removing important contextual nuances that could improve ethical decision making. So, designers must also ensure that AI decision making maintains sensitivity to factors that are important for inclusiveness. For instance, one should ensure that a word processor interacts identically with a human user regardless of that user's gender and ethnicity. But one should also expect that it may operate in an unequal-yet-equitable way by aiding people with visual impairments.

Such expectations are not always met in the context of AI-driven reasoning. Compared to the word processor, AI makes possible a far wider range of decision-making and interaction modalities. Many of these are driven by potentially biased data. Training datasets may contain natural language that carries unfair associations between genders and words that carry normative power in turn (Caliskan, Bryson, and Narayanan 2017). In other contexts and use cases, an equitable approach may *require* differences in communication based on factors such as gender. Consider the case of the virtual teaching assistant that *failed* to discriminate sufficiently well between men and women in its responses to being told that a user was expecting a baby, congratulating the men and ignoring the women (Eicher, Polepeddi, and Goel 2017). A BBC News investigation highlighted an even more egregious example: a mental health chatbot deemed suitable for use by children was unable to understand a child explicitly reporting underage sexual abuse (White 2018). As these cases make clear, the use of AI in human–computer interactions (such as chatbots) requires the correct understanding of both the salient groups to which a user belongs and the characteristics the user embodies when they interact with the software.

Respecting situational fairness is essential for the successful implementation of AI4SG. To achieve it, AI4SG projects need to remove the factors and their proxies that are of ethical importance but irrelevant to an outcome. But the projects also need to include the same factors when these are required, whether for the sake of inclusiveness, safety, or other ethical considerations. The problem of historical biases affecting future decision making is an old one. What is new is the potential that these biases will be embedded in, strengthened, and perpetuated anew by erroneous reinforcement learning mechanisms. This risk is especially pronounced when considered alongside the risk of opacity in AI decision-making systems and their outcomes. We will return to this topic in the next section.

The identification of situational fairness as an essential factor yields now the following best practice:

6)   AI4SG designers should remove from relevant datasets variables and proxies that are irrelevant to an outcome, except when their inclusion supports inclusivity, safety, or other ethical imperatives.

9.3.7 Human-Friendly Semanticization

AI4SG must allow humans to curate and foster their 'semantic capital', which, as I wrote in Floridi et al. (2018), is 'any content that can enhance someone's power to give meaning to and make sense of (*semanticise*) something'. This is crucial to maintain and foster human autonomy. With AI, we may often have the technical capacity to automate meaning- and sense-creation (semanticization), but mistrust or unfairness may also arise if we do so carelessly. From this, two problems emerge.

The first problem is that AI software may define semanticization in a way that diverges from our own choices. This is the case when a procedure arbitrarily defines meanings, for example based on a coin toss. The same problem may arise if AI software supports some kind of semanticization based on pre-existing uses. For example, researchers have developed an application that *predicts the legal meaning* of 'violation' based on past cases (Al-Abdulkarim, Atkinson, and Bench-Capon 2015). If one used the software to *define* the meaning of 'violation',[12] then one would end up limiting the role of judges and justices. They would no longer be able to semanticize (refine and redefine the meaning and the possibility of making sense of) 'violation' when they interpret the law. This is a problem because

---

[12] There is no suggestion that this is the intended use.

past usage does not always predict how we would semanticize the same concepts or phenomena in the future.

The second problem is that, in a social setting, it would be impractical for AI software to define all meanings and senses. Some semanticization is subjective because who or what is involved in the semanticization is also partly constitutive of the process and its outcome. For example, only legally empowered agents can define the legal meaning of 'violation'. The meaning and sense of affective symbols, such as facial expressions, likewise depend on the type of agent showing a given expression. Affective AI can detect an emotion (Martínez-Miranda and Aldea 2005): an AA may state accurately that a human *appears sad*, but it cannot change the meaning of sadness.

The solution to these two problems rests on distinguishing between tasks that should and should not be delegated to an artificial system. AI should be deployed to *facilitate* human-friendly semanticization, but not to provide it itself. This is true, for example, when considering patients with Alzheimer's disease. Research into carer–patient relations highlights three points (Burns and Rabins 2000). First, carers play a critical but burdensome role in reminding patients of the activities in which they participate (such as taking medication). Second, carers also play a critical role in providing patients with meaningful interaction. And third, when carers remind patients to take their medication, the patient–carer relation may become weaker by annoying the patient; the carer then loses some capacity to provide empathy and meaningful support. Consequently, researchers have developed AI software that balances reminding the patient against annoying the patient (Chu et al. 2012). The balance is learned and optimized using reinforcement learning. The researchers designed the system so that caregivers can spend most of their time providing empathic support and preserving a meaningful relationship with the patient. As this example shows, it is possible to use AI to sweep away formulaic tasks whilst sustaining human-friendly semanticization.

As an essential factor for AI4SG, human-centric semanticization underpins the final best practice:

7)   AI4SG designers should not hinder the ability for people to semanticize (that is, to give meaning to, and make sense of) something.

9.4 Conclusion: Balancing Factors for AI4SG

This chapter has analysed seven factors supporting AI4SG and their corresponding best practices. Table 9.2 provides a summary. I argued that the principle of *beneficence* is assumed as a precondition for an AI4SG, so the factors relate to one or more of the other four principles of AI ethics: *nonmaleficence, autonomy, justice,* and *explicability* identified in Chapter 4.

The seven factors suggest that creating successful AI4SG requires striking two kinds of balance: *intra* and *inter*. On the one hand, each single factor in and of itself may require striking an intrinsic balance between the risk of over-intervening and the risk of under-intervening when devising contextual interventions; or between protection-by-obfuscation and protection-by-enumeration of

Table 9.2 Seven factors supporting AI4SG and the corresponding best practices

Factors	Best practices	Ethical principles
Falsifiability and incremental deployment	Identify falsifiable requirements and test them in incremental steps from the lab to the 'outside world'.	Beneficence Nonmaleficence
Safeguards against the manipulation of predictors	Adopt safeguards that (i) ensure non-causal indicators do not inappropriately skew interventions, and when appropriate, limit knowledge of how inputs affect outputs from AI4SG systems to prevent manipulation.	Beneficence Nonmaleficence
Receiver-contextualized intervention	Build decision-making systems in consultation with users interacting with (and impacted by) these systems; with an understanding of user characteristics, the methods of coordination, the purposes and effects of an intervention; and with respect for the user right to ignore or modify interventions.	Beneficence Autonomy
Receiver-contextualized explanation and transparent purposes	Choose an LoA for AI explanation that fulfils the desired explanatory purpose and is appropriate to the system and the receivers. Then, deploy arguments that are rationally and suitably persuasive for the receiver to deliver the explanation. Finally, ensure that the goal (the system's purpose) for which an AI4SG system is developed and deployed is knowable to the receivers of its outputs by default.	Beneficence Explicability
Privacy protection and data subject consent	Respect the threshold of consent established for the processing of datasets of personal data.	Beneficence Nonmaleficence Autonomy
Situational fairness	Remove from relevant datasets variables and proxies that are irrelevant to an outcome, except when their inclusion supports inclusivity, safety, or other ethical imperatives.	Beneficence Justice
Human-friendly semanticization	Do not hinder the ability for people to semanticize (that is, to give meaning to, and make sense of) something.	Beneficence Autonomy

salient differences between people (depending on the purposes and context of a system), and so on. On the other hand, balances are not just specific to a single factor. They are also systemic because they must be struck between multiple factors. Consider the tension between preventing malicious actors from understanding how to 'game' the input data of AI prediction systems versus enabling humans to override genuinely flawed outcomes; or the tension between ensuring the effective disclosure of the reasons behind a decision without compromising the consensual anonymity of data subjects.

For each given case, the overarching question facing the AI4SG community is whether one is morally obliged to (or obliged not to) design, develop, and deploy a specific AI4SG project. This chapter does not seek to answer such a question in the abstract. Resolving the tensions that are likely to arise among and between factors is highly context-dependent. The previous analysis is not meant to cover all potential contexts, not least because this would be inconsistent with the argument for falsifiable hypothesis testing and incremental deployment supported in this article. Nor would a checklist of purely technical 'dos and don'ts' suffice. Rather, the analysis has yielded a set of essential factors that need to be considered, interpreted, and evaluated contextually whenever one is designing, developing, and deploying a specific AI4SG project. The future of AI4SG will likely provide more opportunities to enrich such a set of essential factors. And AI itself may help to manage its own life cycle by providing, in a meta-reflective way, tools for evaluating how best to strike the individual and systemic balances indicated above.

The most pertinent questions to arise from the factors described in this chapter are likely to concern this challenge of balancing the competing needs and claims that the factors and corresponding best practices introduce. This concerns what it is that *legitimates* decision making with and about AI. I shall return to this topic in Chapter 10 as a matter of ethical discussion (for a discussion of its political implications in terms of digital sovereignty, see Floridi (2020b). Here I offer some remarks by way of conclusion.

Questions about trade-offs, balances, and their legitimacy are inevitably intertwined with wider ethical and political challenges regarding who has the power or 'standing' to participate in this process of evaluation, as well as how multiple preferences are measured and aggregated, which Baum outlines in a trichotomic framework (Baum 2020). If we assume that the challenge of balancing factors ought to be at least somewhat participatory in nature, the overview of relevant social choice theorems in Prasad (2018) identifies several background conditions to support effective group decision making. As these analyses suggest, the incorporation of multiple perspectives into the design of AI decision-making systems is likely to be an ethically important step both for AI in general and for AI4SG in particular. So will be efforts to implement forms of co-design.

There is clearly much work still to be done to ensure that
designed in ways that do not merely advance beneficial goal/
challenges, but do so in socially preferable (equitable) /
In this chapter, we looked at the foundation for good pr/
also looked at the foundation for further research into the ethn.
that should undergird AI4SG projects, and hence *the* 'AI4SG project' at ₁.
time has come to discuss how ethical, legal, and policymaking considerations
interact in such a development, in terms of specific recommendations. This is the
topic of the next chapter.

10

How to Deliver a Good AI Society

Some Recommendations

10.0 Summary

Previously, in Chapters 4–6, I analysed the foundational concepts that can ground a future 'Good AI Society'. Chapters 7–9 discussed the challenges, the bad, and the good practices characterizing the use of AI systems. This chapter, along with the next, turns to some constructive and concrete recommendations about how to assess, develop, incentivize, and support good AI. In some cases, these recommendations may be undertaken directly by national or supranational policymakers. In others, changes may be led by other stakeholders ranging from civil society to private actors and sectoral organizations. The hope is that, if adopted, these recommendations may support a firm foundation for the establishment of a Good AI Society.

10.1 Introduction: Four Ways of Delivering a Good AI Society

AI is not another utility that needs to be regulated once it is mature. We made the mistake of thinking so when the Web began to develop in the 1990s and today the mess is obvious. The Web was always going to be a new environment—part of our infosphere, not just another kind of mass media. We should have regulated it accordingly.[1] We should not make the same mistake again. AI is not just a commercial service. It is a powerful force, a new form of smart agency in the infosphere, that is already reshaping our lives, our interactions, and our environments. This new form of agency needs to be steered towards the good of society, everyone in it, and the environments we share. Market forces will be either irrelevant or insufficient. We need a normative approach. This chapter contributes to the ongoing, international, and collaborative effort to development a Good AI Society by proposing twenty recommendations.[2] If adopted, they may help all

---

[1] The rules for a public space are different from the rules for private communication; see Floridi (2014a).

[2] They are the outcome of a project I designed and chaired in 2017 called AI4People. To learn more about the project, see Floridi et al. (2018).

The Ethics of Artificial Intelligence: Principles, Challenges, and Opportunities. Luciano Floridi, Oxford University Press.
© Luciano Floridi 2023. DOI: 10.1093/oso/9780198883098.003.0010

stakeholders seize the opportunities offered by AI, avoid, or at least minimize and counterbalance the risks, respect the principles discussed in Chapter 4, and hence to develop a Good AI Society.

As I wrote in the previous chapters, it is no longer a question whether AI will have a major impact on individuals, societies, and environments. Current debate turns instead on how far this impact will be positive or negative, for whom, in which ways, in which places, and on what timescale. Put another way, in Chapter 4 I observed that the key questions now are *by whom, how, where,* and *when* the positive or negative impacts of AI will be felt. To frame these questions in a more substantive and practical way, I introduce here what may be considered the four chief opportunities for society that AI offers. They are four because they address the four fundamental points in our philosophical anthropology, that is, in our understanding of human dignity and flourishing:

a) *autonomous self-realization*, or who we can become;
b) *human agency*, or what we can do;
c) *individual and societal capabilities*, or what we can achieve; and
d) *societal cohesion*, or how we can interact with each other and the world.

In each case, AI can be used to foster human nature and its potentialities, thus creating opportunities; *underused*, thus creating opportunity costs; or *overused* and *misused*, thus creating risks. Figure 10.1 provides a quick overview, while the following sections offer a more detailed explanation.

As the terminology indicates, the assumption is that the *use* of AI is synonymous with good innovation and positive applications of this technology. However, fear, ignorance, misplaced concerns, or excessive reaction may lead a society to

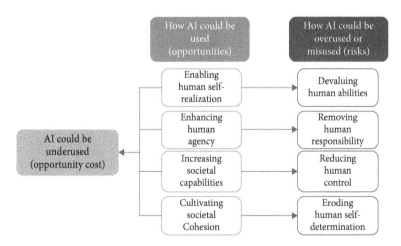

Figure 10.1 AI's opportunities, risks, and costs

underuse AI technologies below their full potential, and for what might be broadly described as the wrong reasons. This could cause significant opportunity costs. It might include, for example, heavy-handed or misconceived regulation, under-investment, or a public backlash akin to that faced by genetically modified crops and nuclear power. As a result, the benefits offered by AI technologies may not be fully realized by society. These dangers arise largely from unintended consequences and relate typically to good intentions gone awry. And of course, one must also consider the risks associated with inadvertent *overuse* or wilful *misuse* of AI technologies, grounded, for example, in misaligned incentives, greed, adversarial geopolitics, or malicious intent. As we saw in Chapters 7 and 8, everything from email scams to full-scale cyber warfare may be accelerated or intensified by the malicious use of AI technologies (Taddeo 2017b). And new evils may be made possible. The possibility of social progress represented by the aforementioned opportunities must be weighed against the risk that malicious manipulation will be enabled or enhanced by AI. Yet a broad risk is that AI may be underused out of fear of overuse, or misused for lack of a clear ethical and legal framework—as we shall see in the rest of this chapter.

10.2 Who We Can Become: Enabling Human Self-Realization without Devaluing Human Abilities

AI may enable self-realization, that is, the ability for people to flourish in terms of their own characteristics, interests, potential abilities or skills, aspirations, and life projects. Much like inventions such as the washing machine, which liberated people (particularly women) from the drudgery of domestic work, the 'smart' automation of other mundane aspects of life may free up yet more time for cultural, intellectual, and social pursuits, and more interesting and rewarding work. More AI could easily mean more human life spent more intelligently. The risk in this case is not the obsolescence of some old skills and the emergence of new ones per se, but the pace at which this is happening and the unequal distributions of the costs and benefits that result.

A very fast devaluation of old skills, and hence a quick disruption of the job market and the nature of employment, can be seen at the level of both the individual and society.

At the level of the individual, jobs are often intimately linked to personal identity, self-esteem, and social role or standing. These are all factors that may be adversely affected by redundancy, even putting to one side the potential for severe economic harm. At the level of society, deskilling in sensitive, skill-intensive domains (such as health care diagnosis or aviation) may create dangerous vulnerabilities in the event of AI malfunction or an adversarial attack. Fostering the development of AI in support of new abilities and skills while also anticipating and mitigating its impact on old ones will require both close study and potentially radical ideas, such as the proposal for some form of 'universal basic income' (which is already growing in popularity and experimental use). In the end, we need some intergenerational solidarity between those disadvantaged today and those advantaged tomorrow to ensure that the disruptive transition between the present and the future will be as fair as possible for everyone. To adopt a terminology that we have sadly come to appreciate during the COVID-19 pandemic, we need to flatten the curve of the social impact of digital technologies— AI included.

10.3 What We Can Do: Enhancing Human Agency without Removing Human Responsibility

AI is providing a growing reservoir of 'smart agency'. Put at the service of human intelligence, such a resource can hugely enhance human agency. We can do more, better, and faster, thanks to the support provided by AI. In this sense of '[human] augmented intelligence', AI could be compared to the impact that engines have had on our lives. The larger the number of people who will enjoy the opportunities and benefits of such a reservoir of smart agency 'on tap', the better our societies will be. Responsibility is therefore essential, in view of what sort of AI we develop, how we use it, and whether we share with everyone its advantages and benefits.

Obviously, the corresponding risk is the absence of such responsibility. This may happen not just because we have the wrong socio-political framework, but also due to a 'black box' mentality according to which AI systems for decision making are seen as being beyond human understanding—and hence, beyond human control. These concerns apply not just to high-profile cases, such as deaths caused by autonomous vehicles. They also apply to more commonplace but still significant uses, such as in automated decisions about parole or creditworthiness. Yet the relationship between the degree and quality of agency that people enjoy and how much agency we delegate to autonomous systems is not zero sum, either pragmatically or ethically. In fact, if developed thoughtfully, AI offers the opportunity to *improve and multiply* the possibilities for human agency. Consider examples of 'distributed morality' in human-to-human systems such as peer-to-peer lending (Floridi 2013). Human agency may be ultimately supported, refined, and expanded by the embedding of 'facilitating frameworks' (designed to improve the likelihood of morally good outcomes) in the set of functions that we delegate to AI systems. If designed effectively, AI systems could amplify and strengthen shared moral systems.

10.4 What We Can Achieve: Increasing Societal Capabilities without Reducing Human Control

AI offers many opportunities for improving and augmenting the capabilities of individuals and society at large. Whether by preventing and curing diseases or optimizing transportation and logistics, the use of AI technologies presents countless possibilities for reinventing society by radically enhancing what humans are collectively capable of. More AI may support better collaboration, and hence more ambitious goals. Human intelligence augmented by AI could find new solutions to old and new problems ranging from a fairer or more efficient distribution of resources to a more sustainable approach to consumption. Precisely because such technologies have the potential to be so powerful and disruptive, they also introduce proportionate risks. Increasingly, there will be processes in which we may not need to be either 'in or on the loop' (that is, as part of the process or at least in control of it) if we can delegate our tasks to AI. But if we rely on the use of AI technologies to augment our own abilities in the wrong way, we may delegate important tasks. Above all, we may delegate crucial decisions to autonomous systems that should remain at least partly subject to human supervision, choice, and rectification. This in turn may reduce our ability to monitor the performance of these systems (by no longer being 'on the loop' either) or prevent or redress the errors and harms that arise ('post loop'). It is also possible that these potential harms may accumulate and become entrenched as more and more functions are delegated to artificial systems. It is therefore imperative to strike a balance between pursuing the ambitious opportunities offered by AI to improve human life and what we can achieve on the one hand, and ensuring that we remain in control of these major developments and their effects on the other.

10.5 How We Can Interact: Cultivating Societal Cohesion without Eroding Human Self-Determination

From climate change and antimicrobial resistance to nuclear proliferation, wars, and fundamentalism, global problems increasingly involve high degrees of coordination complexity. This means they can be tackled successfully only if all stakeholders co-design and co-own the solutions and cooperate to bring them about. AI can hugely help to deal with such coordination complexity with its data-intensive, algorithmic-driven solutions, supporting more societal cohesion and collaboration. For example, we shall see in Chapter 12 efforts to tackle climate change have exposed the challenge of creating a cohesive response, both within societies and between them.

In fact, the scale of the challenge is such that we may soon need to decide how to strike a balance between engineering the climate directly and designing societal frameworks to encourage a drastic cut in harmful emissions. This latter option could be undergirded by an algorithmic system to cultivate societal cohesion. Such a system should not be imposed from the outside; it should be the result of a self-imposed choice, not unlike our choice to not buy chocolate if we had earlier chosen to go on a diet, or to set an alarm to wake up early. 'Self-nudging' to behave in socially preferable ways is the best form of nudging, and the only one that preserves autonomy (Floridi 2015c, 2016f). It is the outcome of human decisions and choices, yet it can rely on AI solutions to be implemented and facilitated. But the risk is that AI systems may erode human self-determination as they may lead to unplanned and unwelcome changes in human behaviours to accommodate the routines that make automation work and people's lives easier. AI's predictive power and relentless nudging, even if unintentional, should be at the service of human self-determination. It should foster societal cohesion, not undermine human dignity or human flourishing.

10.6 Twenty Recommendations for a Good AI Society

Taken together along with their corresponding challenges, the four opportunities outlined above paint a mixed picture about the impact of AI on society and the people in it, and the overall environments they share. Accepting the presence of trade-offs and seizing the opportunities while working to anticipate, avoid, or minimize the risks head-on will improve the prospect for AI technologies to promote human dignity and flourishing. Ensuring that the outcomes of AI are socially preferable (equitable) depends on resolving the tension between incorporating the benefits and mitigating the potential harms of AI—in short, simultaneously avoiding the misuse and underuse of these technologies.

In this context, the value of an ethical approach to AI technologies comes into starker relief. In Chapter 6, I argued that compliance with the law is merely necessary (the least that is required), but significantly insufficient (not the most that can be done). It is the difference between playing according to the rules and playing well to win the game, so to speak. We need an ethical strategy, a soft ethics for the digital society we wish to build. In line with this distinction, what follows are twenty recommendations for a Good AI Society. There are four general areas for action to *assess*, to *develop*, to *incentivize*, and to *support*. Some recommendations may be undertaken directly, by national or European policymakers, for example, working in collaboration with stakeholders where appropriate. For other recommendations, policymakers may play an enabling role to support efforts undertaken or led by third parties.

The assumption is that, to create a Good AI Society, the ethical principles identified in Chapter 4 should be embedded in the default practices of AI. In particular, we saw in Chapter 9 that AI can and should be designed and developed in ways that decrease inequality and further social empowerment, with respect for human dignity and autonomy, to increase the benefits that are equitably shared by all. It is especially important that AI be explicable as explicability is a critical tool for building public trust in, and understanding of, the technology. Creating a Good AI Society requires a multi-stakeholder approach. This is the most effective way to ensure that AI will serve the needs of society by enabling developers, users, and rule makers to all be on board, collaborating from the outset. Inevitably, different cultural frameworks inform attitudes to new technology.

A final comment before presenting the recommendations: the following European approach is meant to complement other approaches. It should not be misunderstood for some sort of endorsement of a Eurocentric perspective. In the same way that I needed to ground ethical considerations in Chapter 8 within a specific legal framework (English criminal law, in that case) without loss of generality, the choice to contextualize the following recommendations within an EU setting is likewise only meant to provide them with a concrete and actionable value. There is nothing in the recommendations that make them particularly EU-only or EU-centred, and they remain universalizable. This is because no matter where we live in the world, we should all be committed to the development of AI technologies in a way that secures people's trust, serves the public interest, strengthens shared social responsibility, and supports the environment.

1) Assess the capacity of existing institutions, such as national civil courts, to redress the mistakes made or harms inflicted by AI systems. This assessment should evaluate the presence of sustainable, majority-agreed foundations for liability from the design stage onwards to reduce negligence and conflicts (see also Recommendation 5).[3]

2) Assess which tasks and decision-making functionalities should not be delegated to AI systems using participatory mechanisms to ensure alignment with societal values and understanding of public opinion. This assessment should consider existing legislation and be supported by ongoing dialogue between all stakeholders (including government, industry, and civil society), to debate how AI will impact society (in concert with Recommendation 17).

3) Assess whether current regulations are sufficiently grounded in ethics to provide a legislative framework that can keep pace with technological

[3] The task of determining accountability and responsibility may be borrowed from lawyers in ancient Rome who would go by the formula 'cuius commoda eius et incommoda' ('the person who derives an advantage from a situation must also bear the inconvenience'). A good 2,200-year-old principle supported by a well-established tradition and elaboration could properly set the starting level of abstraction in this field.

developments. This may include a framework of key principles that would be applicable to urgent and/or unanticipated problems.

4) Develop a framework to enhance the explicability of AI systems that make socially significant decisions. Central to this framework is the ability for individuals to obtain a factual, direct, and clear explanation of the decision-making process, especially in the event of unwanted conse-quences. This is likely to require the development of frameworks specific to different industries; professional associations should be involved in this process alongside experts in science, business, law, and ethics.

5) Develop appropriate legal procedures and improve the digital infrastruc-ture of the justice system to permit the scrutiny of algorithmic decisions in court. This is likely to include the creation of a framework for AI explainability (as indicated in Recommendation 4) specific to the legal system. Examples of appropriate procedures could include the applicable disclosure of sensitive commercial information in intellectual property (IP) litigation. Where disclosure poses unacceptable risks (such as to national security), procedures should include the configuration of AI sys-tems to adopt technical solutions by default (such as zero-knowledge proofs) to evaluate their trustworthiness.

6) Develop auditing mechanisms for AI systems to identify unwanted consequences, such as unfair bias. Auditing should also (perhaps in cooperation with the insurance sector) include a solidarity mechanism to deal with severe risks in AI-intensive sectors. Those risks could be mitigated by multi-stakeholder mechanisms upstream. Pre-digital experience indicates that, in some cases, it may take a couple of decades before society catches up with technology by way of rebalancing rights and protection adequately to restore trust. The earlier that users and governments become involved (as made possible by digital technologies), the shorter this lag will be.

7) Develop a redress process or mechanism to remedy or compensate for a wrong or grievance caused by AI. To foster public trust in AI, society needs a widely accessible and reliable mechanism of redress for harms inflicted, costs incurred, or other grievances caused by the technology. Such a mechanism will necessarily involve a clear and comprehensive allocation of accountability to humans and/or organizations. Lessons could be learnt from the aerospace industry, for example, which has a proven system for handling unwanted consequences thoroughly and ser-iously. The development of this process must follow from the assessment of existing capacity outlined in Recommendation 1. If a lack of capacity is identified, additional institutional solutions should be developed at national and/or EU levels to enable people to seek redress. Such solutions could include:

- an 'AI ombudsperson' to ensure the auditing of allegedly unfair or inequitable uses of AI;
- a guided process for registering a complaint akin to making a Freedom of Information request; and
- the development of liability insurance mechanisms that would be required as an obligatory accompaniment of specific classes of AI offerings in EU and other markets. This would ensure that the relative reliability of AI-powered artefacts, especially in robotics, is mirrored in insurance pricing and therefore in the market prices of competing products.[4]

Whichever solutions are developed, these are likely to rely on the framework for intelligibility proposed in Recommendation 4.

8) Develop agreed-upon metrics for the trustworthiness of AI products and services. These metrics could be the responsibility of either a new organization or a suitable existing one. They would serve as the basis for a system that enables the user-driven benchmarking of all marketed AI offerings. In this way, an index for trustworthy AI can be developed and signalled in addition to a product's price. This 'trust comparison index' for AI would improve public understanding and engender competitiveness around the development of safer, more socially beneficial AI (e.g. 'IwantgreatAI.org'). In the longer term, such a system could form the basis for a broader system of certification for deserving products and services—one that is administered by the organization noted here, and/or by the oversight agency proposed in Recommendation 9. The organization could also support the development of codes of conduct (see Recommendation 18). Furthermore, those who own or operate inputs to AI systems and profit from it could be tasked with funding and/or helping to develop AI literacy programs for consumers, in their own best interest.

9) Develop a new EU oversight agency responsible for the protection of public welfare through the scientific evaluation and supervision of AI products, software, systems, or services. This could be similar, for example, to the European Medicines Agency. Relatedly, a 'post-release' monitoring system for AIs like the one available for drugs, for example, should be developed with reporting duties for some stakeholders and easy reporting mechanisms for other users.

10) Develop a European observatory for AI. The mission of the observatory would be to watch developments, provide a forum to nurture debate and consensus, provide a repository for AI literature and software (including

---

[4] Of course, to the extent that AI systems are 'products', general tort law still applies in the same way to AI as it applies in any instance involving defective products or services that injure users or do not perform as claimed or expected.

concepts and links to available literature), and issue step-by-step recommendations and guidelines for action.

11) Develop legal instruments and contractual templates to lay the foundation for a smooth and rewarding human–machine collaboration in the work environment. Shaping the narrative on the 'Future of Work' is instrumental to winning 'hearts and minds'. In keeping with 'a Europe that protects', the idea of 'inclusive innovation', and efforts to smooth the transition to new kinds of jobs, a European AI Adjustment Fund could be set up along the lines of the European Globalisation Adjustment Fund.

12) Incentivize financially, at the EU level, the development and use of AI technologies within the EU that are socially preferable (not merely acceptable) and environmentally friendly (not merely sustainable, but actually favourable to the environment). This will include the elaboration of methodologies that can help assess whether AI projects are socially preferable and environmentally friendly. In this vein, adopting a 'challenge approach' (see the Defense Advanced Research Projects Agency, DARPA, challenges) may encourage creativity and promote competition in the development of specific AI solutions that are ethically sound and in the interest of the common good.

13) Incentivize financially a sustained, increased, and coherent European research effort tailored to the specific features of AI as a scientific field of investigation. This should involve a clear mission to advance AI4SG to counterbalance AI trends with less focus on social opportunities.

14) Incentivize financially cross-disciplinary and cross-sectoral cooperation and debate concerning the intersections between technology, social issues, legal studies, and ethics. Debates about technological challenges may lag behind the actual technical progress but if they are strategically informed by a diverse multi-stakeholder group, they may steer and support technological innovation in the right direction. Ethics should help seize opportunities and cope with challenges, not simply describe them. It is thus essential that diversity infuses the design and development of AI, in terms of gender, class, ethnicity, discipline, and other pertinent dimensions, to increase inclusivity, toleration, and the richness of ideas and perspectives.

15) Incentivize financially the inclusion of ethical, legal, and social considerations in AI research projects. In parallel, create incentives for regular reviews of legislation to test the extent to which it fosters socially positive innovation. Taken together, these two measures will help ensure that AI technology has ethics at its heart and that policy is oriented towards innovation.

16) Incentivize financially the development and use of lawfully deregulated special zones within the EU. These zones should be used for the empirical testing and development of AI systems. They may take the form of a

'living lab' (or Tokku), building on the experience of existing 'test highways' (or Teststrecken). In addition to aligning innovation more closely with society's preferred level of risk, sandbox experiments such as these contribute to hands-on education and the promotion of accountability and acceptability at an early stage. 'Protection by design' is intrinsic to this kind of framework.

17) Incentivize financially research about public perception and understanding of AI and its applications. Research should also focus on the implementation of structured mechanisms for public consultation to design policies and rules related to AI. This could include the direct elicitation of public opinion via traditional research methods (such as opinion polls and focus groups), along with more experimental approaches (such as providing simulated examples of the ethical dilemmas introduced by AI systems, or experiments in social science labs). This research agenda should not serve merely to measure public opinion. It should also lead to the co-creation of policies, standards, best practices, and rules as a result.

18) Support the development of self-regulatory codes of conduct, for both data and AI-related professions, with specific ethical duties. This would be along the lines of other socially sensitive professions, such as medical doctors or lawyers. In other words, it would involve the attendant certification of 'ethical AI' through trust labels to make sure that people understand the merits of ethical AI and will therefore demand it from providers. Current attention manipulation techniques may be constrained through these self-regulating instruments.

19) Support the capacity of corporate boards of directors to take responsibility for the ethical implications of companies' AI technologies. This could include improved training for existing boards, for example, or the potential development of an ethics committee with internal auditing powers. It could be developed within the existing structure of both one-tier and two-tier board systems, and/or in conjunction with the development of a mandatory form of 'corporate ethical review board'. The ethical review board would be adopted by organizations developing or using AI systems. It would then evaluate initial projects and their deployment with respect to fundamental principles.

20) Support the creation of educational curricula and public awareness activities around the societal, legal, and ethical impact of AI. This may include:
   • school curricula to support the inclusion of computer science among the other basic disciplines that are taught;
   • initiatives and qualification programmes in businesses dealing with AI technology to educate employees on the societal, legal, and ethical impact of working alongside AI;

- a European-level recommendation to include ethics and human rights within the university degrees for data and AI scientists, as well as within other scientific and engineering curricula dealing with computational and AI systems;
- the development of similar programmes for the public at large. These should have a special focus on those involved at each stage of management for the technology, including civil servants, politicians, and journalists;
- engagement with wider initiatives, such as the AI for Good events hosted by the International Telecommunication Union (ITU) and NGOs working on the UN SDGs.

10.7 Conclusion: The Need for Concrete and Constructive Policies

Humanity faces the emergence of a technology that holds much exciting promise for many aspects of human life. At the same time, it seems to pose major threats as well. This chapter—and especially the recommendations in the preceding section—seeks to nudge the tiller in the direction of ethically, socially, and environmentally preferable outcomes from the development, design, and deployment of AI technologies. The recommendations build on the set of five ethical principles for AI synthesized in Chapter 4, and on the identification of both the risks and the core opportunities of AI for society analysed in Chapters 6–9. They are formulated in the spirit of collaboration and in the interest of creating *concrete* and *constructive* responses to the most pressing social challenges posed by AI.

With the rapid pace of technological change, it is tempting to view the political process of contemporary liberal democracies as old-fashioned, out of step, and no longer up to the task of preserving the values and promoting the interests of society and everyone in it. I disagree. The recommendations offered here, which include the creation of centres, agencies, curricula, and other infrastructure, support the case for an ambitious, inclusive, equitable, and sustainable programme of policymaking and technological innovation. This will contribute to securing the benefits and mitigating the risks of AI for all people, as well as for the world that we share. This is also the goal pursued by the next two chapters on the use of AI in support of the UN SDGs and the impact of AI on climate change.

11

The Gambit

AI Impact on Climate Change

11.0 Summary

Previously, in Chapter 4, I presented the ethical principles that provide a framework for AI. One of these principles, *beneficence*, includes sustaining the planet. This and the following chapter further explore that requirement by analysing the positive and negative environmental impacts of AI. The goal is to provide policy recommendations for a path towards a greener and more climate-friendly development of AI—development especially in line with EU values and legislation. The timing is critical because AI is already used today to model events related to climate change and contribute to efforts in combating global warming. It can thus be a great positive force for a fair and sustainable society.

11.1 Introduction: AI's Double-Edged Power

We saw in the previous chapters how AI is a new kind of agency that can be harnessed to solve problems and perform tasks with unmatched success. But it is equally clear that such a new and powerful agency needs to be developed and governed ethically to avoid, minimize, and rectify any negative impact it may have, and to ensure that it benefits humanity and the planet. This holds true also, or perhaps particularly, when it comes to climate change, which is the biggest threat facing humanity in our century (Cowls et al. 2021a). On the one hand, AI can be an extremely powerful tool in the fight against climate change and we need all the help we can get (Ramchurn et al. 2012, Rolnick et al. 2019). On the other hand, there are significant pitfalls (both ethical and environmental) that must be avoided (Mendelsohn, Dinar, and Williams 2006, Anthony, Kanding, and Selvan 2020, Cowls et al. 2021a, Malmodin and Lundén 2018). Understanding these pitfalls is crucial to this end and concrete policy steps can help, as we shall see in this chapter. More specifically, AI presents two crucial opportunities.

The first opportunity is epistemological. AI can help improve and expand our current understanding of climate change by making it possible to process immense volumes of data. This will permit study of existing climate trends, the forecasting of future developments, and predictions about the impact and success (or lack thereof)

The Ethics of Artificial Intelligence: Principles, Challenges, and Opportunities. Luciano Floridi, Oxford University Press.
© Luciano Floridi 2023. DOI: 10.1093/oso/9780198883098.003.0011

of policies. AI techniques have been used to forecast global mean temperature changes (Ise and Oba 2019, Cifuentes et al. 2020); predict climactic and oceanic phenomena such as El Niño (Ham, Kim, and Luo 2019), cloud systems (Rasp, Pritchard, and Gentine 2018), and tropical instability waves (Zheng et al. 2020); better understand aspects of the weather system like rainfall, both generally (Sønderby et al. 2020, Larraondo et al. 2020) and in specific locales such as Malaysia (Ridwan et al. 2020); and further study their knock-on consequences, such as water demand (Shrestha, Manandhar, and Shrestha 2020, Xenochristou et al. 2020). AI tools can also help anticipate the extreme weather events that are more common due to global climate change. For example, AI tools have been used to anticipate heavy rain damage (Choi et al. 2018), wildfires (Jaafari et al. 2019), and downstream consequences such as patterns of human migration (Robinson and Dilkina 2018). In many cases, AI techniques can help improve or expedite existing forecasting and prediction systems. They can automatically label climate modelling data (Chattopadhyay, Hassanzadeh, and Pasha 2020), improve approximations for simulating the atmosphere (Gagne et al. 2020), and separate signals from noise in climate observations (Barnes et al. 2019). All of this is part of an even more general trend: there is virtually no scientific analysis and evidence-based policy that is not powered by advanced digital technologies. AI is becoming part of the necessary tools to advance our scientific understanding in many fields.

The second opportunity is ethical. AI can help deliver greener and more effective solutions, such as improving and optimizing energy generation and use. In this sense, it can proactively contribute to the fight against global warming. Combating climate change effectively requires a vast array of responses related to mitigating the existing effects of climate change and reducing emissions through decarbonization to prevent further warming. For example, a 2018 Microsoft/PwC report estimated that using AI for environmental applications could boost global GDP by between 3.1 and 4.4 per cent; at the same time, the use of AI in this context would also reduce greenhouse gas (GHG) emissions anywhere from 1.5 to 4 per cent by 2030, compared to a 'business as usual' scenario (Microsoft 2018, 8).

In fact, an array of AI-based techniques already plays a key role in many of these responses (Inderwildi et al. 2020, Sayed-Mouchaweh 2020). This includes energy efficiency in industry, for example, especially in the petrochemical sector (Narciso and Martins 2020). Studies have also used AI to understand industrial pollution in China (Zhou et al. 2016), the carbon footprint of concrete used in construction (Thilakarathna et al. 2020), and even energy efficiency in shipping (Perera, Mo, and Soares 2016). Other work has explored the use of AI in electrical grid management (Di Piazza et al. 2020), to forecast building energy usage (Fathi et al. 2020), and to assess the sustainability of food consumption (Abdella et al. 2020). AI can help to predict carbon emissions based on present trends (Mardani et al. 2020, Wei, Yuwei, and Chongchong 2018) along with the impact of interventionist policies like a carbon tax (Abrell, Kosch, and Rausch 2019) or carbon trading systems (Lu et al. 2020). AI could further be used to help monitor the active removal of carbon from the atmosphere through sequestration (Menad et al. 2019).

Beyond this indicative evidence, the growing use of AI to fight climate change can also be seen from the higher vantage point of major institutions and large-scale initiatives. The European Lab for Learning & Intelligent Systems (ELLIS) has a Machine Learning for Earth and Climate Sciences programme that aims to 'model and understand the Earth system with Machine Learning and Process Understanding'.[1] The European Space Agency has also established the Digital Twin Earth Challenge to provide 'forecasting on the impact of climate change and responding to societal challenges'.[2] Several European universities have initiatives and training programmes dedicated to unlocking the power of AI for climate.[3,4] In 2020, a search of Cordis (the European database for funded research) for current projects addressing climate change and AI returned a total of 122 results (Cowls et al. 2021a).[5] Analysis of these 122 projects suggested they represent both geographic and disciplinary breadth. The projects were well spread across the continent, albeit with a clear skew towards western Europe in terms of where they were coordinated. A large majority of projects were related to the natural sciences and/or engineering and technology, but a considerable number were also anchored in social sciences. The breadth of subjects that these projects touched on was vast, spanning domains as diverse as viticulture, mycology, and galactic astronomy.

There is also considerable evidence of private and non-profit initiatives using AI to combat climate change around the world. Microsoft's AI for Earth is a five-year, $50 million initiative established in 2017 to support organizations and researchers using AI and other computational techniques to tackle various aspects of the climate crisis. It currently has sixteen partner organizations.[6] The initiative has released relevant open-source tools[7] and provided grants in the form of cloud computing credits to projects using AI for a variety of purposes ranging from monitoring climate change in the Antarctic to protecting bird populations after hurricanes. Google's AI4SG programme supports twenty organizations using AI to pursue various socially beneficial goals with funding and cloud computing credits. This includes projects seeking to minimize crop damage in India, better manage waste in Indonesia, protect rainforests in the US, and improve air quality

---

[1] https://ellis.eu/programs/machine-learning-for-earth-and-climate-sciences.
[2] https://copernicus-masters.com/prize/esa-challenge/.
[3] https://www.exeter.ac.uk/research/environmental-intelligence/.
[4] https://ai4er-cdt.esc.cam.ac.uk.
[5] Conducted on 30 November 2020, the search of the Cordis research project database used the search string [('climate change' OR 'global warming') AND ('artificial intelligence' OR 'machine learning')], (n = 122).
[6] https://www.microsoft.com/en-us/ai/ai-for-earth-partners.
[7] https://microsoft.github.io/AIforEarth-Grantees/.

in Uganda.[8] Meanwhile, the development company ElementAI's AI for Climate program provided (the company was acquired by ServiceNow in 2020) expertise and partnership opportunities to improve the energy efficiency of manufacturing and business operations. Finally, we shall see in Chapter 12 how there are many AI projects that support the UN SDGs.

However, there are also two main challenges associated with developing AI to combat climate change. One pertains to AI in general: it is the possible exacerbation of some social and ethical problems already associated with AI, such as unfair bias, discrimination, or opacity in decision making. I discussed these problems in Chapters 7 and 8. The other challenge is specific to climate change. It is less understood, and thus one of the main topics of this chapter. It concerns the contribution to global climate change from GHGs emitted by training data and computation-intensive AI systems: the current lack of information about the source and amount of energy used in researching, developing, and deploying AI models makes it difficult to define exactly the carbon footprint of AI.

To address this latter challenge, at the Digital Ethics Lab we specifically studied the carbon footprint of AI research and the factors that influence the GHG emissions of AI at the research and development stage (Cowls et al. 2021a). We also looked at the lack of scientific evidence concerning the trade-off between the emissions required to research, develop, and deploy AI, and the energy and resource efficiency gains that AI can offer. The conclusion was that leveraging the opportunities offered by AI for global climate change is both feasible and desirable. But it will involve a sacrifice (in terms of ethical risks and a potential increase in carbon footprint) in view of a very significant gain (a more effective response to climate change). It is, in other words, a *green gambit*. As I highlighted in Floridi (2014a), this gambit requires responsive and effective governance to become a winning strategy. For this reason, we offered some recommendations for policymakers and AI researchers and developers in the aforementioned work. These recommendations were designed to identify and harness the opportunities of AI for combating climate change while reducing the impact of its development on the environment. This chapter is based on and updates that work.

11.2 AI and the EU's 'Twin Transitions'

In 2020–1, European Commission President Ursula von der Leyen embraced the digital and ecological 'twin transitions' that will shape our future. High-level policy documents highlighted how EU digital initiatives (e.g. 'A Europe Fit for the Digital Age'), including AI, and ecological goals such as the 'European Green

---

[8] https://impactchallenge.withgoogle.com/ai2018.

Deal' can converge. This suggests a helpful starting point for policymaking. The need for financial stimulus resulting from the coronavirus pandemic also opened avenues for tailoring public assistance to promote these 'twin transitions'. The commission saw the two transitions as being deeply interrelated, to the point that the 'European Green Deal' proposal was full of references to the role of digital tools. A roadmap for the Green Deal released in December 2019 noted that:

> digital technologies are a critical enabler for attaining the sustainability goals of the Green Deal in many sectors...[and that technologies] such as artificial intelligence...can accelerate and maximise the impact of policies to deal with climate change and protect the environment specifically in the areas of energy grids, consumer products, pollution monitoring, mobility, and food and agriculture.

The approach of the commission resonates with the idea, which I shall articulate in Chapter 13, of a new marriage between the Green of all our habitats and the Blue of all our digital technologies (Floridi and Nobre 2020). The use of AI to fight climate change is a leading example of such a Green & Blue marriage (Floridi 2019c). Finally, many of the documents produced by the commission to flesh out its digital and environmental vision refer to AI as a key tool, particularly in reference to 'Destination Earth' (an ambitious plan to create a digital model of the Earth and simulate human activity to test the potential effectiveness of Europe's environmental policies). AI is explicitly mentioned as a key component of the Destination Earth initiative. The draft of the proposal for EU legislation on AI also identified AI as a potentially great tool to support sustainable policies (European Commission 2021). In short, the European focus on 'good AI' is in line both with EU values and funding and with scientific efforts around the world. But for all the documents that have been produced by the European Commission in which AI has been identified as a key tool, and for all the opportunities they highlight, they tend to overlook the challenges that must be addressed to ensure the successful and sustainable adoption of AI tools.

11.3 AI and Climate Change: Ethical Challenges

From ethical and privacy concerns to the significant amount of energy that goes into training and deploying AI tools, understanding and taking steps to address those challenges is crucial to ensure the sustainability of AI deployment in the battle against global warming.

A difficulty facing any effort to explain the role that AI can play in combating climate change is determining where the technology is already being used equitably and sustainably. There have been several efforts to create an accurate overview of how AI is being harnessed around the world in climate projects.

However, the rapid pace of technological development has inevitably limited the accuracy of any single survey. Some approaches have focused on the United Nations SDGs (particularly those dealing most specifically with climate-related issues) as a starting point to identify AI projects. I shall analyse this approach in Chapter 12. Here, it is sufficient to anticipate that the University of Oxford's Research Initiative on AIxSDGs[9] includes tens of projects related to Goal 13, which most specifically focuses on climate change. But other databases using the SDGs as a starting point contain far fewer projects. This is a testament to the work that still needs to be done to improve the understanding of the many climate-related areas where AI has been deployed.

Against this background, it is important to recall that a key challenge involves the ethical risks associated with AI more broadly. We have seen in Chapters 7 and 8 that these risks are far more significant in areas such as healthcare and criminal justice, where data privacy is crucial, and decisions have a far greater impact on individuals. Even so, it is nevertheless vital to minimize the ethical risks that may arise when applying AI solutions to climate change. Because AI models are 'trained' using existing datasets, there is a potential for introducing bias into such models due to the datasets chosen for training. Imagine, for example, deploying AI to determine where to set up charging stations for electric vehicles. Using the existing driving patterns of electric cars could skew the data towards a wealthier demographic due to the relatively higher prevalence of electric vehicle use among higher income brackets. That, in turn, would create an additional hurdle to increasing electric car use in less wealthy areas.

Another potential ethical pitfall concerns the erosion of human autonomy. Tackling climate change requires large-scale coordinated action, including systemic changes to individual behaviour. A careful balance must be struck here between protecting individual autonomy and implementing large-scale, climate-friendly policies and practices.

Finally, there is the problem of protecting individual and group privacy (Floridi 2014c). In control systems designed to decrease carbon footprints in a range of contexts, such as energy storage (Dobbe et al. 2019), industrial heating and cooling (Aftab et al. 2017), and precision agriculture (Liakos et al. 2018), the effectiveness of AI systems depends on granular data about energy demands often available in real time. While many AI solutions deployed in the battle against climate change rely on non-personal data, such as meteorological and geographical data, some strategies for limiting emissions may require data pertaining to human behaviour. This tension was highlighted in a survey[10] of thirteen EU countries produced by the Vodafone Institute for Society and Communications. The survey

---

[9] This is a project I directed in collaboration with the Saïd Business School to provide a database of AI projects that support the SDGs; see https://www.aiforsdgs.org.
[10] https://www.vodafone-institut.de/wp-content/uploads/2020/10/VFI-DE-Pulse_Climate.pdf.

showed that while Europeans are broadly willing to share their data to help protect the environment, a clear majority (53 per cent) would do so only under strict conditions of data protection.

11.4 AI and Climate Change: Digital Carbon Footprint

Perhaps the greatest challenge associated with the use of AI in addressing climate change is assessing and accounting for the carbon footprint of the technology itself. After all, it is of little help if AI solutions contribute to alleviating one aspect of climate change while exacerbating another. In the sense of both training models and uses, AI can consume vast amounts of energy and generate GHG emissions (García-Martín et al. 2019, Cai et al. 2020). A significant share of the carbon footprint generated by AI is associated with the computing power necessary to train ML systems.

Such systems are trained by being fed vast quantities of data, which requires correspondingly powerful data centres. Those data centres need energy to operate, in turn. I recall reminding people in the past that the heat of a laptop on your legs was a clear sign of environmental impact. Today, after the advent of deep learning, a type of ML that involves algorithms learning from huge amounts of data, the computing power required for model training has doubled every 3.4 months. This has resulted in growing energy demand. The increase in energy consumption associated with training larger models and with the widespread adoption of AI has been in part mitigated by hardware efficiency improvements. But depending on where and how energy is sourced, stored, and delivered, the rise of compute-intensive AI research can have significant negative environmental effects.

Many factors contribute to the carbon footprint of AI. One of these is the computing power necessary to train ML models. With the emergence of deep learning as a central technique for AI systems since 2012, the computing power required for model training has seen an exponential rise (Amodei and Hernandez 2018). The result is growing energy demand and hence carbon emissions. Its carbon footprint remains relative to where and how electricity is sourced, stored, and delivered. As an example, let us consider GPT-3, the third-generation, autoregressive language model that uses deep learning to produce human-like text. Its development is problematic from an environmental perspective. According to documentation published in May 2020, GPT-3 required an amount of computational power (compute) several orders of magnitude higher than its predecessor GPT-2, which was published only one year prior. Due to lack of information pertaining to the training conditions and development process of GPT-3, a number of researchers using different methodologies have attempted to estimate the cost of a single training run (Anthony, Kanding, and Selvan 2020). Several factors need to be tracked to determine the carbon footprint of an AI system, including the type of hardware used, the duration of a training run, the number of neural networks trained, the time of day, memory usage, and energy resources used by the energy grid supplying the electricity (Henderson et al. 2020). Missing some of these data can skew carbon assessments. Thus, one can estimate the cost of a single training run for GPT-3, but the publication does not reveal how many models were trained to achieve publishable results. Consider, too, that it is common for AI researchers to train thousands of models first (Schwartz et al. 2020).

Despite all these constraints, using information pertaining to the amount of computing power and type of hardware that was used by researchers at OpenAI to train GPT-3 (Brown et al. 2020), making assumptions as to the rest of the model training conditions (for more information, see Cowls et al. (2021a)), and using Lacoste et al.'s (2019) carbon impact calculator, we estimated that a single training run of GPT-3 would have produced 223,920 kg of CO_2 (or equivalent, CO_2eq). Had the cloud provider been Amazon Web Services, the training run would have produced 279,900 kg CO_2eq. That is without considering the providers' accounting and offsetting techniques to achieve 'net zero' emissions. By comparison, a typical passenger car in the United States emits about 4,600 kg of CO_2eq per year, meaning that a single training run using Microsoft Azure would emit as much as forty-nine cars do in a year (EPA 2016). Furthermore, geography is important. It is ten times more costly in terms of CO_2eq to train a model using energy grids in South Africa than in France, for example.

The increasing availability of massive quantities of data has been a major factor fuelling the rise of AI. So, too, have new methods designed to leverage Moore's law, according to which microchip performance doubles every two years. The introduction of chips with multiple processor cores massively accelerated that development (Thompson et al. 2020). This innovation has enabled the development of increasingly complex AI systems, but it has also significantly increased the amount of energy needed to research, train, and operate them. The trend is well known and major data centre operators, such as cloud providers like Microsoft Azure and Google Cloud, have taken significant steps to reduce their carbon footprint by investing in energy-efficient infrastructure, switching to renewable energy, recycling waste heat, and other similar measures. Both providers have leveraged AI to reduce the energy consumption of their data centres—in some cases by up to 40 per cent (Evans and Gao 2016, Microsoft 2018).

The demand for data centres, which are key to the ICT sector and the operation of AI in research and production settings, has also grown substantially in recent years. On the one hand, the energy consumption of data centres has remained relatively stable (Avgerinou, Bertoldi, and Castellazzi 2017, Shehabi et al. 2018, Jones 2018, Masanet et al. 2020). The International Energy Agency reports that, if current efficiency trends in hardware and data centre infrastructure can be maintained, global data centre energy demand (currently 1 per cent of global electricity demand) can remain nearly flat through 2022 despite a 60 per cent increase in service demand. On the other hand, even in the EU, where energy-efficient cloud computing has become a primary issue on the political agenda, the European Commission estimates a 28 per cent increase in the energy consumption of data centres by 2030 (European Commission 2020). A source of uncertainty is the lack of transparency regarding the data required to calculate GHG emissions of on-premises data centres as well as cloud vendors. Also, calculating the carbon footprint of AI involves more than just data centres. It thus remains unclear whether increased energy efficiency in data centres will offset the rapidly rising demand for computational power. It is further unclear whether such efficiency gains will be realized equally around the world.

For all these reasons, it is crucial to assess the carbon footprint of various AI solutions used in different aspects of understanding climate change or in developing strategies to address specific aspects of it. But this, too, is problematic. Easy-to-use techniques for monitoring and controlling the carbon emissions of AI research and development are only now beginning to appear. Still, some approaches seem promising. The goal is to track several factors during model training phases to help assess and control emissions. The factors include the type of hardware used, the training duration, the energy resources used by the energy grid supplying the electricity, memory usage, and others.

Nevertheless, even the lower hurdles to reducing AI's carbon footprint are difficult to clear due to the lack of widespread adoption of such approaches and thus to the lack of information in many AI research publications. That can also lead to unnecessary carbon emissions when other researchers seek to reproduce the results of AI studies. Some papers do not provide their code, while others provide insufficient information about the training conditions of their models. Additionally, the number of experiments run by researchers before achieving publishable results is underreported. Some experiments require the training of thousands of models during research and development phases only to achieve modest performance improvements. Massive amounts of computational power can go into fine-tuning. One example here is a research paper by Google Brain, which described the training of over 12,800 neural networks to achieve a 0.09 per cent improvement in accuracy (Fedus, Zoph, and Shazeer 2021). Modern AI research has tended to focus on producing deeper and more accurate models at the detriment of energy efficiency.

Focusing heavily on accuracy over efficiency improvements tends to create a high barrier to entry, since only research groups that are very well funded can afford the computational power required. Research teams from smaller organizations or those in developing countries are thus sidelined. It also institutionalizes an attitude of 'the bigger, the better' and incentivizes incremental improvements even if they are negligible in terms of practical utility. Some researchers are seeking to lower the computational burden and energy consumption of AI through algorithmic improvements and building more efficient models. And it is also vital to consider how even if training AI models is energy intensive, many of these models alleviate (or replace altogether) tasks that would otherwise require more time, space, human effort, and energy.

What the field needs to reconsider is its commitment to computer-intensive research for its own sake. It should move away from performance metrics that focus exclusively on accuracy improvements while ignoring their environmental costs. The EU has a vital role to play here. Given the positive role that AI can have in the battle against climate change and given Europe's goals for both climate change and digitization, the EU would be a perfect sponsor in addressing the complexities associated with the technology's own contribution to the problem and in meeting the need for coordinated, multilevel policymaking to ensure the successful adoption of AI solutions. That is why this chapter and the following recommendations are written from an EU perspective. As I already stressed before, it is not because the EU is the only or even the best actor in this area. Rather, it is a sufficiently significant actor that can make a difference and lead by example.

11.5 Thirteen Recommendations in Favour of AI against Climate Change

The following recommendations focus on the two broad objectives suggested above. First, there is the objective of harnessing the opportunities presented by AI to combat climate change in ways that are ethically sound. And second, there is the objective of minimizing the size of AI's carbon footprint. The recommendations urge all relevant stakeholders to assess existing capacities and potential opportunities, incentivize the creation of new infrastructure, and develop new approaches to allow society to maximize the potential of AI in the context of climate change—all while minimizing ethical and environmental drawbacks.

11.5.1 Promoting Ethical AI in the Fight against Climate Change

Performing comprehensive surveys and holding global conferences does not seem sufficient to gather, document, and analyse the use of AI to combat climate change. More needs to be done to identify and promote such efforts. The European Strategy for Data notes that a current lack of data also hinders the use of data for the public good. There is a need for legislative and regulatory steps to encourage business-to-business and business-to-government data sharing to promote the development of more and better AI-based solutions (either as for-profit products and services or as efforts to tackle climate-related issues without a profit incentive).

Given the European Union's goals for both climate change and digitization, it would be an ideal sponsor of such incentivization efforts. With the agreement that parts of the Coronavirus Recovery Fund should specifically be dedicated to combat climate change and go towards digital transition, there seems to be plenty of scope for these recommendations to become reality. The EU is also perfectly positioned to ensure that steps are taken to prevent bias and discrimination from creeping into AI tools, and to ensure that AI metrics are transparent to all stakeholders.

1) Create incentives for a world-leading initiative (an observatory) to document evidence of AI being used to combat climate change around the world, derive best practices and lessons learned, and disseminate the findings among researchers, policymakers, and the public.

2) Develop standards of quality, accuracy, relevance, and interoperability for data for inclusion in the forthcoming Common European Green Deal data space; identify aspects of climate action for which more data would be most beneficial; and explore, in consultation with domain experts and civil society organizations, how these data could be pooled in a common global climate data space.

3) Create incentives for collaboration between data providers and technical experts in the private sector with domain experts from civil society. These should occur in the form of 'challenges' aimed at ensuring that the data in the Common European Green Deal data space are utilized effectively against climate change.

4) Create incentives for the development of sustainable, scalable responses to climate change that incorporate AI technology, drawing on earmarked Recovery Fund resources.

5) Develop mechanisms for the ethical auditing of AI systems, which should be deployed in high-stakes climate change contexts where personal data may be used and/or individual behaviour may be affected. Ensure that clear, accessible statements regarding what metrics AI systems are optimized for, and why this is justified, are made available prior to the deployment of these systems. The possibility for affected stakeholders to question and contest system design and outcomes should also be guaranteed.

11.5.2 Gauging and Auditing the Carbon Footprint of AI: Researchers and Developers

There are many immediate steps that can be taken by those in the research and development field to ensure that the carbon footprint of AI is both properly gauged and kept in check. Indeed, many steps have already been taken, such as encouraging paper submissions to include source code for the purpose of ensuring reproducibility. Systematic and accurate measurements to evaluate the energy consumption and carbon emissions of AI are also needed for research activities. Recommendations 6 and 7 are key to normalizing the disclosure of information pertaining to the carbon footprint of AI, enabling researchers and organizations to include environmental considerations when choosing research tools.

6) Develop conference and journal checklists that include the disclosure of, *inter alia*, energy consumption, computational complexity, and experiments (e.g. number of training runs, and models produced) to align the field on common metrics.

7) Assess the carbon footprint of AI models that appear on popular libraries and platforms, such as PyTorch, TensorFlow, and Hugging Face, to inform users about their environmental costs.

8) Create incentives for the initiation of efficiency metrics for AI research and development (including model training) by promoting efficiency improvements and objectives in journals, at conferences, and at challenges.

11.5.3 Gauging and Controlling the Carbon Footprint of AI: Policymakers

When it comes to accessing computational power and making AI research more accessible and affordable, policymakers also have a vital role to play in levelling the playing field. One example is a proposal by researchers in the United States to nationalize cloud infrastructure to give more researchers affordable access. A European equivalent could enable researchers in the EU to compete more effectively on a global scale while ensuring that such research takes place on an efficient and sustainable platform.

9) Develop greener, smarter, and cheaper data infrastructure (e.g. European research data centres) for researchers and universities across the EU.

10) Assess AI and its underlying infrastructure (e.g. data centres) when formulating energy management and carbon mitigation strategies to ensure that the European AI sector becomes sustainable as well as uniquely competitive.

11) Develop carbon assessment and disclosure standards for AI to help the field align on metrics, increase research transparency, and communicate carbon footprints effectively via methods such as adding carbon labels to AI-based technologies and models listed in online libraries, journals, and leader boards.

12) Incentivize diverse research agendas by funding and rewarding projects that diverge from the current trend of computer-intensive AI research to explore energy-efficient AI.

13) Incentivize energy-efficient and green research by making EU funding conditional on applicants measuring and reporting their estimated energy consumption and GHG emissions. Funding could fluctuate according to environmental efforts made (e.g. the usage of efficient equipment or renewable electricity, a Power Usage Effectiveness of <1.5).

11.6 Conclusion: A More Sustainable Society and a Healthier Biosphere

AI represents only part of the 1.4 per cent of global GHG emissions associated with ICT (Malmodin and Lundén 2018). However, there is a risk that current trends in AI research and development may quickly accelerate its carbon footprint. Depending on future efficiency gains and the diversification of energy sources, estimates indicate that the ICT sector will be responsible for anywhere between 1.4 per cent (assuming stagnant growth) to 23 per cent of global emissions by 2030 (Andrae and Edler 2015, Malmodin and Lundén 2018, C2E2 2018, Belkhir and Elmeligi 2018, Jones 2018, Hintemann and Hinterholzer 2019). In this wider context, keeping the carbon footprint of AI under control depends on systematic and accurate measurements along with continued energy-efficiency gains as global demand rises. In the fight against climate change, the positive impact of AI can be very significant. But it is crucial to identify and mitigate the potential ethical and environmental pitfalls associated with the technology. The EU's commitment to defending human rights, combating climate change, and promoting the digital transition opens vast opportunities to make sure that AI can realize its potential. The right policies are crucial. If they are properly designed and implemented by policymakers, it will be possible to harness the power of AI while mitigating its negative impact—paving the way for a fair, sustainable society, and a healthier biosphere. This is a point that holds true not only for climate change but for all the seventeen SDGs set by the UN, as I shall argue in the next chapter.

12
AI and the UN Sustainable Development Goals

12.0 Summary

Previously, in Chapter 11, I analysed the positive and negative impact of AI on climate change and offered some recommendations to increase the former and decrease the latter. I mentioned that climate change is one of the areas where AI is being used to support the UN SDGs. As we saw in Chapter 9, initiatives relying on AI to deliver socially beneficial outcomes (so-called AI4SG) are on the rise. However, existing attempts to understand and foster AI4SG initiatives have so far been limited by the lack of normative analyses and a shortage of empirical evidence. Following the analyses provided in Chapters 9–11, this chapter addresses these limits by supporting use of the United Nations' SDGs as a benchmark for tracing the scope and spread of AI4SG. The chapter also presents in more detail a database of AI4SG projects (already mentioned in Chapter 11) collected using this benchmark. I discuss several key insights, including the extent to which different SDGs are being addressed. The goal of the chapter is to facilitate the identification of pressing problems that, if left unaddressed, risk hampering the effectiveness of AI4SG initiatives.

12.1 Introduction: AI4SG and the UN SDGs

The SDGs were set by the United Nations General Assembly in 2015 to integrate the economic, social, and environmental dimensions of sustainable development.[1] They are internationally agreed priorities for socially beneficial action, and thus constitute a sufficiently empirical and reasonably uncontroversial benchmark to evaluate the positive social impact of AI4SG globally. Using the SDGs to evaluate AI4SG applications means equating AI4SG with AI that supports the SDGs (AI × SDGs). This move, AI4SG = AI×SDGs (Cowls et al. 2021b), may seem restrictive because there is undoubtedly a multitude of examples of socially good

---

[1] United Nations Development Programme 2015, 'Sustainable Development Goals', https://www.undp.org/content/undp/en/home/sustainable-development-goals.html.

The Ethics of Artificial Intelligence: Principles, Challenges, and Opportunities. Luciano Floridi, Oxford University Press.

uses of AI outside the scope of the SDGs. Nonetheless, the approach offers five significant advantages.

First, the SDGs offer clear, well-defined, and shareable boundaries to *positively* identify what is socially good AI (what should be done as opposed to what should be avoided). However, they should not be understood as indicating what it is *not* socially good AI.

Second, the SDGs are internationally agreed-upon goals for development. They have begun informing relevant policies worldwide, so they raise fewer questions about the relativity and cultural dependency of values. While inevitably improvable, they are nonetheless the closest thing we have to a humanity-wide consensus on what ought to be done to promote positive social change, advance better standards of living, and conserve our natural environment.

Third, the existing body of research on SDGs already includes studies and metrics on how to measure progress in attaining each of the seventeen goals and the 169 associated targets defined in the 2030 Agenda for Sustainable Development.[2] These metrics can be applied to evaluate the impact of AI×SDGs (Vinuesa et al. 2020).

Fourth, focusing on the impact of AI-based projects across different SDGs can improve existing efforts. It can also lead to new synergies between projects addressing different SDGs, further leveraging AI to gain insights from large and diverse data sets. Ultimately, it can pave the way to more ambitious collaborative projects.

Finally, understanding AI4SG in terms of AI×SDGs enables better planning and resource allocation once it becomes clear which SDGs are under-addressed and why.

12.2 Assessing Evidence of AI×SDGs

In view of the advantages of using the UN SDGs as a benchmark for assessing AI4SG, at the Digital Ethics Lab we conducted an international survey of AI×SDG projects. Running between July 2018 and November 2020, the survey involved collecting data on AI×SDG projects that met the following five criteria:

1) only projects that addressed (even if not explicitly) at least one of the seventeen SDGs;
2) only real-life, concrete projects relying on some actual form of AI (symbolic AI, neural networks, ML, smart robots, natural language processing, etc.) rather than merely referring to AI, which is a not insignificant problem among AI start-ups more generally;[3]

---

[2] United Nations Development Programme 2015, 'Sustainable Development Goals', https://www.undp.org/content/undp/en/home/sustainable-development-goals.html.

[3] Ram, Allya, 4 March 2019, 'Europe's AI Start-ups Often Do Not Use AI, Study Finds', *Financial Times*, https://www.ft.com/content/21b19010-3e9f-11e9-b896-fe36ec32aece.

3) only projects built and used 'in the field' for at least six months, as opposed to theoretical projects or research projects yet to be developed (e.g. patents or grant programmes);

4) only projects with demonstrably positive impact, for example documented through a web site, a newspaper article, a scientific article, an NGO report, etc.; and

5) only projects with no or minimal evidence of counter-indications, negative side-effects, or significant counter-effects.

Requirements (c) and (d) were crucial to unearth concrete examples of AI×SDG, that is, projects with a proven record of robust, positive impact (as opposed to identifying research projects or tools developed in laboratories and trained on data that may prove to be inadequate or unfeasible when the technology is deployed outside controlled environments). No constraints were assumed about who developed the project, where or by whom it was used, who supported it financially, or whether the project was open source, except for projects conducted solely by commercial entities with entirely proprietary systems. These latter projects were excluded.

The projects were discovered via a combination of resources, including academic databases (ArXiv and Scopus), government press releases, patent filings, report tracking, public commitments to the UN SDGs made by organizations, and existing databases (including those at ITU and the Inter-American Development Bank's fAIr LAC partnership). This approach built on existing work by Vinuesa et al. (2020), who used an expert elicitation process to ascertain which of the SDGs could potentially be affected by AI, by offering empirical evidence of actual benefits already being felt with respect to various SDGs.

From a larger pool, the survey identified 108 projects matching these criteria. The data about the AI×SDG projects collected in this study are publicly available in the database (https://www.aiforsdgs.org/all-projects). This is part of the Oxford Research Initiative on Sustainable Development Goals and Artificial Intelligence (https://www.aiforsdgs.org/) that I directed in collaboration with Oxford's Saïd Business School. We presented the first results from our research in September 2019 at a side event during the annual UN General Assembly, then again in 2020. The database we created was merged in 2023 with the database of AI for Sustainable Development Goals (AI4SDGs) Think Tank (available here: https://ai-for-sdgs.academy/)> The outcome of that research was published in Mazzi and Floridi (2023).

The analysis (see Figure 12.1) shows that every SDG is already being addressed by at least one AI-based project. It indicates that the use of AI×SDGs is an increasingly global phenomenon with projects operating from five continents. But also, the phenomenon may not be equally distributed across the SDGs. Goal 3 ('Good Health and Well-Being') leads the way, while Goals 5 ('Gender Equality'),

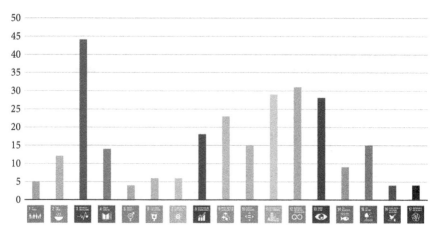

Figure 12.1 A survey sample of 108 AI projects addressing the SDGs

16 ('Peace, Justice, and Strong Institutions'), and 17 ('Partnerships for the Goals') appear to be addressed by fewer than five projects.

It is important to note that use of AI to tackle at least one of the SDGs does not necessarily correspond to success. Note also that a project could address multiple SDGs simultaneously *or* on different timescales and in different ways. Moreover, even a complete success for a given project would be exceedingly unlikely to result in the eradication of all the challenges associated with an SDG. This is chiefly because each SDG concerns entrenched challenges that are widespread and structural in nature. This is well reflected by the way SDGs are organized: all seventeen goals have several targets, and some targets in turn have more than one metric of success. The survey shows which SDGs are being addressed by AI at a high level. However, a more finely grained analysis is required to assess the extent of the positive impact of AI-based interventions with respect to specific SDG indicators, as well as possible cascade effects and unintended consequences. As I shall indicate in the conclusion, much research still needs to be done.

The unequal allocation of efforts detected by the survey may be due to the constraints of our survey criteria. But given the degree of systematic analysis and search conducted, it more likely signals underlying divergence in how suitable it is to use AI technology to address each goal. For instance, the suitability of AI for a given problem also rests on the ability to formalize that problem at a useful level of abstraction (Floridi 2008a). It may be that goals such as 'Gender Equality' or 'Peace and Justice and Strong Institutions' are harder to formalize than problems that pertain more directly to the allocation of resources, such as 'Affordable and Clean Energy' or 'Clean Water and Sanitation'.

We also observed a different allocation of efforts along geographical lines. For example, projects based in South America mainly pursued the goals of 'Reduced Inequalities', 'Quality Education', and 'Good Health and Well-Being' (twenty-five out of the 108 projects). The more detailed questions prompted by the survey, such as what explains the observed divergence and how it may be overcome or what may explain the different geographical distribution of projects, will require further work. This is being addressed by our current research.

It is worth stressing that, although one criterion for the survey was that the projects must have already demonstrated positive impact, in many cases this impact was 'only' local or at an early stage. Questions therefore remain about how best to—or indeed in each case *whether* to—scale up existing solutions to apply them at regional or even global levels. The idea of scaling up solutions is attractive. This is because it implies that demonstrable success in one domain or area can be replicated elsewhere, reducing the costs of duplication (not to mention the computationally intense and hence environmentally problematic training of AI systems). Indeed, as we highlight below, learning lessons from successes and failures is another critical area for future research.

But in asking how successes can be scaled up, it is important to not overlook the fact that most of the projects in our survey already represent a scaling down of existing technology. More specifically, most examples of $AI \times SDG$ reflect the repurposing of existing AI tools and techniques (developed *in silico* in academic or industrial research contexts) for the specific problem at hand. This can in part explain why some areas (such as 'Good Health and Well-Being') are seeing more $AI \times SDG$ projects flourish than others (such as 'Gender Equality'), where tools and techniques are relatively lacking or not yet equally mature. This also suggests that $AI \times SDG$ involves first a 'funnelling in' where numerous (*in silico* and/or *in vivo*) options are considered to address a particular SDG target in a particular place. This is followed by a 'fanning out' that involves the spread and iterative adoption of verified successes in adjacent domains and areas.

The analysis suggests that the 108 projects meeting the criteria cohere with the seven essential factors for socially good AI identified in Chapter 9: falsifiability and incremental deployment; safeguards against the manipulation of predictors; receiver-contextualized intervention; receiver-contextualized explanation and transparent purposes; privacy protection and data subject consent; situational fairness; and human-friendly semanticization. Each factor relates to at least one of the five ethical principles of AI—beneficence, nonmaleficence, justice, autonomy, and explicability—identified in the comparative analysis provided in Chapter 4.

This coherence is crucial: $AI \times SDGs$ cannot be inconsistent with ethical frameworks guiding the design and evaluation of any kind of AI. We also saw in Chapters 4 and 11 that the principle of *beneficence* is of relevance when considering $AI \times SDGs$, as it states that the use of AI should benefit humanity and the natural world. $AI \times SDG$ projects should therefore respect and implement this principle. But while beneficence is a necessary condition for $AI \times SDGs$ projects to succeed, it is not sufficient. The beneficent impact of an $AI \times SDGs$ project may be offset by the creation or amplification of other risks or harms (see Chapters 5, 7, 8, and 11).

Ethical analyses informing the design, development, and deployment (including monitoring) of AI×SDGs initiatives play a central role in mitigating foreseeable risks involving unintended consequences and possible misuses of the technology. Here, a specific example may help to clarify the point.

12.3 AI to Advance 'Climate Action'

As I anticipated in Chapter 11 but in terms of the current focus, the thirteenth goal, 'Climate Action' (SDG 13), ranks fourth in the Oxford database with twenty-eight of the 108 initiatives tackling it. This is despite the ethical and environmental problems linked to the use of AI, that is, the intense computational requirements (and therefore energy consumption) required by training successful deep learning systems (Dandres et al. 2017, Strubell, Ganesh, and McCallum 2019, Cowls et al. 2021a).

To explore the extent to which AI is already being developed to tackle SDG 13, along with specifically how this is occurring, one may cross-reference the initiatives in the dataset that were coded as addressing the 'Climate Action' goal with the areas of prospective thirty-five use cases across thirteen domains identified in a large-scale scoping effort undertaken by Rolnick et al. (2019). As Figure 12.2 details, at least one initiative in our dataset addresses eight of the thirteen aspects of climate action identified by Rolnick and colleagues.

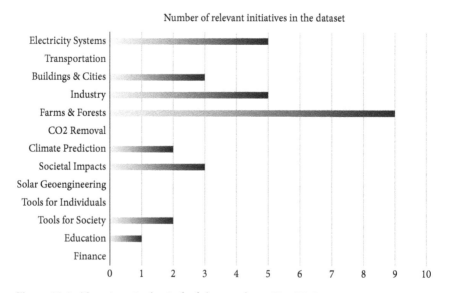

Number of relevant initiatives in the dataset

Figure 12.2 AI projects in the Oxford dataset about AI × SDGs

Note: they are organized according to domains of climate crisis response as identified by Rolnick et al. (2019)

Projects relying on AI to support 'climate action' in our dataset are based across several countries. This suggests reasonable geographic spread, but it is important to note that most of these countries (Australia, France, Germany, Japan, Slovenia, South Korea, the UAE, the UK, and the US) are considered part of the Global North. Only four projects were based in the Global South, specifically in Argentina, Peru, and Chile. This is not, of course, to suggest that these initiatives are not having an impact elsewhere in the world; to take one example, Global Forest Watch is a UK-based project that is attempting to track and protect forests worldwide. Nonetheless, this finding highlights the risk that projects based (and funded) in one part of the world may not necessarily be responsive to actual needs elsewhere.

Overall, this case study provides promising preliminary evidence that AI is in fact being used to tackle climate change and associated problems. As the cross-referencing effort above shows, this dovetails with wider research suggesting that AI could and should be developed and used for this purpose. As Rolnick et al. (2019) show, AI could support efforts to mitigate climate change in thirteen existing and potential domains ranging from CO_2 removal, transport optimization, to forestry protection. The potential for AI to support climate action has also been recognized by a consortium of academics, NGOs, and energy companies who wrote to the UK government in 2019 to call for the establishment of an international centre for 'AI, Energy and Climate'.[4]

The previous overview indicates that there are already 'boots on the ground' using AI to tackle the climate crisis, even if such efforts are only at an early stage. Given the strict criteria applied in our sampling process (e.g. that projects must have had evidence of positive impact), our evidence shows positive direction. At the same time, it highlights that there is much more to be done with several existing gaps towards which prospective initiatives could orient their efforts.

12.4 Conclusion: A Research Agenda for AI × SDGs

A growing number of projects are using AI4SG by addressing the UN SDGs. AI technologies are not a panacea. But they can be an important part of the solution and help address major challenges, both social and environmental, facing humanity today. If designed well, AI technologies can foster the delivery of socially good outcomes at an unprecedented scale and efficiency. Therefore, it is crucial to provide a coherent structure within which new and existing AI × SDG projects can thrive.

---

[4] Priyanka Shrestha, 2019, 'Leading Energy and Tech Groups Call for International Centre for AI, Energy and Climate', *Energy Live News*, 20 August 2019, https://www.businessgreen.com/news/3080630/essential-ai-top-business-groups-call-for-creation-of-international-centre-for-ai-energy-and-climate

The next steps in understanding AI4SG in terms of AI×SDGs are to analyse what factors determine the success or failure of AI×SDG projects, particularly with respect to their specific impacts on the ground; to explain gaps and discrepancies between the use of AI to tackle different SDGs and indicators, as well as mismatches between where projects are based and where SDG-related need is greatest; and to clarify what roles key stakeholders could play to advance the success of AI×SDG projects and address important gaps or discrepancies. Inevitably, all of this will need to be based on a multidisciplinary approach. It will have to involve deeper investigation of the AI×SDGs projects in the locations and communities where they are both developed and deployed. And it will require a broader perspective, at least in terms of what sort of human project we want to design and pursue in the twenty-first century. This is the topic of the next and final chapter.

13

Conclusion

The Green and the Blue

13.0 Summary

Previously, in Chapters 1–12, I analysed the nature of AI, its positive and negative impact, the ethical issues arising from it, and what measures may be taken to ensure that a good AI society is more likely to develop. This final chapter draws some general conclusions and offers a view of what may be coming: a move from the ethics of artificial agency to the politics of social actions, to pursue a human project based on the marriage between the green of all our environments and the blue of all our digital technologies.

13.1 Introduction: From the Divorce of Agency and Intelligence to the Marriage of Green and Blue

Sometimes we forget that life without good politics, reliable science, and robust technology soon becomes 'solitary, poor, nasty, brutish, and short', to borrow the phrase from Thomas Hobbes's *Leviathan*. The COVID-19 crisis has tragically reminded us that nature can be merciless. Only human ingenuity and goodwill can improve and safeguard the living standards of billions of people and their environments. Today, much of this ingenuity is busy delivering an epochal revolution: the transformation of an exclusively analogue world into one that is also increasingly digital. The effects are already widespread. This is the first pandemic when a new habitat, the infosphere, has helped overcome the dangers of the biosphere. We have been living onlife (both online and offline) for some time, but the pandemic has made the onlife experience a reality of no return for the whole planet.

In the previous chapters, I have argued that the development of AI is an important factor in this epochal revolution. AI should be interpreted as the engineering of artefacts to do things that would require intelligence if we were able to do them at all. This is illustrated by a classic example that I have used more than once: while only as intelligent as a toaster, a smartphone can beat almost anyone at chess. In other words, AI is an unprecedented divorce between the ability to complete tasks or solve problems successfully in view of a goal and any need to

The Ethics of Artificial Intelligence: Principles, Challenges, and Opportunities. Luciano Floridi, Oxford University Press.

be intelligent in doing so. This successful divorce has become possible only in recent years, thanks to skyrocketing quantities of data, gigantic computational power at ever lower costs, very sophisticated statistical tools, and the transformation of our habitats into increasingly AI-friendly places, through a process I defined as enveloping. The more we live in the infosphere and onlife, the more we share our everyday realities with engineered forms of agency, and the more AI can deal with an increasing number of problems and tasks. There is no limit to AI but human ingenuity.

From this historical and ecological perspective, AI is an amazing technology, a new form of agency that can be a powerful force for good in two main ways. It can help us know, understand, and foresee more and better the many challenges that are becoming so pressing, especially climate change, social injustice, and global poverty. AI's successful management of data and processes can accelerate the virtuous circle between more information, better science, and improved policies. Yet knowledge is power only when translated into action. AI can be a remarkable force for good here, too, helping us improve the world and not just our interpretation of it. The pandemic has reminded us how the problems we face are complex, systemic, and global. We cannot solve them individually. We need to *coordinate* so we do not get in each other's way, *collaborate* so we each do our part, and *cooperate* so we work together more, better, and internationally. AI can enable us to deliver these 3Cs more efficiently (through more results with fewer resources), efficaciously (through better results), and innovatively (through new results).

There is a 'but' here. We have seen that human ingenuity without goodwill can be dangerous. If AI is not controlled and steered equitably and sustainably, it can exacerbate social problems due to bias or discrimination; erode human autonomy and responsibility; and magnify past problems ranging from the digital divide and the unfair allocation of wealth to the development of a culture of mere distraction— that of *panem et digital circenses*. AI risks going from part of the solution to part of the problem. Therefore ethical initiatives such as those described in Chapter 4 and, ultimately, good international regulations are essential to ensure that AI remains a powerful force for good.

AI4SG is part of a new marriage between the Green of all our habitats (whether natural, synthetic, and artificial, from the biosphere to the infosphere, from urban environments to economic, social, and political circumstances) and the Blue of our digital technologies (from mobile phones to social platforms, from the Internet of Things to Big Data, from AI to future quantum computing). With all its advantages, the marriage between the Green and the Blue counterbalances the divorce between Agency and Intelligence with all its risks. It is our responsibility to design and manage both successfully. The pandemic has made clear that what is at stake is not so much digital innovation as it is good governance of the digital. Technologies multiply and improve daily. To save our planet and ourselves (from ourselves), we can and must use them much better. Just think of the spread of COVID-19-related disinformation on social media, or the ineffectiveness of the so-called coronavirus apps. The pandemic could also be interpreted been the dress rehearsal of what should be the human project for the twenty-first century: a strong and fruitful marriage between the Green and the Blue. We can make it a success together by relying on more and better philosophy, not less.

13.2 The Role of Philosophy as Conceptual Design

For some time, the frontier of cyberspace has been the human/machine divide. Today, we have moved inside the infosphere. Its all-pervading nature also depends on the extent to which we accept its digital nature as integral to our reality and transparent to us (in the sense that it is no longer perceived as present). What matters is not moving bits instead of atoms. This is an outdated, communication-based interpretation of the information society that owes too much to mass-media sociology. Instead, what matters is the far more radical fact that our understanding and conceptualization of the essence and fabric of reality is changing. Indeed, we have begun to accept the virtual as partly real and the real as partly virtual. Thus, the information society is better seen as a neo-manufacturing society in which raw materials and energy have been superseded by data and information, the new digital gold, and the real source of added value. Aside from communication and transactions, the creation, design, and management of information are all key to a proper understanding of our predicament and the development of a sustainable infosphere. Such understanding requires a new narrative. That is, it requires a new sort of realistic and reliable story that we tell ourselves to make sense of our predicament and design the human project we wish to pursue. This may seem like an anachronistic step in the wrong direction. Until recently, there was much criticism of 'big narratives' ranging from Marxism and Neo-liberalism to the so-called 'end of history'. But the truth is that such a criticism, too, was just another narrative, and it did not work. A systematic critique of grand narratives is inevitably part of the problem that it tries to solve. Understanding why there are narratives, what justifies them, and what better narratives may replace them is a less juvenile and more fruitful way ahead.

Information and communication technologies (ICTs) are creating the new informational environment in which future generations will spend most of their time. Previous revolutions in the creation of wealth (especially the agricultural and the industrial ones) led to macroscopic transformations in our social and political structures and architectural environments. These occurred often without much foresight, and usually with deep conceptual and ethical implications. Whether understood in terms of wealth creation or in terms of a reconceptualization of our own selves, the information revolution is no less dramatic. We shall be in serious trouble if we do not take seriously the fact that we are constructing new environments that will be inhabited by future generations.

In view of this important change in the sort of ICT-mediated interactions that we will increasingly enjoy with other agents (whether biological or artificial) and in our self-understanding, an ethical approach is vital to tackle the new challenges posed by ICTs. This must be an approach that does not privilege the natural or untouched, but treats as authentic and genuine all forms of existence and behaviour, even those based on artificial, synthetic, hybrid, and engineered artefacts. The task is to formulate an ethical framework that can treat the infosphere as a new environment worthy of the moral attention and care of the human agents inhabiting it.

Such an ethical framework must address and solve the unprecedented challenges arising in the new environment. It must be an *e-nvironmental* ethics for the whole infosphere, as I have argued for some time with little success (Floridi 2013). This sort of *synthetic* (both in the sense of holistic or inclusive, and in the sense of artificial) *e-nvironmentalism* will require a change in how we perceive ourselves and our roles with respect to reality, what we consider worthy of our respect and care, and how we might negotiate a new alliance between the natural and the artificial. It will require serious reflection on the human project and a critical review of our current narratives at individual, social, and political levels. These are all pressing issues that deserve our full and undivided attention.

Unfortunately, I suspect it will take some time and a whole new kind of education and sensitivity before we realize that the infosphere is a common space—one that needs to be preserved to the advantage of all. Philosophy as conceptual design (Floridi 2019d) should contribute not only with a change in perspective but also with constructive efforts that may be translated into policies. It should help us improve our self-understanding and develop a society that can take care of both humanity and nature.

13.3 Back to 'the Seeds of Time'

In Chapter 2, we saw how Galileo thought nature was like a book written in mathematical symbols that could be read by science. This might have been a metaphorical stretch at the time, but today the world we live in is certainly becoming more and more a book written in digits, one that can be read and expanded by computer and data science. Within this book, digital technologies are increasingly successful because they are the true natives of the infosphere, like fish in the sea. This also explains why AI applications are better than us at an increasing number of tasks: we are mere analogue organisms trying to adapt to such a new habitat by living onlife. The epochal change of our environment into a mixed infosphere that is both analogue and digital, along with the fact that we are sharing the infosphere with increasingly smart, autonomous, and social AAs, has profound consequences. Some of these 'seeds of time' (to rely again on Shakespeare's metaphor, introduced in Chapter 3) are still undetectable. We shall discover them only in time. Others are barely discernible. And still others are in front of our eyes. Let me start with these.

AI agents can be soft (apps, webots, algorithms, software of all kinds) or hard (robots, driverless cars, smart watches, and gadgets of all kinds). These agents are replacing human ones in areas that were thought off limits for any technology just a few years ago. Artificial agents are cataloguing images, translating documents, interpreting radiographies, flying drones, extracting new information from huge masses of data, and doing many other things that only white-collar workers were supposed to be able to do. Brown-collar workers in agriculture and blue-collar workers in industry have been feeling the digital pressure for decades. Services are just the new target. So, many white collar jobs will also disappear or be completely transformed. How many and how quickly, we can only reasonably guess— but the disruption is likely to be profound. Wherever humans work like interfaces today, that job is at risk. For example, humans currently work as interfaces between a GPS and a car, between two documents in different languages, between some ingredients and a dish, between symptoms and the corresponding disease. At the same time, new jobs will appear. New interfaces will be needed between services provided by computers, between web sites, between AI applications, between the outcomes of AI, and so forth. Someone will have to check that an approximately good translation is a sufficiently reliable translation, and take care of it. Many tasks will also remain too expensive for AI applications, even assuming they will be doable by AI. Consider Amazon, for instance. We saw in Chapter 2 that the company provides 'access to more than 500,000 workers from 190 countries',[1] so-called Turks, which are also defined by Amazon as 'artificial artificial [sic] intelligence'. The repetition here is indicative: these are mindless jobs paid pennies. This is not the sort of job you may wish for your children, yet it is still a job of some sort that many people need and cannot turn down. Clearly, AI risks polarizing our society even further, unless we provide better legal and ethical frameworks. Polarization will occur especially between the few people above the machines (the new capitalists) and the many below the machines (the new proletariat). Taxes will also go with jobs, although this is a bit further in the future. No workers means no taxpayers—this is obvious, and the companies that take advantage of the AI-fication of tasks will not be as generous as with their former employees when it comes to supporting social welfare. Something will have to be done to make companies and well-off people pay more taxes. Legislation will thus play an influential role also in determining which jobs will have to be

---

[1] https://requester.mturk.com/create/projects/new.

kept 'human'. Driverless trains will remain a rarity also because of legislative reasons,[2] even though they are vastly easier to manage than driverless taxis or buses. Inevitably, regulations will contribute significantly to how we design the future of our infosphere and protect both humanity and the planet.

On a brighter note, many tasks that disappear will not make the corresponding jobs vanish. Gardeners helped by one of the many robot lawnmowers already available will have more time to do other things instead of cutting the grass. And many tasks will not actually disappear. Instead, they will simply be relocated onto our shoulders as users. We already push the buttons in the elevator (that job is gone). We are growing increasingly used to scanning goods at the supermarket (cashier jobs are going). And we will certainly do more jobs ourselves in the future. More generally, there will be a growing need for managers, carers, and curators of digital environments and smart agents. These new herds will need human shepherds (Heideggerian pun intended) or what I like to call 'green collars'. The point deserves further analysis.

13.4 Green Collars Needed

On 26 April 2015 the House of Commons' Science and Technology Committee of the British Parliament published online the responses to its inquiry on 'algorithms in decision-making'.[3] The responses varied in length, detail, and approach, but appeared to share at least one feature: acknowledgement that human intervention may be unavoidable, even welcome, when it comes to trusting algorithmic decisions. This was sensible and it remains good news.

Automation has transformed agriculture and industry. Today, brown and blue collars are a minority. About 90 per cent of American jobs are in services and government. Most of us deal with data and software, not with bioware or hardware. The trouble is that computers eat data and software for breakfast. So, the digital revolution is challenging white-collar jobs everywhere. This is not because the digital makes technology intelligent—if that were so, I would still have a chance playing chess against my idiotic smart phone. It is because the digital makes tasks stupid by decoupling them from any intelligence needed to perform them successfully. And wherever the digital divorces a task from intelligence, an algorithm can step in and replace us. The result is rapid and widespread unemployment today, but also new jobs tomorrow. The long term is brighter. According to the World Bank, for example, the world will need 80 million healthcare workers by 2030, which is double the number in 2013.

In a society increasingly pervaded by algorithms and automated processes, the question addressed by the committee was how we can trust such brainless technologies when they regularly make decisions for us and instead of us. Note that this really is about you and me. Since automation replaced brown collars, potatoes might face the risk of mishandling. Once blue collars go, robots might paint cars the wrong colour. Now that white collars are being replaced, everyone may be at the mercy of an algorithm's mistake, an unfair identification of responsibility, a biased decision, or any other Kafkian mess concocted by a computer. Examples abound. We saw in the previous chapters that the risk is real and serious. The solution is to put some human intelligence back in place. This could be done in at least four ways: *before, in, on,* and *after the loop.*

Trust is based on deliverance, transparency, and accountability. You trust your doctor when she does what she is supposed to do. You are, or at least can be, informed about what she does, and she is responsible if anything goes wrong. The same holds true for algorithms. We can trust them when it is clear what they are supposed to deliver, and it is transparent whether they are delivering it. If there is any problem, we can trust that someone is causally accountable (or at least morally responsible), if not legally liable. Therefore we need humans before, in, on, and after the loop. We need humans before the loop because we want to design the right sort of algorithms and minimize risks. Humans should be in the loop because sometimes even the best algorithm can go wrong, get fed the wrong data, or be misused. We need control so that some consequential decisions are not entirely left to mindless machines. Humans should be on the loop because while crucial decisions may be too complex or time-sensitive for any human to make, it is our intelligent supervision that should check and manage processes that are both complex and fast. Humans should also be after the loop because there are always issues that we would like to redress or rectify, or different choices to make. The fact that a decision was made by an algorithm provides no grounds for giving up our right to appeal to human insight and understanding. So, we need *design, control, transparency,* and *accountability* operationalized by humans. And all this with all the help we can get from digital technologies themselves. You see why the responses by the committee were good news. There is plenty of intelligent work to be done in the future, but it will not be white collars who fill the new positions. It will be experts who can take care of the new digital environments and its AAs. Algorithms are the new herd. Our future jobs will be in the shepherding industry. The age of green collars is coming.

13.5 Conclusion: Humanity as a Beautiful Glitch

What about the 'seeds' less obvious, the consequences barely discernible, when AI will no longer be in the hands of researchers, technicians, and managers but 'democratized' in the pockets of billions of people? Here I can only be even more abstract and tentative. Along with predictive tools that can anticipate and manipulate human decisions, AI offers a historic opportunity to rethink human exceptionalism as not mistaken, but rather misdirected. Our intelligent behaviour will be challenged by the smart behaviour of AIs, which can adapt more successfully in the infosphere. Our autonomous behaviour will be challenged by the predictability and manipulability of our rational choices, and by the development of artificial autonomy. And our sociability will be challenged by its artificial counterpart, as represented by artificial companions, holograms or mere voices, 3D servants or human-like sex robots. These counterparts can be both attractive to humans and sometimes indistinguishable from them. How all this will play out is unclear. But one thing seems predictable: the development of AAs will not lead to any scaremongering realization of some dystopian sci-fi scenario, a possibility that is irresponsibly distracting. *Terminator* is not coming. In fact, in this book I argued that AI is an oxymoron: smart technologies will be as stupid as our old technologies. But AI will invite us to reflect more seriously and less complacently on who we are, could be, and would like to become, and thus our responsibilities and self-understanding. It will deeply challenge our identity and 'exceptionalism', in terms of what we mean by considering ourselves somewhat 'special' even after the fourth revolution (Floridi 2014a), according to which we are not at the centre of the universe (Copernicus), of the biosphere (Darwin), of the mental space (Freud), and now of the infosphere (Turing). Here, I am not arguing that our exceptionalism is incorrect. I am suggesting that AI will make us realize that our exceptionalism lies in the unique and perhaps irreproducible way that we are successfully dysfunctional. We are as unique as a *hapax legomenon* in Galileo's book of nature, that is, as an expression that occurs only once in a text, like the expression 'gopher wood', which refers to the primary building material for Noah's ark and appears only once in the whole Bible. With a more digital and contemporary metaphor, we are a *beautiful glitch* in the great software of the universe, not the ultimate application. We shall remain a bug, a uniquely successful mistake, while AI will become more and more of a feature in Galileo's mathematical book of nature. Such a beautiful glitch will be increasingly responsible for nature and history. In short, Shakespeare was right:

> Men at some time are masters of their fates.
> The fault, dear Brutus, is not in our stars
> But in ourselves, that we are underlings.
>
> Shakespeare, *Julius Caesar*, 1.2

But we shall not be able to become the masters of our fate without rethinking another form of agency, the political one. Hence *The Politics of Information*, which is the topic of the next volume (see also Floridi 2023).

References

Abadi, Martin, Andy Chu, Ian Goodfellow, H. Brendan Mcmahan, Ilya Mironov, Kunal Talwar, and Li Zhang. 2016. 'Deep learning with differential privacy.' CCS'16: ACM SIGSAC Conference on Computer and Communications Security, 24 October 2016.

Abdella, Galal M., Murat Kucukvar, Nuri Cihat Onat, Hussein M. Al-Yafay, and Muhammet Enis Bulak. 2020. 'Sustainability assessment and modeling based on supervised machine learning techniques: The case for food consumption.' *Journal of Cleaner Production* 251:119661.

Abebe, Rediet, Solon Barocas, Jon Kleinberg, Karen Levy, Manish Raghavan, and David G. Robinson. 2020. 'Roles for computing in social change.' Proceedings of the 2020 Conference on Fairness, Accountability, and Transparency, pp. 252–60.

Abrell, Jan, Mirjam Kosch, and Sebastian Rausch. 2019. *How Effective Was the UK Carbon Tax? A Machine Learning Approach to Policy Evaluation.* Rochester, NY: Social Science Research Network.

Adams, John. 1787. *A Defence of the Constitutions of Government of the United States of America.* London: C. Dilly.

Aftab, Muhammad, Chien Chen, Chi-Kin Chau, and Talal Rahwan. 2017. 'Automatic HVAC control with real-time occupancy recognition and simulation-guided model predictive control in low-cost embedded system.' *Energy and Buildings* 154:141–56.

Aggarwal, Nikita. 2020. 'The norms of algorithmic credit scoring.' *The Cambridge Law Journal* 80:42–73.

Al-Abdulkarim, Latifa, Katie Atkinson, and Trevor Bench-Capon. 2015. 'Factors, issues and values: Revisiting reasoning with cases.' In Proceedings of the 15th international conference on artificial intelligence and law, pp. 3–12.

Alaieri, Fahad, and André Vellino. 2016. 'Ethical decision making in robots: Autonomy, trust and responsibility.' International Conference on Social Robotics. In Social Robotics: 8th International Conference, ICSR 2016, Kansas City, MO, USA, November 1–3, 2016 Proceedings 8, pp. 159–68. Springer International Publishing, 2016.

Alazab, Mamoun, and Roderic Broadhurst. 2016. 'Spam and criminal activity.' *Trends and Issues in Crime and Criminal Justice (Australian Institute of Criminology)* 526 (2016):1–20.

Algorithm Watch. 2020. 'The AI ethics guidelines global inventory.' https://algorithmwatch. org/en/project/ai-ethics-guidelines-global-inventory/.

Allen, Anita. 2011. *Unpopular Privacy: What Must We Hide?* Oxford: Oxford University Press.

Allo, Patrick. 2010. *Putting Information First: Luciano Floridi and the Philosophy of Information.* Oxford: Wiley-Blackwell.

Alterman, Hyman. 1969. *Counting People: The Census in History.* New York: Harcourt, Brace & World.

Alvisi, Lorenzo, Allen Clement, Alessandro Epasto, Silvio Lattanzi, and Alessandro Panconesi. 2013. 'Sok: The evolution of sybil defense via social networks.' 2013 IEEE Symposium on Security and Privacy. In 2013 IEEE symposium on security and privacy, pp. 382–96. IEEE, 2013.

Ammanath, Beena. 2022. *Trustworthy AI: A Business Guide for Navigating Trust and Ethics in AI*. Hoboken: John Wiley & Sons, Inc.

Amodei, Dario, and Danny Hernandez. 2018. 'AI and compute.' https://openai.com/blog/ai-and-compute/.

Ananny, Mike, and Kate Crawford. 2018. 'Seeing without knowing: Limitations of the transparency ideal and its application to algorithmic accountability.' *New Media & Society* 20 (3):973–89.

Andrae, Anders, and Tomas Edler. 2015. 'On global electricity usage of communication technology: Trends to 2030.' *Challenges* 6 (1):117–57.

Andrighetto, Giulia, Guido Governatori, Pablo Noriega, and Leendert W. N. van der Torre. 2013. *Normative Multi-Agent Systems*. Vol. 4. Schloss Dagstuhl-Leibniz-Zentrum fuer Informatik. https://drops.dagstuhl.de/opus/volltexte/2012/3535/.

Angwin, Julia, Jeff Larson, Surya Mattu, and Kirchner Lauren. 2016. 'Machine Bias.' In Ethics of data and analytics, pp. 254–64. Auerbach Publications, 2016.

Anthony, Lasse F. Wolff, Benjamin Kanding, and Raghavendra Selvan. 2020. 'Carbontracker: Tracking and predicting the carbon footprint of training deep learning models.' arXiv preprint arXiv:2007.03051.

Applin, Sally A, and Michael D Fischer. 2015. 'New technologies and mixed-use convergence: How humans and algorithms are adapting to each other.' 2015 IEEE international symposium on technology and society (ISTAS).

Archbold, John Frederick. 1991. *Criminal Pleading, Evidence and Practice*. London: Sweet & Maxwell.

Arkin, Ronald C. 2008. 'Governing lethal behavior: Embedding ethics in a hybrid deliberative/reactive robot architecture.' Proceedings of the 3rd ACM/IEEE International Conference on Human Robot Interaction, pp. 121–28.

Arkin, Ronald C., and Patrick Ulam. 2012. 'Overriding ethical constraints in lethal autonomous systems.' Georgia Inst of Tech Atlanta Mobile Robot Lab.

Arkoudas, Konstantine. 2023. 'ChatGPT is no stochastic parrot. But it also claims that 1 is greater than 1.' Medium (also forthcoming in *Philosophy & Technology*), https://medium.com/@konstantine_45825/chatgpt-is-no-stochastic-parrot-but-it-also-claims-that-1-is-greater-than-1-e3cd1fc303e0.

Arnold, Matthew, Rachel K. E. Bellamy, Michael Hind, Stephanie Houde, Sameep Mehta, Aleksandra Mojsilovic, Ravi Nair, Karthikeyan Natesan Ramamurthy, Darrell Reimer, Alexandra Olteanu, David Piorkowski, Jason Tsay, and Kush R. Varshney. 2019. 'FactSheets: Increasing trust in AI services through supplier's declarations of conformity.' arXiv:1808.07261 [cs].

Arora, Sanjeev, and Boaz Barak. 2009. *Computational Complexity: A Modern Approach*. Cambridge: Cambridge University Press.

Ashworth, Andrew. 2010. 'Should strict criminal liability be removed from all imprisonable offences?' *Irish Jurist (1966–)*:1–21.

Avgerinou, Maria, Paolo Bertoldi, and Luca Castellazzi. 2017. 'Trends in data centre energy consumption under the European Code of Conduct for Data Centre Energy Efficiency.' *Energies* 10 (10):1470.

Bambauer, Jame, and Tal Zarsky. 2018. 'The algorithmic game.' *Notre Dame Law Review* 94 (1):1–47.

Banjo, Omotayo. 2018. 'Bias in maternal AI could hurt expectant black mothers.' *Motherboard* 17 August.

Barnes, Elizabeth A., James W. Hurrell, Imme Ebert-Uphoff, Chuck Anderson, and David Anderson. 2019. 'Viewing forced climate patterns through an AI lens.' *Geophysical Research Letters* 46 (22):13389–98.

Barocas, Solon, and Andrew D. Selbst. 2016. 'Big data's disparate impact.' *California Law Review* 104 (3):671–732.

Bartneck, Christoph, Tony Belpaeme, Friederike Eyssel, Takayuki Kanda, Merel Keijsers, and Selma Šabanović. 2020. *Human–Robot Interaction: An Introduction*. Cambridge: Cambridge University Press.

Bartneck, Christoph, Christoph Lütge, Alan Wagner, and Sean Welsh. 2021. *An Introduction to Ethics in Robotics and AI*. Cham: Springer.

Baum, Seth D. 2020. 'Social choice ethics in artificial intelligence.' *AI & Society* 35 (1):165–176.

Baumer, Eric P. S. 2017. 'Toward human-centered algorithm design.' *Big Data & Society* 4 (2):205395171771885.

Beauchamp, Tom L., and James F. Childress. 2013. *Principles of Biomedical Ethics*. 7th ed. New York: Oxford University Press.

Beer, David. 2017. 'The social power of algorithms.' *Information, Communication & Society* 20 (1):1–13.

Beijing Academy of Artificial Intelligence. 2019. 'Beijing AI principles.' https://www.wired. com/beyond-the-beyond/2019/06/beijing-artificial-intelligence-principles/.

Belkhir, Lotfi, and Ahmed Elmeligi. 2018. 'Assessing ICT global emissions footprint: Trends to 2040 & recommendations.' *Journal of Cleaner Production* 177:448–63.

Bendel, Oliver. 2019. 'The synthetization of human voices.' *Ai & Society* 34 (1):83–9.

Bender, Emily M., Timnit Gebru, Angelina McMillan-Major, and Shmargaret Shmitchell. 2021. 'On the dangers of stochastic parrots: Can language models be too big.' Proceedings of the 2021 ACM Conference on Fairness, Accountability, and Transparency, pp. 610–623.

Benjamin, Ruha. 2019. *Race after Technology: Abolitionist Tools for the New Jim Code*. Medford, MA: Polity.

Benkler, Yochai. 2019. 'Don't let industry write the rules for AI.' *Nature* 569 (7754):161–2.

Berk, Richard, Hoda Heidari, Shahin Jabbari, Michael Kearns, and Aaron Roth. 2018. 'Fairness in criminal justice risk assessments: The state of the art.' *Sociological Methods &Research* :004912411878253.

Bilge, Leyla, Thorsten Strufe, Davide Balzarotti, and Engin Kirda. 2009. 'All your contacts are belong to us: Automated identity theft attacks on social networks.' Proceedings of the 18th International Conference on World Wide Web, pp. 551–560.

Bilgic, Mustafa, and Raymond Mooney. 2005. 'Explaining recommendations: Satisfaction vs. promotion.' In Beyond personalization workshop, IUI, vol. 5, p. 153. 2005.

Binns, Reuben. 2018a. 'Algorithmic accountability and public reason.' *Philosophy & Technology* 31 (4):543–56.

Binns, Reuben. 2018b. 'Fairness in machine learning: Lessons from political philosophy.' arXiv:1712.03586 [cs].

Bishop, J. Mark. 2021. 'Artificial intelligence is stupid and causal reasoning will not fix it.' *Frontiers in Psychology* 11:2603.

Blacklaws, Christina. 2018. 'Algorithms: Transparency and accountability.' *Philosophical Transactions of the Royal Society A: Mathematical, Physical and Engineering Sciences* 376 (2128):20170351.

Blackman, Reid. 2022. *Ethical Machines: Your Concise Guide to Totally Unbiased, Transparent, and Respectful AI*. Boston, MA: Harvard Business Review Press.

Blyth, Colin R. 1972. 'On Simpson's Paradox and the Sure-Thing Principle.' *Journal of the American Statistical Association* 67 (338):364–6.

Boland, H. 14 October 2018. 'Tencent executive urges Europe to focus on ethical uses of artificial intelligence.' *The Telegraph*.

Borges, Jorge Luis. 2000. *The Library of Babel*. Boston, MA: David R. Godine.

Borji, Ali. 2023. 'A categorical archive of ChatGPT failures.' arXiv preprint arXiv:2302.03494.

Boshmaf, Yazan, Ildar Muslukhov, Konstantin Beznosov, and Matei Ripeanu. 2012. 'Key challenges in defending against malicious socialbots.' Presented as part of the 5th {USENIX} Workshop on Large-Scale Exploits and Emergent Threats.

Boshmaf, Yazan, Ildar Muslukhov, Konstantin Beznosov, and Matei Ripeanu. 2013. 'Design and analysis of a social botnet.' *Computer Networks* 57 (2):556–78.

Boutilier, Craig. 2002. 'A POMDP formulation of preference elicitation problems.' AAAI/IAAI, pp. 239–246.

boyd, danah, and Kate Crawford. 2012. 'Critical questions for big data: Provocations for a cultural, technological, and scholarly phenomenon.' *Information Communication & Society* 15 (5):662–79. doi: 10.1080/1369118X.2012.678878.

Bradshaw, Jeffrey M., Stuart Dutfield, Pete Benoit, and John D. Woolley. 1997. 'KAoS: Toward an industrial-strength open agent architecture.' *Software agents* 13:375–418.

British Academy, The Royal Society. 2017. 'Data management and use: Governance in the 21st century—A joint report by the British Academy and the Royal Society.' https://royalsociety.org/topics-policy/projects/data-governance/

Broadhurst, Roderic, Donald Maxim, Paige Brown, Harshit Trivedi, and Joy Wang. 2019. 'Artificial intelligence and crime.' Available at SSRN 3407779.

Brown, Tom B., Benjamin Mann, Nick Ryder, Melanie Subbiah, Jared Kaplan, Prafulla Dhariwal, Arvind Neelakantan, Pranav Shyam, Girish Sastry, and Amanda Askell. 2020. 'Language models are few-shot learners.' arXiv preprint arXiv:2005.14165.

Brundage, Miles, Shahar Avin, Jack Clark, Helen Toner, Peter Eckersley, Ben Garfinkel, Allan Dafoe, Paul Scharre, Thomas Zeitzoff, and Bobby Filar. 2018. 'The malicious use of artificial intelligence: Forecasting, prevention, and mitigation.' arXiv preprint arXiv:1802.07228.

Brundage, Miles, Shahar Avin, Jasmine Wang, Haydn Belfield, Gretchen Krueger, Gillian Hadfield, Heidy Khlaaf, Jingying Yang, Helen Toner, and Ruth Fong. 2020. 'Toward trustworthy AI development: Mechanisms for supporting verifiable claims.' arXiv preprint arXiv:2004.07213.

Brundtland, Gro Harlem. 1987. *The Brundtland Report*. World Commission on Environment and Development. Oxford: Oxford University Press.

Buhmann, Alexander, Johannes Paßmann, and Christian Fieseler. 2019. 'Managing algorithmic accountability: Balancing reputational concerns, engagement strategies, and the potential of rational discourse.' *Journal of Business Ethics* 163 (2):265–280.

Burgess, Matt. 2017. 'NHS DeepMind deal broke data protection law, regulator rules.' *Wired UK*, 3 July.

Burke, Robin. 2017. 'Multisided fairness for recommendation.' *arXiv:1707.00093*

Burns, Alistair, and Peter Rabins. 2000. 'Carer burden in dementia.' *International Journal of Geriatric Psychiatry* 15 (S1):S9–13.

Burrell, Jenna. 2016. 'How the machine 'thinks:' Understanding opacity in machine learning algorithms.' *Big Data & Society* 3 (1):2053951715622512.

C2E2. 2018. 'Greenhouse gas emissions in the ICT sector.' https://c2e2.unepdtu.org/collection/c2e2-publications/, last modified 2018.

Cabinet Office, Government Digital Service. 2016. 'Data science ethical framework.' https://www.gov.uk/government/publications/data-science-ethical-framework

Cai, Han, Chuang Gan, Tianzhe Wang, Zhekai Zhang, and Song Han. 2020. 'Once-for-all: Train one network and specialize it for efficient deployment.' arXiv:1908.09791 [cs, stat].

Caldwell, M., J. T. A. Andrews, T. Tanay, and L. D. Griffin. 2020. 'AI-enabled future crime.' *Crime Science* 9 (1):1–13.

Caliskan, Aylin, Joanna J. Bryson, and Arvind Narayanan. 2017. 'Semantics derived automatically from language corpora contain human-like biases.' *Science* 356 (6334):183–6.

Callaway, Ewen. 2020. ''It will change everything': Deepmind's AI makes gigantic leap in solving protein structures.' *Nature* 588:203–4.

Campbell, Murray, A. Joseph Hoane Jr, and Feng-hsiung J. Hsu. 2002. 'Deep blue.' *Artificial Intelligence* 134 (1–2):57–83.

Carton, Samuel, Jennifer Helsby, Kenneth Joseph, Ayesha Mahmud, Youngsoo Park, Joe Walsh, Crystal Cody, C. P. T. Estella Patterson, Lauren Haynes, and Rayid Ghani. 2016. 'Identifying police officers at risk of adverse events.' In Proceedings of the 22nd ACM SIGKDD international conference on knowledge discovery and data mining, pp. 67–76. 2016.

Cath, Corinne N. J., Ludovica Glorioso, and Mariarosaria Taddeo. 2017. 'NATO CCD COE workshop on "Ethics and Policies for Cyber Warfare"—a report.' In *Ethics and Policies for Cyber Operations*, edited by Mariarosaria Taddeo and Ludovica Glorioso, 231–41. Cham: Springer International Publishing.

Cath, Corinne, Sandra Wachter, Brent Mittelstadt, Mariarosaria Taddeo, and Luciano Floridi. 2018. 'Artificial intelligence and the "good society": The US, EU, and UK approach.' *Science and Engineering Ethics* 24 (2):505–28.

CDC. 2019. 'Pregnancy mortality surveillance system: Maternal and infant health.' Last modified 16 January 2019. https://www.cdc.gov/reproductivehealth/maternal-mortality/pregnancy-mortality-surveillance-system.htm

Chajewska, Urszula, Daphne Koller, and Ronald Parr. 2000. 'Making rational decisions using adaptive utility elicitation.' In AAAI/IAAI, pp. 363–369. 2000.

Chakraborty, Abhijnan, Gourab K. Patro, Niloy Ganguly, Krishna P. Gummadi, and Patrick Loiseau. 2019. 'Equality of voice: Towards fair representation in crowdsourced top-k recommendations.' In Proceedings of the Conference on Fairness, Accountability, and Transparency, pp. 129–138. 2019.

Chameau, Jean-Lou, William F. Ballhaus, Herbert S. Lin, Globally, Committee on Ethical and Societal Implications of Advances in Militarily Significant Technologies that are Rapidly Changing and Increasingly Accessible, Computer Science and Telecommunications Board, Board on Life Sciences, Technology Committee on Science, Ethics Center for Engineering, National Research Council, and National Academy of Engineering. 2014. *Foundational Technologies*. National Academies Press (US). https://nap.nationalacademies.org/catalog/18750/emerging-and-readily-available-technologies-and-national-security-a-framework

Chantler, Nic, and Roderic Broadhurst. 2008. 'Social engineering and crime prevention in cyberspace.' *Proceedings of the Korean Institute of Criminology*:65–92.

Chattopadhyay, Ashesh, Pedram Hassanzadeh, and Saba Pasha. 2020. 'Predicting clustered weather patterns: A test case for applications of convolutional neural networks to spatio-temporal climate data.' *Scientific Reports* 10 (1):1317.

Chen, Ying-Chieh, Patrick S. Chen, Ronggong Song, and Larry Korba. 2004. 'Online gaming crime and security issue-cases and countermeasures from Taiwan.' PST, pp. 131–136.

Chen, Ying-Chieh, Patrick S. Chen, Jing-Jang Hwang, Larry Korba, Ronggong Song, and George Yee. 2005. 'An analysis of online gaming crime characteristics.' *Internet Research* 15 (3):246–261.

China State Council. 8 July 2017. 'State council notice on the issuance of the Next Generation Artificial Intelligence Development Plan.' Retrieved 18 September 2018, from http://www.gov.cn/zhengce/content/2017-07/20/content_5211996.htm. Translation by Creemers, R., Webster, G., Triolo, P. and Kania, E. https://www.newamerica.org/documents/1959/translation-fulltext-8.1.17.pdf.

Choi, Changhyun, Jeonghwan Kim, Jongsung Kim, Donghyun Kim, Younghye Bae, and Hung Soo Kim. 2018. 'Development of heavy rain damage prediction model using machine learning based on big data.' *Advances in Meteorology.*

Christian, Jon. 2023. 'Amazing "jailbreak" bypasses ChatGPT's ethics safeguards.' *Futurism*, https://futurism.com/amazing-jailbreak-chatgpt.

Chu, Yi, Young Chol Song, Richard Levinson, and Henry Kautz. 2012. 'Interactive activity recognition and prompting to assist people with cognitive disabilities.' *Journal of Ambient Intelligence and Smart Environments* 4 (5):443–59.

Chu, Zi, Steven Gianvecchio, Haining Wang, and Sushil Jajodia. 2010. 'Who is tweeting on Twitter: human, bot, or cyborg?' Proceedings of the 26th Annual Computer Security Applications Conference, pp. 21–30.

Chui, Michael, James Manyika, Mehdi Miremadi, Nicolaus Henke, Rita Chung, Pieter Nel, and Sankalp Malhotra. 2018. 'Notes from the AI frontier: Insights from hundreds of use cases.' McKinsey Global Institute.

Cifuentes, Jenny, Geovanny Marulanda, Antonio Bello, and Javier Reneses. 2020. 'Air temperature forecasting using machine learning techniques: A review.' *Energies* 13 (16):4215.

Clarke, Arthur Charles. 1967. *The Nine Billion Names of God.* San Diego, CA: Harcourt.

Cliff, Dave, and Linda Northrop. 2012. 'The global financial markets: An ultra-large-scale systems perspective.' Monterey workshop. Oxford, UK, March 19–21, 2012, Revised Selected Papers 17, pp. 29–70. Springer Berlin Heidelberg, 2012.

Cobb, Matthew. 27 February 2020. 'Why your brain is not a computer.' *The Guardian.*

Cobb, Matthew. 2020. *The Idea of the Brain: A History.* London: Profile Books.

Cobbe, Karl, Vineet Kosaraju, Mohammad Bavarian, Mark Chen, Heewoo Jun, Lukasz Kaiser, Matthias Plappert, Jerry Tworek, Jacob Hilton, and Reiichiro Nakano. 2021. 'Training verifiers to solve math word problems.' arXiv preprint arXiv:2110.14168.

Coeckelbergh, Mark. 2020. *AI Ethics.* The MIT Press Essential Knowledge Series. Cambridge, MA: The MIT Press.

Cohen, Julie. 2000. 'Examined lives: Informational privacy and the subject as object.' *Stan. L. Rev.* 52 (1999):1373.

Corbett-Davies, Sam, and Sharad Goel. 2018. 'The measure and mismeasure of fairness: A critical review of fair machine learning.' arXiv:1808.00023 [cs].

Corea, Francesco. Aug 29 2018. 'AI knowledge map: How to classify AI technologies, a sketch of a new AI technology landscape.' *Medium—Artificial Intelligence*, Https://Medium.Com/@Francesco_Ai/Ai-Knowledge-Map-How-To-Classify-Ai-Technologies-6c073b969020.

Cowls, Josh, Marie-Thérèse Png, and Yung Au. unpublished. 'Some tentative foundations for "global" algorithmic ethics.'

Cowls, Josh, Andreas Tsamados, Mariarosaria Taddeo, and Luciano Floridi. 2021a. 'The AI gambit—leveraging artificial intelligence to combat climate change: Opportunities, challenges, and recommendations.' *Ai & Society*, 1–25.

Cowls, Josh, Andreas Tsamados, Mariarosaria Taddeo, and Luciano Floridi. 2021b. 'A definition, benchmark and database of AI for social good initiatives.' *Nature Machine Intelligence* 3 (2):111–15.

Crain, Matthew. 2018. 'The limits of transparency: Data brokers and commodification.' *New Media & Society* 20 (1):88–104.

Crawford, Kate. 2016. 'Artificial intelligence's white guy problem.' *The New York Times* 25 (06):5.

Crawford, Kate, and Jason Schultz. 2014. 'Big data and due process: Toward a framework to redress predictive privacy harms.' *BCL Rev.* 55:93.

Cummings, Mary. 2012. 'Automation bias in intelligent time critical decision support systems.' AIAA 1st Intelligent Systems Technical Conference, 2012.

Dahl, E. S. 2018. 'Appraising black-boxed technology: The positive prospects.' *Philosophy & Technology* 31 (4):571–91.

Danaher, John. 2017. 'Robotic rape and robotic child sexual abuse: Should they be criminalised?' *Criminal Law and Philosophy* 11 (1):71–95.

Dandres, Thomas, Nathan Vandromme, Glasha Obrekht, Andy Wong, Kim Khoa Nguyen, Yves Lemieux, Mohamed Cheriet, and Réjean Samson. 2017. 'Consequences of future data center deployment in Canada on electricity generation and environmental impacts: A 2015–2030 prospective study.' *Journal of Industrial Ecology* 21 (5):1312–22.

Danks, David, and Alex John London. 2017. 'Algorithmic bias in autonomous systems.' Twenty-Sixth International Joint Conference on Artificial Intelligence, August 2017, vol. 17, pp. 4691–4697.

Darling, Kate. 2015. '"Who's Johnny?" Anthropomorphic framing in human-robot interaction, integration, and policy.' *Robot Ethics* 2.

Datta, Amit, Michael Carl Tschantz, and Anupam Datta. 2015. 'Automated experiments on ad privacy settings.' *Proceedings on Privacy Enhancing Technologies* 2015 (1):92–112.

Datta, Anupam, Shayak Sen, and Yair Zick. 2016. 'Algorithmic transparency via quantitative input influence: Theory and experiments with learning systems.' In 2016 IEEE symposium on security and privacy (SP), pp. 598–617. May 2016.

Davenport, Thomas, and Ravi Kalakota. 2019. 'The potential for artificial intelligence in healthcare.' *Future Healthcare Journal* 6 (2):94.

Davis, Ernest, and Gary Marcus. 2019. *Rebooting AI: Building Artificial Intelligence We Can Trust*. New York: Pantheon Books.

De Angeli, Antonella. 2009. 'Ethical implications of verbal disinhibition with conversational agents.' *PsychNology Journal* 7 (1).

De Angeli, Antonella, and Sheryl Brahnam. 2008. 'I hate you! Disinhibition with virtual partners.' *Interacting with Computers* 20 (3):302–10.

De Fauw, Jeffrey, Joseph R. Ledsam, Bernardino Romera-Paredes, Stanislav Nikolov, Nenad Tomasev, Sam Blackwell, Harry Askham, Xavier Glorot, Brendan O'Donoghue, Daniel Visentin, George van den Driessche, Balaji Lakshminarayanan, Clemens Meyer, Faith Mackinder, Simon Bouton, Kareem Ayoub, Reena Chopra, Dominic King, Alan Karthikesalingam, Cían O. Hughes, Rosalind Raine, Julian Hughes, Dawn A. Sim, Catherine Egan, Adnan Tufail, Hugh Montgomery, Demis Hassabis, Geraint Rees, Trevor Back, Peng T. Khaw, Mustafa Suleyman, Julien Cornebise, Pearse A. Keane, and Olaf Ronneberger 2018. 'Clinically applicable deep learning for diagnosis and referral in retinal disease.' *Nature Medicine* 24 (9):1342–50.

de Lima Salge, Carolina Alves, and Nicholas Berente. 2017. 'Is that social bot behaving unethically?' *Communications of the ACM* 60 (9):29–31.

Declaration, G7. 2017. G7 Declaration on Responsible State Behavior in Cyberspace. Lucca.

Delamaire, Linda, Hussein Abdou, and John Pointon. 2009. 'Credit card fraud and detection techniques: A review.' *Banks and Bank Systems* 4 (2):57–68.

Delcker, J. 3 March 2018. 'Europe's silver bullet in global AI battle: Ethics.' *Politico* https://www.politico.eu/article/europe-silver-bullet-global-ai-battle-ethics/.

Delmas, Magali A., and Vanessa Cuerel Burbano. 2011. 'The drivers of greenwashing.' *California Management Review* 54 (1):64–87.

Demir, Hilmi. 2012. *Luciano Floridi's Philosophy of Technology: Critical Reflections*. Dordrecht; London: Springer.

Dennett, D. C. 1987. *The Intentional Stance*. Cambridge, MA; London: MIT Press.

Dennis, Louise, Michael Fisher, Marija Slavkovik, and Matt Webster. 2016. 'Formal verification of ethical choices in autonomous systems.' *Robotics and Autonomous Systems* 77:1–14.

Di Piazza, A., M. C. Di Piazza, G. La Tona, and M. Luna. 2021. 'An artificial neural network-based forecasting model of energy-related time series for electrical grid management.' *Mathematics and Computers in Simulation* 184:294–305.

Diakopoulos, Nicholas, and Michael Koliska. 2017. 'Algorithmic transparency in the news media.' *Digital Journalism* 5 (7):809–28.

Dignum, Virginia. 2019. *Responsible Artificial Intelligence: How to Develop and Use AI in a Responsible Way.* Cham: Springer.

Dignum, Virginia, Maite Lopez-Sanchez, Roberto Micalizio, Juan Pavón, Marija Slavkovik, Matthijs Smakman, Marlies van Steenbergen, Stefano Tedeschi, Leon van der Toree, Serena Villata, Tristan de Wildt, Matteo Baldoni, Christina Baroglio, Maurizio Caon, Raja Chatila, Louise Dennis, Gonzalo Génova, Galit Haim, and Malte S. Kließ. 2018. 'Ethics by design: Necessity or curse?' AAAI/ACM Conference, 2018, pp. 60–66.

DiMatteo, Larry A., Cristina Poncibò, and Michel Cannarsa. 2022. *The Cambridge Handbook of Artificial Intelligence: Global Perspectives on Law and Ethics.* Cambridge, UK; New York, NY: Cambridge University Press.

Ding, Jeffrey. 2018. 'Deciphering China's AI dream.' *Future of Humanity Institute Technical Report* https://www.fhi.ox.ac.uk/wp-content/uploads/Deciphering_Chinas_AI-Dream.pdf.

Dobbe, Roel, Oscar Sondermeijer, David Fridovich-Keil, Daniel Arnold, Duncan Callaway, and Claire Tomlin. 2019. 'Toward distributed energy services: Decentralizing optimal power flow with machine learning.' *IEEE Transactions on Smart Grid* 11 (2):1296–306.

Döring, Nicola, M. Rohangis Mohseni, and Roberto Walter. 2020. 'Design, use, and effects of sex dolls and sex robots: Scoping review.' *Journal of Medical Internet Research* 22 (7):e18551.

Doshi-Velez, Finale, and Been Kim. 2017. 'Towards a rigorous science of interpretable machine learning.' arXiv:1702.08608 [cs, stat].

Dremliuga, Roman, and Natalia Prisekina. 2020. 'The concept of culpability in criminal law and AI systems.' *Journal of Politics and Law* 13:256.

Dubber, Markus Dirk, Frank Pasquale, and Sunit Das. 2020. *The Oxford Handbook of Ethics of AI.* New York: Oxford University Press. Oxford handbooks online http://dx.doi.org/10.1093/oxfordhb/9780190067397.001.0001, accessed 2 July 2020.

Durante, Massimo. 2017. *Ethics, Law and the Politics of Information: A Guide to the Philosophy of Luciano Floridi.* The International Library of Ethics, Law and Technology. Dordrecht: Springer.

Dworkin, Ronald M. 1967. 'The model of rules.' *The University of Chicago Law Review* 35 (1):14–46.

Edmonds, Bruce, and Carlos Gershenson. 2015. 'Modelling complexity for policy: Opportunities and challenges.' In *Handbook on Complexity and Public Policy.* Cheltenham, UK: Edward Elgar Publishing.

EDPS Ethics Advisory Group. 2018. 'Towards a digital ethics.' https://edps.europa.eu/sites/edp/files/publication/18-01-25_eag_report_en.pdf.

Edsger, Dijkstra. 1984. The Threats to Computing Science, 1984, manuscript EWD898, available at https://www.cs.utexas.edu/~EWD/transcriptions/EWD08xx/EWD898.html.

Edwards, Lilian, and Michael Veale. 2017. 'Slave to the algorithm? Why a right to explanation is probably not the remedy you are looking for.' *Duke Law & Technology Review* 16 (1):18–84.

EGE. 2018. 'European Commission's European Group on Ethics in Science and New Technologies, Statement on Artificial Intelligence, Robotics and "Autonomous" Systems.' https://ec.europa.eu/info/news/ethics-artificial-intelligence-statement-ege-released-2018-apr-24_en.

Eicher, Bobbie, Lalith Polepeddi, and Ashok Goel. 2017. 'Jill Watson doesn't care if you're pregnant: Grounding AI ethics in empirical studies.' In Proceedings of the 2018 AAAI/ACM Conference on AI, Ethics, and Society, pp. 88–94. 2018.

EPA, US. 2016. 'Greenhouse gas emissions from a typical passenger vehicle.' Overviews and Factsheets. Last modified 12 January 2016. https://www.epa.gov/greenvehicles/greenhouse-gas-emissions-typical-passenger-vehicle#:~:text=typical%20passenger%20vehicle%3F-,A%20typical%20passenger%20vehicle%20emits%20about%204.6%20metric%20tons%20of,8%2C887%20grams%20of%20CO2

Epstein, Robert. 2016. 'The empty brain.' Aeon, 18 May.

Estevez, David, Juan G. Victores, Raul Fernandez-Fernandez, and Carlos Balaguer. 2017. 'Robotic ironing with 3D perception and force/torque feedback in household environments.' 2017 IEEE/RSJ International Conference on Intelligent Robots and Systems (IROS), pp. 6484–6489.

Etzioni, Amitai. 1999. 'Enhancing privacy, preserving the common good.' Hastings Center Report 29 (2):14–23.

Eubanks, Virginia. 2017. Automating Inequality: How High-Tech Tools Profile, Police, and Punish the Poor. New York, NY: St. Martin's Press.

European Commission. 8 April 2019. 'Ethics guidelines for trustworthy AI.' https://ec.europa.eu/digital-single-market/en/news/ethics-guidelines-trustworthy-ai.

European Commission. 2020. 'Energy-efficient cloud computing technologies and policies for an eco-friendly cloud market.' Last modified 2020. https://digital-strategy.ec.europa.eu/en/library/energy-efficient-cloud-computing-technologies-and-policies-eco-friendly-cloud-market

European Commission. 2021. 'Proposal for a regulation laying down harmonised rules on artificial intelligence (Artificial Intelligence Act).' https://digital-strategy.ec.europa.eu/en/library/proposal-regulation-laying-down-harmonised-rules-artificial-intelligence

Evans, Richard, and Jim Gao. 2016. 'DeepMind AI reduces Google Data Centre cooling bill by 40%.' Last modified 2016. https://www.deepmind.com/blog/deepmind-ai-reduces-google-data-centre-cooling-bill-by-40

Ezrachi, A., and M. Stucke. 2017. 'Two artificial neural networks meet in an online hub and change the future (of competition, market dynamics and society) July 1, 2017 Oxford Legal Studies.' Research Paper 24.

Faltings, Boi, Pearl Pu, Marc Torrens, and Paolo Viappiani. 2004. 'Designing example-critiquing interaction.' Proceedings of the 9th International Conference on Intelligent User Interfaces, pp. 22–29.

Fang, Fei, Thanh H. Nguyen, Rob Pickles, Wai Y. Lam, Gopalasamy R. Clements, Bo An, Amandeep Singh, Milind Tambe, and Andrew Lemieux. 2016. 'Deploying PAWS: Field Optimization of the Protection Assistant for Wildlife Security.' Twenty-Eighth IAAI Conference, 5 March 2016, vol. 30, no. 2, pp. 3966–3973.

Farmer, J. Doyne, and Spyros Skouras. 2013. 'An ecological perspective on the future of computer trading.' Quantitative Finance 13 (3):325–46.

Fathi, Soheil, Ravi Srinivasan, Andriel Fenner, and Sahand Fathi. 2020. 'Machine learning applications in urban building energy performance forecasting: A systematic review.' Renewable and Sustainable Energy Reviews 133:110287.

Fedus, William, Barret Zoph, and Noam Shazeer. 2021. 'Switch transformers: Scaling to trillion parameter models with simple and efficient sparsity.' arXiv preprint arXiv:2101.03961.

Ferguson, Christopher J., and Richard D. Hartley. 2009. 'The pleasure is momentary...the expense damnable? The influence of pornography on rape and sexual assault.' *Aggression and Violent Behavior* 14 (5):323–9.

Ferrara, Emilio. 2015. '"Manipulation and abuse on social media" by Emilio Ferrara with Ching-man Au Yeung as coordinator.' *ACM SIGWEB Newsletter* (Spring):1–9.

Ferrara, Emilio, Onur Varol, Clayton Davis, Filippo Menczer, and Alessandro Flammini. 2016. 'The rise of social bots.' *Communications of the ACM* 59 (7):96–104.

Floridi, Luciano. 1999. *Philosophy and Computing: An Introduction.* London; New York: Routledge.

Floridi, Luciano. 2003. 'Informational realism.' In *Selected Papers from Conference on Computers and Philosophy Volume 37*, edited by John Weckert and Yeslam Al-Saggaf, 7–12. Australian Computer Society. https://dl.acm.org/doi/10.5555/1082145.1082147

Floridi, Luciano. 2004. 'LIS as applied philosophy of information: A reappraisal.' *Library Trends* 52 (3):658–65.

Floridi, Luciano. 2005a. 'The ontological interpretation of informational privacy.' *Ethics and Information Technology* 7 (4):185–200.

Floridi, Luciano. 2005b. 'The philosophy of presence: From epistemic failure to successful observation.' *Presence: Teleoperators & Virtual Environments* 14 (6):656–67.

Floridi, Luciano. 2006. 'Four challenges for a theory of informational privacy.' *Ethics and Information Technology* 8 (3):109–19.

Floridi, Luciano. 2008a. 'The method of levels of abstraction.' *Minds and Machines* 18 (3):303–29.

Floridi, Luciano. 2008b. 'Understanding epistemic relevance.' *Erkenntnis* 69 (1):69–92.

Floridi, Luciano. 2010a. *The Cambridge Handbook of Information and Computer Ethics.* Cambridge, UK; New York: Cambridge University Press.

Floridi, Luciano. 2010b. *Information: A Very Short Introduction.* Oxford: Oxford University Press.

Floridi, Luciano. 2011. *The Philosophy of Information.* Oxford: Oxford University Press.

Floridi, Luciano. 2012a. 'Big data and their epistemological challenge.' *Philosophy & Technology* 25 (4):435–7.

Floridi, Luciano. 2012b. 'Distributed morality in an information society.' *Science and Engineering Ethics* 19 (3):727–43.

Floridi, Luciano. 2013. *The Ethics of Information.* Oxford: Oxford University Press.

Floridi, Luciano. 2014a. *The Fourth Revolution: How the Infosphere Is Reshaping Human Reality.* Oxford: Oxford University Press.

Floridi, Luciano, ed. 2014b. *The Onlife Manifesto: Being Human in a Hyperconnected Era.* New York: Springer.

Floridi, Luciano. 2014c. 'Open data, data protection, and group privacy.' *Philosophy & Technology* 27 (1):1–3.

Floridi, Luciano. 2014d. 'Technoscience and ethics foresight.' *Philosophy & Technology* 27 (4):499–501.

Floridi, Luciano. 2015a. '"The right to be forgotten": A philosophical view.' *Jahrbuch für Recht und Ethik—Annual Review of Law and Ethics* 23 (1):30–45.

Floridi, Luciano. 2015b. 'Should you have the right to be forgotten on Google? Nationally, yes. Globally, no.' *New Perspectives Quarterly* 32 (2):24–9.

Floridi, Luciano. 2015c. 'Toleration and the design of norms.' *Science and Engineering Ethics* 21 (5):1095–123.

Floridi, Luciano. 2016a. 'Faultless responsibility: On the nature and allocation of moral responsibility for distributed moral actions.' *Philosophical Transactions of the Royal Society A: Mathematical, Physical and Engineering Sciences* 374 (2083):20160112.

Floridi, Luciano. 2016b. 'Mature information societies: A matter of expectations.' *Philosophy & Technology* 29 (1):1–4.

Floridi, Luciano. 2016c. 'On human dignity as a foundation for the right to privacy.' *Philosophy & Technology* 29 (4):307–12.

Floridi, Luciano. 2016d. 'Should we be afraid of AI.' *Aeon Essays* https://aeon.co/essays/true-ai-is-both-logically-possible-and-utterly-implausible.

Floridi, Luciano. 2016e. 'Technology and democracy: Three lessons from Brexit.' *Philosophy & Technology* 29 (3):189–93.

Floridi, Luciano. 2016f. 'Tolerant paternalism: Pro-ethical design as a resolution of the dilemma of toleration.' *Science and Engineering Ethics* 22 (6):1669–88.

Floridi, Luciano. 2017a. 'Infraethics: On the conditions of possibility of morality.' *Philosophy & Technology* 30 (4):391–4.

Floridi, Luciano. 2017b. 'The logic of design as a conceptual logic of information.' *Minds and Machines* 27 (3):495–519.

Floridi, Luciano. 2017c. 'Robots, jobs, taxes, and responsibilities.' *Philosophy & Technology* 30 (1):1–4.

Floridi, Luciano. 2017d. 'The rise of the algorithm need not be bad news for humans.' *Financial Times,* May 4, 2017. https://www.ft.com/content/ac9e10ce-30b2-11e7-9555-2 3ef563ecf9a

Floridi, Luciano. 2018a. 'Soft ethics and the governance of the digital.' *Philosophy & Technology* 31 (1):1–8.

Floridi, Luciano. 2018b. 'What the maker's knowledge could be.' *Synthese* 195 (1):465–81.

Floridi, Luciano. 2019a. 'Autonomous vehicles: From whether and when to where and how.' *Philosophy & Technology* 32 (4):569–73.

Floridi, Luciano. 2019b. 'Establishing the rules for building trustworthy AI.' *Nature Machine Intelligence* 1 (6):261–2.

Floridi, Luciano. 2019c. 'The green and the blue: Naïve ideas to improve politics in a mature information society.' In *The 2018 Yearbook of the Digital Ethics Lab*, edited by Carl Öhman and David Watson, 183–221. Cham: Springer International Publishing.

Floridi, Luciano. 2019d. *The Logic of Information: A Theory of Philosophy as Conceptual Design*. Oxford: Oxford University Press.

Floridi, Luciano. 2019e. 'Translating principles into practices of digital ethics: Five risks of being unethical.' *Philosophy & Technology* 32 (2):185–93.

Floridi, Luciano. 2019f. 'What the near future of artificial intelligence could be.' *Philosophy & Technology* 32 (1):1–15.

Floridi, Luciano. 2020a. 'AI and its new winter: From myths to realities.' *Philosophy & Technology* 33:1–3.

Floridi, Luciano. 2020b. 'The fight for digital sovereignty: What it is, and why it matters, especially for the EU.' *Philosophy & Technology* 33 (3):369–78.

Floridi, Luciano (ed.). 2021. *Ethics, Governance, and Policies in Artificial Intelligence*. Cham: Springer.

Floridi, Luciano, Josh Cowls, Thomas C. King, and Mariarosaria Taddeo. 'How to design AI for social good: seven essential factors.' *Science and Engineering Ethics* 26:1771–96.

Floridi, Luciano. 2021. 'The European legislation on AI: A brief analysis of its philosophical approach.' *Philosophy & Technology* 34 (2):215–22.

Floridi, Luciano. 2023. *The Green and the Blue: Naive Ideas to Improve Politics in an Information Society.* New York: Wiley.

Floridi, Luciano, and Massimo Chiriatti. 2020. 'GPT-3: Its nature, scope, limits, and consequences.' *Minds and Machines*:1–14.

Floridi, Luciano, and Josh Cowls. 2019. 'A unified framework of five principles for AI in society.' *Harvard Data Science Review*, https://hdsr.mitpress.mit.edu/pub/l0jsh9d1/release/8

Floridi, Luciano, Josh Cowls, Monica Beltrametti, Raja Chatila, Patrice Chazerand, Virginia Dignum, Christoph Luetge, Robert Madelin, Ugo Pagallo, Francesca Rossi, Burkhard Schafer, Peggy Valcke, and Effy Vayena. 2018. 'AI4People: An ethical framework for a good AI society: Opportunities, risks, principles, and recommendations.' *Minds and Machines* 28 (4):689–707.

Floridi, Luciano, Josh Cowls, Thomas C. King, and Mariarosaria Taddeo. 2020. 'How to design AI for social good: Seven essential factors.' *Science and Engineering Ethics* 26 (3):1771–96.

Floridi, Luciano, Matthias Holweg, Mariarosaria Taddeo, Javier Amaya Silva, Jakob Mökander, and Yuni Wen. 2022. 'CapAI-A procedure for conducting conformity assessment of AI systems in line with the EU Artificial Intelligence Act.' Available at SSRN 4064091.

Floridi, Luciano, and Phyllis Illari. 2014. The *Philosophy of Information Quality*. Cham: Springer.

Floridi, Luciano, Sylvie Kauffman, Lidia Kolucka-Zuk, Frank LaRue, Sabine Leutheusser-Schnarrenberger, José-Luis Piñar, Peggy Valcke, and Jimmy Wales. 2015. *The Advisory Council to Google on the Right to be Forgotten*. Final Report. https://archive.google.com/advisorycouncil/

Floridi, Luciano, and Tim Lord Clement-Jones. 20 March 2019. 'The five principles key to any ethical framework for AI.' *New Statesman*, https://www.aithics.co/post/the-five-principles-for-ai.

Floridi, Luciano, and Kia Nobre. 2020. 'The green and the blue: How AI may be a force for good.' OECD, available online. https://www.oecd-forum.org/posts/the-green-and-the-blue-how-ai-may-be-a-force-for-good

Floridi, Luciano, and Jeff W. Sanders. 2004. 'On the morality of artificial agents.' *Minds and Machines* 14 (3):349–79.

Floridi, Luciano, and Mariarosaria Taddeo. 2014. *The Ethics of Information Warfare*. New York: Springer.

Floridi, Luciano, and Mariarosaria Taddeo. 2016. 'What is data ethics?' *Philosophical Transactions of the Royal Society A: Mathematical, Physical and Engineering Sciences* 374 (2083).

Floridi, Luciano, Mariarosaria Taddeo, and Matteo Turilli. 2009. 'Turing's imitation game: Still an impossible challenge for all machines and some judges––An evaluation of the 2008 Loebner Contest.' *Minds and Machines* 19 (1):145–50.

Freier, Nathan G. 2008. 'Children attribute moral standing to a personified agent.' Proceedings of the SIGCHI Conference on Human Factors in Computing Systems, pp. 343–352.

Freitas, Pedro Miguel, Francisco Andrade, and Paulo Novais. 2013. 'Criminal liability of autonomous agents: From the unthinkable to the plausible.' International Workshop on AI Approaches to the Complexity of Legal Systems.

Freud, S. 1955. 'A difficulty in the path of psycho analysis.' 135–44, *The Standard Edition of the Complete Psychological Works of Sigmund Freud*, Vol. 17: (1917–1919) https://pep-web.org/search/document/SE.017.0135A?page=P0135

Friedman, Batya, and Helen Nissenbaum. 1996. 'Bias in computer systems'. *ACM Transactions on Information Systems (TOIS)* 14 (3):330–47.

Friis, Jan Kyrre Berg Olsen, Stig Andur Pedersen, and Vincent F. Hendricks. 2013. *A Companion to the Philosophy of Technology*. Blackwell Companions to Philosophy. Chichester, UK; Malden, MA: Wiley-Blackwell.

Fuster, Andreas, Paul Goldsmith-Pinkham, Tarun Ramadorai, and Ansgar Walther. 2017. 'Predictably unequal? The effects of machine learning on credit markets'. *The Journal of Finance* 77 (1):5–47.

Future of Life Institute. 2017. 'The Asilomar AI Principles'. https://futureoflife.org/open-letter/ai-principles/.

Gagne, David John, Hannah M. Christensen, Aneesh C. Subramanian, and Adam H. Monahan. 2020. 'Machine learning for stochastic parameterization: Generative adversarial networks in the Lorenz '96 Model'. *Journal of Advances in Modeling Earth Systems* 12 (3):e2019MS001896.

Gajane, Pratik, and Mykola Pechenizkiy. 2018. 'On formalizing fairness in prediction with machine learning'. arXiv:1710.03184 [cs, stat].

Ganascia, Jean-Gabriel. 2010. 'Epistemology of AI revisited in the light of the philosophy of information'. *Knowledge, Technology & Policy* 23 (1):57–73.

García-Martín, Eva, Crefeda Faviola Rodrigues, Graham Riley, and Håkan Grahn. 2019. 'Estimation of energy consumption in machine learning'. *Journal of Parallel and Distributed Computing* 134:75–88.

Gauci, Melvin, Jianing Chen, Wei Li, Tony J. Dodd, and Roderich Gross. 2014. 'Clustering objects with robots that do not compute'. Proceedings of the 2014 International Conference on Autonomous Agents and Multi-Agent Systems, pp. 421–428.

Gebru, Timnit, Jamie Morgenstern, Briana Vecchione, Jennifer Wortman Vaughan, Hanna Wallach, Hal Daumé III, and Kate Crawford. 2020. 'Datasheets for Datasets'. arXiv:1803.09010 [cs].

Ghani, Rayid. 2016. 'You say you want transparency and interpretability?' *Rayid Ghani*. http://www.rayidghani.com/2016/04/29/you-say-you-want-transparency-and-interpretability/

Gillis, Talia B., and Jann Spiess. 2019. 'Big data and discrimination'. *University of Chicago Law Review* 86 (2):459–488.

Gless, Sabine, Emily Silverman, and Thomas Weigend. 2016. 'If robots cause harm, who is to blame? Self-driving cars and criminal liability'. *New Criminal Law Review* 19 (3):412–36.

Goel, Ashok, Brian Creeden, Mithun Kumble, Shanu Salunke, Abhinaya Shetty, and Bryan Wiltgen. 2015. 'Using Watson for enhancing human-computer co-creativity'. In 2015 AAAI fall symposium series. 2015.

Gogarty, Brendan, and Meredith Hagger. 2008. 'The laws of man over vehicles unmanned: The legal response to robotic revolution on sea, land and air'. *Journal of Law and Information Science* 19:73.

Golder, Scott A., and Michael W. Macy. 2011. 'Diurnal and seasonal mood vary with work, sleep, and daylength across diverse cultures'. *Science* 333 (6051):1878–81.

González-González, Carina Soledad, Rosa María Gil-Iranzo, and Patricia Paderewski-Rodríguez. 2021. 'Human–robot interaction and sexbots: A systematic literature review'. *Sensors* 21 (1):216.

Goodfellow, Ian, Jean Pouget-Abadie, Mehdi Mirza, Bing Xu, David Warde-Farley, Sherjil Ozair, Aaron Courville, and Yoshua Bengio. 2014. 'Generative adversarial networks'. *Communications of the ACM* 63 (11):139–44.

Goodhart, Charles A. E. 1984. 'Problems of monetary management: The UK experience.' In *Monetary Theory and Practice*, 91–121. Springer.

Graeff, Erhardt. 5 May 2013. 'What we should do before the social bots take over: Online privacy protection and the political economy of our near future.' https://dspace.mit.edu/handle/1721.1/123463

Green, Ben. 2019. '"Good" isn't good enough.' Proceedings of the AI for Social Good Workshop at NeurIPS, vol. 16.

Green, Ben, and Yiling Chen. 2019. 'Disparate interactions: An algorithm-in-the-loop analysis of fairness in risk assessments.' In Proceedings of the conference on fairness, accountability, and transparency, pp. 90–99. 2019.

Green, Ben, and Salomé Viljoen. 2020. 'Algorithmic realism: Expanding the boundaries of algorithmic thought.' FAT* '20: Conference on Fairness, Accountability, and Transparency, 27 January 2020, pp. 19–31.

Gregor, Shirley, and Izak Benbasat. 1999. 'Explanations from intelligent systems: Theoretical foundations and implications for practice.' *MIS Quarterly* 23:497–530.

Grgić-Hlača, Nina, Elissa M. Redmiles, Krishna P. Gummadi, and Adrian Weller. 2018. 'Human perceptions of fairness in algorithmic decision making: A case study of criminal risk prediction.' arXiv:1802.09548 [cs, stat].

Grote, Thomas, and Philipp Berens. 2020. 'On the ethics of algorithmic decision-making in healthcare.' *Journal of Medical Ethics* 46 (3):205–11.

Grut, Chantal. 2013. 'The challenge of autonomous lethal robotics to international humanitarian law.' *Journal of Conflict and Security Law* 18 (1):5–23.

Hage, Jaap. 2018. 'Two concepts of constitutive rules.' *Argumenta* 4 (1):21–39.

Hagendorff, Thilo. 2020. 'The ethics of AI ethics: An evaluation of guidelines.' *Minds and Machines* 30 (1):99–120.

Hager, Gregory D., Ann Drobnis, Fei Fang, Rayid Ghani, Amy Greenwald, Terah Lyons, David C. Parkes, Jason Schultz, Suchi Saria, Stephen F. Smith, and Milind Tambe. 2019. 'Artificial intelligence for social good.' arXiv:1901.05406 [cs].

Hallevy, Gabriel. 2011. 'Unmanned vehicles: Subordination to criminal law under the modern concept of criminal liability.' *Journal of Law, Information and Science* 21:200.

Ham, Yoo-Geun, Jeong-Hwan Kim, and Jing-Jia Luo. 2019. 'Deep learning for multi-year ENSO forecasts.' *Nature* 573 (7775):568–72.

Haque, Albert, Michelle Guo, Alexandre Alahi, Serena Yeung, Zelun Luo, Alisha Rege, Jeffrey Jopling, Lance Downing, William Beninati, Amit Singh, Terry Platchek, Arnold Milstein, and Li Fei-Fei. 2017. 'Towards vision-based smart hospitals: A system for tracking and monitoring hand hygiene compliance.' In Machine Learning for Healthcare Conference, pp. 75–87. PMLR, 2017.

Harwell, Drew. 2020. 'Dating apps need women. Advertisers need diversity. AI companies offer a solution: Fake people.' *Washington Post*. https://cacm.acm.org/news/242027-dating-apps-need-women-advertisers-need-diversity-ai-companies-offer-a-solution-fake-people/fulltext

Hauer, Tomas. 2019. 'Society caught in a labyrinth of algorithms: Disputes, promises, and limitations of the new order of things.' *Society* 56 (3):222–30.

Haugen, Geir Marius Sætenes. 2017. 'Manipulation and deception with social bots: Strategies and indicators for minimizing impact.' NTNU.

Hay, George A, and Daniel Kelley. 1974. 'An empirical survey of price fixing conspiracies.' *The Journal of Law and Economics* 17 (1):13–38.

Hayward, Keith J., and Matthijs M. Maas. 2020. 'Artificial intelligence and crime: A primer for criminologists.' *Crime, Media, Culture*:1741659020917434.

Hegel, Georg Wilhelm Friedrich. 2009. *The Phenomenology of Spirit*. The Cambridge Hegel Translations. Cambridge: Cambridge University Press.

Henderson, Peter, Jieru Hu, Joshua Romoff, Emma Brunskill, Dan Jurafsky, and Joelle Pineau. 2020. 'Towards the systematic reporting of the energy and carbon footprints of machine learning.' *Journal of Machine Learning Research* 21 (248):1–43.

Henderson, Peter, Koustuv Sinha, Nicolas Angelard-Gontier, Nan Rosemary Ke, Genevieve Fried, Ryan Lowe, and Joelle Pineau. 2018. 'Ethical challenges in data-driven dialogue systems.' AIES '18: AAAI/ACM Conference on AI, Ethics, and Society, pp. 123–129, 27 December 2018.

Henry, Katharine E., David N. Hager, Peter J. Pronovost, and Suchi Saria. 2015. 'A targeted real-time early warning score (TREWScore) for septic shock.' *Science Translational Medicine* 7 (299):299ra122-2.

Herlocker, Jonathan L., Joseph A. Konstan, and John Riedl. 2000. 'Explaining collaborative filtering recommendations.' In Proceedings of the 2000 ACM conference on Computer supported cooperative work, pp. 241–250. 2000.

Hilbert, Martin. 2016. 'Big data for development: A review of promises and challenges.' *Development Policy Review* 34 (1):135–74.

Hildebrandt, Mireille. 2008. 'Ambient intelligence, criminal liability and democracy.' *Criminal Law and Philosophy* 2:163–80.

Hill, Robin K. 2016. 'What an algorithm is.' *Philosophy & Technology* 29 (1):35–59.

Hine, Emmie, and Luciano Floridi. 2022. 'Artificial intelligence with American values and Chinese characteristics: A comparative analysis of American and Chinese governmental AI policies.' *AI & Society*, 1–22.

Hintemann, Ralph, and Simon Hinterholzer. 2019. 'Energy consumption of data centers worldwide.' The 6th International Conference on ICT for Sustainability (ICT4S), Lappeenranta.

HLEGAI. 18 December 2018. 'High Level Expert Group on Artificial Intelligence, EU: Draft ethics guidelines for trustworthy AI.' https://ec.europa.eu/digital-single-market/en/news/draft-ethics-guidelines-trustworthy-ai.

HLEGAI. 8 April 2019. 'High Level Expert Group on Artificial Intelligence, EU: Ethics guidelines for trustworthy AI.' https://ec.europa.eu/digital-single-market/en/news/ethics-guidelines-trustworthy-ai.

Hoffmann, Anna Lauren, Sarah T. Roberts, Christine T. Wolf, and Stacy Wood. 2018. 'Beyond fairness, accountability, and transparency in the ethics of algorithms: Contributions and perspectives from LIS.' *Proceedings of the Association for Information Science and Technology* 55 (1):694–6.

House of Lords Artificial Intelligence Committee. 16 April 2017. 'AI in the UK: Ready, willing and able?' Report of Session 2017–19, HL Paper 100.

Howe, Bill, Julia Stoyanovich, Haoyue Ping, Bernease Herman, and Matt Gee. 2017. 'Synthetic data for social good.' arXiv preprint arXiv:1710.08874.

Hu, Margaret. 2017. 'Algorithmic Jim Crow.' *Fordham Law Review* 86:633.

Hutson, Matthew. 2019. 'Bringing machine learning to the masses.' *Science* 365 (6452):416–17.

ICO. 2020. 'ICO and the Turing consultation on explaining AI decisions guidance.' Last modified 30 March 2020. https://ico.org.uk/for-organisations/uk-gdpr-guidance-and-resources/artificial-intelligence/explaining-decisions-made-with-artificial-intelligence/

IEEE. 2017. 'Ethically aligned design: A vision for prioritizing human well-being with autonomous and intelligent systems, version 2.' https://standards.ieee.org/news/2017/ead_v2.html.

Inderwildi, Oliver, Chuan Zhang, Xiaonan Wang, and Markus Kraft. 2020. 'The impact of intelligent cyber-physical systems on the decarbonization of energy.' *Energy & Environmental Science* 13 (3):744–71.

Information Commissioner's Office. 2017. 'Royal Free—Google DeepMind trial failed to comply with data protection law.' Last modified 3 July 2017. https://www.pslhub.org/ learn/investigations-risk-management-and-legal-issues/investigations-and-complaints/ investigation-reports/other-reports-and-enquiries/ico-royal-free-%E2%80%93-google-deepmind-trial-failed-to-comply-with-data-protection-law-july-2017-r869/

Ise, Takeshi, and Yurika Oba. 2019. 'Forecasting climatic trends using neural networks: An experimental study using global historical data.' *Frontiers in Robotics and AI* 6.

Jaafari, Abolfazl, Eric K. Zenner, Mahdi Panahi, and Himan Shahabi. 2019. 'Hybrid artificial intelligence models based on a neuro-fuzzy system and metaheuristic optimization algorithms for spatial prediction of wildfire probability.' *Agricultural and Forest Meteorology* 266–7:198–207.

Jagatic, Tom N., Nathaniel A. Johnson, Markus Jakobsson, and Filippo Menczer. 2007. 'Social phishing.' *Communications of the ACM* 50 (10):94–100.

James, Gareth, Daniela Witten, Trevor Hastie, and Robert Tibshirani. 2013. *An Introduction to Statistical Learning.* New York: Springer.

Janoff-Bulman, Ronnie. 2007. 'Erroneous assumptions: Popular belief in the effectiveness of torture interrogation.' *Peace and Conflict: Journal of Peace Psychology* 13 (4):429–35.

Jezard, Adam. 11 April 2018. 'China is now home to the world's most valuable AI start-up.' https://www.weforum.org/agenda/2018/04/chart-of-the-day-china-now-has-the-worlds-most-valuable-ai-startup/.

Jobin, Anna, Marcello Ienca, and Effy Vayena. 2019. 'The global landscape of AI ethics guidelines.' *Nature Machine Intelligence* 1 (9):389–99.

Joh, Elizabeth E. 2016. 'Policing police robots.' *UCLA Law Review Discourse* 64:516.

Jones, Nicola. 2018. 'How to stop data centres from gobbling up the world's electricity.' *Nature* 561 (7722):163–7.

Karppi, Tero. 2018. '"The computer said so": On the ethics, effectiveness, and cultural techniques of predictive policing.' *Social Media + Society* 4 (2):205630511876829.

Karras, Tero, Samuli Laine, and Timo Aila. 2019. 'A style-based generator architecture for generative adversarial networks.' arXiv:1812.04948 [cs, stat].

Katell, Michael, Meg Young, Dharma Dailey, Bernease Herman, Vivian Guetler, Aaron Tam, Corinne Binz, Daniella Raz, and P. M. Krafft. 2020. 'Toward situated interventions for algorithmic equity: Lessons from the field.' FAT* '20: Conference on Fairness, Accountability, and Transparency, 27 January 2020.

Kaye, Jane, Edgar A. Whitley, David Lund, Michael Morrison, Harriet Teare, and Karen Melham. 2015. 'Dynamic consent: A patient interface for twenty-first century research networks.' *European Journal of Human Genetics* 23 (2):141–6.

Kerr, Ian R. 2003. 'Bots, babes and the californication of commerce.' *University of Ottawa Law and Technology Journal* 1:285.

Kerr, Ian R., and Marcus Bornfreund. 2005. 'Buddy bots: How Turing's fast friends are undermining consumer privacy.' *Presence: Teleoperators & Virtual Environments* 14 (6):647–55.

King, Gary, and Nathaniel Persily. 2020. 'Unprecedented Facebook URLs dataset now available for academic research through social science One.' *Social Science One* 13.

King, Thomas C., Nikita Aggarwal, Mariarosaria Taddeo, and Luciano Floridi. 2019. 'Artificial intelligence crime: An interdisciplinary analysis of foreseeable threats and solutions.' *Science and Engineering Ethics* 26:89–120.

Kizilcec, René. 2016. 'How much information?' Proceedings of the 2016 CHI Conference on Human Factors in Computing Systems (pp. 2390–5).

Klee, Robert. 1996. *Introduction to the Philosophy of Science: Cutting Nature at Its Seams*. Oxford: Oxford University Press.

Kleinberg, Jon, Sendhil Mullainathan, and Manish Raghavan. 2016. 'Inherent trade-offs in the fair determination of risk scores.' arXiv:1609.05807 [cs, stat].

Kortylewski, Adam, Bernhard Egger, Andreas Schneider, Thomas Gerig, Andreas Morel-Forster, and Thomas Vetter. 2019. 'Analyzing and reducing the damage of dataset bias to face recognition with synthetic data.' Proceedings of the IEEE Conference on Computer Vision and Pattern Recognition Workshops, 2019.

Labati, Ruggero Donida, Angelo Genovese, Enrique Muñoz, Vincenzo Piuri, Fabio Scotti, and Gianluca Sforza. 2016. 'Biometric recognition in automated border control: A survey.' *ACM Computing Surveys* 49 (2):1–39.

Lacoste, Alexandre, Alexandra Luccioni, Victor Schmidt, and Thomas Dandres. 2019. 'Quantifying the carbon emissions of machine learning.' arXiv preprint arXiv:1910.09700.

Lagioia, Francesca, and Giovanni Sartor. 2019. 'AI systems under criminal law: A legal analysis and a regulatory perspective.' *Philosophy & Technology*:1–33.

Lakkaraju, Himabindu, Everaldo Aguiar, Carl Shan, David Miller, Nasir Bhanpuri, Rayid Ghani, and Kecia L. Addison. 2015. 'A machine learning framework to identify students at risk of adverse academic outcomes.' In Proceedings of the 21th ACM SIGKDD international conference on knowledge discovery and data mining, pp. 1909–1918.

Lambrecht, Anja, and Catherine Tucker. 2019. 'Algorithmic bias? An empirical study of apparent gender-based discrimination in the display of STEM career ads.' *Management Science* 65 (7):2966–81.

Larraondo, Pablo R., Luigi J. Renzullo, Albert I. J. M. Van Dijk, Inaki Inza, and Jose A. Lozano. 2020. 'Optimization of deep learning precipitation models using categorical binary metrics.' *Journal of Advances in Modeling Earth Systems* 12 (5):e2019MS001909.

Larson, Brian. 2017. 'Gender as a variable in natural-language processing: Ethical considerations.' Proceedings of the First ACL Workshop on Ethics in Natural Language Processing, 2017.

Lee, K., and P. Triolo. December 2017. 'China's artificial intelligence revolution: Understanding Beijing's structural advantages—Eurasian Group.' https://www.eurasia-group.net/live-post/ai-in-china-cutting-through-the-hype.

Lee, Michelle Seng Ah, and Luciano Floridi. 2020. 'Algorithmic fairness in mortgage lending: From absolute conditions to relational trade-offs.' *Minds and Machines* 31 (1): 165–191.

Lee, Michelle Seng Ah, Luciano Floridi, and Alexander Denev. 2020. 'Innovating with confidence: Embedding AI governance and fairness in a financial services risk management framework.' *Berkeley Technology Law Journal* 34 (2):1–19.

Lee, Min Kyung. 2018. 'Understanding perception of algorithmic decisions: Fairness, trust, and emotion in response to algorithmic management.' *Big Data & Society* 5 (1):205395171875668.

Lee, Min Kyung, Ji Tae Kim, and Leah Lizarondo. 2017. 'A human-centered approach to algorithmic services: Considerations for fair and motivating smart community service management that allocates donations to non-profit organizations.' Proceedings of the 2017 CHI conference on human factors in computing systems, pp. 3365–3376. 2017

Lee, Richard B., and Richard Heywood Daly. 1999. *The Cambridge Encyclopedia of Hunters and Gatherers*. Cambridge: Cambridge University Press.

Legg, Shane, and Marcus Hutter. 2007. 'A collection of definitions of intelligence.' In *Advances in Artificial General intelligence: Concepts, Architecture, and Algorithms*, edited by Ben Goertzel and Pei Wang, 17–24. IOS.

Lepri, Bruno, Nuria Oliver, Emmanuel Letouzé, Alex Pentland, and Patrick Vinck. 2018. 'Fair, transparent, and accountable algorithmic decision-making processes: The premise, the proposed solutions, and the open challenges.' *Philosophy & Technology* 31 (4):611–27.

Lessig, Lawrence. 1999. *Code: And Other Laws of Cyberspace.* New York: Basic Books.

Lewis, Dev. 2019. 'Social credit case study: City citizen scores in Xiamen and Fuzhou.' Medium: Berkman Klein Center Collection 8.

Liakos, Konstantinos G., Patrizia Busato, Dimitrios Moshou, Simon Pearson, and Dionysis Bochtis. 2018. 'Machine learning in agriculture: A review.' *Sensors* 18 (8):2674.

Liang, Huiying, Brian Y. Tsui, Hao Ni, Carolina C. S. Valentim, Sally L. Baxter, Guangjian Liu, Wenjia Cai, Daniel S. Kermany, Xin Sun, Jiancong Chen, Liya He, Jie Zhu, Pin Tian, Hua Shao, Lianghong Zheng, Rui Hou, Sierra Hewett, Gen Li, Ping Liang, Xuan Zang, Zhiqi Zhang, Liyan Pan, Huimin Cai, Rujuan Ling, Shuhua Li, Yongwang Cui, Shusheng Tang, Hong Ye, Xiaoyan Huang, Waner He, Wenqing Liang, Qing Zhang, Jianmin Jiang, Wei Yu, Jianqun Gao, Wanxing Ou, Yingmin Deng, Qiaozhen Hou, Bei Wang, Cuichan Yao, Yan Liang, Shu Zhang, Yaou Duan, Runze Zhang, Sarah Gibson, Charlotte L. Zhang, Oulan Li, Edward D. Zhang, Gabriel Karin, Nathan Nguyen, Xiaokang Wu, Cindy Wen, Jie Xu, Wenqin Xu, Bochu Wang, Winston Wang, Jing Li, Bianca Pizzato, Caroline Bao, Daoman Xiang, Wanting He, Suiqin He, Yugui Zhou, Weldon Haw, Michael Goldbaum, Adriana Tremoulet, Chun-Nan Hsu, Hannah Carter, Long Zhu, Kang Zhang, and Huimin Xia. 2019. 'Evaluation and accurate diagnoses of pediatric diseases using artificial intelligence.' *Nature Medicine* 25 (3):433–438.

Lin, Tom C. W. 2016. 'The new market manipulation.' *Emory LJ* 66:1253.

Lipworth, Wendy, Paul H. Mason, Ian Kerridge, and John P. A. Ioannidis. 2017. 'Ethics and epistemology in big data research.' *Journal of Bioethical Inquiry* 14 (4):489–500.

Liu, Jenny X., Yevgeniy Goryakin, Akiko Maeda, Tim Bruckner, and Richard Scheffler. 2017. 'Global Health Workforce Labor Market Projections for 2030.' *Human Resources for Health* 15 (1):11. doi: 10.1186/s12960-017-0187-2.

Lodder, Jerry M. 2008. 'Binary arithmetic: From Leibniz to Von Neumann.' *Resources for Teaching Discrete Mathematics*:168–78.

Lu, Haonan, Mubarik Arshad, Andrew Thornton, Giacomo Avesani, Paula Cunnea, Ed Curry, Fahdi Kanavati, Jack Liang, Katherine Nixon, Sophie T. Williams, Mona Ali Hassan, David D. L. Bowtell, Hani Gabra, Christina Fotopoulou, Andrea Rockall, and Eric O. Aboagye. 2019. 'A mathematical-descriptor of tumor-mesoscopic-structure from computed-tomography images annotates prognostic- and molecular-phenotypes of epithelial ovarian cancer.' *Nature Communications* 10 (1):764.

Lu, Hongfang, Xin Ma, Kun Huang, and Mohammadamin Azimi. 2020. 'Carbon trading volume and price forecasting in China using multiple machine learning models.' *Journal of Cleaner Production* 249:119386.

Luccioni, Alexandra, Victor Schmidt, Vahe Vardanyan, and Yoshua Bengio. 2021. 'Using artificial intelligence to visualize the impacts of climate change.' *IEEE Computer Graphics and Applications* 41 (1):8–14.

Luhmann, Niklas, and John Bednarz. 1995. *Social Systems, Writing Science.* Stanford, CA: Stanford University Press.

Lum, Kristian, and William Isaac. 2016. 'To predict and serve?' *Significance* 13 (5):14–19.

Lynskey, Orla. 2015. *The Foundations of EU Data Protection Law.* Oxford Studies in European Law. Oxford, New York: Oxford University Press.

Magalhães, João Carlos. 2018. 'Do algorithms shape character? Considering algorithmic ethical subjectivation.' *Social Media + Society* 4 (2):205630511876830.

Malhotra, Charru, Vinod Kotwal, and Surabhi Dalal. 2018. 'Ethical framework for machine learning.' 2018 ITU Kaleidoscope: Machine Learning for a 5G Future (ITU K), November 2018.

Malmodin, Jens, and Dag Lundén. 2018. 'The energy and carbon footprint of the global ICT and E&M sectors 2010–2015.' *Sustainability* 10 (9):3027.

Manheim, David, and Scott Garrabrant. 2018. 'Categorizing variants of Goodhart's Law.' arXiv preprint arXiv:1803.04585.

Mano, M. Morris. 1979. Digital *Logic and Computer Design*. Englewood Cliffs, NJ: Prentice-Hall.

Manzoni, Alessandro. 2016. *The Betrothed*. London: Penguin Books.

Mardani, Abbas, Huchang Liao, Mehrbakhsh Nilashi, Melfi Alrasheedi, and Fausto Cavallaro. 2020. 'A multi-stage method to predict carbon dioxide emissions using dimensionality reduction, clustering, and machine learning techniques.' *Journal of Cleaner Production* 275:122942.

Marrero, Tony. 2016. 'Record Pacific cocaine haul brings hundreds of cases to Tampa court.' *Tampa Bay Times*, 10 September:2016.

Martin, Kirsten. 2019. 'Ethical implications and accountability of algorithms.' *Journal of Business Ethics* 160 (4):835–50.

Martínez-Miranda, Enrique, Peter McBurney, and Matthew J. W. Howard. 2016. 'Learning unfair trading: A market manipulation analysis from the reinforcement learning perspective.' 2016 IEEE Conference on Evolving and Adaptive Intelligent Systems (EAIS), pp. 103–109.

Martínez-Miranda, Juan, and Arantza Aldea. 2005. 'Emotions in human and artificial intelligence.' *Computers in Human Behavior* 21 (2):323–41.

Masanet, Eric, Arman Shehabi, Nuoa Lei, Sarah Smith, and Jonathan Koomey. 2020. 'Recalibrating global data center energy-use estimates.' *Science* 367 (6481):984–6.

Mayson, Sandra G. 2019. 'Bias in, bias out.' *Yale Law Journal* 128:2218–2300.

Mazzini, Gabriele. forthcoming. 'A system of governance for artificial intelligence through the lens of emerging intersections between AI and EU law.' In *Digital Revolution: New Challenges for Law*, edited by A. De Franceschi, R. Schulze, M. Graziadei, O. Pollicino, F. Riente, S. Sica, and P. Sirena. SSRN: https://ssrn.com/abstract=3369266.

Mazzi, Francesca and Luciano Floridi (ed.) 2023. *The Ethics of Artificial Intelligence for the Sustainable Development Goals*. Cham: Springer.

McAllister, Amanda. 2016. 'Stranger than science fiction: The rise of AI interrogation in the dawn of autonomous robots and the need for an additional protocol to the UN convention against torture.' *Minnesota Law Review* 101:2527.

McBurney, Peter, and Matthew J. Howard. 2015. Learning unfair trading: A market manipulation analysis from the reinforcement learning perspective. arXiv.org.

McCarthy, John. 1997. 'Review of Kasparov vs. Deep Blue by Monty Newborn.' *Science*, 6 June.

McCarthy, John, Marvin L. Minsky, Nathaniel Rochester, and Claude E. Shannon. 2006. 'A proposal for the Dartmouth summer research project on artificial intelligence, August 31, 1955.' *AI magazine* 27 (4):12.

McFarlane, Daniel. 1999. 'Interruption of people in human-computer interaction: A general unifying definition of human interruption and taxonomy.' Office of naval research Arlington VA, 1997.

McFarlane, Daniel, and Kara Latorella. 2002. 'The scope and importance of human interruption in human-computer interaction design.' *Human-Computer Interaction* 17:1–61.

McKelvey, Fenwick, and Elizabeth Dubois. 2017. 'Computational propaganda in Canada: The use of political bots.' https://demtech.oii.ox.ac.uk/wp-content/uploads/sites/12/2017/06/Comprop-Canada.pdf

Menad, Nait Amar, Abdolhossein Hemmati-Sarapardeh, Amir Varamesh, and Shahaboddin Shamshirband. 2019. 'Predicting solubility of CO2 in brine by advanced machine learning systems: Application to carbon capture and sequestration.' *Journal of CO2 Utilization* 33:83–95.

Mendelsohn, Robert, Ariel Dinar, and Larry Williams. 2006. 'The distributional impact of climate change on rich and poor countries.' *Environment and Development Economics* 11 (2):159–78.

Meneguzzi, Felipe Rech, and Michael Luck. 2009. 'Norm-based behaviour modification in BDI agents.' AAMAS 1:177–184.

Microsoft. 2018. 'The carbon benefits of cloud computing: A study on the Microsoft Cloud.' https://www.microsoft.com/en-us/download/details.aspx?id=56950

Milano, Silvia, Mariarosaria Taddeo, and Luciano Floridi. 2019. 'Ethical aspects of multi-stakeholder recommendation systems.' *The Information Society* 37 (1):35–45.

Milano, Silvia, Mariarosaria Taddeo, and Luciano Floridi. 2020. 'Recommender systems and their ethical challenges.' *AI & Society* 35 (4):957–67.

Milano, Silvia, Mariarosaria Taddeo, and Luciano Floridi. 2021. 'Ethical aspects of multi-stakeholder recommendation systems.' *The Information Society* 37 (1):35–45.

Mill, John Stuart. 1861. *Considerations on Representative Government.* 2nd ed. London: Parker, Son, and Bourn.

Mittelstadt, Brent Daniel, Patrick Allo, Mariarosaria Taddeo, Sandra Wachter, and Luciano Floridi. 2016. 'The ethics of algorithms: Mapping the debate.' *Big Data & Society* 3 (2): 2053951716679679.

Mnih, Volodymyr, Koray Kavukcuoglu, David Silver, Andrei A. Rusu, Joel Veness, Marc G. Bellemare, Alex Graves, Martin Riedmiller, Andreas K. Fidjeland, and Georg Ostrovski. 2015. 'Human-level control through deep reinforcement learning.' *Nature* 518 (7540):529–33.

Mohanty, Suchitra, and Rahul Bhatia. 2017. 'Indian court's privacy ruling is blow to government.' *Reuters*, 25 August. Accessed 13 April 2019.

Mojsilovic, Aleksandra. 2018. 'Introducing AI Explainability 360 toolkit.' In Proceedings of the 3rd ACM India Joint International Conference on Data Science & Management of Data (8th ACM IKDD CODS & 26th COMAD), pp. 376–379. 2021.

Mokander, Jakob, and Luciano Floridi. 2021. 'Ethics-based auditing to develop trustworthy AI.' *Minds and Machines* 31 (2):323–327.

Mökander, Jakob, Jessica Morley, Mariarosaria Taddeo, and Luciano Floridi. forthcoming. 'Ethics-based auditing of automated decision-making systems: Nature, scope, and limitations.' *Science and Engineering Ethics* 27 (4):44.

Möller, Judith, Damian Trilling, Natali Helberger, and Bram van Es. 2018. 'Do not blame it on the algorithm: An empirical assessment of multiple recommender systems and their impact on content diversity.' *Information, Communication & Society* 21 (7):959–77.

Moor, James H. 1985. 'What is computer ethics?' *Metaphilosophy* 16 (4):266–75.

Moore, Jared. 2019. 'AI for not bad.' *Frontiers in Big Data* 2:32.

Morley, Jessica, Josh Cowls, Mariarosaria Taddeo, and Luciano Floridi. 2020. 'Ethical guidelines for COVID-19 tracing apps.' *Nature* 582:29–31.

Morley, Jessica, Luciano Floridi, Libby Kinsey, and Anat Elhalal. 2020. 'From what to how: An initial review of publicly available AI ethics tools, methods and research to translate principles into practices.' *Science and Engineering Ethics* 26 (4):2141–68.

Morley, Jessica, Caio C. V. Machado, Christopher Burr, Josh Cowls, Indra Joshi, Mariarosaria Taddeo, and Luciano Floridi. 2020. 'The ethics of AI in health care: A mapping review.' *Social Science & Medicine* 260:113172.

Morley, Jessica, Caroline Morton, Kassandra Karpathakis, Mariarosaria Taddeo, and Luciano Floridi. 2021. 'Towards a framework for evaluating the safety, acceptability and efficacy of AI systems for health: An initial synthesis.' arXiv preprint arXiv:2104.06910.

Moroney, Laurence. 2020. *AI and Machine Learning for Coders: A Programmer's Guide to Artificial Intelligence*. Sebastopol, CA: O'Reilly.

Murgia, Madhumita. 2018. 'DeepMind's move to transfer health unit to Google stirs data fears.' *Financial Times,* November 13, 2018.

Narciso, Diogo A. C., and F. G. Martins. 2020. 'Application of machine learning tools for energy efficiency in industry: A review.' *Energy Reports* 6:1181–99.

Neff, Gina, and Peter Nagy. 2016a. 'Automation, algorithms, and politics—talking to bots: Symbiotic agency and the case of Tay.' *International Journal of Communication* 10:17.

Neff, Gina, and Peter Nagy. 2016b. 'Talking to bots: Symbiotic agency and the case of Tay.' *International Journal of Communication* 10:4915–31.

Neufeld, Eric, and Sonje Finnestad. 2020. 'In defense of the Turing test.' *AI & Society* 35: 819–827.

Nield, Thomas. 5 January 2019. 'Is deep learning already hitting its limitations? And is another ai winter coming?' *Towards Data Science* https://towardsdatascience.com/is-deep-learning-already-hitting-its-limitations-c81826082ac3.

Nietzsche, Friedrich Wilhelm. 2008. *Twilight of the Idols, or How to Philosophize with a Hammer*. Oxford: Oxford University Press.

Nijhawan, Lokesh P., Manthan Janodia, Muddu Krishna, Kishore Bhat, Laxminarayana Bairy, Nayanabhirama Udupa, and Prashant Musmade. 2013. *Informed Consent: Issues and Challenges* 4.

Nissenbaum, Helen. 2009. *Privacy in Context: Technology, Policy, and the Integrity of Social Life*. Stanford, CA: Stanford University Press.

Nissenbaum, Helen. 2011. 'A contextual approach to privacy online.' *Daedalus* 140 (4):32–48.

Noble, Safiya Umoja. 2018. *Algorithms of Oppression: How Search Engines Reinforce Racism*. New York: New York University Press.

Nordling, Linda. 2018. 'Europe's biggest research fund cracks down on "ethics dumping".' *Nature* 559 (7712):17.

Nunamaker, Jay F., Douglas C. Derrick, Aaron C. Elkins, Judee K. Burgoon, and Mark W. Patton. 2011. 'Embodied conversational agent-based kiosk for automated interviewing.' *Journal of Management Information Systems* 28 (1):17–48.

Obermeyer, Ziad, Brian Powers, Christine Vogeli, and Sendhil Mullainathan. 2019. 'Dissecting racial bias in an algorithm used to manage the health of populations.' *Science* 366 (6464):447–53.

Ochigame, Rodrigo. 2019. 'The invention of "ethical AI": How big tech manipulates academia to avoid regulation.' *Economies of Virtue* 49.

OECD. 2019. 'Forty-two countries adopt new OECD principles on artificial intelligence.' https://www.oecd.org/science/forty-two-countries-adopt-new-oecd-principles-on-artificial-intelligence.htm.

Olhede, S. C., and P. J. Wolfe. 2018a. 'The growing ubiquity of algorithms in society: Implications, impacts and innovations.' *Philosophical Transactions of the Royal Society A: Mathematical, Physical and Engineering Sciences* 376 (2128):20170364.

Olhede, Sofia, and Patrick Wolfe. 2018b. 'The AI spring of 2018.' *Significance* 15 (3):6–7.

Olteanu, Alexandra, Carlos Castillo, Fernando Diaz, and Emre Kiciman. 2016. 'Social data: Biases, methodological pitfalls, and ethical boundaries.' *Frontiers in Big Sata* 2:13.

Oswald, Marion. 2018. 'Algorithm-assisted decision-making in the public sector: Framing the issues using administrative law rules governing discretionary power.' *Philosophical Transactions of the Royal Society A: Mathematical, Physical and Engineering Sciences* 376 (2128):20170359.

Pagallo, Ugo. 2011. 'Killers, fridges, and slaves: A legal journey in robotics.' *AI & Society* 26 (4):347–54.

Pagallo, Ugo. 2015. 'Good onlife governance: On law, spontaneous orders, and design.' In *The Onlife Manifesto*, 161–77. Cham: Springer.

Pagallo, Ugo. 2017. 'From automation to autonomous systems: A legal phenomenology with problems of accountability.' 26th International Joint Conference on Artificial Intelligence, IJCAI 2017.

Paraschakis, Dimitris. 2017. 'Towards an ethical recommendation framework.' 11th International Conference on Research Challenges in Information Science (RCIS), May 2017, pp. 211–220.

Paraschakis, Dimitris. 2018. 'Algorithmic and ethical aspects of recommender systems in e-commerce.' Malmö University. Faculty of Technology and Society, 2018.

Partnership on AI. 2018. 'Tenets of the Partnership on AI.' https://partnershiponai.org/about/

Pedreshi, Dino, Salvatore Ruggieri, and Franco Turini. 2008. 'Discrimination-aware data mining.' Proceedings of the 14th ACM SIGKDD International Conference on Knowledge Discovery and Data Mining, 24 August 2008, pp. 560–568.

Perera, Lokukaluge P., B. Mo, and Guedes Soares. 2016. 'Machine intelligence for energy efficient ships: A big data solution.' In *Maritime Engineering and Technology III*, edited by Guedes Soares and T. A. Santos, 1:143–50.

Perez, Ethan, Sam Ringer, Kamilė Lukošiūtė, Karina Nguyen, Edwin Chen, Scott Heiner, Craig Pettit, Catherine Olsson, Sandipan Kundu, and Saurav Kadavath. 2022. 'Discovering language model behaviors with model-written evaluations.' arXiv preprint arXiv:2212.09251.

Perrault, Raymond, Shoham Yoav, Erik Brynjolfsson, Clark Jack, John Etchmendy, Barbara Grosz, Lyons Terah, Manyika James, Mishra Saurabh, and Niebles Juan Carlos. 2019. Artificial Intelligence Index Report 2019. https://aiindex.stanford.edu/report/

Pirolli, Peter. 2007. *Information Foraging Theory: Adaptive Interaction with Information.* Oxford: Oxford University Press.

Pirolli, Peter, and Stuart Card. 1995. 'Information foraging in information access environments.' *Proceedings of the SIGCHI Conference on Human Factors in Computing Systems* 51–8.

Pirolli, Peter, and Stuart Card. 1999. 'Information foraging.' *Psychological Review* 106 (4):643.

Pontifical Academy for Life. 2020. 'Rome call for an AI ethics.' https://www.romecall.org/.

Popkin, Richard H. 1966. *The Philosophy of the Sixteenth and Seventeenth Centuries.* New York, London: Free Press; Collier-Macmillan.

Prasad, Mahendra. 2018. 'Social choice and the value alignment problem.' *Artificial Intelligence Safety and Security*, 291–314.

Prates, Marcelo O. R., Pedro H. Avelar, and Luís C. Lamb. 2019. 'Assessing gender bias in machine translation: A case study with Google Translate.' *Neural Computing and Applications* 32:6363–6381.

Price, W. Nicholson, and I. Glenn Cohen. 2019. 'Privacy in the age of medical big data.' *Nature Medicine* 25 (1):37.

Puaschunder, Julia M. 2020. 'The potential for artificial intelligence in healthcare.' Available at SSRN 3525037.

Rachels, James. 1975. 'Why privacy is important.' *Philosophy & Public Affairs* 4 (4):323–33.

Rahwan, Iyad. 2018. 'Society-in-the-loop: Programming the algorithmic social contract.' *Ethics and Information Technology* 20 (1):5–14.

Ramchurn, Sarvapali D., Perukrishnen Vytelingum, Alex Rogers, and Nicholas R. Jennings. 2012. 'Putting the "smarts" into the smart grid: A grand challenge for artificial intelligence.' *Communications of the ACM* 55 (4):86–97.

Ras, Gabrielle, Marcel van Gerven, and Pim Haselager. 2018. 'Explanation methods in deep learning: Users, values, concerns and challenges.' arXiv:1803.07517 [cs, stat].

Rasp, Stephan, Michael S. Pritchard, and Pierre Gentine. 2018. 'Deep learning to represent subgrid processes in climate models.' *Proceedings of the National Academy of Sciences* 115 (39):9684–9.

Ratkiewicz, Jacob, Michael Conover, Mark Meiss, Bruno Gonçalves, Snehal Patil, Alessandro Flammini, and Filippo Menczer. 2011. 'Truthy: Mapping the spread of astroturf in microblog streams.' Proceedings of the 20th International Conference Companion on World Wide Web, pp. 249–252.

Rawls, John. 1955. 'Two concepts of rules.' *The Philosophical Review* 64 (1):3–32.

Reddy, Elizabeth, Baki Cakici, and Andrea Ballestero. 2019. 'Beyond mystery: Putting algorithmic accountability in context.' *Big Data & Society* 6 (1):205395171982685.

Reed, Chris. 2018. 'How should we regulate artificial intelligence?' *Philosophical Transactions of the Royal Society A: Mathematical, Physical and Engineering Sciences* 376 (2128):20170360.

Rehm, Matthias. 2008. ' "She is just stupid": Analyzing user–agent interactions in emotional game situations.' *Interacting with Computers* 20 (3):311–25.

Reisman, Dillon, Jason Schultz, Kate Crawford, and Meredith Whittaker. 2018. 'Algorithmic impact assessments: A practical framework for public agency accountability.' AI Now Institute.

Richardson, Rashida, Jason Schultz, and Kate Crawford. 2019. 'Dirty data, bad predictions: How civil rights violations impact police data, predictive policing systems, and justice.' *NYUL Rev. Online* 94:15.

Ridwan, Wanie M., Michelle Sapitang, Awatif Aziz, Khairul Faizal Kushiar, Ali Najah Ahmed, and Ahmed El-Shafie. 2020. 'Rainfall forecasting model using machine learning methods: Case study Terengganu, Malaysia.' *Ain Shams Engineering Journal* 12 (2): 1651–1663.

Robbins, Scott. 2019. 'A misdirected principle with a catch: Explicability for AI.' *Minds and Machines* 29 (4):495–514.

Roberts, Huw, Josh Cowls, Emmie Hine, Francesca Mazzi, Andreas Tsamados, Mariarosaria Taddeo, and Luciano Floridi. 2021. 'Achieving a "good AI society": Comparing the aims and progress of the EU and the US.' *Science and Engineering Ethics* 27 (6):68.

Roberts, Huw, Josh Cowls, Emmie Hine, Jessica Morley, Mariarosaria Taddeo, Vincent Wang, and Luciano Floridi. 2021. 'China's artificial intelligence strategy: Lessons from the European Union's "ethics-first" approach.' Available at SSRN 3811034.

Roberts, Huw, Josh Cowls, Jessica Morley, Mariarosaria Taddeo, Vincent Wang, and Luciano Floridi. 2021. 'The Chinese approach to artificial intelligence: An analysis of policy, ethics, and regulation.' *AI & Society* 36 (1):59–77.

Robinson, Caleb, and Bistra Dilkina. 2018. 'A machine learning approach to modeling human migration.' Proceedings of the 1st ACM SIGCAS Conference on Computing and Sustainable Societies, 20 June 2018, pp. 1–8.

Rolnick, David, Priya L. Donti, Lynn H. Kaack, Kelly Kochanski, Alexandre Lacoste, Kris Sankaran, Andrew Slavin Ross, Nikola Milojevic-Dupont, Natasha Jaques, and Anna Waldman-Brown. 2019. 'Tackling climate change with machine learning.' arXiv preprint arXiv:1906.05433.

Rosenblueth, Arturo, and Norbert Wiener. 1945. 'The role of models in science.' *Philosophy of Science* 12 (4):316–21.

Ross, Casey, and Ike Swetlitz. 2017. 'IBM pitched Watson as a revolution in cancer care. It's nowhere close.' STAT. Last modified 5 September 2017.

Rossler, Beate. 2015. *The Value of Privacy*. New York: John Wiley & Sons.

Rubel, Alan, Clinton Castro, and Adam Pham. 2019. 'Agency laundering and information technologies.' *Ethical Theory and Moral Practice* 22 (4):1017–41.

Rumbelow, Jessica. 2023. 'SolidGoldMagikarp (plus, prompt generation).' AI Alignment Forum https://www.alignmentforum.org/posts/aPeJE8bSo6rAFoLqg/solidgoldmagikarp-plus-prompt-generation.

Russell, Stuart J., and Peter Norvig. 2018. *Artificial Intelligence: A Modern Approach*. 4th ed. Upper Saddle River: Pearson.

Samuel, Arthur L. 1960. 'Some moral and technical consequences of automation: A refutation.' *Science* 132 (3429):741–2.

Sandvig, Christian, Kevin Hamilton, Kerry Karahalios, and Cedric Langbort. 2016. 'When the algorithm itself is a racist: Diagnosing ethical harm in the basic components of software.' *International Journal of Communication* 10:4972–90.

Saxena, Nripsuta, Karen Huang, Evan DeFilippis, Goran Radanovic, David Parkes, and Yang Liu. 2019. 'How do fairness definitions fare? Examining public attitudes towards algorithmic definitions of fairness.' arXiv:1811.03654 [cs].

Sayed-Mouchaweh, Moamar. 2020. *Artificial Intelligence Techniques for a Scalable Energy Transition: Advanced Methods, Digital Technologies, Decision Support Tools, and Applications*. Cham: Springer.

Schott, Ben. 4 February 2010. 'Bluewashing.' *The New York Times*.

Schuchmann, Sebastian. 17 August 2019. 'Probability of an approaching AI winter.' Towards Data Science https://towardsdatascience.com/probability-of-an-approaching-ai-winter-c2d818fb338a.

Schwartz, Roy, Jesse Dodge, Noah A. Smith, and Oren Etzioni. 2020. 'Green AI.' *Communications of the ACM* 63 (12):54–63.

Searle, John R. 2018. 'Constitutive rules.' *Argumenta* 4 (1):51–4.

Selbst, Andrew D., Danah Boyd, Sorelle A. Friedler, Suresh Venkatasubramanian, and Janet Vertesi. 2019. 'Fairness and abstraction in sociotechnical systems.' Proceedings of the conference on fairness, accountability, and transparency, pp. 59–68.

Seymour, John, and Philip Tully. 2016. 'Weaponizing data science for social engineering: Automated E2E spear phishing on Twitter.' *Black Hat USA* 37:1–39.

Shaffer, Gregory C., and Mark A. Pollack. 2009. 'Hard vs. soft law: Alternatives, complements, and antagonists in international governance.' *Minnesota Law Review* 94:706–99.

Shah, Hetan. 2018. 'Algorithmic accountability.' *Philosophical Transactions of the Royal Society A: Mathematical, Physical and Engineering Sciences* 376 (2128):20170362.

Shannon, Claude E., and Warren Weaver. 1975. *The Mathematical Theory of Communication*. Urbana, IL: University of Illinois Press.

Shannon, Claude E., and Warren Weaver. 1998. *The Mathematical Theory of Communication*. Urbana/Chicago, IL: University of Illinois Press.

Sharkey, Noel, Marc Goodman, and Nick Ross. 2010. 'The coming robot crime wave.' *Computer* 43 (8):115–16.

Shehabi, Arman, Sarah J. Smith, Eric Masanet, and Jonathan Koomey. 2018. 'Data center growth in the United States: Decoupling the demand for services from electricity use.' *Environmental Research Letters* 13 (12):124030.

Shin, Donghee, and Yong Jin Park. 2019. 'Role of fairness, accountability, and transparency in algorithmic affordance.' *Computers in Human Behavior* 98:277–84.

Shortliffe, Edward H., and Bruce G. Buchanan. 1975. 'A model of inexact reasoning in medicine.' *Mathematical Biosciences* 23 (3):351–79.

Shrestha, Manish, Sujal Manandhar, and Sangam Shrestha. 2020. 'Forecasting water demand under climate change using artificial neural network: A case study of Kathmandu Valley, Nepal.' *Water Supply* 20 (5):1823–33.

Sibai, Fadi N. 2020. 'AI crimes: A classification.' 2020 International Conference on Cyber Security and Protection of Digital Services (Cyber Security), pp. 1–8.

Silver, David, Thomas Hubert, Julian Schrittwieser, Ioannis Antonoglou, Matthew Lai, Arthur Guez, Marc Lanctot, Laurent Sifre, Dharshan Kumaran, Thore Graepel, Timothy Lillicrap, Karen Simonyan, and Demis Hassabis. 2018. 'A general reinforcement learning algorithm that masters chess, shogi, and Go through self-play.' *Science* 362 (6419):1140–4.

Simon, Herbert A. 1996. *The Sciences of the Artificial.* 3rd ed. Cambridge, MA; London: MIT Press.

Sipser, Michael. 2012. *Introduction to the Theory of Computation.* 3rd ed. Boston, MA: Cengage Learning.

Sloan, Robert H., and Richard Warner. 2018. 'When is an algorithm transparent? Predictive analytics, privacy, and public policy.' *IEEE Security & Privacy* 16 (3):18–25.

Solis, Gary D. 2016. *The Law of Armed Conflict: International Humanitarian Law in War.* Cambridge: Cambridge University Press.

Solove, Daniel J. 2008. *Understanding Privacy.* Cambridge, MA; London: Harvard University Press.

Sønderby, Casper Kaae, Lasse Espeholt, Jonathan Heek, Mostafa Dehghani, Avital Oliver, Tim Salimans, Shreya Agrawal, Jason Hickey, and Nal Kalchbrenner. 2020. 'MetNet: A neural weather model for precipitation forecasting.' arXiv:2003.12140 [physics, stat].

Spatt, Chester. 2014. 'Security market manipulation.' *Annual Review of Financial Economics* 6 (1):405–18.

Stilgoe, Jack. 2018. 'Machine learning, social learning and the governance of self-driving cars.' *Social Studies of Science* 48 (1):25–56.

Strathern, Marilyn. 1997. ' "Improving ratings": Audit in the British University system.' *European Review* 5 (3):305–21.

Strickland, Eliza. 2019. 'How IBM Watson overpromised and underdelivered on AI health care.' *IEEE Spectrum* 56 (4):24–31.

Strubell, Emma, Ananya Ganesh, and Andrew McCallum. 2019. 'Energy and policy considerations for deep learning in NLP.' arXiv preprint arXiv:1906.02243.

Swearingen, Kirsten, and Rashmi Sinha. 2002. 'Interaction design for recommender systems.' Designing Interactive Systems, vol. 6, no. 12, pp. 312–334. New York: ACM Press.

Szegedy, Christian, Wojciech Zaremba, Ilya Sutskever, Joan Bruna, Dumitru Erhan, Ian Goodfellow, and Rob Fergus. 2014. 'Intriguing properties of neural networks.' arXiv:1312.6199 [cs].

Tabuchi, Hiroko, and David Gelles. 2019. 'Doomed Boeing jets lacked 2 safety features that company sold only as extras.' *The New York Times*, 2019-04-05T00:55:24.836Z, Business. Accessed 13 April 2019.

Taddeo, M. 2009. 'Defining trust and e-trust.' *International Journal of Technology and Human Interaction* 5 (2):23–35.

Taddeo, Mariarosaria. 2010. 'Modelling trust in artificial agents, a first step toward the analysis of e-trust.' *Minds and Machines* 20 (2):243–57.

Taddeo, Mariarosaria. 2014. 'The struggle between liberties and authorities in the information age.' *Science and Engineering Ethics* 21 (5):1125–1138.

Taddeo, Mariarosaria. 2017a. 'Deterrence by norms to stop interstate cyber attacks.' *Minds and Machines* 27 (3):387–92.

Taddeo, Mariarosaria. 2017b. 'The Limits of Deterrence Theory in Cyberspace.' *Philosophy & Technology* 31 (3):339–55.

Taddeo, Mariarosaria. 2017c. 'Trusting digital technologies correctly.' *Minds and Machines* 27 (4):565–8.

Taddeo, Mariarosaria, and Luciano Floridi. 2005. 'Solving the symbol grounding problem: A critical review of fifteen years of research.' *Journal of Experimental & Theoretical Artificial Intelligence* 17 (4):419–45.

Taddeo, Mariarosaria, and Luciano Floridi. 2007. 'A praxical solution of the symbol grounding problem.' *Minds and Machines* 17 (4):369–89.

Taddeo, Mariarosaria, and Luciano Floridi. 2011. 'The case for e-trust.' *Ethics and Information Technology* 13 (1):1–3.

Taddeo, Mariarosaria, and Luciano Floridi. 2015. 'The debate on the moral responsibilities of online service providers.' *Science and Engineering Ethics* 22:1575–1603.

Taddeo, Mariarosaria, and Luciano Floridi. 2018a. 'How AI can be a force for good.' *Science* 361 (6404):751–2.

Taddeo, Mariarosaria, and Luciano Floridi. 2018b. 'Regulate artificial intelligence to avert cyber arms race.' *Nature* 556 (7701):296–8.

Taddeo, Mariarosaria, Tom McCutcheon, and Luciano Floridi. 2019. 'Trusting artificial intelligence in cybersecurity is a double-edged sword.' *Nature Machine Intelligence* 1 (12):557–60.

Tan, Zhi Ming, Nikita Aggarwal, Josh Cowls, Jessica Morley, Mariarosaria Taddeo, and Luciano Floridi. 2021. 'The ethical debate about the gig economy: A review and critical analysis.' *Technology in Society* 65:101594.

Taylor, Linnet, and Dennis Broeders. 2015. 'In the name of development: Power, profit and the datafication of the global South.' *Geoforum* 64:229–37.

Taylor, Linnet, Luciano Floridi, and Bart van der Sloot. 2016. *Group Privacy: New Challenges of Data Technologies*. Cham: Springer.

Taylor, Linnet, and Ralph Schroeder. 2015. 'Is bigger better? The emergence of big data as a tool for international development policy.' *GeoJournal* 80 (4):503–18.

The Economist. 27 October 2014. 'Waiting on hold: Ebola and big data.'

Thelisson, Eva, Kirtan Padh, and L. Elisa Celis. 2017. 'Regulatory mechanisms and algorithms towards trust in AI/ML.' Proceedings of the IJCAI 2017 workshop on explainable artificial intelligence (XAI), Melbourne, Australia, pp. 19–21.

Thilakarathna, P. S. M., S. Seo, K. S. Kristombu Baduge, H. Lee, P. Mendis, and G. Foliente. 2020. 'Embodied carbon analysis and benchmarking emissions of high and ultra-high strength concrete using machine learning algorithms.' *Journal of Cleaner Production* 262:121281.

Thompson, Neil C., Kristjan Greenewald, Keeheon Lee, and Gabriel F. Manso. 2020. 'The computational limits of deep learning.' arXiv preprint arXiv:2007.05558.

Tickle, A. B., R. Andrews, M. Golea, and J. Diederich. 1998. 'The truth will come to light: Directions and challenges in extracting the knowledge embedded within trained artificial neural networks.' *IEEE Transactions on Neural Networks* 9 (6):1057–68.

Toffler, Alvin. 1980. *The Third Wave*. London: Collins.

Tonti, Gianluca, Jeffrey M. Bradshaw, Renia Jeffers, Rebecca Montanari, Niranjan Suri, and Andrzej Uszok. 2003. 'Semantic web languages for policy representation and reasoning: A comparison of KAoS, Rei, and Ponder.' The Semantic Web-ISWC 2003: Second International Semantic Web Conference, Sanibel Island, FL, USA, October 20–23, 2003. Proceedings 2, pp. 419–437. Springer Berlin Heidelberg.

Torpey, John. 2000. The Invention of the Passport: Surveillance, Citizenship and the State. Cambridge: Cambridge University Press.

Tsamados, Andreas, Nikita Aggarwal, Josh Cowls, Jessica Morley, Huw Roberts, Mariarosaria Taddeo, and Luciano Floridi. 2021. 'The ethics of algorithms: Key problems and solutions.' AI & Society 37 (1):215–30.

Turilli, Matteo, and Luciano Floridi. 2009. 'The ethics of information transparency.' Ethics and Information Technology 11 (2):105–12.

Turing, A. M. 1950. 'Computing machinery and intelligence.' Mind 59 (236):433–60.

Turing, Alan. 1951. 'Alan Turing's lost radio broadcast rerecorded—On the 15th of May 1951 the BBC broadcasted a short lecture on the radio by the mathematician Alan Turing.' BBC Radio https://www.youtube.com/watch?v=cMxbSsRntv4.

Turner Lee, Nicol. 2018. 'Detecting racial bias in algorithms and machine learning.' Journal of Information, Communication and Ethics in Society 16 (3):252–60.

United Nations Human Rights Council. 2012. U.N. Human Rights Council: First Resolution on Internet Free Speech. https://www.eff.org/deeplinks/2012/07/un-human-rights-council-resolution-internet-and-human-rights-step-right-direction

Université de Montréal. 2017. 'Montreal Declaration for Responsible AI.' https://www.montrealdeclaration-responsibleai.com/.

Uszok, Andrzej, Jeffrey Bradshaw, Renia Jeffers, Niranjan Suri, Patrick Hayes, Maggie Breedy, Larry Bunch, Matt Johnson, Shriniwas Kulkarni, and James Lott. 2003. 'KAoS policy and domain services: Toward a description-logic approach to policy representation, deconfliction, and enforcement.' Proceedings POLICY 2003. IEEE 4th International Workshop on Policies for Distributed Systems and Networks, pp. 93–96.

Valiant, Leslie G. 1984. 'A theory of the learnable.' Communications of the ACM 27:1134–42.

Van de Poel, Ibo, Jessica Nihlén Fahlquist, Neelke Doorn, Sjoerd Zwart, and Lamber Royakkers. 2012. 'The problem of many hands: Climate change as an example.' Science and Engineering Ethics 18 (1):49–67.

van Lier, Ben. 2016. 'From high frequency trading to self-organizing moral machines.' International Journal of Technoethics (IJT) 7 (1):34–50.

Van Riemsdijk, M. Birna, Louise A. Dennis, Michael Fisher, and Koen V. Hindriks. 2013. 'Agent reasoning for norm compliance: A semantic approach.' Proceedings of the 2013 International Conference on Autonomous Agents and Multi-Agent Systems, pp. 499–506.

Van Riemsdijk, M. Birna, Louise Dennis, Michael Fisher, and Koen V. Hindriks. 2015. 'A semantic framework for socially adaptive agents: Towards strong norm compliance.' Proceedings of the 2015 International Conference on Autonomous Agents and Multiagent Systems, pp. 423–432.

Vanderelst, Dieter, and Alan Winfield. 2018a. 'An architecture for ethical robots inspired by the simulation theory of cognition.' Cognitive Systems Research 48:56–66.

Vanderelst, Dieter, and Alan Winfield. 2018b. 'The dark side of ethical robots.' Proceedings of the 2018 AAAI/ACM Conference on AI, Ethics, and Society, pp. 317–322.

Veale, Michael, and Reuben Binns. 2017. 'Fairer machine learning in the real world: Mitigating discrimination without collecting sensitive data.' Big Data & Society 4 (2):205395171774353.

Vedder, Anton, and Laurens Naudts. 2017. 'Accountability for the use of algorithms in a big data environment.' International Review of Law, Computers & Technology 31 (2):206–24.

Veletsianos, George, Cassandra Scharber, and Aaron Doering. 2008. 'When sex, drugs, and violence enter the classroom: Conversations between adolescents and a female pedagogical agent.' *Interacting with Computers* 20 (3):292–301.

Vieweg, Stefan. 2021. *AI for the Good: Artificial Intelligence and Ethics*. Cham: Springer.

Vinuesa, Ricardo, Hossein Azizpour, Iolanda Leite, Madeline Balaam, Virginia Dignum, Sami Domisch, Anna Felländer, Simone Daniela Langhans, Max Tegmark, and Francesco Fuso Nerini. 2020. 'The role of artificial intelligence in achieving the Sustainable Development Goals.' *Nature Communications* 11 (1):1–10.

Vodafone Institute for Society and Communications. 2018. 'New technologies: India and China see enormous potential—Europeans more sceptical.' https://www.vodafone-institut.de/digitising-europe/digitisation-india-and-china-see-enormous-potential/.

Voeneky, Silja, Philipp Kellmeyer, Oliver Mueller, and Wolfram Burgard. 2022. *The Cambridge Handbook of Responsible Artificial Intelligence: Interdisciplinary Perspectives*. Cambridge, UK; New York, NY: Cambridge University Press.

Wachter, Sandra, Brent Mittelstadt, and Luciano Floridi. 2017a. 'Transparent, explainable, and accountable AI for robotics.' *Science Robotics* 2 (6):eaan6080.

Wachter, Sandra, Brent Mittelstadt, and Luciano Floridi. 2017b. 'Why a right to explanation of automated decision-making does not exist in the general data protection regulation.' *International Data Privacy Law* 7 (2):76–99.

Walch, Kathleen. 20 October 2019. 'Are we heading for another AI winter soon?' Forbes https://www.forbes.com/sites/cognitiveworld/2019/10/20/are-we-heading-for-another-ai-winter-soon/#783bf81256d6.

Wang, Dayong, Aditya Khosla, Rishab Gargeya, Humayun Irshad, and Andrew H. Beck. 2016. 'Deep learning for identifying metastatic breast cancer.' arXiv preprint arXiv:1606.05718.

Wang, Gang, Manish Mohanlal, Christo Wilson, Xiao Wang, Miriam Metzger, Haitao Zheng, and Ben Y. Zhao. 2012. 'Social Turing tests: Crowdsourcing sybil detection.' arXiv preprint arXiv:1205.3856.

Wang, Shuang, Xiaoqian Jiang, Siddharth Singh, Rebecca Marmor, Luca Bonomi, Dov Fox, Michelle Dow, and Lucila Ohno-Machado. 2017. 'Genome privacy: Challenges, technical approaches to mitigate risk, and ethical considerations in the United States: Genome privacy in biomedical research.' *Annals of the New York Academy of Sciences* 1387 (1):73–83.

Wang, Yilun, and Michal Kosinski. 2018. 'Deep neural networks are more accurate than humans at detecting sexual orientation from facial images.' *Journal of Personality and Social Psychology* 114 (2):246.

Warren, Samuel D., and Louis D. Brandeis. 1890. 'The right to privacy.' *Harvard Law Review* 4 (5):193–220.

Watson, David S., and Luciano Floridi. 2020. 'The explanation game: A formal framework for interpretable machine learning.' *Synthese* 198 (10):9211–9242.

Watson, David, Limor Gultchin, Ankur Taly, and Luciano Floridi. 2021. 'Local explanations via necessity and sufficiency: Unifying theory and practice.' arXiv preprint arXiv:2103.14651.

Watson, David S., Jenny Krutzinna, Ian N Bruce, Christopher E. M. Griffiths, Iain B. McInnes, Michael R. Barnes, and Luciano Floridi. 2019. 'Clinical applications of machine learning algorithms: Beyond the black box.' *BMJ* 1886.

Webb, Helena, Menisha Patel, Michael Rovatsos, Alan Davoust, Sofia Ceppi, Ansgar Koene, Liz Dowthwaite, Virginia Portillo, Marina Jirotka, and Monica Cano. 2019. '"It would be pretty immoral to choose a random algorithm": Opening up algorithmic interpretability and transparency.' *Journal of Information, Communication and Ethics in Society* 17 (2):210–28.

Wei, Sun, Wang Yuwei, and Zhang Chongchong. 2018. 'Forecasting CO2 emissions in Hebei, China, through moth-flame optimization based on the random forest and extreme learning machine.' *Environmental Science and Pollution Research* 25 (29):28985–97.

Weiss, Gerhard, ed. 2013. *Multiagent Systems*. 2nd ed. Intelligent Robotics and Autonomous Agents. Cambridge, MA: The MIT Press.

Weizenbaum, Joseph. 1976. *Computer Power and Human Reason: From Judgment to Calculation*. San Francisco: W. H. Freeman.

Weller, Adrian. 2019. 'Transparency: Motivations and challenges.' arXiv:1708.01870 [cs].

Wellman, Michael P., and Uday Rajan. 2017. 'Ethical issues for autonomous trading agents.' *Minds and Machines* 27 (4):609–24.

Wexler, James. 2018. 'The what-if tool: Code-free probing of machine learning models.' Google AI blog.

Whitby, Blay. 2008. 'Sometimes it's hard to be a robot: A call for action on the ethics of abusing artificial agents.' *Interacting with Computers* 20 (3):326–33.

White, Geoff. 2018. 'Child advice chatbots fail sex abuse test.' Technology, 11 December 2018. Accessed 13 April 2019. BBC https://www.bbc.co.uk/news/technology-46507900

Whitman, Madisson, Chien-yi Hsiang, and Kendall Roark. 2018. 'Potential for participatory big data ethics and algorithm design: A scoping mapping review.' The 15th Participatory Design Conference, 2018.

Wiener, Norbert. 1950. *The Human Use of Human Beings: Cybernetics and Society*. London: Eyre and Spottiswoode.

Wiener, Norbert. 1954. *The Human Use of Human Beings: Cybernetics and Society*. Revised ed. Boston, MA: Houghton Mifflin.

Wiener, Norbert. 1960. 'Some moral and technical consequences of automation.' *Science* 131 (3410):1355–8.

Wiener, Norbert. 1989. *The Human Use of Human Beings: Cybernetics and Society*. Rev. ed. London: Free Association.

Williams, Rebecca. 2017. 'Lords select committee, artificial intelligence committee, written evidence (AIC0206).' http://data.parliament.uk/writtenevidence/committeeevidence. svc/evidencedocument/artificial-intelligence-committee/artificial-intelligence/written/ 70496.html#_ftn13.

Winfield, Alan. 18 April 2019. 'An updated round up of ethical principles of robotics and AI.' http://alanwinfield.blogspot.com/2019/04/an-updated-round-up-of-ethical.html.

Winner, Langdon. 1980. 'Do artifacts have politics?' *Modern Technology: Problem or Opportunity?* 109 (1):121–36.

Wong, Pak-Hang. 2019. 'Democratizing algorithmic fairness.' *Philosophy & Technology* 33: 225–244.

Wooldridge, Michael J. 2009. *An Introduction to MultiAgent Systems*. 2nd ed. Chichester, UK: John Wiley & Sons.

Xenochristou, Maria, Chris Hutton, Jan Hofman, and Zoran Kapelan. 2020. 'Water demand forecasting accuracy and influencing factors at different spatial scales using a Gradient Boosting Machine.' *Water Resources Research* 56 (8):e2019WR026304.

Xian, Zhengzheng, Qiliang Li, Xiaoyu Huang, and Lei Li. 2017. 'New SVD-based collaborative filtering algorithms with differential privacy.' *Journal of Intelligent & Fuzzy Systems* 33 (4):2133–44.

Xu, Depeng, Shuhan Yuan, Lu Zhang, and Xintao Wu. 2018. 'FairGAN: Fairness-aware Generative Adversarial Networks.' 2018 IEEE International Conference on Big Data (Big Data), pp. 570–575, December 2018.

Yadav, Amulya, Hau Chan, Albert Jiang, Eric Rice, Ece Kamar, Barbara Grosz, and Milind Tambe. 2016. 'POMDPs for assisting homeless shelters: Computational and deployment challenges.' Autonomous Agents and Multiagent Systems: AAMAS 2016 Workshops, Visionary Papers, Singapore, Singapore, May 9–10, 2016, Revised Selected Papers, pp. 67–87. Springer International Publishing.

Yadav, Amulya, Hau Chan, Albert Xin Jiang, Haifeng Xu, Eric Rice, and Milind Tambe. 2016. 'Using social networks to aid homeless shelters: Dynamic influence maximization under uncertainty.' *AAMAS* 16:740–48.

Yadav, Amulya, Bryan Wilder, Eric Rice, Robin Petering, Jaih Craddock, Amanda Yoshioka-Maxwell, Mary Hemler, Laura Onasch-Vera, Milind Tambe, and Darlene Woo. 2018. 'Bridging the gap between theory and practice in influence maximization: Raising awareness about HIV among homeless youth.' *IJCAI* 5399–5403.

Yampolskiy, Roman V. 2018. *Artificial Intelligence Safety and Security*. Chapman and Hall/CRC. https://www.taylorfrancis.com/books/edit/10.1201/9781351251389/artificial-intelligence-safety-security-roman-yampolskiy

Yang, Guang-Zhong, Jim Bellingham, Pierre E. Dupont, Peer Fischer, Luciano Floridi, Robert Full, Neil Jacobstein, Vijay Kumar, Marcia McNutt, Robert Merrifield, Bradley J. Nelson, Brian Scassellati, Mariarosaria Taddeo, Russell Taylor, Manuela Veloso, Zhong Lin Wang, and Robert Wood. 2018. 'The grand challenges of *Science Robotics*.' *Science Robotics* 3 (14):eaar7650.

Yu, Meng, and Guodong Du. 2019. 'Why are Chinese courts turning to AI?' *The Diplomat* 19.

Zerilli, John, Alistair Knott, James Maclaurin, and Colin Gavaghan. 2019. 'Transparency in algorithmic and human decision-making: Is there a double standard?' *Philosophy & Technology* 32 (4):661–83.

Zheng, Gang, Xiaofeng Li, Rong-Hua Zhang, and Bin Liu. 2020. 'Purely satellite data-driven deep learning forecast of complicated tropical instability waves.' *Science Advances* 6 (29):eaba1482.

Zhou, Na, Chuan-Tao Zhang, Hong-Ying Lv, Chen-Xing Hao, Tian-Jun Li, Jing-Juan Zhu, Hua Zhu, Man Jiang, Ke-Wei Liu, He-Lei Hou, Dong Liu, Ai-Qin Li, Guo-Qing Zhang, Zi-Bin Tian, and Xiao-Chun Zhang. 2019. 'Concordance study between IBM Watson for oncology and clinical practice for patients with cancer in China.' *The Oncologist* 24 (6):812–19.

Zhou, Wei, and Gaurav Kapoor. 2011. 'Detecting evolutionary financial statement fraud.' *Decision Support Systems* 50 (3):570–5.

Zhou, Yadi, Fei Wang, Jian Tang, Ruth Nussinov, and Feixiong Cheng. 2020. 'Artificial intelligence in COVID-19 drug repurposing.' *The Lancet Digital Health* 2 (12): e667–e676.

Zhou, Zhifang, Tian Xiao, Xiaohong Chen, and Chang Wang. 2016. 'A carbon risk prediction model for Chinese heavy-polluting industrial enterprises based on support vector machine.' *Chaos, Solitons & Fractals* 89:304–15.

Index

For the benefit of digital users, indexed terms that span two pages (e.g., 52–53) may, on occasion, appear on only one of those pages.